Early Childhood Literature

W9-ADS-358

Early Childhood Literature

For Love of
Child and Book

Eileen M. Burke
Trenton State College

Allyn and Bacon, Inc.
Boston London Sydney Toronto

Series Editor: *Jeffery W. Johnston*
Production Coordinator: *Sandy Stanewick*
Editorial and Production Services: *TKM Productions*
Cover Coordinator: *Linda Dickinson*

Library of Congress Cataloging-in-Publication Data

Burke, Eileen M.
    Early childhood literature.

    Includes bibliographies and index.
    1. Children — Books and reading. 2. Children's
literature — Study and teaching. I. Title.
Z1037.A1B86 1986   028.5'34   85-9095
ISBN 0-205-08596-2

Printed in the United States of America

10 9 8 7 6 5 4 3   90 89 88

To my mother, Catherine M. Burke

Contents

Chapter 4
The Feel of Literature: Design and Graphic Variations   69

Chapter 5
The Sound of Literature: Song and Poetry   83

Foreword

There are many reasons for us to bring literature into the lives of young children. Literature enhances children's knowledge of the world. It allows children to tap a wide range of human emotions and experiences, and it stimulates curiosity and reflective thought.

As educators, we often focus on the literary qualities in children's stories and poems. We are concerned that children develop an appreciation of various types of literature. We are very much aware of the role literature plays in the development of reading and writing abilities; and we recognize that exposure to the language of stories and poems is critical to children's development of vocabulary and their sense of story.

It is unlikely that children are aware of the many ways that literature contributes to their development. Most often, they simply view activities with literature as pleasurable events during the day. For them, the sheer joy of sharing literature is quite enough. It is the joy in the sharing of literature—the immense pleasure that it offers children—that comes through so vividly in this volume. Eileen Burke has managed to tell the story of children and their literature in a manner that blends scholarship with a sensitivity to why literature is such a powerful medium.

A careful observer of children, Burke offers numerous anecdotes about young children's experiences with books. These help provide a context for the reader to place the many strategies provided for using literature in the classroom. In every instance, Burke's suggestions are grounded in sound principles of child development, an understanding of how children learn and make sense of their world, and a thorough knowledge of literature for children.

Teachers will be informed and inspired by the ideas in this book. Most important, readers of *Early Childhood Literature* cannot help but take a hard look at the place that children's literature plays in the school program and in the very lives of the children they care about.

Dorothy S. Strickland
Teachers College
Columbia University

Preface

The early years of childhood are pristine, rich in potential, experimental, crucial, precious, and vulnerable to shaping. They cry out for the richest, deepest, fullest of experiences. They are developmentally prime time.

For most young children, no matter what problems confront them, each day brings some new adventure. For the three to eight year old, the focus of this book, some of these adventures are contacts with, or extensions of contacts with, books. It is during these years that books are still new—a source of excitement, delight, and surprise.

To form the strongest foundation for a lifetime of adventures with literature the nursery and primary-grade child needs a careful, enthusiastic, broad introduction to literature. Although literature is no substitute for first-hand direct learning, it offers a sumptuous lode of rich vicarious experiences to young children. It can powerfully grip their minds and emotions, effecting a total engagement of thought and feeling. Such engagement is the internalization psychologists speak of and the learning teachers yearn to incite in all children.

Although not exclusive to young children, certain genres, for developmental and sometimes historical reasons, belong especially to them. The nursery rhymes, the books to "feel," the alphabet, counting, and concept books, the picture books, and much of traditional literature are very particularly theirs. Indeed in the case of traditional literature, it is generally agreed that these early years are peak years. At the end of this age span, interest in fairy tales lessens and factual books begin to be preferred by many children.

Other preferences wax and wane during early years; some even take root, shaped by the child's holistic development and the quality and quantity of books shared and available. There is a time when young children need to "feel" books, a point-and-say time when naming the picture is vital, a time when Mother Goose and her family are most needed and loved, a time for acknowledging what is in the world and a time for imagining what is beyond it. These times will overlap; indeed, they may run concomitantly for months. Their duration is less important, however, than their recognition and nurturance.

Of one such time, Sam Sebesta and William Iverson say in *Literature for Thursday's Child,* "If you miss this stage [simple picture books and object books], with children, something is lost that can never be regained. The idea that pictures can convey reality, that books are windows to the world, must be introduced early and with care" (Chicago: Science Research Associates, 1975, p. 134).

We owe young children provision for *every* literary time and stage.

Early Childhood Literature: For the Love of Child and Book is dedicated to the greater use of literature with and by young children. It is predicated upon the child's fundamental right to, and need of, literature and upon the splendor of today's literature that clamors to be shared. It seeks to do what it can to create an epidemic of bibliophilism among all young children so that they may be afflicted with book loving all of their lives.

Acknowledgments

I would like to express my appreciation to Mary Yates, Coordinator of Early Childhood Education at Trenton State College, and to Gwendolyn Jones, colleague, mentor, storyteller, and former first-grade teacher, for reviewing portions of this manuscript; to Thomas P. Daily, principal of Lawrenceville Elementary School, and his faculty; to Dr. Dorothy Rubin whose professional beliefs have influenced my thinking; to Dr. Susan Glazer for her utilization of a language–literature approach even in clinical practice; to Elizabeth Strouse, Susan Welsh, Eleanore Dunker, Carol Satz, Joan Queripel, and many other teachers whose classrooms continuously reveal rich encounters between children and books; to Karol Zielinski and Margaret Quinlan for their support; to Regina C. Muehleisen for sharing her time and talent; to Debbie Varrassee whose competence and patience throughout the completion of the manuscript deserve very special recognition; to Milton, Catherine, and Nancy Kay Austin and to my mother without whose patience and support this manuscript would not have been completed.

E. B.

Early Childhood
Literature

Chapter 1

Young Children: Growing Up

In early childhood, life itself is new. Each day is a fresh quest on the journey to "Somewhere."

Could you tell me the way to Somewhere—
Somewhere, Somewhere
I have heard of a place called Somewhere—
But know not where it can be.
It makes no difference,
Whether or not
I go in dreams
Or trudge on foot;
Would you tell me the way to Somewhere,
The Somewhere meant for me.

From "Somewhere" in *Bells and Grass* by Walter de la Mare. Copyright 1942 by Walter de la Mare; ©renewed 1969 by Richard de la Mare. Reprinted by permission of Viking Penguin Inc.

As young children travel to their personal Somewhere that marks their achievement as deeply compassionate, productive, thinking persons, they do so holistically—questioning, feeling, companioning as they go forth. For research and analytical purposes, educators may talk of the cognitive, affective, and psychomotor domains and speak of physical, social, emotional, and intellectual development as though they were separate entities, but the young child is neither an assemblage of domains or developments nor simply the synthesis of them. A child is a holistic being—greater than the sum of any set of psychological or physical categories

In reaching out for their own special Somewhere, young children from three to eight years of age exhibit an array of appealing, enlivening, and sometimes confusing behaviors.

Notable Behaviors

The anecdotes that follow are accounts of happenings in classrooms and in school and public libraries; they exemplify some of the more notable behaviors of young children. They also represent the rich encounters that can occur when a child meets a book.

Curious

A young child's curiosity is a dynamic force; it propels him or her to marvel, query, investigate, and discover.

"A spider is not an insect?" John asks dubiously. His tone implies the judgment, "It's got to be. What else could it be?" All the other children look at Mr. Jackson as though they had not really heard him correctly. After all, they have just finished a unit on insects and they are experts.

John repeats, "It's *got* to be an insect."

"How can we find out for sure?" asks Mr. Jackson.

"Look it up!"

"Ask Miss Brown. She knows everything."

"I got an uncle who works in a laboratory with animals. Maybe he knows."

In the meantime, John has headed to the library. The first book does not help very much but eventually he and his friends conclude that insects, by definition, have six legs; spiders have eight. Spiders are *not* insects.

John still wonders. "Do *all* spiders have eight legs? I've got to see Miss Brown," says John as he walks toward the library again.

Mr. Jackson nods. John's curiosity is ignited.

•◆•

Throughout a child's early years, curiosity will be endlessly reignited and kept aflame if parents and teachers follow these guidelines:

- Honor the child's questions by being attentive.
- Show enthusiasm about books.
- Share stories.
- Insure that a wide variety of books is available.

- Provide time to browse in libraries, question subject matter, and discuss books.
- Supply, *when needed*, a few prods to help stir a book search and satisfy a wonder.

Fortunately today no curriculum area lacks a cache of varied books with which to arouse curiosity, clarify concepts, document generalizations, and extend understandings. From *The Cloud Book* by Tomie de Paola, Franklyn Branley's more technical *Comets*, Tana Hoban's *Shapes and Things*, May Garelick's *Where Does the Butterfly Go When It Rains*, Gail Gibbons's *The Post Office Book*, Fulvio Testa's *If You Take a Pencil*, to Donald Crews's *Freight Train*, literature can enrich and enhance the curriculum as it enchants the curious young child.

Active

Young children need to jump, hop, dance, skip, become "angels-in-the-snow," play Stepping Stone and tag, run, catch, toss a beanbag and ball, ride tricycles and bicycles, walk the balance beam, and march.

"Now, let me," says Becky, a first grader who is ready to share her story.

She marches forth. "This is my favoritest book. I can read it and I can sing it. I'll show you."

She begins, "Oh, a-hunting I will go." Soon everyone is humming or singing along, and as Mrs. Johnson watches the shoes tapping, hands clapping, and heads swaying to the rhythm, she beckons the children forward. Led by Becky, the youngsters parade the boundaries of the classroom in a happy, festive fashion. Following the lively prance everyone sits down while Becky emphatically announces that she wants more "singing books" like that.

For young children there are many more singing books like John Langstaff's *Oh, A-Hunting We Will Go*. There are also dancing, clapping, tapping books, and even books to be drummed to like Barbara Emberley's *Drummer Hoff*. These are books that set muscles working. Vocal muscles are stirred to use by the repeated lines of Beatrice Schenk de Regniers's *May I Bring a Friend?* and by the lilt and delicious refrain of Maurice Sendak's *Chicken Soup with Rice* or many of the songs in Clyde Watson's *Father Fox's Feast of Songs*; leg muscles try "animal and insect walking" to poems like those in Aileen Fisher's *Cricket in a Thicket*; arm muscles hold up the toys and presents (or pictures of such) mentioned in Phyllis McGinley's *The Year Without a Santa Claus*; laugh muscles respond to William Cole's *Oh! What Nonsense!* and Bruce Degan's *Jamberry*.

Language and action, action and language — this is a happy, vital combination for the young child

Experimental

Young children constantly examine, experiment, and test.

✻ Laughter ripples through the third grade. Miss Johnson is sharing some verses from *Peter Piper's Practical Principles of Plain and Perfect Pronunciation.*

"How about Butchie's bouncing basketball?" asks Jimmy.

"Where'd you hear that?" asks Jackie suspiciously. "It's not in the book."

"Course not. I just made it up," brags Jimmy.

•◆•

Peter Piper has triggered "Butchie's bouncing basketball." Young children revel in such linguistic fun. The poems of Merriam, Ciardi, McCord, Prelutsky, Hoberman, Kuskin, and others evoke not only alliteration that twists the tongue but similes and metaphors that turn pictures on in young minds.

On their way to Somewhere, young children must try out hosts of new words and new tasks. Recipe books like Eva Moore's *The Great Banana Cookbook for Boys and Girls* and project books like Harlow Rockwell's *I Did It* involve children in simple activities that satisfy and deepen their need for experimentation.

Impatient

The impatience of young children and their hunger for experiences are poetically distilled in Marchette Chute's poem.

✻
_____

I'm always told to hurry up —
Which I'd be glad to do,
If there were not so many things
That need attending to.

From *Around and About*, by Marchette Chute, copyright 1957 (E.P. Dutton), renewed 1985. By permission of the author. ✻

_____

Today's young children live in a world of great stimulation; such a world intensifies their natural impatience for a taste of everything — *now.* Certain genres in children's literature recognize this impatience;

bedtime stories like the all-time favorite *Goodnight Moon* (Margaret W. Brown) still the natural impatience against sleep and rest by focusing on the gentle ritual of bidding everything and everyone good night. Adventure stories such as Arnold Adoff's *Where Wild Willie* and Irene Haas's *The Maggie B* respond to children's impatience for more and more experiences.

In addition there is the impatience literal young children sometimes feel with adults.

> *Melissa, a four-year-old, was playing "baby." She had her shoes and socks off. The teacher called to her, "Melissa, put on your shoes and socks! You know you can't run around without your shoes and socks."*
>
> *Melissa, disgusted, said under her breath, "Don't she know babies don't wear no shoes?"*[1]

Egocentric

Early years are ego-centered. Young children need a gradual introduction into recognizing the viewpoints of others. David's reaction in the following anecdote is typical of the young child.

> *I had occasion to re-visit a preschool where I had once taught kindergarten. There I met David, the four-year-old and younger brother of one of my former charges. I bent over and warmly said to David, "You're Chuckie's brother."*
> *He gazed up at me with serious eyes, shook his head from side to side, and said solemnly, "Uh, uh! Chuckie's my brother!"*[2]

Concerns and pangs suffered by the young child while learning to live with friends and siblings are many, as are the books that deal with such concerns. Books like *Let's Be Enemies* (Janice May Udry), *Nobody Ever Asked Me If I Wanted a Baby Sister* (Martha Alexander), *I Love My Baby Sister (Most of the Time)* (Elaine Edelman), *To Hilda for Helping* (Margot Zemach), and a host of others nudge the young child along the sometimes lengthy and uphill route from self-centeredness to other-centeredness.

Imaginative

The imagination of young children radiates as they construct, chant, dance, clap, explore, dramatize, draw, and discuss.

"'Eye hugs?' What does that mean?" pipes up Bernie as the teacher shares *My Grandson Lew* by Charlotte Zolotow.

"My dad gives me bear hugs not eye hugs. I'd rather have bear hugs," says Jean.

"What are bear hugs?" asks Leslie.

"You know—a r-r-r-eal big tight squeeze."

"Oh," exclaims Leslie, a bit wistfully, "It must be nice to have both kinds."

"Are there eye kisses too?" asks Sue.

●◆●

Children respond to linguistic beauty with appreciation and enthusiasm. This enthusiasm sometimes leads them to fresh and delightful word coinages of their own, as it did for Sue in the example above.

Imagination surfaces in more than linguistic creations, however. For example, many are the doting relatives who purchase a toy for the very young child only to find that the child's imagination and attention are prodded more by the packaging and its manipulativeness than the gift itself. A story version of this phenomenon that seven- or eight-year-olds would appreciate is Gauch's *Christina Katerina & the Box.* Christina manages to dream up and enact all sorts of uses for a refrigerator packing box. For three- and four-year-olds, Watanabe's *I Can Build a House* tells something of the same tale.

An additional phenomenon typical of many young children is the imaginary friend they sometimes create for themselves. These are the years children are as likely to walk with imaginary friends as with real ones and enjoy dressing up and playing out different roles. Such imaginary characters as Martha Alexander's *Blackboard Bear* are as real and comforting to young children as are James and John in Janice Udry's *Let's Be Enemies.*

Imitative

By modeling their parents, older siblings, babysitters, and teachers, young children demonstrate how much learning is accomplished through imitation.

❋ Mr. Deare watched two children dramatizing *Look What I Can Do,* Jose Aruego's lively tale of the carabaos who challenge and imitate each other. As the children giggled, Mr. Deare heard Jimmy comment, "Hey, this is like that other story. You know, the one about the chick."

Jack looked puzzled. "You know, the chick who couldn't swim," continued Jimmy.

Mr. Deare supplied, "*The Chick and the Duckling.*"

"Yup, that's right." Both boys grinned as they continued their jolly dramatizing.

Then they said to each other, "Let's do that one next."

●◆●

In these two books, and others such as Frank Asch's *Just Like Daddy,* young children appreciate the fun in imitation and the results of over-imitation.

Enthusiastic

The bubbling effervescence of young children as they giggle, goggle, query, and quest is delightfully invigorating for their caretakers.

"Susie, are you comfortable there?" asks the librarian, looking dubiously at the three-and-a-half-year-old who clearly needs another cushion to prop her up. Settled a moment later Susie reaches for the record player and listens to her story with obvious absorption. After a few minutes, Susie reports, "I like that *Chicken Soup with Rice*. I r-e-a-l-l-y l-i-k-e i-t. Where's the book?"

"Right here," responds the librarian.

Record player on, book in lap, immersed in Maurice Sendak, Susie does not speak again until she wriggles off the cushion and, with book in hand, confronts the librarian.

"That's got to be 'Chicken Soup'" says she, pointing to those exact words.

The librarian nods. "How did you know, Susie?"

"Cause that's the way the story starts and I see it there," she jabs the page, "and there and there and here and y' know what?"

"What?"

"I can hardly wait to read it myself."

●◆●

Young children greet with great enthusiasm their own discoveries and welcome their teacher's ideas for fresh learning. "Now I think we'll have a song. Let's try *Frog Went A-Courtin'*," says the teacher and every face breaks into a smile. Or the teacher frames her eyes and the children instantly smile, curl their fingers around their eyes, and chant, "These are grandmother's glasses...," Simon Says, a classroom skit, a new arithmetic game, the latest adventure of Piet Potter or Ramona—all are greeted with enthusiastic expectancy.

Adult-Dependent

For the structure that healthful growing and learning demand, children need adult guidance. Continuously involved in exploration, young children seek answers to their questions whether adults help or not. Their seeking, exploring and experimenting are not always as fruitful as they might be because young children lack the ability to analyze, test, or reflect upon their observations.[3]

Parents of young children might do well to model the behavior of Frances's mother and father in Russell Hoban's Frances stories. Patient, loving, firm, and full of gentle humor, they offer the type of adult guidance and modeling young children need—the kind that enables young children to do better and more effectively that which they will continuously attempt to do anyway.

Unpredictable

The major manifestation of unpredictability in young children may be the development of each child. The works of Erikson, White, Havighurst, Piaget, and the developmental psychologists in general have enabled those who guide young children to identify the sequence and the major characteristics of each developmental stage, age, or task. Yet the pace of such sequencing is personal and the intensity and essence of every experience leaves a unique impression on each child, differentiating each individual from his or her agemates.

"This book doesn't have any words. Can it *tell* you a story when it has no words?" asks Miss Campbell as she holds up a copy of Raymond Briggs's *The Snowman*.

"Sure," pipes up Tommy.

"How?"

"The pictures tell you."

"How?"

Tommy's expression is nonplussed, and his words are tinged with annoyance.

"You know...they show different things."

As Miss Campbell waits, Tommy says, "You know, like, here...." Tommy points to a picture. "The Snowman's taking his hat off and then he's in the house, and then he's looking at the cat and...." His story continues, "...and he's running so fast, his hat comes off." As Tommy proceeds from one illustration to the other, he proves he is alert and attentive to graphic detail.

Mary interrupts, "Oh, I like that picture," she says, indicating the figures of the Snowman and the boy as they fly through the snowstorm.

"Why?" queries Miss Campbell, thinking that the double-spread picture looks cold and bleak.

"Cause I like *big* pictures and cause it's soft and swirly like snow. It's a soft, swirly picture," Mary continues, dipping into metaphor.

Miss Campbell smiles at Mary's unpredictable response. Pictures create impressions — highly individual ones — as well as tell stories, Miss Campbell reminds herself.

In summary, in their journey to Somewhere, young children continuously exhibit curiosity, activity, experimentation, impatience, egocentricism, imagination, imitation, enthusiasm, dependence on adults, and unpredictability. To such behaviors, some genres and books are especially responsive, as shown in Table 1.1.

TABLE 1.1 *Genres and Books Responsive to the Characteristics of Young Children*

Characteristics of Young Children	Genres	Selected Texts Responsive to These Characteristics
Curious	Concept books Information books Realistic books	Tasha Tudor. *Around the Year.* 3–5 Lorna Balian. *Where in the World Is Henry?* 5–8 Millicent Selsam. *Is This a Baby Dinosaur? and Other Science Picture Puzzles.* 5–8 Anne and Harlow Rockwell. *The Supermarket.* 3–5 Marguerite De Angeli. *Yonie Wondernose.* 5–8
Active	Poetry Arts, Crafts books Sports books Cookbooks	Harlow Rockwell. *I Did It.* 5–8 Alvin Schwartz. *The Rainy Day Book.* 3–5 Peter Spier. *London Bridge Is Falling Down.* 3–5 Jill Krementz. *A Very Young Skater.* 5–8 Eva Moore. *The Seabury Cookbook for Boys and Girls.* 5–8
Experimental	Puzzle books Science books Hobby books	*Ed Emberley's Drawing Book: Make a World.* 5–8 Anne Rockwell. *Games and How to Play Them.* 5–8 Hou-tien Cheng. *Scissor Cutting for Beginners.* 5–8
Impatient	Realistic books Fables, folktales	Ruth Krauss *The Carrot Seed.* 3–5 Aesop. "The Crow and the Water Jug" *Once in a Wood.* 5–8
Egocentric	Realistic books (about friendship) Fables	Peter Wezel *The Good Bird.* 3–5 Nonny Hogrogian. *Carrot Cake* 5–8 Tobi Tobias. *The Quitting Deal.* 5–8

(continued)

TABLE 1.1 *Continued*

Characteristics of Young Children	Genres	Selected Texts
		Responsive to These Characteristics
Imaginative	Career books Humorous books Poetry	Miriam Young. *If I Drove a Truck.* 5–8 Aliki. *Keep Your Mouth Closed, Dear.* 3–5 Mary Ann Hoberman. *Nuts to You and Nuts to Me.* 3–8
Imitative	Animal books Biographies Realistic books	Clyde R. Bulla. *Keep Running Allen!* 5–8 Roger Duvoisin. *Donkey-Donkey.* 5–8 Aliki. *The Story of William Penn.* 5–8 Ingri and Edgar D'Aulaire. *Abraham Lincoln.* 5–8
Enthusiastic	Poetry Song books Plays	Aileen Fisher. "The Package," *Up a Windy Hill.* 3–5 Robert Louis Stevenson. "The Swing," *A Child's Garden of Verses.* 3–8 Maurice Sendak. *The Sign on Rosie's Door.* 5–8
Adult-Dependent	Realistic books Animal books	Charlotte Zolotow. *My Grandson Lew.* 5–8 Charlotte Zolotow. *If You Listen.* 5–8 Russell Hoban. *Bedtime for Frances.* 5–8 Crescent Dragonwagon. *Will It Be Okay?* 5–8
Unpredictable	Humorous books	Harry Allard. *Miss Nelson Is Missing.* 5–8 Lorna Balian. *Humbug Witch.* 3–5 John Goodall. *Paddy's New Hat.* 3–5

Younger children in the age range of three to eight years can listen to and appreciate what slightly older children can read; younger children can enjoy the music of the language while not fully understanding the content; younger children respond to the most obvious meaning of the text while older children can begin to sense the more-than-one layer of meaning inherent in the tale; younger children respond somewhat indiscriminately to visual and verbal beauty while older children begin to develop preferences in art, writing styles, and genres. For all these reasons, the age categories of three to five years and five to eight years are flexible. Only the knowledge of each child and each book can *guarantee* the success of a child–book meeting.

Developmental Changes

The study of children aged three through eight is a saga so dynamic as to be almost awesome. The amount of living and learning characteristic of these years is phenomenal. Changes that typify this age span are presented in Table 1.2.

TABLE 1.2 *Developmental Characteristics of Three- and Eight-Year-Old Children*

Three Years Old	Eight Years Old
Physical	
Much jumping, swinging, climbing, running (large-muscle coordination)	Continued large-muscle activity done with better coordination
	Concentration on small-muscle tasks like simple model construction, rock collection, and simple sewing, cooking, and handwriting activities
Plays with large blocks, large balls	Plays with large and small items including pick-up sticks, small Lego pieces
Tricycles	Bicycles
May push and shove	"Play" punches and wrestles; tries lifting small weights; beginning to gain skill in activities requiring good motor coordination
Temporary teeth	Permanent teeth
Not yet ready for many visual tasks	Developing ability to function in a variety of tasks involving near and far vision

(continued)

TABLE 1.2 *Continued*

Three Years Old	Eight Years Old
Social	
Playing next to each other	Playing with each other
May have imaginative companions	Comfortable with group activities or team activities
Frustrated due to inability to enter into games of older siblings and their friends	Enjoys spontaneous and supervised activity
Beginning to cope with society's social phrases such as "please" and "thank you"	Growing in the use of such phrases (or becoming conditioned to being reminded to use them)
Needs much adult guidance and structure	Growing independence and self-reliance within limits set by adults
Imitative behavior in language, manner, and habits; dons adult clothes to play "dress-up"	Simple, original classroom skits or team choral verse renditions
Emotional	
Many emotional swings	Growing emotional stability
Very vulnerable to the emotional climate of home and school	Greater resilience to emotional variations in home and school but still in great need of consistency in both places
Anxious in the face of inconsistent demands	
Wants praise for good behavior	Wants recognition for self-control, self-discipline, responsible behavior
Needs love and affection; very parent-dependent	Needs love and affection
The world revolves around him or her	Can project his or her own feelings toward others and toward characters in books
Sharing is difficult	Admires characters who cope
Language	
Has mastered basic syntactical structures	Uses basic syntactical structures with more variation and facility
Increases vocabulary principally through direct experience	Increases vocabulary by direct and vicarious (including book) experiences
Starting to build connotational meaning	Connotational, associational meaning grows at great rate
Very dependent on language around him or her; this is the "buffet" from which child chooses what he or she needs	Social speech; development toward true dialogue

Three Years Old	Eight Years Old
Language accompanies activity and is oftentimes a monologue even though the child thinks he or she is talking to someone else (Piaget's collective monologue)	
Literal understanding of language	Growing understanding of figurative uses of language
	Evidence of self-monitoring own behavior and language

Intellectual

Full of questions and wonder but finds answers largely by trial and error although he or she is begining to use some symbols to think	Becomes increasingly skilled in processing and using language symbols and mental images
Especially in need of concrete experiences upon which to base conclusions	Concrete experiences still greatly needed but sometimes now used to confirm conclusions rather than generate them
Not ready for meaningful self evaluation	Is capable of self-reflection regarding own behavior and in some cases as related to situational problems
Slapstick humor, simple large tactile puzzles	Enjoys codes, ciphers, visual puzzles, riddles
Perceptual stimulation critical; perceptual experience dictates conceptual knowledge	Perceptual stimulation still shapes concepts but he or she will sometimes question perceptions
Accepts appearances in making judgments	Logical thinking beginning
	Some classifying, sequencing, subordinating, and other organizational skills beginning to develop

Moral

Moral behavior very much shaped by the reinforcements and corrections received from parents, and other adults who are significant in his or her life	Adult reinforcement and correction still very potent but peers are beginning to affect child's sense of right and wrong
Moral behavior also shaped by the modeling of the adults who matter to the child	

Holistic Development

The span from three to eight years of age arches many differences yet the entire period is also characterized by similarities. For the holistic development of the child, much depends upon the way people treat the child. The trust, confidence, and self-worth needed by each child are shaped by those about him or her. Such nurturing is vital as the child struggles between attachment and separation.

In trying to satisfy the dual needs for psychological safety and adventure, nothing succeeds so well as:

- The supportive love and affection of those near the child
- Rich, social interactions with others
- Diverse, direct experiences.

It is in this environment that the young child builds clear concepts, social and emotional health, personality integration, and a positive view of self that will support more and more investigation and richer, deeper learning.

The Young Child and Television

Perception is the basis of concept formation. The potency of television in affording young and especially vulnerable children many perceptual experiences cannot be overestimated. Such potency is at least partially based upon the readiness of the young child to believe his or her perceptions.

Preschool children are probably more likely than older children to believe the immediate perceptual stimulus from the visual media and to have difficulty distinguishing real from unreal. They may retain less than older children from any one media exposure, but the repetition that occurs in the mass media probably eventually enables preschoolers to learn and retain much of the pervasive content.[4]

From Piaget's work, we know that preschool children will rely on their *perceptual* experience even if they have some *conceptual* knowledge that contradicts it. "This feature of the child's cognitive development might lead him to believe and accept what is presented in the media even when it is contradicted by verbal or conceptual knowledge."[5]

Not the least of the concerns about the young child's television viewing hours is the resultant reduction in direct learning experiences at a time when such experiences are especially critical.

In addition to the "world view" shaped for young children by television and the reduction in direct experiencing for which television is responsible, abundant research supports the conclusion that a causal relationship exists between the amount of television aggression a child sees and the aggressive thought and behavior he or she later exhibits. (See the works of A. D. Leifer, R. M. Liebert, J. M. Neal, E. S. Davidson, N. S. Schwartzberg, A. H. Stein, and L. K. Friedrich.) Further, although a research synthesis shows only a small negative correlation between television and school learning, it appears that viewing television more than ten hours a week has a definite negative effect on achievement which is especially adverse for females and children with high IQs.[6]

In a more positive vein, the portrayal of children in wheelchairs on television has been helpful in modifying young children's attitudes and behaviors toward those who are physically disabled.[7]

Clearly the influence of television upon young children is powerful and indisputable. Teachers are well advised to share the results of studies with parents, and both home and school should shoulder responsibility for recommending and monitoring children's television hours.

Summary

The notable behaviors of young children from three to eight years of age are curiosity, activity, experimentation, impatience, egocentrism, imagination, imitation, enthusiasm, adult-dependency, and unpredictability. These behaviors are characteristic of a period that is developmental prime time—a period when young children grow toward physical control, social ease, emotional stability, linguistic facility, intellectual questing, and moral understanding.

There are genres and books especially responsive to young children and their holistic development. The media-saturated environment of today's young children spurs critical questions about their perceptions and the formation of their concepts. The influential role of television cannot be overemphasized. It is a critical responsibility of adults to monitor the quality and quantity of the young child's television viewing.

DISCUSSION ACTIVITIES

• After considering the notable behaviors identified in this chapter, observe a three-year-old and an eight-year-old child (or any two children within this age span). What evidences of the notable behaviors do you find? What other behaviors would you add to this list?

• Select and read three books from Table 1.1. Then share the books with children from three to eight years old. Note each child's response. Was the sharing successful in generating an enthusiastic reaction? Did some children respond with great enthusiasm? Did some children have little or no enthusiasm? How do you account for these differences?

• Read a study of young children's television viewing habits and their effects (see page 15). Share the findings with others who are reading similar studies. What are the implications of these findings for a child's holistic development and literary development?

NOTES

1. Margaret Rasmussen, ed., *Listen! The Children Speak* (Washington, D.C.: United States National Committee of the World Organization for Early Childhood Education, 1979), p. 37

2. Ibid., p. 11.

3. Kenneth D. Wann, Miriam Selchen Dore, and Elizabeth Ann Liddle, *Fostering Intellectual Development in Young Children* (New York: Teachers College Press, 1962), p. 64.

4. Aletha Huston Stein, "Mass Media and Young Children's Development," in *Early Childhood Education,* ed. Ira J. Gordon, The Seventy-First Yearbook of the National Society for the Study of Education (Chicago: The Society, 1972), p. 183.

5. Ibid.

6. Patricia A. Williams, Edward H. Haertel, Geneva D. Haertel, and Herbert J. Walberg, "The Impact of Leisure-Time Television on School Learning: A Research Synthesis," *American Educational Research Journal,* Vol. 19, No. 1 (Spring 1982): 19–50.

7. Nancy Rubin Glauberman, "The Influence of Positive T.V. Portrayals on Children's Behavior and Attitude toward the Physically Disabled," Ph.D. dissertation, Columbia University Teachers College, 1980.

PROFESSIONAL BIBLIOGRAPHY

Almy, Millie, with Chittenden, Edward, and Miller, Paula. *Young Children's Thinking: Studies of Some Aspects of Piaget's Theory.* New York: Teachers College Press, 1966.

Britton, James. *Language and Learning.* Middlesex, England: The Penguin Books, Ltd., 1970.

Butler, Dorothy, and Clay, Marie. *Reading Begins at Home.* London: Heinemann Educational Books, Ltd., 1979.

Cazden, Courtney B. *Child Language and Education.* New York: Holt, Rinehart and Winston, 1972.

Chambers, Aidan. *Introducing Books to Children.* London: Heinemann Educational Books, Ltd., 1973.

Durkin, Dolores. *Children Who Read Early.* New York: Teachers College Press, 1966.
——. *Teaching Young Children to Read.* Boston: Allyn and Bacon, 1972.
Gardner, D. Bruce. *Development in Early Childhood: The Preschool Years.* New York: Harper & Row, Publishers, Inc., 1964.
Gesell, Arnold; Ilg, Frances L.; and Ames, Louisa Bates. *Infant & Child in the Culture of Today.* Rev. ed. New York: Harper & Row, Publishers, Inc., 1943.
Gibson, Janice T. *Growing Up: A Study of Children.* Reading, Mass.: Addison-Wesley Publishing Company, 1978.
Glauberman, Nancy Rubin. "The Influence of Positive Portrayals on Children's Behavior and Attitude toward the Physically Disabled," Ph.D. dissertation. New York: Columbia University Teachers College, 1980.
Higgins, James E. *Beyond Words: Mystical Fancy in Children's Literature.* New York: Teachers College Press, 1970.
Larrick, Nancy. *Children's Reading Begins at Home.* Winston-Salem, N.C.: Starstream Products, 1980.
Lavatelli, Celia Stendler. *Piaget's Theory Applied to an Early Childhood Curriculum.* Boston: A Center for Media Development, Inc., 1970.
Lee, Catherine. *The Growth and Development of Children.* 2d ed. London: Longman Group Limited, 1977.
Lefevre, Carl A. *Linguistics, English, and the Language Arts.* New York: Teachers College Press, 1970.
McDermott, Gerald. "Caldecott Award Acceptance." *The Horn Book Magazine* 51 (August 1975).
Portland Public Schools. *Improving Motor-Perceptual Skills.* Corvallis, Oregon: Continuing Education Publications, 1970.
Pulaski, Mary Ann Spencer. *Understanding Piaget: An Introduction to Children's Cognitive Development.* New York: Harper & Row, Publishers, Inc., 1971.
Rasmussen, Margaret, Ch. *Listen! The Children Speak.* Washington, D.C.: United States National Committee of World Organization for Early Childhood Education, 1979.
Rosen, Connie, and Rosen, Harold. *The Language of Primary School Children.* Middlesex, England: Penguin Books, Inc., 1973.
Russell, David. *Children's Thinking.* Boston: Ginn and Company, 1956.
Sarafino, Edward P., and Armstrong, James W. *Child and Adolescent Development.* Glenview, Ill.: Scott, Foresman and Company, 1980.
Smith, Lillian. *The Unreluctant Years.* Chicago: American Library Association, 1953.
Smith, William Jay. *Laughing Time.* New York: Delacorte Press, 1953.
Spodek, Bernard. *Early Childhood Education.* Englewood Cliffs, N.J.: Prentice-Hall, 1973.
Stein, Aletha Huston. "Mass Media and Young Children's Development." In *Early Childhood Education,* edited by Ira J. Gordon. The Seventy-First Yearbook of the National Society for the Study of Education. Chicago: The Society, 1972.
Strickland, Dorothy S. "Promoting Language and Concept Development." In *Literature and Young Children,* edited by Bernice E. Cullinan and Carolyn

W. Carmichael. Urbana, Ill.: National Council of Teachers of English, 1977.

Wann, Kenneth D.; Dorn, Miriam Selchen; and Liddle, Elizabeth Ann. *Fostering Intellectual Development in Young Children.* New York: Teachers College Press, 1962.

Weber, Evelyn. *Early Childhood Education: Perspectives on Change.* Belmont, Calif.: Wadsworth Publishing Company, Inc., 1970.

Wilkinson, Andrew. *The Foundations of Language: Talking and Reading in Young Children.* London: Oxford University Press, 1971.

————. *Language and Education.* London: Oxford University Press, 1975.

Williams, Patricia A.; Haertel, Edward H; Haertel, Geneva D.; and Walberg, Herbert H. "The Impact of Leisure-Time Television on School Learning: A Research Synthesis." *American Educational Research Journal,* Vol. 19, No. 1 (Spring 1982): 19–50.

Yardley, Alice. *Exploration and Language.* New York: Citation Press, 1973.

✿CHILDREN'S BOOKS

Adoff, Arnold. *Where Wild Willie.* Illus. by Emily McCully. New York: Harper & Row, Publishers, Inc., 1978.

Aesop. "The Crow and the Water Jug," *Once in a Wood.* Adapted and illus. by Eve Rice. New York: Greenwillow Books, 1979.

Alexander, Martha. *Blackboard Bear.* Illus. by author. New York: Dial Press, 1969.

————. *Nobody Ever Asked Me If I Wanted a Baby Sister.* New York: Dial Press, 1971.

Aliki. *Keep Your Mouth Closed, Dear.* New York: Dial Press, 1966.

————. *The Story of William Penn.* Englewood Cliffs, N.J.: Prentice-Hall, 1964.

Allard, Harry. *Miss Nelson Is Missing.* Illus. by James Marshall. Boston: Houghton Mifflin Co., 1977.

Anno, Mitsumasa. *Anno's Alphabet.* New York: T.Y. Crowell Co., 1975.

————. *Anno's Animals.* New York: William Collins, Publishers, 1979.

————. *Anno's Counting Book.* New York: T.Y. Crowell Co., 1977.

————. *Anno's Counting House.* New York: Philomel Books, 1982.

————. *Anno's Journey.* New York: Collins/World, 1978.

Aruego, Jose. *Look What I Can Do.* Totowa, N.J.: Charles Scribner's Sons, 1971.

Asch, Frank. *Just Like Daddy.* Illus. by author. Englewood Cliffs, N.J.: Prentice-Hall, 1981.

Avi. *Emily Upham's Revenge.* Pictures by Paul Zelinsky. New York: Pantheon Books, 1978.

Balian, Lorna. *Humbug Witch.* Nashville: Abingdon Press, 1965.

————. *Where in the World Is Henry?* Nashville: Abingdon Press, 1980.

Beyer, Evelyn. "Jump or Jiggle," *Another Here and Now Story Book.* Edited by Lucy Spraque Mitchell. New York: E. P. Dutton & Co., Inc., 1937.

Branley, Franklyn M. *Comets.* New York: Thomas Y. Crowell Co., 1984.

Briggs, Raymond. *The Snowman.* New York: Random House, 1978.

Brown, Marc. *Your First Garden Book.* Boston: Little, Brown & Co., 1981.

Brown, Margaret W. *Goodnight Moon.* Illus. by Clement Hurd. New York: Harper & Row, Publishers, Inc., 1947.

Bulla, Clyde R. *Keep Running Allen!* Illus. by Satomi Ichikawa. New York: Harper & Row, Publishers, Inc., 1978.

Cheng, Hou-Tien. *Scissor Cutting for Beginners.* New York: Holt, Rinehart and Winston, 1978.

Cole, William, comp. *Oh! What Nonsense!* Illus. by Tomi Ungerer. New York: Viking Press, Inc., 1966.

Crews, Donald. *Freight Train.* Illus. by author. New York: Greenwillow Books, 1978.

d'Aulaire, Ingri, and d'Aulaire, Edgar. *Abraham Lincoln.* Rev. ed. New York: Doubleday & Co., Inc., 1957.

De Angeli, Marguerite. *Yonie Wondernose.* New York: Doubleday & Co., Inc., 1944.

Degan, Bruce. *Jamberry.* Illus. by author. New York: Harper & Row, Publishers, Inc., 1983.

de Paola, Tomie. *The Cloud Book.* New York: Holiday House Inc., 1975.

de Regniers, Beatrice Schenk. *May I Bring a Friend?* Illus. by Beni Montresor. New York: Atheneum Publishers, 1964.

———. *It Does Not Say Meow and Other Animal Riddle Rhymes.* New York: Seabury Press, 1972.

Dragonwagon, Crescent. *Will It Be Okay?* Illus. by Ben Schecter. New York: Harper & Row, Publishers, Inc., 1977.

Duvoisin, Roger. *Donkey-Donkey.* New York: Parents Magazine Press, 1940.

———. *Petunia.* New York: Alfred A. Knopf Inc., 1950.

Edelman, Elaine. *I Love My Baby Sister (Most of the Time).* Illus. by Wendy Watson. New York: Lothrop, Lee & Shepard Books, 1984.

Emberley, Barbara. *Drummer Hoff.* Illus. by Ed Emberley. Englewood Cliffs, N.J.: Prentice-Hall, 1967.

Emberley, Ed. *Ed Emberley's Drawing Book: Make a World.* Boston: Little, Brown & Co., 1972.

Farber, Norma. *How Does It Feel to Be Old?* Illus. by Trina Schart Hyman. New York: E. P. Dutton & Co., Inc. 1979.

Fisher, Aileen. *Cricket in a Thicket.* Illus. by Feodor Rojankovsky. New York: Charles Scribner's Sons, 1963.

———. "The Package," *Up a Windy Hill.* New York: Abelard-Schuman Ltd., 1953 (orig. 1933).

Garelick, May. *Where Does the Butterfly Go When It Rains?* Illus. by Leonard Weisgard. New York: W. R. Scott, 1961.

Gauch, Patricia Lee. *Christina Katerina & the Box.* Illus. by Doris Burn. New York: Coward, McCann & Geoghegan, Inc., 1971.

Geisel, Theodor [Dr. Seuss]. *Horton Hatches the Egg.* New York: Random House, Inc., 1940.

Gibbons, Gail. *The Post Office Book: Mail and How It Moves.* New York: Thomas Y. Crowell Co, 1982.

Ginsburg, Mirra. *The Chick and the Duckling.* Illus. by Jose Aruego and Ariane Aruego. New York: Macmillan Publishing Co., Inc., 1972.

Goodall, John S. *Paddy's New Hat*. New York: Atheneum Publishers, 1980.

Greenaway, Kate. "Jump-jump-jump," *Marigold Garden*. New York and London: Frederick Warne and Company, 1885.

Gwynne, Fred. *A Chocolate Moose for Dinner*. New York: E. P. Dutton & Co., 1976.

———. *The King Who Rained*. New York: E. P. Dutton and Co., 1970.

———. *The Maggie B*. Illus. by author. New York: Atheneum Publishers, 1975.

Hoban, Russell. *Bedtime for Frances*. Illus. by Garth Williams. New York: Harper & Row, Publishers, Inc., 1960.

———. *A Birthday for Frances*. Illus. by Lillian Hoban. New York: Harper & Row, Publishers, Inc., 1968.

Hoban, Tana. *Shapes and Things*. New York: Macmillan Co., 1970.

Hoberman, Mary Ann. *Nuts to You and Nuts to Me*. Illus. by Ronni Solbert. New York: Alfred A. Knopf Inc., 1974.

Hogrogian, Nonny. *Carrot Cake*. Illus. by author. New York: Greenwillow Books, 1977.

Jackson, Leroy. "O It's Hippity Hop to Bed," *The Peter Patter Book*. Chicago: Rand McNally & Company, 1918.

Kellogg, Steven. *Much Bigger Than Martin*. New York: Dial Press, 1976.

Kessler, Ethel, and Kessler, Leonard. *What's Inside the Box?* New York: Dodd, Mead & Co., 1976.

Krauss, Ruth. *The Carrot Seed*. Illus. by Johnson Crockett. New York: Harper & Row, Publishers, Inc., 1945.

Krementz, Jill. *A Very Young Circus Flyer*. New York: Alfred A. Knopf, 1979.

———. *A Very Young Dancer*. New York: Alfred A. Knopf, 1976.

———. *A Very Young Rider*. New York: Alfred A. Knopf, 1977.

———. *A Very Young Skater*. New York: Alfred A. Knopf, 1979.

Kuskin, Karla. *Roar and More*. New York: Harper & Row, Publishers, Inc., 1956.

Langstaff, John. *Frog Went A-Courtin'*. Illus. by Feodor Rojankovsky. New York: Harcourt Brace Jovanovich, Inc., 1955.

———. *Oh, A-Hunting We Will Go*. Illus. by Nancy Winslow Parker. New York: Atheneum Publishers, 1974.

Lobel, Arnold. *Frog and Toad All Year*. New York: Harper & Row, Publishers, Inc., 1976.

———. *Frog and Toad Together*. New York: Harper & Row, Publishers, Inc. 1972.

McDermott, Gerald. *The Stonecutter*. New York: Viking Books, 1975.

MacDonald, Golden. *The Little Island*. Illus. by Leonard Weisgard. New York: Doubleday & Co., Inc., 1946.

McGinley, Phyllis. *The Year Without a Santa Claus*. Philadelphia: J. B. Lippincott Co., 1957

Mitchell, Cynthia. *Playtime*. Illus. bv Satomi Ichikawa. New York: Collins & World, 1979.

Moore, Eva. *The Great Banana Cookbook for Boys and Girls*. Illus. by Susan Russo. Boston: Houghton Mifflin Co., 1983.

———. *The Seabury Cookbook for Boys and Girls*. Illus. by Talivaldis Stubis. New York: Seabury Press, Inc., 1971.

Morrison, Bill. *Squeeze a Sneeze.* Boston: Houghton Mifflin Co., 1977.

Ness, Evaline. *Sam, Bangs, and Moonshine.* New York: Holt, Rinehart and Winston, 1966.

O'Neill, Mary. *Hailstones and Halibut Bones: Adventures in Color.* Illus. by Leonard Weisgard. New York: Doubleday & Co., Inc., 1961.

Pearson, Susan. *Molly Moves Out.* Illus. by Steven Kellogg. New York: Dial Press, 1979.

Peter Piper's Practical Principles of Plain and Perfect Pronunciation. New York: Dover Publications Inc., 1970. Unabridged and unaltered republication of the work published by Le Roy Phillips in Boston in 1911 from the first American edition, Lancaster, Mass., 1830.

Rockwell, Anne. *Games and How to Play Them.* New York: Thomas Y. Crowell Co., 1973.

Rockwell, Anne, and Rockwell, Harlow. *The Supermarket.* New York: Macmillan Publishing Co., Inc., 1979.

Rockwell, Harlow. *I Did It.* New York: Macmillan Publishing Co., Inc., 1974.

Schwartz, Alvin. *The Rainy Day Book.* New York: Simon & Schuster, Inc., 1973.

Selsam, Millicent. *Is This a Baby Dinosaur? and Other Science Picture Puzzles.* New York: Harper & Row, Publishers, Inc., 1972.

Sendak, Maurice. *Chicken Soup with Rice* in the Nutshell Library. New York: Harper & Row, Publishers, Inc., 1962.

———. *The Sign on Rosie's Door.* New York: Harper & Row, Publishers, Inc., 1960.

Shedlock, Marie L., ret. "Hafiz, the Stone-Cutter," *The Art of the Story Teller.* 3d ed., revised. New York: Dover Publications, Inc., 1951 (original 1915).

Smith, Kay. *Parakeets and Peach Pits.* Illus. by Jose Aruego. Bergenfield, N.J.: Parents Magazine Press, 1970.

Spier, Peter. *Crash! Bang! Boom!* New York: Doubleday & Co., Inc., 1972.

———. *London Bridge Is Falling Down.* New York: Doubleday & Co., 1967.

Stevenson, Robert L. "The Swing," *A Child's Garden of Verses.* Illus. by Jessie W. Smith. New York: Charles Scribner's Sons, 1905.

Testa, Fulvio. *If You Take a Pencil.* New York: Dial Press, 1982.

Tobias, Tobi. *The Quitting Deal.* Illus. by Trina Schart Hyman. New York: Viking Press, 1975.

Tudor, Tasha. *Around the Year.* New York: Henry Z. Walck Inc., 1957.

Udry, Janice May. *Let's Be Enemies.* Illus. by Maurice Sendak. New York: Harper & Row, Publishers, Inc., 1961.

Vincent, Gabrielle. *Ernest and Celestine's Picnic.* New York: Greenwillow Books, 1982.

Waber, Bernard. *The Snake: A Very Long Story.* Boston: Houghton Mifflin, 1978.

Watanabe, Shigeo. *I Can Build a House.* Illus. by Uasuo Ohtomo. New York: Philomel Books, 1983.

Watson, Clyde. *Father Fox's Feast of Songs.* Illus. by Wendy Watson. New York: Philomel Books, 1983.

Wells, Rosemary. *Benjamin and Tulip.* New York: Dial Press, 1973.

———. *Stanley and Rhoda.* New York: Dial Press, 1978.

Wezel, Peter. *The Good Bird.* New York: Harper & Row, Publishers, Inc., 1966.

Young, Miriam. *If I Drove a Truck.* Illus. by Robert Quackenbush. New York: Lothrop, Lee & Shepard Books, 1967.

Zemach, Margot. *To Hilda for Helping.* New York: Farrar, Straus & Giroux, 1977.

Zolotow, Charlotte. *If You Listen.* Illus. by Marc Simont. New York: Harper & Row, Publishers, Inc., 1980.

———. *My Grandson Lew.* Illus. by William Pene du Bois. New York: Harper & Row, Publishers, Inc., 1974.

Young Children: Growing Up with Literature

RICH ENCOUNTERS

A teacher held up a leaf devastated by the gypsy moth only to hear two second graders say with a giggle, "That was The Very Hungry Caterpillar."

•◆•

The seal on the cover of May I Bring a Friend? *proudly tooted his horn. As Dad shared the book jacket, illustrations, and verse story, his son happily joined in on the refrain. A gaggle of giggles erupted at the final turnabout. Still chuckling, Dad said, "I bet I know what friend you'd bring to the King."*

The boy looked at his father then grinned, "Yep, a dolphin," and they smiled together as they thought about the feature they viewed on television about dolphins a few weeks before.

Literature and the Needs of Young Children

Young children have a number of critical basic needs that books and stories can help to meet. (For more discussion on human needs, see Abraham Maslow's *Motivation and Personality*, rev. ed., New York: Harper and Row, 1970, pp. 35–38.)

Need to Know

Children have a *need to know* and stories are a wonderful source of information for them. The pothole in the vicinity of the school leads to questions about how roads are built, which Gail Gibbons's *New Road!* can clarify; the sudden dearth of paper needed for a mural leads to observations about how important paper is and makes a look at Gibbons's *Paper, Paper Everywhere* relevant and satisfying; or a hiccup interrupts a lesson and children ask "What causes hiccups?" which Berger's *Why I Cough, Sneeze, Shiver, Hiccup and Yawn* can answer.

Teachers can capitalize on this need to know not only by supplying books responsive to young children's questions but by nurturing and honoring the subsequent discussion and paraphrases of the children themselves. Such paraphrases are an excellent indication of how much information children have really internalized.

Need to Accept and to Give Love

Stories give children characters to relate to, to "try on," to love, and young children *need to accept and give love.* A sharing of E. B. White's *Charlotte's Web* seldom leaves dry eyes among third graders; Charlotte the spider is loved and so is Wilbur the pig. Children generally find Frances, Corduroy, Peter of *Peter's Chair,* Frog and Toad, George and Martha, Little Bear, Curious George, and many others very lovable. They know too that they themselves are loved. The very act of story sharing, a gift of adult time, is a testimony to young children that others care about them.

Teachers sharing stories soon find that it is a small step from discussing a book to discussing the fears, angers, joys, and problems children find in their own lives. Books move many children to reflect and to speak of their concerns; young children need time to do both.

Need to Belong

Stories core around human relationships. Children need to know how to manage such relationships; they *need to belong.* Stories about families like *The Quarreling Book* (Charlotte Zolotow), *Peter's Chair* (Ezra Keats), *A Chair for My Mother* (Vera B. Williams), *Smartest Bear and His Brother Oliver* (Alice Bach), and the *Frances* books (Russell Hoban) help children relate to and understand the interplay of ideas and feelings among family members. Stories like *Let's Be Enemies* (Janice Udry), *Will I Have a Friend?* (Miriam Cohen), *Everett Anderson's Friend* (Lucille Clifton), *Frog and Toad Together* (Arnold Lobel), and *Amos and Boris* (William Steig) acquaint children with characters who are initiating or maintaining friendships. Such stories and the discussions they generate help to nurture social, emotional, and moral development. The discovery of the ideas and feelings of others shows children bits of themselves. The painful process of learning that I cannot have everything I want (things and people must be shared) and that I cannot have many things I want *when* I want them (I may have to wait) needs easing for children.

Acting out the roles in these tales spurs understanding of what living demands if relationships are to be happy and harmonious. Such playacting also helps reading comprehension[1] and refines intellectual skills.[2]

Need to Achieve and to Feel Self-Esteem

Children *need to achieve and to feel self-esteem*, and stories help children build a sense of achievement. In scores of folktales it is the expectation of the achievement of the protagonist that glues many children to the story. Katy in *Katy and the Big Snow* (Virginia Lee Burton) copes with the big snow, and *Swimmy* (Leo Lionni) copes with the big fish. Jack succeeds in *Jack and the Beanstalk* (Joseph Jacobs), *Leo the Late Bloomer* (Robert Kraus) finally blooms, and *Crow Boy* (Taro Yashima) at last earns the respect of his peers Young children need such character models — human, animal, or machine — to help build their own feelings of "I can" and to combat the "too little," "too young," "too small," and "just wait" rebuffs they continuously meet. When this vicarious experiencing of feelings of achievement and self-esteem arrives clothed in adventure, so much the happier.

Need for Beauty, Order, and Harmony

Through both language and content, stories help supply the *need* young children have *for beauty, order, and harmony.* Language is a miracle to young children. On the tongue of a gifted storyteller, and even those who are not so gifted, the music of language — its grace and flow — can transport young listeners to the never-never land of fantasy or clothe the everyday world of fact with fresh labels and images. Beautiful language feeds children's need for beauty.

It is in the consistent structure of many folk and fairy tales that young children begin to acquire a sense of story, perceive a linear order, and develop genre expectations. They begin to discover the order of time when they read books about seasons and holidays; these stories present them with anchors that corroborate their personal experiences. Selsam's *Benny's Animals* helps children begin to appreciate hierarchical order, and even in the very simple adventures of *George and Martha* the order of cause and effect is clearly indicated. Together order and beauty create a harmony that young children appreciate even though they cannot articulate it.

Through the part stories play in meeting their needs, children make meaning; that is, they bring meaning to each story situation and accumulate more in the process.

The Young Child: Making Meaning

Meaning: Unique to Each Child

Roger Brown defines meaning as "...the total disposition make use of and react to form."[3] Children bring such total disposition to story-sharing sessions; this disposition, shaped by each child's total development, grows and intensifies as the child hears or reads. In this process the child becomes disposed to read or hear more, reacting and responding to the form and content, whatever it be, in his or her own unique and unpredictable fashion. The uniqueness of the response is due in part to the singularity of each child, for after all

As long as I live
I shall always be
Myself and no other,
Just me.

From "Me" in *Bells and Grass* by Walter de la Mare. Copyright 1942 by Walter de la Mare; © renewed 1969 by Richard de la Mare. Reprinted by permission of Viking Penguin Inc.

But the originality of the child's response is also due to the special way his or her emotions and thoughts are caught up by the story. The grip of thoughts and emotions, which is the glory of literature, is dependent on the child, the story, and the way the story is shared. In short, what sparks a child–book friendship is a mix of child, story, and sharing. This triadic relationship is dynamic with the disposition (or meaning) intensifying as more of the story is shared. When the sharing is done by people who matter to the child, the personal meaning developed and the impact on him or her may be life-long.

Making meaning is dependent on a number of factors. Although according to Applebee, children below seven years of age retell a story in whole or in part with little understanding of the overall structure,[4] numerous experiences in reprocessing and reproducing stories help young children, over time, to gain a story grammar—an awareness of the typical elements in a story. In turn, this recognition helps the child savor and comprehend stories more fully.[5]

Certainly in the making of meaning the comprehending-composing or reading–writing processes reinforce each other. These have been researched by many, including Graves and Hansen.[6] Whether children can write *before* their reading experiences give them the visual images of words they will need to compose is questionable, but there is no question that both processes are vital in helping young children shape meaning from their own knowledge and experiences.

It is from the child's background of experiences shaped by his or her environment that meaning is made. As shown in Figure 2.1, the

FIGURE 2.1 *Growing Awareness of Story Grammar*

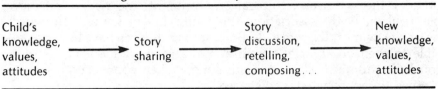

child's knowledge, values, and attitudes are the background against which stories are shared and extended and from which an awareness of story grammar develops, increasing story expectancy and enjoyment and creating *new* meaning.

Meaning: Dependent on Experience

Dorothy White observed of her daughter Carol, "Over and over again I see that her reading enjoyment is contingent upon the range of her previous experience."[7] Ideas emerge from the many experiences children have. Children sift out the similarities and differences among such experiences and begin to fashion ideas. The early classifying of their sensory-emotional experiences according to some similar characteristic leads children to generalize, then to name. With labeling, comes the beginning of order. Indeed, the abilities to compare, organize, and generalize are basic. The quality of these generalizations is dependent on the nature of the early experiences that induced them—their dynamism, clarity, and diversity.

A book offers young children experiences to categorize, contrast, and judge against all other ideas coming their way. Such comparisons illuminate personal history and may trigger debate or even rejection if the concept contradicts experience. (Recall from Chapter 1, John was ready to debate the inclusion of spiders in insectdom.)

Inspired is the teacher (and the author and illustrator) who can so involve children in a story that each child *experiences* the adventure; *he* or *she becomes* the protagonist. Careful observation of children yields situations such as the following: Jim, the hero of the mystery story, is coping with the clues in the story. George, the third-grade reader of the story, links the clues to a solution before the story's climax and says, as though Jim were a close and living friend, "Sorry, Jim, I beat you."

Meaning: Dependent on Environment

Rich literary encounters require rich literary environments. All of us are brought up vulnerable to myriad influences—familial, social, and cultural. The richer the home in diverse stimulation and the broader the social and cultural environment, the richer and more plentiful will be the associations the young child makes with the words he or she hears and later reads. Book-loving children have books accessible to them in libraries and in homes and in schools—books to be touched, thumbed, clasped, read, sung, talked about, laughed over, clapped to, appreciated, and shared.

Children continuously relate what life and their imaginations provide to what the book says or shows. Zoo visits enrich books about animals, and books about animals enrich zoo visits. *Mike Mulligan's Mary Ann* (Virginia Lee Burton) makes the excavation down the street more understandable; David Macaulay's *Cathedral* introduces the older child to architecture, to the interdependence of craftspeople, and to humanity's desire to create fitting places of worship.

Here again, children are unpredictable but alert to their environment. David Macaulay's *Cathedral* might well be questioned as a logical choice for nursery-school shelves, but one nursery teacher enlightens us.

☆ Joey ran excitedly from his blocks to the teacher's desk one day asking, "Where is it? Where is it?"

"Where is what?" the teacher asked.

"You know, that big book with pictures of big buildings—churches."

The teacher looked nonplussed so Joey ran to the bookshelves and hunted impatiently. Finally, he pulled out *Cathedral*, ran back to his blocks, set *Cathedral* standing, chevron style on the carpet, and after finding the page picturing the buttresses, proceeded to block-build the buttresses of his own cathedral.

●◆●

Meaning-Making: Dynamic

The outside dynamic forces in the lives of young children are by no means the only ones at work; the children themselves provide motion and change. Children form concepts from experiences that leave them with a potpourri of perceptions and memories. The sifting out and the shaping of perceptions and memories into a more or less reliable structure on which to build concepts is a continuous and lively activity of all children.

Sometimes the dynamism of a literary experience is best seen in the quality and quantity of the post-sharing experiences in which young children engage—the enthusiasm of their construction of Jack's beanstalk, the ingenuity of the animal masks for Verna Aardema's *Who's in Rabbit's House?*, or the enactment of one of Ernest and Celestine's adventures.

Meaning-Making: Reality and Fantasy

If meaning is somewhat dependent on the images that experience conjures, the fuller and more diverse these images, the deeper the meaning. Surely it requires fantasy *and* reality to shape such images.

Marvelous are the informational books available to children; their narrative and pictures help to answer the young child's questions about the world and spur him or her to ask more. Equally wonderful are the books of fantasy "...which recognize the 'inner child' and so reach out to him leading him forth to share experience beyond his immediate, tangible horizons."[8] In helping children to savor other worlds, these books help them construct new horizons for themselves.

Literature of reality and fantasy offers children a mix and balance that expand their images and enlarge their associations. There are books that deliberately juxtapose fact and fiction permitting children to contrast the two. Simon's *Animal Fact/Animal Fable*, for example, takes advantage of challenge and suspense and invites the child to chuckle at the *fable* and the funny illustration that accompanies it after which the page is turned and *fact* is presented. An older child will enjoy *Come Away From the Water, Shirley* by John Burningham who juxtaposes, on opposite pages, Shirley's real, parent-directed world with her fantasy world of pirates, adventures, and treasures.

Meaning-Making: Art

Artists use their tools of line, color, shape, texture, and general composition to interpret texts in their own highly personal fashion. Viewers interpret artistic works just as personally. "Our experience of a picture is something we create within ourselves."[9]

Ezra Keats's collages, Brian Wildsmith's vivid colors, Kay Chorao's pastels, Margot Zemach's versatile lines, Ed Emberley's textures, Leo Lionni's collage and paper stamping, Peter Spier's great detail—all bespeak a personal interpretation; each will elicit a different response from children as they see, hear, or read the story. The meaning tne children make—the dispositions they intensify—will result from the fusion of graphic and literary elements.

It is not only the vitality of the child's experience and environment, the balance between the word and the picture and between fantasy and reality, that shape his or her disposition and initial response, it is also the quality of the writing. Though the young child certainly does not analyze this, it is an author's ability to weave the elements of literature into gripping stories that guarantees a young child's undivided attention.

The Story: The Making of Literature

Young children know that they like or dislike what they hear or read and readily offer evaluative statements such as, "I liked it," "It's nice," or "It's good."[10] Rarely are these statements analytical. However, the importance of the nature and quality of the special blending of literary elements presented by the writer, whether or not it is analyzed with or by children, cannot be disallowed. Literature of course is far greater than the sum of its literary elements, but it is to these components we must look if we are to judge quality.

Characterization

High-quality books for young children are marked by characters who are believable, simply delineated, motorically and verbally active, and free of stereotypes.

For example, *Owliver*, Robert Kraus's charming and independent little owl, is believable. He listens to his parents, gives their suggestions a try, then makes his own decisions. *Owliver* represents a delightful balance between obedience and independence. Simply delineated in narrative and art, the character Owliver is an actor from beginning to end—a teasing mimic. Active, experimenting, full of curiosity and enthusiasm, Owliver, in fact, exhibits all the notable behaviors mentioned in Chapter 1. His activity reveals his character and makes him the believable, nonstereotypical protagonist that he is.

The one-dimensional characters of folktales and fairy tales are understood and loved, but children soon learn to appreciate fuller characters who change as a story builds. Sam in *Sam, Bangs and Moonshine* (Evaline Ness) not only learns the difference between real (truth) and moonshine (fantasy) but also acts to rectify the aftermath of her daydreaming. Her motivations for fantasizing are clear and understandable. Sam is not the simple character Owliver is and young children who appreciate the former learn, as they hear and read more stories, to appreciate the latter.

Plot

Plot is the order of actions or events in a story that mirror the conflict generated when the characters vie with self, others, nature, or society. In Miranda Hapgood's *Martha's Mad Day*, Martha is her own worst enemy. In the fable *The Town Mouse and Country Mouse* (by the same author), the conflict is the result of two very different viewpoints about life styles. Conflict in Lonzo Anderson's *The Day the Hurricane Happened* focuses on a family's behavior during a hurricane, and in

Unhurry Harry, by Eve Merriam, Harry fights an uphill battle against all the cultural-social pressure for haste.

In high-quality books for young children, the plot, whether achieved through events leading to a surprising climax (*Simple Pictures Are Best* by Nancy Willard) or a series of actions that generate continuous suspense (*The Honeybee and the Robber* by Eric Carle) must meet certain criteria:

- The plot should be simply but clearly delineated. For instance, actions must dovetail, as in William Steig's *Sylvester and the Magic Pebble,* and the cause-effect sequence must be logically revealed, as in Gerald McDermott's *Arrow to the Sun.*
- The plot must be focal (as in Pat Hutchins's *Don't Forget the Bacon*). Many subplots or subconflicts confuse the young child.
- The plot should shape the behavior of characters and be shaped by them, as well as reveal a good deal of action, as in John Goodall's tales of Paddy Pork.

However plot is woven, it must offer the characters opportunities to change, to grow, to act, and to cope if the minds and emotions of young children are to be caught and held.

Setting

The setting—the where and when of the story—is a literary element of varying emphasis. Sometimes cultural, temporal, or spatial factors are focal; sometimes they are merely incidental. In books such as Taro Yashima's *Crow Boy,* Robert McCloskey's *One Morning in Maine,* Phyllis Krasilovsky's *The Cow Who Fell in the Canal,* Rumer Godden's *The Old Woman Who Lived in a Vinegar Bottle,* and Muriel Feelings's *Moja Means One,* setting in cultural or temporal terms is core to the plot. In the Obadiah stories, too, the Nantucket Quaker setting is evident in illustration, dress, and language.

In Gian Paolo Ceserani's *Marco Polo* and in Mitsumasa Anno's *Anno's Italy* and *Anno's Britain,* setting looms important. In the former, highly detailed illustrations of the late part of the thirteenth century augment the historical account, and in the latter two titles, the story *is* the setting. In a book like Roger Duvoisin's *Snowy and Woody,* a consciousness of setting is developed because a contrast of two places is basic to the plot.

Time and space concepts are slow in developing in young children. To very young children all stories are "now." As they grow a bit older, time and space become dichotomized—the time is "now" and "long ago," the space is "here" or "there." Time and space concepts later become increasingly differentiated. Young children become conscious of time not only when the tale is set in the past but also when the hero or heroine has to meet deadlines, as in certain mystery stories. Also such stories as James Stevenson's *That Terrible Halloween Night,* Cheli Ryan's *Hildilid's Night,* and Robert McCloskey's *One Morning in Maine* bring an awareness of time because actions take place within a strong temporal frame—night or morning.

Discussing the settings reinforced by illustrations in the text *before* the story is shared sometimes helps young children to form and confirm concepts of place. Such discussion also nourishes growing awareness of time changes, especially when children begin to verbalize differences in terms of their own experiences. Aliki's *A Medieval Feast* is rich in fostering a contrast for third graders between the text and preparation for our Thanksgiving Day. It could easily lead to research on the culinary preparation for a presidential visit by George Washington or the current president of the United States.

Style

According to Virginia Hamilton, "No one really knows what style is but I think it must be a writer's personality which means to me a public self that the writer feels comfortable having the reader recognize."[11] The special way an author uses words to relate his or her tale renders possible a quick trip of the imagination, a slow but persistent hold on it, or no spur to the imagination at all. Through use of figurative language, humor, imagery, rhythm, rhyme, and various literary forms, an author succeeds in presenting a story in language so suitable to it that the total effect engages, even rivets, the reader's attention. This is style. Patricia Cianciolo credits style as "that component of fiction and non-fiction which elicits particular responses from the reader. Therein lies its importance."[12]

Storywriters and storytellers can create music; they can also preserve it. In sharing stories with young children this music of language must be treasured for the sake of the tale and the sake of the child. Young children's responses to what Owen Egan calls "traditional language" should not be denied them. In speaking of a number of Irish folktales untouched by rewriters, Egan says, "There is a striking song-like quality in the [original] writing, a great reliance on the rhythms and cadences of spoken language."[13] The young child responds enthusiastically to such lyric quality.

Children may be unaware of its potency but it is style that first attracts their ears, turns up the corners of their lips, and focuses their eyes on the teller or tale. It also nudges the young child to linguistic experimentation and creativity.

Theme

Theme is the heart of the tale. The themes of literature are basic ideas about problems inherent in the human condition. The way the author and illustrator think and feel about problems is the motivation and purpose of the story.

Am I my brother's (sister's) keeper? Horton in Dr. Seuss's *Horton Hatches the Egg* has to answer that when Lazy Mayzie leaves her egg untended. Lilly Etts in *Sidewalk Story* not only faces the same question, but she also has the problem of how to answer "yes."

Can I be content being myself? Donkey-Donkey, in the story by the same name by Roger Duvoisin, learns that being true to oneself makes for happiness.

In Janice Udry's *Let's Be Enemies*, John and James quarrel but make up and resume their fast friendship by day's end. They learn that it's playing *together* that counts.

Alexander in Judith Viorst's *Alexander and the Terrible, Horrible, No Good, Very Bad Day* fights his own frustration with life's annoyances.

Themes are the foundation of literature. There are a focal few but the variations of them are legion. Young children perceive themes dimly so gripped are they by the plight of the story's hero and heroine.

Format

The size, shape, binding, type style, illustrations, quality and type of paper and reproduction, as well as the cover and jacket designs are part of a book's format. Each of these elements must be appropriate to the content of the story and should be attractive to the child.

The graphics of Karla Kuskin's *Roar and More* give the text a charm and credibility that appeal to young readers; the sounds shout through the print. The beautiful full-page illustrations by Leo and Diane Dillon in Margaret Musgrove's *Ashanti to Zulu* enhance the well-documented text and offer a rich visualization of African traditions. The alphabet guessing game book, by Elting and Folsom, *Q Is For Duck*, gives answers to such questions as "Why is E for Whale?" on the page after the question. This format captivates children by challenging them to respond to the question and enabling them to find out immediately whether their response is accurate. The "holey" aftermath of the caterpillar in Carle's *The Very Hungry Caterpillar* is a clever idea in format that generates the interest of children and marks the main idea.

Nothing substitutes for a basically sound plot and full characters, but format can certainly help to attract the young reader to the story and help to maintain interest. See Chapter 4 for more books of unusual and diverse design.

Bridging Child and Story

The potency of the child's initial meeting with a book cannot be over-estimated. Careful consideration of children's preferences prior to the sharing and the manner of the story sharing itself are amply repaid.

Story Preferences of Young Children

What kinds of books do young children want to hear and read? They certainly do have preferences. These must be considered in story selection and respected just as literary components must be weighed. Generally young children expect their stories to contain:

• *Action* The active bodies and minds of young children demand action in their stories. They want book characters who are lively.

• *Dialogue* Young children like characters who not only act but talk. Characters are more believable when they converse. Indeed, long before young children begin reading, they have known and appreciated the cartoon "balloons" that hold the dialogue of the comic strips they enjoy.

• *Surprise* Plots in stories for young children need to be direct and uncomplicated but also exciting. Children expect their stories to be the herbs and spices of their lives; they anticipate surprise. Whether surprise comes about via an unusual resolution of the conflict or a change in the behavior of a character or the intriguing language in the telling is immaterial. For the story sharer, surprise is often created or heightened by utilizing to the fullest all the intonational features possible as well as a keen sense of timing.

• *Brevity* Young children prefer short stories that they can hear at one sitting. Some books can charm children into lengthier attention spans but initially tales should be short. Indeed, interspersing even short tales with riddles, short poems, or fingerplays is ideal for very young audiences who have to grow into lengthier picture books and on to story books.

• *Humor* Humor helps to rivet attention and cohere the audience. There is probably no more effective social glue than a chuckle or laugh and nothing that links the young child so closely to the text.

• *Imagery* It is imagery in a story that will give young children the mental pictures that create the feeling of "being there," of being the pro-tagonist, of experiencing for themselves actions that are the story. To interest young children, images must be simple and analogies clear.

• *Contagious Cadence* In a special way, young children respond to rhyme and intonation in every story. If they can feel the rhythm, tap it, clap it, join in on the stressed words, dance to it, march to it, or sing to it, they will make the story their own. The younger the children, the more likely they are to respond to the cadence of words with body movement. There are stories in children's literature that have been built upon a song; these sell themselves. Children usually crown the sharing of such stories with a rendition of the song.

• *Repetition* Young children find comfort in repetition. When it is integral to a story, repetition combines the ease and security of the familiar with the chance to participate.

• *Happy Endings* Young children want tales to end happily. As they grow and cope with more and more of life's problems, reality balances this expectation of ideal happiness and the resolution of life's complexities in not wholly-happy endings can be accepted. If children have met in life and in books enough persons who enrich and afford them models of behavior in diverse situations, they are likely to be able to cope with not-so-happy endings. For the very young child, this time is not yet. For the five- to eight-year-old, the time may be beginning.

• *Illustrations* Although the well-prepared storyteller can always command attention, the media-conscious child of today generally expects to see as well as hear a story. See Chapter 7 for selection criteria and a discussion of picture books.

Some titles that exemplify these preferences of young children follow in Table 2.1.

Selection Criteria

In addition to major literary criteria and children's preferences, consideration in story selection ought to be given to the following:

• Stories must appeal emotionally to children. Young children probably *feel* things more intently than they *think* them, therefore the emotional strength and attraction of a story is a major consideration in making a selection. Stories with solid, clear plots, believable characters, and authentic setting, mood, and style suitable to the tale are likely to make an emotional impact. When overall story quality, children's preferences, and their background experiences are considered, this emotional appeal is likely to be present.

• Stories for very young nonreading children need to be within their understanding and listening comprehension. A knowledge of the developmental characteristics of young children (see Chapter 1), their home backgrounds, and their school or nursery "history" help those who are selecting stories for children to identify tales within young children's

TABLE 2.1 *Story Preferences of Young Children and Selected Titles*

Children's Story Preferences	Selected Titles
Action	Jill Krementz. *A Very Young Gymnast.* 5–8 Rachel Isadora. *My Ballet Class.* 5–8 Clyde Watson. *Catch Me and Kiss Me and Say It Again.* 5–8
Dialogue	Harry Allard and James Marshall. Books about *The Stupids.* 3–8 Sue Breitner. *The Bookseller's Advice.* 5–8 Patricia MacLachlan. *Through Grandpa's Eyes.* 5–8 Maurice Sendak. *Pierre.* 3–5 Charlotte Zolotow. *My Grandson Lew.* 5–8
Surprise	Franz Bonn. *The Children's Theatre.* 5–8 Aardema, Verna. *Who's in Rabbit's House?* 5–8 Robert Crowther. *The Most Amazing Hide-and-Seek Counting Book.* 3–5 Jan Pienkowski *The Haunted House.* 3–5
Brevity	Marc Brown, comp. *Finger Rhymes.* 3–5 Beatrice de Regniers. *It Does Not Say Meow and Other Animal Riddle Rhymes.* 5–8 Arnold Lobel. *Owl at Home.* 5–8 Arnold Lobel. *Frog and Toad Together.* 5–8 James Marshall. *George and Martha.* 3–8
Humor	Aliki. *Keep Your Mouth Closed, Dear.* 5–8 Tomie de Paola. *Fin M'Coul.* 5–8 Rosemary Wells. *Good Night, Fred.* 3–5
Imagery	Aileen Fisher. *I Stood Upon a Mountain.* 5–8 Mary O'Neill. *Hailstones and Halibut Bones.* 3–8
Contagious Cadence	Many titles of Dr. Seuss. 3–8 Tom Glazer. *Do Your Ears Hang Low?* 3–8 Ogden Nash. *Custard and Company.* Sel. by Quentin Blake. 3–8 Christina Rossetti. *Sing-Song.* 3–8 Maurice Sendak. *Chicken Soup with Rice.* 3–8
Repetition	Mirra Ginsburg. *Good Morning, Chick.* 3–5 Mirra Ginsburg. *How the Sun Was Brought Back to the Sky.* 5–8 Robert Quackenbush. *Old McDonald Had a Farm.* 3–8 Nonny Hogrogian. *Rooster Brother.* 5–8
Happy Endings	Grimm Brothers. *The Bremen Town Musicians. Cinderella. Hansel and Gretel.* 3–8 Phyllis McGinley. *The Plain Princess.* 5–8 Jay Williams. *The Practical Princess.* 5–8
Illustrations	See Chapter 7

abilities to understand and enjoy. The child *reader* in this age group should be given a good deal of freedom to choose titles.

• Young children are especially vulnerable to stereotypes in book characters. The fewer such characters they encounter the better. Here it must be noted that the one-dimensional characters of much of traditional literature may seem close to being stereotypes. In speaking of these characters, Iona and Peter Opie call them "stock figures. They are either altogether good or altogether bad and there is no evolution of character."[14] One-dimensional characters are more like the figures in the morality plays of medieval times each of whom represented a moral virtue. It may be that the mix of characters, bad, good, and evil, in traditional stories presents an overall balance that contributes to a "world view" upon which children can build.

• Young children ought to meet all types of stories. They do appreciate change. Poetry, song, adventure stories, folk and fairy tales, informational books all need to be shared: it is via story sharing that the child's awareness and appreciation of a variety of genres develop. When parents and teachers are constantly confronted with young children who request the same book again and again, it is difficult to remember that children do indeed want change. Unhinging the child may be achieved through presenting stories of the same type concomitantly with a totally new form but just as exciting a tale. For instance, a *Nate the Great* (Marjorie Weinman Sharmat) adventure can be accompanied by Millicent Selsam's *Tyrannosaurus Rex*, for older children in this age range.

Settings for Story Sharing

The who, what, how, where, and when of story sharing loom large in determining whether or not the child-book meeting marks a friendship or a passing acquaintance. The maxim "He has half the deed done, who has made a beginning" (Horace's *Epistles*, Book I, line 40) is pertinent here. When a child is introduced to a book, a memory begins. Memories lodge deep; their introductions should be carefully planned. It behooves storyteller and writer to recognize the potency of a worthy introduction.

Who The importance to human development of the "significant others" in one's life has been documented innumerable times. In John Bowlby's works, and most recently in Selma Fraiberg's *Every Child's Birthright*, the effects of an unloved infancy and childhood are personal tragedy and probable social problems. Stories presented by significant others in a child's life—parents, grandparents, family members, and later the teachers who become the significant others in a child's *school* life—are likely to be remembered. The child who comes to school after years of Mother Goose has been shared as he or she sat on the lap of a grandparent, parent, or other loving adult is prepared to chuckle when the teacher shares the nonsense verse of David McCord, William Jay Smith, Shel Silverstein, Mary Ann Hoberman, or John Ciardi. (See Chapter 5.) That child also has learned that words can label funny actions, scenes, and feelings, and has acquired an awareness of some of the things that can be done with words that tickle the funny bone.

Young children want to be near those they love and they love storytellers. Whether this derives from love of teller or love of tale is sometimes difficult to determine since children are likely to think those they love always tell good stories and good stories must be told by those they love.

Interest in storytellers carries over to storywriters. Children are entranced by the people who write their books and they want to learn more about them. Witness the great popularity of Lee Bennett Hopkins's books, *Books Are by People* and *More Books by More People.* Fortunate children who receive autographed copies of books with a personal message are wonderstruck. One such child looking at the Veronica that Roger Duvoisin drew for her said, "He drew it specially for me — just for me — just for me in my very own book." Agog, she walked slowly away hugging the pink Veronica spread across two pages — not just any Veronica but *her* Veronica!

What Not only is the person who introduces the book important but what is introduced is critical. Although the child should be involved in the selection of books from early years, the quality of the content for a young child is primarily the parent and teacher's responsibility. Today for the caring adult, the right book is less a puzzle than it once was. A rich, comprehensive set of general and special selection aids help parents and teachers know what is available and how to make the best books accessible. (See Chapter 11 and other chapter bibliographies.)

No book is likely to be the right book for the child if the adult does not know the child as well as the book. The Stupids are hilariously funny to some children; others prefer the gentle humor of Frog and Toad. Teachers are fortunate; from their observations, conversations, story times, and story talks as well as from the administration of such things as interest inventories, they learn about each child. With knowledge of both children and books, the teacher is likely to serve stories that will be remembered, questioned, loved, actively sought, as well as thought about and felt keenly.

How Stories shared by adults who love the book *and* the child are likely to be enthusiastically received even if the sharer is not a Ruth Sawyer or a Marie Shedlock. Still, those who care about children and literature will want to perfect their story-sharing technique. Aids abound; they range from the cassettes and records of great story-tellers to very practical sequential suggestions on story reading and storytelling. (See Chapter 3.)

With the possible exception of poetry, the storytellers' enthusiasm is more important than their memory of the exact words of the story. Their involvement in the story, their feeling for it radiates and the children catch this glow. The first rule for a prospective story-teller, then, might be: Love your story. Affection for a story permeates any rendition, as does affection for the child permeate any selection process.

Strategies to enhance the communication of enthusiasm are numerous. Witness the delighted surprise mirrored on young faces as the teacher telling *Caps for Sale* (Esphyr Slobodkina) turns a large flannel-board tree around and children see mischievous monkeys dangling among its branches. Listen to the applause of first graders as a teacher manipulates the four hand-puppets in Paul Galdone's *The Three Little Pigs* and they are told they can be the puppeteers tomor-row. Listen and watch as children enter into Seymour Chwast's *The House That Jack Built* by popping up with the verse as it accumulates, or observe as children sit mesmerized by a very special home-made story told by a lover of words and tales.

When   The universal love of story precludes any likelihood that a teller of tales will be stopped by children unless the selection is really unsuitable or the presentation very poor. In all but rare cases, *when* you tell a story to children is less important than *what* you tell them, *how* you tell them, and *who* you are. Obviously, however, children engaged in a very engrossing participatory activity are going to respond less enthusiastically (if at all) to an announcement about storytelling than children not so engaged.

Although storytelling time is any time a teller has a story to tell, *regular story hours* for young children are often and wisely scheduled. *Their very regularity gives to these sessions the importance they deserve* and they generate happy anticipation in the children.

Teachers must also be aware that there are prime times for teaching and learning as well as for book sharing. To capitalize on the interest of a child or class is to recognize a prime time. Mr. Jackson (from Chapter 1) certainly knew this. Johnny was definitely vacci-nated with bibliophilism because Mr. Jackson recognized a prime time. The decision about when a child should be introduced to a story is contingent upon more than curriculum, however, and relates to his or her needs. Caring teachers recognize snippets of time in the class-room schedule when a story or poetry break would be wise and they

Eve Merriam, Mary Ann Hoberman, or Karla Kuskin to break the pace or, in rare instances, to defuse a troubled environment. Having a poetry collection at hand is a spur to linguistic, aesthetic, and emotional development and therefore to good classroom climate.

The timing of when to introduce a book is most critical in the case of bibliotherapy. *Bibliotherapy* is the knowledge of oneself that comes from reading. The child with a persistent emotional or developmental problem needs help that bibliotherapy is unlikely to accomplish unaided. However, whatever help books *can* give needs to be made available as the child copes with his or her problem. Accomplishing the appropriate matching requires skill on the teacher's or parent's part. There are a number of selection aids that make this more likely, principally Dreyer's *The Bookfinder*. See also the books cited in Chapter 9.

Where   Just as stories can be told or read any time, they can be told or read any place—in the lap of a loving adult or in a circle around the teacher. As long as the teller and hearer are not distracted, the story can be communicated. The same is true for the older child-reader. A nook, a carrel, special corners or tables that offer space, time, and quiet give assurance of comparative freedom from distraction. Such space may be difficult to find in today's world; adults in the home and school may have to be particularly inventive about providing it.

There are, of course, *prime* settings for book introductions too. Quiet and time are of major importance but settings with books on a shelf or table—with comfortable chairs or floor space and with adequate light, temperature, and ventilation encourage reading and listening. Special care must be taken of the conditions under which the young child reads so that ocular development is nurtured and eye strain is prevented.

If the teacher plans to act out the story or have the children dramatize it, then space is vital. For such "story living," *location* is critical. A puppet show or dramatization requires enough space for children to move about, pick up a prop, or change simple scenery. Except for this type of book involvement, however, the child and teller or the child and book require only enough space to communicate to each other.

Summary

All young children are constantly engaged in making meaning from their experiences and their environment. Such meaning is unique and personal for each child and the process itself is dynamic.

From story sharing and story extensions children add to and modify their view of the world, generating new meanings for themselves. In making meaning from literature and acquiring a sense of story, young children utilize reality and fantasy stories and the graphic arts as well as the literary components of plot, characterization, setting, style, theme, and format.

Young children have preferences. They prefer stories that are active, full of conversation, brief, and humorous—stories with surprises, happy endings, and linguistic features that delight their ears.

The who, what, how, when, and where of story sharing can help to determine whether a child and a book form a lasting friendship.

DISCUSSION ACTIVITIES

• Observe a small group of three- to eight-year-old children over several days for one to two hours as they engage in different activities. Record their questions; use a tape recorder if necessary. Can you categorize their questions? Do the questions suggest any topics of permanent interest? Take the list of questions to the card catalog of the children's room of a school or public library. How many books can you find that address the interests of young children and would be helpful in answering their questions?

• Focus on any one of the basic needs of children. Compile a list of ten books that are especially suitable in meeting this need of children aged three through five or five through eight. Select one title from your list and plan how this book might be best prepared for presentation to children.

• Select any two fictional books mentioned in this chapter and paraphrase the plot: Describe the characters, style, format, and identify the setting and theme. After reviewing the literary standards in this chapter, would you label the two books "high quality"? Why? Why not?

• What types of teacher behavior would be most productive in helping young children to develop a "sense of story"?

NOTES

1. G. Michael Miller and George Mason, "Dramatic Improvisation: Riskfree Role Playing for Improving Reading Performance," *Reading Teacher*, Vol. 37, No. 2 (November 1983): 131.

2. Thomas Daniel Yawkey, "More on Play as Intelligence in Children," *Journal of Creative Behavior*, Vol. 13, No. 4 (1979): 247.

3. Roger Brown, *Words and Things* (New York: The Free Press, 1958), p. 109.

4. Arthur N. Applebee, *The Child's Concept of Story* (Chicago: University of Chicago Press, 1978), p. 123ff.

5. Muriel K. Rand, "Story Schema: Theory, Research and Practice," *Reading Teacher,* Vol. 37, No. 4 (January 1984): 381.

6. Donald H. Graves and Jane Hansen, "The Relationship of Reading to Writing," project in progress at University of New Hampshire, 1982.

7. Dorothy White, *Books Before Five* (New York: Oxford University Press, 1956), p. 29.

8. James E. Higgins, *Beyond Words: Mystical Fancy in Children's Literature* (New York: Teachers College Press, 1970), p. 1.

9. Peggy Whalen Levitt, "Picture Play in Children's Books: A Celebration of Visual Awareness," *Wilson Library Bulletin* (October 1980): 106.

10. Applebee, *The Child's Concept of Story,* pp. 99–100.

11. Virginia Hamilton, "Writing the Source: In Other Words," *The Horn Book,* Vol 54, No. 6 (December 1978): 618.

12. Patricia Cianciolo, ed., *Picture Books for Children* (Chicago: American Library Association, 1973), p. 2.

13. Owen Egan, "In Defense of Traditional Language: Folktales and Reading Texts," *The Reading Teacher,* Vol. 37, No. 3 (December 1983): 232.

14. Iona Opie and Peter Opie, *The Classic Fairy Tales* (New York: Oxford University Press, 1974), p. 18.

✡ PROFESSIONAL BIBLIOGRAPHY

Applebee, Arthur N. *The Child's Concept of Story.* Chicago: University of Chicago Press, 1978.

Babbitt, Natalie. "Happy Endings? Of Course, and Also Joy," *The New York Times Book Review,* Part 2, November 8, 1970, pp. 1, 50.

Brown, Roger. *Words and Things.* New York: The Free Press, 1958.

Chambers, Aidan. *Introducing Books to Children.* London: Heinemann Educational Books, Ltd., 1973.

Cianciolo, Patricia, ed. *Picture Books for Children.* Chicago: American Library Association, 1973.

de la Mare, Walter. *Bells and Grass.* New York: Viking Press, 1947.

Dreyer, Sharon Spredemann. *The Bookfinder: A Guide to Children's Literature about the Needs and Problems of Youth Aged 2–15.* Circle Pines, Minn.: American Guidance Service, 1981.

Egan, Owen. "In Defense of Traditional Language: Folktales and Reading Texts," *The Reading Teacher*, Vol. 37, No. 3 (December 1983): 228–233.

Fraiberg, Selma. *Every Child's Birthright: in Defense of Mothering*. New York: Basic Books, Inc., 1977.

Graves, Donald H., and Hansen, Jane. "The Relationship of Reading to Writing." Project in progress at University of New Hampshire, 1982.

Hamilton, Virginia. "Writing the Source: In Other Words," *The Horn Book*, Vol. LIV, No. 6 (December 1978): 618.

Higgins, James E. *Beyond Words: Mystical Fancy in Children's Literature*. New York: Teacher's College Press, 1970.

Hopkins, Lee Bennett. *Books Are by People*. New York: Citation Press, 1969.

———. *More Books by More People*. New York: Citation Press, 1974.

MacCann, Donnarae, and Richard, Olga. *The Child's First Books: A Critical Study of Pictures and Texts*. New York: The H. W. Wilson Company, 1973.

Miller, G. Michael, and Mason, George. "Dramatic Improvisation: Risk-free Role Playing for Improving Reading Performance," *Reading Teacher*, Vol. 37, No. 2 (November 1983): 128–131.

Opie, Iona , and Opie, Peter. *The Classic Fairy Tales*. New York: Oxford University Press, 1974.

Rand, Muriel K. "Story Schema: Theory, Research and Practice," *Reading Teacher*, Vol. 37, No. 4 (January 1984): 377–382.

Whalen-Levitt, Peggy. "Picture Play in Children's Books: A Celebration of Visual Awareness," *Wilson Library Bulletin* (October 1980): 102–107.

White, Dorothy. *Books Before Five*. New York: Oxford University Press, 1956.

Yawkey, Thomas Daniel. "More on Play as Intelligence in Children," *Journal of Creative Behavior*, Vol. 13, No. 4 (1979): 247–262.

CHILDREN'S BOOKS

Aardema, Verna. *Who's in Rabbit's House?* Illus. by Leo Dillon and Diane Dillon. New York: Dial Press, 1977.

Aliki. *Keep Your Mouth Closed, Dear*. New York: Dial Press, 1966.

———. *A Medieval Feast*. Illus. by author. New York: Thomas Y. Crowell, 1983.

Allard, Harry. *The Stupids Step Out*. Illus. by James Marshall. Boston: Houghton Mifflin Company, 1974.

Allard, Harry, and Marshall, James. *The Stupids Have a Ball*. Illus. by James Marshall. Boston: Houghton Mifflin Company, 1978.

Anderson, Lonzo. *The Day the Hurricane Happened*. Illus. by Ann Grafalconi. New York: Charles Scribner's Sons, 1974.

Anno, Mitsumasa. *Anno's Britain*. Illus. by author. New York: Philomel Books, 1982.

———. *Anno's Italy*. Illus. by author. New York: Philomel Books, 1980.

Bach, Alice. *Smartest Bear and His Brother Oliver*. Pictures by Steven Kellogg. New York: Harper & Row, Publishers, Inc., 1975.

Berger, Melvin. *Why I Cough, Sneeze, Shiver, Hiccup and Yawn.* Illus. by Holly Keller. New York: Thomas Y. Crowell Co., 1983.

Bond, Michael. *A Bear Called Paddington.* Illus. by Peggy Fortnum. Boston: Houghton Mifflin Company, 1960.

Bonn, Franz. *The Children's Theatre.* New York: Viking Press, 1979.

Breitner, Sue. *The Bookseller's Advice.* Illus. by Jane Chambless-Rigie. New York: Viking Books, 1981.

Brown, Marc, comp. *Finger Rhymes.* New York: E. P. Dutton & Co., Inc., 1980.

Burningham, John. *Come Away From the Water, Shirley.* New York: Thomas Y. Crowell Company, 1977.

Burton, Virginia Lee. *Katy and the Big Snow.* Illus. by author. Boston: Houghton Mifflin Co., 1943.

——. *Mike Mulligan and His Steam Shovel.* New York: Houghton Mifflin Co., 1939, renewed 1967.

Carle, Eric. *The Honeybee and the Robber.* Illus. by author. New York: Philomel Books, 1981.

——. *The Very Hungry Caterpillar.* Cleveland, Ohio: Collins World, 1969.

Ceserani, Gian Paolo. *Marco Polo.* Illus. by Piero Ventura. New York: G. P. Putnam's Sons, 1977.

Chwast, Seymour. *The House That Jack Built.* New York: Random House, 1973.

Cleary, Beverly. *Ramona the Pest.* Illus. by Louis Darling. New York: William Morrow & Co., Inc., 1968.

Clifton, Lucille. *Everett Anderson's Friend.* Illus. by Ann Grifalconi. New York: Holt, Rinehart and Winston, Inc., 1976.

Cohen, Miriam. *When Will I Read?* Illus. by Lillian Hoban. New York: Greenwillow Books, 1977.

——. *Will I Have a Friend?* Illus. by Lillian Hoban. New York: Macmillan Publishing Co., Inc., 1967.

Crowther, Robert. *The Most Amazing Hide-and-Seek Counting Book.* New York: Viking Press, 1978.

de la Mare, Walter. *Bells and Grass.* New York: Viking Press, 1942.

de Paola, Tomie. *Fin M'Coul.* New York: Holiday House, 1981.

de Regniers, Beatrice. *It Does Not Say Meow and Other Animal Riddle Rhymes.* New York: Seabury Press, 1972.

——. *May I Bring a Friend?* Illus. by Beni Montresor. New York: Atheneum Publishers, 1964.

Duvoisin, Roger. *Donkey-Donkey.* New York: Parents Magazine Press, 1940.

——. *Snowy and Woody.* New York: Alfred A. Knopf, 1979.

——. *Veronica.* New York: Alfred A. Knopf, 1961.

Elting, Mary, and Folsom, Michael. *Q Is For Duck.* Pictures by Jack Kent. New York: Houghton Mifflin/Clarion Books, 1980.

Feelings, Muriel. *Moja Means One: A Swahili Counting Book.* Illus. by Tom Feelings. New York: Dial Press, 1971.

Fisher, Aileen. *I Stood Upon a Mountain.* Illus. by Blair Lent. New York: Harper and Row, Publishers, Inc., 1979.

Freeman, Don. *Corduroy.* New York: Viking Books, 1968.

Galdone, Paul. *The Three Little Pigs.* New York: The Seabury Press, Inc., 1970.

———. *The Town Mouse and the Country Mouse.* New York: McGraw-Hill Co., 1971.

Geisel, Theodor [Dr. Suess]. *Horton Hatches the Egg.* New York: Random House, Inc., 1940.

Gibbons, Gail. *New Road!* Illus. by author. New York: Harper & Row, Publishers, Inc., 1983.

———. *Paper, Paper Everywhere.* Illus. by author. New York: Harcourt, Brace Jovanovich, Inc., 1983.

Ginsburg, Mirra. *Good Morning, Chick.* Illus. by Byron Barton. New York: Greenwillow Books, 1980.

———. *How the Sun Was Brought Back to the Sky.* Illus. by Jose Aruego and Ariane Dewey. New York: Macmillan Publishing Co., Inc., 1975.

Glazer, Tom. *Do Your Ears Hang Low?* Illus. by Mila Lazarevich. New York: Doubleday & Co., 1980.

Godden, Rumer. *The Old Woman Who Lived in a Vinegar Bottle.* Illus. by Mairi Heddewick. New York: Viking Press, 1972.

Goodall, John S. *The Adventures of Paddy Pork.* Illus. by author. New York: Harcourt Brace Jovanovich, 1968.

Grimm Brothers. *The Bremen Town Musicians.* Illus. by Paul Galdone. New York: McGraw Hill Book Co., 1968.

———. *Cinderella.* Illus. by Nonny Hogrogian. New York: Greenwillow Books, 1981.

———. *Hansel and Gretel.* Trans. by Charles Scribner. Illus. by Adrienne Adams. New York: Charles Scribner's Sons, 1975.

Hapgood, Miranda. *Martha's Mad Day.* Illus. by Emily McCully. New York: Crown Publishers, 1977.

Hoban, Russell. *Bedtime for Frances.* Illus. by Garth Williams. New York: Harper & Row, Publishers, Inc., 1960.

———. *A Birthday for Frances.* Illus. by Lillian Hoban. New York: Harper & Row, Publishers, Inc., 1968.

Hogrogian, Nonny. *Rooster Brother.* Illus. by author. New York: Macmillan Publishing Co., Inc., 1974.

Hurd, Edith Thacher. *I Dance in My Red Pajamas.* Pictures by Emily Arnold McCully. New York: Harper & Row, Publishers, Inc., 1982.

Hutchins, Pat. *Don't Forget the Bacon.* New York: Greenwillow Books, 1976.

Isadora, Rachel. *My Ballet Class.* New York: Greenwillow Books, 1980.

Jacobs, Joseph. *Jack and the Beanstalk.* Illus. by Margery Gill. New York: Henry Z. Walck Inc., 1975.

Keats, Ezra Jack. *Peter's Chair.* New York: Harper & Row, Publishers, Inc., 1967.

———. *Whistle for Willie.* New York: Viking Press, 1964.

Kellogg, Steven. *Pinkerton Behave!* New York: Dial Press, 1979.

———. *A Rose for Pinkerton.* New York: Dial Press, 1981.

Krasilovsky, Phyllis. *The Cow Who Fell in the Canal.* Illus. by Peter Spier. New York: Doubleday & Company, Inc., 1953.

Kraus, Robert. *Leo the Late Bloomer.* Illus. by Jose Aruego. New York: Windmill Books, Inc., 1971.

——— *Owliver.* Illus. by Jose Aruego and Ariane Dewey. New York: Windmill Books, Inc., 1974.

Krementz, Jill. *A Very Young Gymnast.* New York: Alfred A. Knopf, 1978.

Kuskin, Karla. *Roar and More.* New York: Harper & Row, Publishers, Inc., 1956.

Lionni, Leo. *Frederick.* New York: Pantheon Books, Inc., 1967.

———. *Swimmy.* New York: Pantheon Books, Inc., 1963.

Lobel, Arnold. *Frog and Toad Together.* New York: Harper & Row, Publishers, Inc., 1972.

———. *Owl at Home.* New York: Harper & Row, Publishers, Inc., 1975.

Macaulay, David. *Cathedral.* Boston: Houghton Mifflin Company, 1973.

McCloskey, Robert. *One Morning in Maine.* New York: Viking Press, 1952.

McDermott, Gerald. *Arrow to the Sun.* Illus. by author. New York: Viking Press, 1974.

McGinley, Phyllis. *The Plain Princess.* Illus. by Helen Stone. Philadelphia: J. B. Lippincott Company, 1945.

———. *The Year Without a Santa Claus.* Illus. by Kurt Werth. Philadelphia: J. B. Lippincott Company, 1956.

MacLachlan, Patricia. *Through Grandpa's Eyes.* Illus. by Deborah Ray. New York: Harper & Row, Publishers, Inc., 1980.

Marshall, James. *George and Martha.* Boston: Houghton Mifflin Co., 1972.

Mathis, Sharon. *Sidewalk Story.* Illus. by Leo Carty. New York: Viking Press, 1971.

Merriam, Eve. *Unhurry Harry.* Illus. by Gail Owens. New York: Four Winds Press, 1978.

Minarik, Else Holmelund. *Little Bear.* Illus. by Maurice Sendak. New York: Harper & Row, Publishers, Inc., 1957.

Musgrove, Margaret. *Ashanti to Zulu: African Traditions.* Illus. by Leo Dillon and Diane Dillon. New York: Dial Press, 1976.

Nash, Ogden. *Custard and Company.* Sel. by Quentin Blake. Boston: Little, Brown & Co., 1980.

Ness, Evaline. *Sam, Bangs and Moonshine.* Illus. by author. New York: Holt, Rinehart and Winston, 1966.

O'Dell, Scott. *Island of the Blue Dolphins.* Boston: Houghton Mifflin Company, 1960.

O'Neill, Mary. *Hailstones and Halibut Bones: Adventures in Color.* Illus. by Leonard Weisgard. New York: Doubleday & Co., Inc., 1961.

Perrault, Charles. *Cinderella.* Illus. by Paul Galdone. New York: McGraw-Hill, 1978.

Pienkowski, Jan. *The Haunted House.* New York: E. P. Dutton & Co., Inc., 1979.

Piper, Watty. *The Little Engine That Could.* Illus. by George Hauman and Doris Hauman. New York: Platt & Munk, Publishers, 1954 (1930).

Quackenbush, Robert. *Old MacDonald Had a Farm.* New York: Harper & Row, Publishers, Inc., 1972.

Rey, Hans Augusto. *Curious George.* Boston: Houghton Mifflin Co., 1941.

Rossetti, Christina. *Sing-Song.* Illus. by Arthur Hughes. New York: Dover Publications, 1969 (Macmillan, 1952).

Ryan, Cheli D. *Hildilid's Night.* Illus. by Arnold Lobel. New York: Macmillan Company, 1974.

Selsam, Millicent. *Benny's Animals and How He Put Them in Order.* Illus. by Arnold Lobel. New York: Harper & Row, Publishers, Inc., 1966.

———. *Tyrannosaurus Rex.* New York: Harper & Row, Publishers, Inc., 1978.

Sendak, Maurice. *Chicken Soup with Rice.* New York: Harper & Row, Publishers, Inc., 1962.

———. *Pierre.* (Nutshell Library.) New York: Harper & Row, Publishers, Inc., 1962.

———. *Where the Wild Things Are.* New York: Harper & Row, Publishers, Inc., 1963.

Sharmat, Marjorie Weinman. *Nate the Great.* Illus. by Marc Simont. New York: Coward, McCann & Geoghegan, Inc., 1972.

Simon, Seymour. *Animal Fact/Animal Fable.* Illus. by Diane de Groat. New York: Crown Publishers, 1979.

Slobodkina, Esphyr. *Caps for Sale.* Reading, Mass.: Addison-Wesley, 1947.

Sobol, Donald J. *Encyclopedia Brown Tracks Them Down.* Illus. by Leonard Shortall. Nashville: Thomas Nelson Inc., 1971.

Steig, William. *Amos and Boris.* New York: Farrar, Straus & Giroux, Inc., 1971.

———. *Sylvester and the Magic Pebble.* New York: Windmill Books, 1969.

Stevenson, James. *That Terrible Halloween Night.* Illus. by author. New York: Greenwillow Books, 1980.

Udry, Janice May. *Let's Be Enemies.* Illus. by Maurice Sendak. New York: Harper & Row, Publishers, Inc., 1961.

Vincent, Gabrielle. *Ernest and Celestine's Picnic.* New York: Greenwillow Books, 1982.

Viorst, Judith. *Alexander and the Terrible, Horrible, No Good, Very Bad Day.* Illus. by Ray Cruz. New York: Atheneum Publishers, 1972.

Vreuls, Diane. *Sums: A Looking Game.* New York: Viking Press, 1977.

Watson, Clyde. *Catch Me and Kiss Me and Say It Again.* Illus. by Wendy Watson. New York: William Collins Publishers, Inc., 1978.

Wells, Rosemary. *Goodnight, Fred.* New York: Dial Press, 1981.

White, E. B. *Charlotte's Web.* Illus. by Garth Williams. New York: Harper & Row, Publishers, Inc., 1952.

Willard, Nancy. *Simple Pictures Are Best.* Illus. by Tomie de Paola. New York: Harcourt Brace Jovanovich Inc., 1977.

Williams, Jay. *The Practical Princess and Other Liberating Fairy Tales.* Illus. by Rick Schreiter. New York: Parents Magazine Press, 1978.

Williams, Vera B. *A Chair for My Mother.* New York: Greenwillow Books, 1982.

Yashima, Taro. *Crow Boy.* New York: Viking Press, 1955.

Zolotow, Charlotte. *My Grandson Lew.* Illus. by William Pene du Bois. New York: Harper & Row, Publishers, Inc., 1974.

———. *The Quarreling Book.* Illus. by Arnold Lobel. New York: Harper & Row, Publishers, Inc., 1963.

Chapter 3

Story Sharing

RICH ENCOUNTERS

The first-grade teacher secured the simply made tagboard and placed four hand-puppets, the three pigs and a wolf, behind it.

The six-year-olds settled into their semicircle and heard, "Once upon a time when pigs spoke rhyme...."

After the fate of the first pig, there were choruses of determined voices, "Then I'll huff, and I'll puff, and I'll blow your house in," in strong, menacing tones.

Soon the voices in unison exclaimed, "No, no, by the hair of my chinny chin chin."

The teacher continued with Joseph Jacobs's version of "The Story of the Three Little Pigs." When the last remaining pig thwarted the wolf by building a house of bricks, there were many happy, satisfied, "good-for-him" looks from the children. Soon the expressions became anxious, however, when the pig was caught—at first atop the apple tree and then in the rolling butter churn. The wolf got his just desserts, however, and when the pig put the lid on the "make-believe" (but very much "believed-in") pot there were some exclamations of "Good," nods of yes, and agreement that he was a "big, baaaaaaaaad wolf." In a moment, all of these exclamations were quickly replaced by, "Can we put on a play?" "I want to be the wolf." "Can I be a pig?"

●◆●

The teacher is in her storytelling chair; the storytelling rug has been spread. Children have just completed the finger play "Grandfather's Glasses," and are ready to listen.

"Once there was a boy named Danny," the teacher begins. The nursery school youngsters then meet Mrs. Hen, Mrs. Goose, Mrs. Goat, and Mrs. Cow and hear Danny ask each of them if she could give him something for his mother's birthday. The children quickly learn the repetition of the greeting–request–response–thank-you form of Marjorie Flack's Ask Mr. Bear, but the ending takes them by surprise. They grin at Mr. Bear's answer and when the teacher asks, reaching out her arms, what a bear hug is, THEY SHOW HER.

Story Sharing—Eons Old

Stories and story sharing are eons old. When traditional tales are shared with young children the heritage of centuries becomes part of their lives, for despite the variety and number of tellings the core of the stories has remained intact. Tales themselves cross time, countries, and cultures. The existence and variety of names for storytellers mark the focal value cultures accord the role: gleemen, ollami, shenachies, minnesingers, minstrels, troubadours, bards.

Young children are not unique in their joy of story. They join the weary warriors of old, the court company of medieval times, and their own curious counterparts in homes and classrooms in the enjoyment of spun tales. Stories grip the spirits of children, enabling them to associate the past tale with present personal experiences and to enact past and present tales with verve and joy.

It is fitting that the treasury of tales was entrusted to young children. When the oral sharing of stories among adults was replaced by more sophisticated reading, child nurturers the world over continued to share stories with children. Cribs and cradles, nurseries and playrooms became the repositories of oral literature. Indeed, it is still the crib and cradle, the home nursery and later the nursery school that best sustain the tradition. How fortunate is the young child whose own home and schoolroom house enthusiastic tale sharers.

Story Power

The awed, surprised, sorrowful, angry, happy, excited expressions that chase across the faces of children listening intently to a story advertise the power of stories to stir emotions. Such effects are overt and ephemeral.

Longer-lasting effects, seemingly peripheral and serendipitous, are legion. Snippets of language remain in the child long after a story is shared only to burst out unexpectedly in a discussion, as happened in the anecdote of Eric Carle's *The Very Hungry Caterpillar*. The likening of a problem confronted by a story hero to a child's own life is remarked upon and pondered. The joy of group choral reading later leads to "Remember the poem we did at Halloween? We did that with loud and soft voices."

Variations in Story-Sharing Styles

Story sharers differ in style. Marie Shedlock, Gudrun Thorne Thomsen, Augusta Baker, and Ellin Greene believe strongly in the art of storytelling as a *listening* experience. Baker and Greene, for example, state that various realia may entertain "the child but they do not speak to the inner child."[1] These storytellers emphasize the voice as the instrument of the taleteller. It is through the carefully cultivated use of voice that the heart is warmed and memories are born. Classroom teachers who read and tell stories learn to use their voices to vivify their tales.

There are other story sharers who have penetrated the hearts of a people and collected their stories. When they share these folktales, in addition to attention-getting articulation, they may use native rhythm instruments, "talking sticks," native dress, or cultural artifacts as focals to their story sharing.

Still other sharers, most notably in classrooms and libraries, who work with young children use puppets, masks, chalkboards, story boards (flannel, felt, or magnetic), transparencies, magic tricks, music, records, tapes, slides, filmstrips or films, pantomime, improvisation, props, or costumes to present parts of or the whole story.

No matter what the style of presentation, story sharers are united in their desire to breathe life into the tale with all the means at hand and heart.

Story sharing as an art is experiencing a resurgence. Organizations such as the National Association for the Preservation and Perpetuation of Storytelling (NAPPS) and the National Story League seek to preserve the art of storytelling and share the riches of the oral tradition. Project Storytelling: Classics of the Oral Tradition is a project originally funded by the National Endowment for the Humanities and currently expanded under the direction of CEMREL Inc., St. Louis, Missouri. The Project involves teachers, librarians, and parents in storytelling and in sharing a wide range of stories with children—stories as different as "The Three Little Pigs" and *Beowulf*, and *The Iliad*. These groups give testimony to the existence of people eager to collect and share tales and a growing recognition of the art and serious craft of storytelling.

Releasing Story Power

Good storytellers release the power that is found in good tales. Together, good tales and good tellers create rich encounters. There are three basics for rich encounters.

- *Share stories.* The first condition needed for rich encounters is story sharing. For a literary treasure to become a joy, it must be shared. Here young children are dependent on adults or older siblings. In scheduled story hours young children generally meet a balance of literature—an integration of prose and poetry, finger plays and dramatic plays, rhymes and choral verse, and sometimes art and music. Such an integration encourages young children to respond to literature in a variety of ways.

• *Make books accessible.* Young children need to see and hold books, to gaze at and feel books before they can giggle or marvel over the pictures or become engrossed over the words. The home, classroom, and school and public library collections ought to be familiar. Indeed, if books—numerous, diverse, and appealing—were as accessible as television, is it not possible that children might turn the pages as eagerly as they turn the dial?

• *Provide modeling.* The potency of modeling as a way of learning for young children must be understood and utilized. To see parents and teachers reading and enjoying books is a lesson young children do not forget. Some school systems have made modeling a part of the curriculum. In programs such as USSR (Uninterrupted, Sustained, Silent Reading),[2] and variations thereof, time is allocated during the school day for *everyone*—principal, teachers, staff, and children—to enjoy a favorite book. When children see everyone concentrating on and delighting in a variety of books, they want books too.

Modes of Story Sharing

There are three major modes of story sharing: storytelling, story reading, and story living. Once selected, should the story be told, read, enacted, or some combination of the three? The checklist presented in Table 3.1 may help effect a decision.

The advantages of the various modes of presentation are inherent in the questions in the checklist. The face-to-face presentation of *storytelling,* without even the book between teller and child, is the most personal, the most intimate, and possibly the most emotional of all story-sharing modes. The laugh, smile, tear, or anger spurred by the storyteller's skill etch large on the child's board of experience. To deprive a child of the beauty of illustrations in picture books or an exact rendering of a poem, however, is unthinkable; here the advantages of reading *and* viewing are quickly apparent.

There are still other times when plot, characters, and mood demand dramatization—where props, gestures, and actions (sometimes exaggerated) are necessary to breathe life into the story. The goal of all story presentation is to bring the story to life in order that it may become part of the life of each listener.

Teachers of young children ought to guard against the idea that they *must* resort to all sorts of aids and gimmicks to share a story. A tale

TABLE 3.1 *Checklist for Type of Presentation*

	Examples
Storytelling	
1. Does the story beg to be heard? Does it sound musical, lyrical, rhythmic? Do the words sparkle with freshness? Do they "spell" pictures in the mind? Are the linguistic features of simple imagery, rhythm, rhyme, repetition, alliteration, and onomatopoeia prominent?	Nonny Hogrogian. *One Fine Day.* 3–8. Jack Prelutsky. *Toucans Two.* 3–8. Robert Quackenbush. *Go Tell Aunt Rhody.* 3–8. Maurice Sendak. *Chicken Soup with Rice.* 3–8.
2. Is there a verbal *humor* that must be heard?	Arlene Mosel. *Tikki Tikki Tembo.* 3–8. Judith Barrett. *Cloudy with a Chance of Meatballs.* 5–8.
3. Can the presentation of character and plot best be accomplished through the words, intonation, and personel style of the storyteller? Are the uniquenesses of the characters most apparent in the dialogue?	Judith Viost. *I'll Fix Anthony.* 3–8.
4. Does the plot build toward a powerful climax that can be made more dramatic by intonation?	Mercer Mayer. *What Do You Do with a Kangaroo?* 5–8.
5. Is the story of sufficient literary quality to warrant the time to prepare it for telling?	
6. How long will it take to share the story? Is such a time span suitable to a young audience?	
7. Does the story grow in richness as the teller shares and reshares it? Does it have "repeatability"?	Cumulative tales
8. Do the actions in the story meld together smoothly, forming a clear sequence	Paul Galdone. *The Gingerbread Boy.* 3–5. Anne Rockwell. *The Old Woman and Her Pig.* 3–5.

(continued)

TABLE 3.1 *Continued*

	Examples
that will not tax the listening comprehension of young children?	

A resounding "yes" to all of these questions suggests that the story be told.

Story Reading

9. Is the story one in which pictures and text need simultaneous presentation? Are the pictures critical to the story? Do they "tell" the story or share equally with the narrative the task of communicating the story? Are the illustrations, if not critical to the story, too beautiful to miss?

   The Stupids stories. 5–8.
   Lorna Balian. *Humbug Witch*. 3–8.

10. Does the story line require careful, verbatim presentation.

    All verse stories. 3–8.
    Maurice Sendak. *Pierre*. 3–8.
    Geoffrey Chaucer. *Chanticleer and the Fox*. 3–8.
    Arnold Lobel. *The Rose in My Garden*. 3–8.

11. Is the story of such a length as to prohibit *telling* it?

12. Is the story in poetry form? (Here memorization or reading is necessary to faithful presentation.)

    Clement Moore. *The Night Before Christmas*. 3–8.

13. Can the pictures easily be shared as the story is read?

    Don Freeman. *The Chalk Box Story*. 3–8.

A "yes" to questions 9–13 warrants story reading.

Story Living

14. Is the story one of a few simple actions which can be easily dramatized via simple puppets, flannel-board, chalk rhythm instruments?

    The Mr. Grumpy stories. 3–5.
    Esphyr Slobodkina. *Caps for Sale*. 3–8.
    Strega Nona stories. 3–8.

15. Does the story suggest gestural or postural presentation?

    Florence Heide. *The Shrinking of Treehorn*. 7–8.

	Examples
16. Are the book personalities few in number and so vivid and strong that they invite enactment?	Grimm Brothers. *King Grisly Beard.* 5–8.
17. Does the mood require props costumes, or gestures to sustain it?	Historical and holiday books. 3–8.
18. Does the story unfold through strong dialogue?	Marjorie Flack. *Ask Mr. Bear.* 3–8.

A "yes" to questions 14–18 warrants story living.

---

well loved and well known by the story sharer can be effectively and beautifully shared via the human voice unaided. In the process, listening skills are honed.

Classroom in Readiness

A classroom is ready for story sharing when the following criteria have been met:

- The setting is semi-circular to allow for maximal eye contact.
- The children are comfortable and anticipatory.
- The atmosphere is intimate and personal.
- Floor spaces are marked or indicated verbally.
- The story sharer is well prepared.
- The story sharer cares about the child and the tale.

According to Jackie Torrence, a well known teller of tales, "One simple way to select a story is to think about how it feels as you read it. If it feels right, that's the one to tell. The most important thing about the selection of a story is never to waste time on a story you dislike."[3]

Sharers who understand young children and their interests have a variety of stories available of varying lengths and types and are not likely to lose the attention of their listeners. The age-old magic of a worthy tale rarely fails to enchant afresh each new audience.

Preparation for Sharing

Storytelling According to Augusta Baker and Ellin Greene, a storyteller must "live with [the] story until the characters and the setting become as real to you as people and places you know. You must know it so well that it can be told as if it were a personal reminiscence."[4] Such immersion in a story involves much practice. Some suggestions for achieving such involvement include:

- Read the entire story three or four times. Internalize the basic story line.
- Learn those words indigenous to the tale — repetitive phrases and stage setters; for example, "Beyond the sun, moon, and stars," "It was yesterday and yet today."
- Tape the story and note which portions need to be modified.
- Practice the story aloud (if possible, rehearse it in front of one child) and make necessary adjustment in intonation and pacing.
- Prepare reminder cards, if needed.
- Time the presentation.

Given the teacher's usual time constraints, it is probable that the types of preparation described here will be reserved for a few tales each year. This should cause no concern. One of the greatest storytellers is said to have prepared only three new stories a year but these were planned with great meticulousness. Just as children love repetition *in* a story, they also love repetition *of* stories. A well-prepared tale will not suffer from repeated renditions; it will in fact grow more loved. It is the skilled story sharer who never tires of repetition and contrives to bring love and enthusiasm to *each* rendition. (See Appendix I for a *guide* to storytelling preparation written by Gwendolyn Jones, a former first-grade teacher and a professional storyteller. Mrs. Jones is currently teaching graduate and undergraduate children's literature courses. In her guide, she relates how she "internalizes" her stories — a must for all story sharers.)

Story Reading The story reader as well as the storyteller must know the whole story well so that intonation flows naturally. If pictures are to be shown, they should be effectively integrated with the narrative and visible to all children.

Story Living After determining that certain stories ought to be dramatized, story sharers need to proceed through the following steps:

- Identify and practice the voice changes and the appropriate gestures that make the story live.

- Identify and practice the use of any props that best catch the plot, characters, or mood.
- Practice the sequencing of cumulative tales so that the sharing is smooth and invites the participation of children.
- Where characters and dialogue of the story are simple, and the plot uncomplicated, hand puppets or a flannel-board may be used to retell the story after it is first shared by telling or reading.
- Stories, such as Virginia Burton's *The Little House,* can be shared via voice and simple chalk drawings which mirror the changes in the little house and its settings.
- If the characters engage in simple movement and dialogue against a static background, a presentation of felt figures on a storyboard is ideal.
- If the story involves only two or three characters and can be represented in terms of a few focal actions, pantomime may be used.

Presentation

Storytelling   When *telling* a story, the following guidelines are helpful:

- Informally gather the children together and be sure they are comfortable.
- Make certain the children can hear.
- Maintain eye contact with all children.
- Consciously use pitch, stress, juncture, and pace to create and sustain the mood.
- Use a confidential tone unless the story dictates otherwise.
- Articulate clearly.
- Keep the story moving.
- Delay discussion — preferably until after the story is finished.
- At the conclusion, encourage story talk and extension activities.

Story Reading   When *reading* a story, the following guidelines are helpful, in addition to the previous suggestions:

- Make certain the illustrations are visible to all.
- Preferably share the story at one sitting. If this is not possible, ask a child to summarize the story before continuing to the next part. Do some picture reviewing too.

Story Living   When *enacting* a story, the following guidelines, in addition to previous suggestions, are helpful:

- Be sure that props are readily available and sharing tools are handy. Involve young children in the creation of these aids whenever possible.
- Provide sufficient space and time for enactment.
- Check to see that the audience is comfortable and can see the story unfold.

If the children are to participate in the actual presentation:

- Be sure the children are instructed on how to participate. Sometimes this is best done by a beckoning gesture while sharing the story; sometimes it is best "rehearsed" briefly beforehand. When the presentation is designed to teach children the story, as in a finger play, demonstrate slowly enough for young children to follow.
- Use story and poem content to stir *natural gesture* and *movement*. In poems such as "Jump or Jiggle" and "Little Charlie Chipmunk" and in the story "The Snooks Family," there are movements natural to the story and children need little invitation to move according to the words. Sometimes the participation is simply supplying sound effects, as in "The King with a Terrible Temper" where a verbal response is mandated whenever the king, queen, princess, and prince are mentioned.

Story Extensions

Story extensions span a range from the simple retelling of a story by children to inviting them to join in on the refrain (if they have not spontaneously done so during the second sharing) to elaborate puppet or dramatic performances. Such extensions may be linguistic, dramatic, artistic, or any combination thereof.

The nature and quality of story extensions reflect the power in stories to stir the imagination. According to Eileen Colwell, a well known storyteller, "Stories provide a stimulus to the imagination which cannot be found elsewhere.... The child's imagination must be stimulated from an early age if he is to develop as a person.... Imagination enables him to see a landscape he has never seen, to take part in adventures he may never experience...."[5]

Linguistic Extensions   Beyond the simple repetition of the refrain are the choral verse, choral play, and even choral creations. Stories in verse from the simple nursery rhymes to the cumulative tales to the folk song-stories invite verbal participation and even verbal continuation. Old Mother Hubbard and her dog can have all sorts of additional adventures. Dividing the class into narrator and characters and inviting children's suggestions and self-evaluation is fun as well as linguistically sound.

Having children act out their own version of a story quickly reveals whatever most impressed them, the story's relevancy to their own experiences, and how stimulating to their imaginations the tale is.

Dramatic Extensions The simple, untutored renditions of "Three Billy Goats Gruff," "The Three Bears," "The Three Pigs," "Jack and the Beanstalk," and other simple folktales are experiences no child should be deprived of. Such stories stir appropriate movement and gesture and adlibbing.

These extensions can range from quick improvisation to elaborate productions. "Hansel and Gretel" can be simply enacted or more sophisticatedly rendered to the music of the operetta. Jay Williams's *Practical Princess* begs to be played and Lorna Balian's *The Humbug Witch* can be pantomimed with a few props. Diane Wolkstein's *A Cool Ride in the Sky* offers a chance for some happy slapstick and a play on words. José Aruego's *Look What I Can Do!* does the same in a simpler fashion. Many of John Langstaff's books can be initially heard to a soft hum in the background and, when read a second time, choral versed and climaxed with the song. This is the great potential of dramatic extensions; the range of possibilities is limited only by the imaginations of the author and the players. Some of the approaches used in Readers Theatre[6] can be applied by teachers of young readers to effect a dynamic oral dramatic event. Simple folktales and narrative poems can be quickly and happily read with verve and gusto.

Artistic Extensions Artistic extensions can be accomplished by one child or by a group of children. A classroom full of children can create a delightful bulletin board teeming with jolly, pink, three-dimensional pigs, depicting Arnold and Anita Lobel's *A Treeful of Pigs*. One child or many can create additional ball scenes for *The Stupids Have a Ball* (Allard and Marshall) and effect their own second book of the Stupid Family's adventures. By making and wearing simple paper-bag masks, children can become the animal actors in Verna Aardema's *Who's in Rabbit's House?* or in one of Arnold Lobel's *Fables*. Twenty-two children hear Tomi Ungerer's *The Beast of Monsieur Racine* and twenty-two beasts are crayoned onto a long strip of folded paper to create a leporello of beasts. (A leporello is an accordion-folded paper that contains pictures, stories, or records. The first joint project of the International Board of Books for Young People (IBBY) and the International Reading Association (IRA) was a leporello of ten bears in full color, the work of some of the world's most famous illustrators/authors.)

Media as Story Sharer

Local or regional radio programs, tape cassettes, and audio reels of children's tales, when well presented and faithful to their sources, stir the imagination and young children are forced to sculpt their own characters, paint their own setting, and visualize the plot in their own way. The face-to-face encounter of the storyteller is missed but imagination flourishes.

Powerful as television is, televised tales lack the intimacy of person-to-person sharing, the potential for participation, and the personal challenge to the imagination as well as the facial, postural message the listener gives the teller when tale-sharing strikes the heart. It robs the child of the opportunity to create pictures of his or her own; however, such deprivation *may* be more apparent than real. Television does afford young children the opportunity to see their creations confirmed *if* pre-television sharing and discussions have elicited from them their perceptions of the story or, if the story is unknown, have generated some hypotheses based on the title. Comparison and evaluation then spring forth naturally.

When a "televersion" introduces rather than confirms a story, it may accelerate the child's search for the book but it can also alienate the child from the book or offer him or her a distorted version that may remain forever uncorrected. Therefore, parents and teachers need to read carefully the announcements of television productions, know the groups and sponsors who give thought to preserving the original story, and set aside pre- and post-television talk time with young children.

Summary

Stories and the sharing of them are eons old. Such sharing can stir the feelings, imagination, and intellects of young children in powerful ways.

In addition to the sharer's preference and the listeners' ages, the mode of sharing a particular story depends on factors relating to the richness of the language, the dependency of the narrative on illustrations to communicate the tale, and the dramatic potential of the story.

Story sharers differ in their styles of presentation. Some prefer to utilize voice only and others employ props, native dress, musical accompaniment, pedagogical tools (chalkboard, flannel-boards, etc.) to share the story.

For all types of sharing, telling, reading, and living, careful preparation is needed. Linguistic, dramatic, and artistic story extensions offer children a chance to share the emotion the story stirred and in so doing to stretch their imaginations.

DISCUSSION ACTIVITIES

• Using the checklist provided in this chapter (Table 3.1) and the preparation suggestions by Gwendolyn Jones in Appendix I, select a story to tell to children. Share it with one child and evaluate your performance in terms of:
    a. the child's attention throughout the presentation
    b. the child's comments following the story
    c. your own feelings about the sharing session.

• Using the checklist provided in this chapter (Table 3.1) and Appendix I, select a book to read to children. Practice coordinating reading the text and sharing the pictures. Identify places where "reflective, savor time" is vital. Indicate several possible extensions for the story and work with children as they extend the story.

• Share a story with children in whatever mode you consider most suitable after using the checklist in this chapter (Table 3.1). Tape the children's comments as they discuss the story and their work in extending it. Are there any indications that children are growing in appreciating and understanding story structure? How do you know?

NOTES

1. Augusta Baker and Ellin Greene, *Storytelling: Art and Technique* (New York: York: R. R. Bowker Company, 1977), p. xii.

2. The concept of Uninterrupted Sustained Silent Reading (USSR) was introduced by Dr. Lyman Hunt in 1970. Sustained Silent Reading (SSR) and Drop Everything and Read (DEAR) are variations of the same concept.

3. Jackie Torrence, "Storytelling," *The Horn Book Magazine* Vol. LIX, No. 3 (June 1983): 285.

4. Augusta Baker and Ellin Greene, *Storytelling: Art and Technique* (New York: R. R. Bowker Company, 1977), p. 43.

5. Eileen Colwell, "What Is Storytelling?" *The Horn Book Magazine* Vol. LIX, No. 3 (June 1983): 267.

6. Readers Theatre is a group of people who perform dramatic extensions. One person presents a dynamic interpretive reading of a poem, tale, play, or song as others in the group mime the actions.

PROFESSIONAL BIBLIOGRAPHY
COMPILATIONS OF STORIES AND LISTS OF STORIES*

Babbitt, Ellen C., ret. "The Monkey and the Crocodile," *Jataka Tales*. Englewood Cliffs, N.J.: Prentice-Hall, Inc., 1940. Orig. 1912.

* See Chapter 9 for compilations of folk and fairy tales.

Baker, Virginia. *Young Years*. New Haven, Conn.: Home Library Press, 1960.

Brooke, L. Leslie. *Golden Goose Book*. Illus. by author. New York: Frederick Warne & Co., Inc., 1905.

Cathon, Laura, ed. *Stories to Tell to Children: A Selected List*. 8th ed. Pittsburgh: University of Pittsburgh Press for Carnegie Library of Pittsburgh, 1974.

Chapman, Gaynor, sel. and illus. *Aesop's Fables*. New York: Atheneum Publishers, 1971.

de la Mare, Walter. *Tales Told Again*. New York: Alfred A. Knopf, 1959.

de Regniers, Beatrice Schenk. *The Giant Book*. Illus. by William Lahey Cummings. New York: Atheneum Publishers, 1966.

Dobbs, Rose. *Once-Upon-A-Time Story Book*. Illus. by Flavia Gag. New York: Random House, 1958.

Farjeon, Eleanor. *The Little Bookroom*. New York: Henry Z. Walck Inc., 1956.

Fenner, Phyllis. *The Giggle Box*. Pictures by William Steig. New York: Alfred A. Knopf, 1950.

Fillmore, Parker, ret. *The Shepard's Nosegay*. New York: Harcourt, Brace, World, Inc., 1958.

Flax, Zena, ed. and designer. *The Old-Fashioned Children's Storybook*. New York: Simon & Schuster, 1979.

Greene, Ellin. *Stories: A List of Stories to Tell and to Read Aloud*. Rev. ed. New York: The New York Public Library, 1965.

Grimm Brothers. *Household Stories*, trans. by Lucy Crane, illus. by Walter Crane. New York: McGraw-Hill, 1966 (1886) (Kinder and Hausmarchen, 1812).

Hardendorff, Jeanne D. *Stories to Tell: A List of Stories with Annotations*. 5th ed. Baltimore: Enoch Pratt Free Library, 1965.

Hutchinson, Veronica, sel, *Candle-Light Stories*. Illus. by Lois Lenski. New York: Minton, Balch and Co., 1928.

Iarusso, Marilyn. *Stories: A List of Stories to Tell and to Read Aloud*. 7th ed. New York: New York Public Library, 1977.

Jacobs, Joseph, ed. *English Fairy Tales*. Illus. by John D. Batten. Facsimile edition. New York: Dover Publications, Inc., 1968 (original 1894).

———. *More English Fairy Tales*. Illus. by John D. Batten. Fascimile edition. New York: Dover Publications, Inc., 1968 (original 1894).

Kipling, Rudyard. *Just So Stories*. New York: Doubleday & Co., Inc., 1972. Orig. 1902.

Lang, Andrew. *The Blue Fairy Book*. Illus. by Reisie Lonette. New York: Random House, 1959 (original 1889). (Dover Publications, Inc. publishes Lang's Violet, Yellow, Orange, Pink, Brown, Crimson, Green, Grey, Lilac, Olive and Red Fairy Books.)

Meek, Alfred David, and Meek, Mary Elizabeth, sel. *The Twelve Dancing Princesses and Other Fairy Tales*. Bloomington & London: Indiana University Press, 1964.

Montgomerie, Norah, ret. and illus. *Twenty-five Fables*. New York: Atheneum Publishers, 1971.

Provenson, Alice, and Provenson, Martin. *The Provenson Book of Fairy Tales*. New York: Random House, 1971.

Tashjian, Virginia A., sel. "The King with a Terrible Temper," *With a Deep Sea Smile.* Illus. Rosemary Wells. Boston: Little Brown and Company, 1974.
————,sel. "The Snooks Family," *Juba This and Juba That.* Boston: Little, Brown and Company, 1969.

PROFESSIONAL BOOKS

GENERAL

American Library Association. *Storytelling: Readings, Bibliographies, Resources.* Chicago: ALA, 1978.
Baker, Augusta, and Greene, Ellin, *Storytelling: Art and Technique.* New York: R. R. Bowker Company, 1977.
Bauer, Caroline Fuller. *Handbook for Storytellers.* Chicago: American Library Association, 1977.
Bechtel, Louise Seaman. *Books in Search of Children.* New York: The Macmillan Company, 1940.
Burrell, Arthur. *A Guide to Story Telling.* London: Sir Isaac Pitman & Sons, Ltd., 1926. Republished by Gryphon Books, Ann Arbor, Michigan, 1971.
Butler, Cynthia. "When the Pleasurable is Measurable," *Language Arts* Vol. 57, No. 8 (November/December 1980): 882–885.
Butler, Dorothy. *Babies Need Books.* New York: Atheneum Publishers, 1980.
Butler, Francelia. *Sharing Literature with Children.* New York: David McKay Co., Inc., 1977.
Chambers, Aidan. *Introducing Books to Children.* New York: Heineman Educational Books, Ltd., 1975.
Chambers, Dewey W. *The Oral Tradition: Storytelling and Creative Drama.* Dubuque, Iowa: William C. Brown Company, 1977.
————. "Storytelling, the Neglected Art," *Elementary English* Vol. 43 (November 1966): 715–719.
————. *Storytelling and Creative Drama.* Dubuque, Iowa: William C. Brown, 1970.
Chukovsky, Kornei. *From Two to Five.* Trans. and edited by Miriam Morton. Berkeley: University of California Press, 1974.
Colwell, Eileen. *Storytelling.* Salem: Merrimack Publishers (Bodley Head), 1983.
Coody, Betty. *Using Literature with Young Children.* Dubuque, Iowa: William C. Brown, 1973.
Cundiff, R. E., and Webb, B. *Story Telling for You.* Yellow Springs, Ohio: Antioch, 1957.
Groff, Patrick. "Let's Update Storytelling," *Language Arts* Vol. 54, No. 3 (March 1977): 272–277, 286.
Hazard, Paul. *Books, Children and Men.* Boston: The Horn Book, 1932.

Johnson, Ferne, ed. *Start Early for an Early Start: You and the Young Child.* Chicago: American Library Association, 1976.

MacDonald, Margaret Read, comp. *The Storyteller's Source Book: A Subject, Title and Motif Index to Folklore Collections for Children.* Detroit: Gale Research, 1982.

Moore, Vardine. *Pre-School Story Hour.* 2nd ed. Metuchen, N.J.: The Scarecrow Press, Inc., 1972.

Pellowski, Anne. *The World of Storytelling.* New York: R. R. Bowker Co., 1977.

Ross, Ramon. *The Storyteller.* 2d ed. Columbus, Ohio: Charles E. Merrill Co., 1980.

Sawyer, Ruth. *The Way of the Storyteller.* New York: Viking Press, 1962.

Schimmel, Nancy. *Just Enough to Make a Story: A Sourcebook for Storytelling.* Berkeley, Calif.: Sister's Choice Press, 1978.

Shedlock, Marie L. *The Art of the Story Teller.* 3d ed., rev. New York: Dover Publications, Inc., 1951. Orig. 1915.

Smith, Lillian. *The Unreluctant Years.* Chicago: American Library Association, 1953.

Tooze, Ruth. *Storytelling.* Englewood Cliffs, N.J.: Prentice-Hall, 1959.

Wilson, Jane B. *The Story Experience.* Metuchen, N.J.: The Scarecrow Press, Inc., 1979.

Ziskind, Sylvia. *Telling Stories to Children.* New York: The H. W. Wilson Company, 1976.

RECORDINGS

Baker, Augusta. "Storytelling." In Prelude (six mini-seminars, three cassettes) Series 1. New York: Children's Book Council, 1975.

STORYTELLING "TIPS"

Morrow, Lesley Mandel. *Super Tips for Storytelling.* Instructor Publications Inc., 1979, 1981.

FINGER PLAYS

Fletcher, Helen T. *Fingerplay Poems for Children.* Darien, Conn.: Teachers Publishing Co., 1964.

Grayson, Marion. *Let's Do Fingerplays.* Washington: Robert B. Luce, 1962.

Jacobs, Frances E. *Finger Plays and Action Rhymes.* New York: Lothrop, Lee & Shepard Co., 1941.

Poulsson, Emilie. *Finger Plays for Nursery and Kindergarten.* New York: Dover Publications, 1971.

Scott, Louise B., and Thompson, Jesse V. *Rhymes for Fingers and Flannelboards.* New York: McGraw-Hill Book Co., 1960.

CHILDREN'S BOOKS

STORIES TO BE TOLD, POEMS (COLLECTIONS) TO BE SHARED

Aliki. *Go Tell Aunt Rhody*. Illus. by author. New York: Macmillan Publishing Co., 1974.

Barrett, Judith. *Cloudy with a Chance of Meatballs*. Illus. by Ron Barrett. New York: Atheneum Publishers, 1978.

Bodecker, N. M. *It's Raining Said John Twaining*. New York: Atheneum Publishers, 1973.

Brown, Marcia. *The Three Billy Goats Gruff*. Illus. by author. New York: Harcourt, 1957.

Charlip, Remy. *Fortunately*. Illus. by author. New York: Parents Magazine Press, 1964.

Flack, Marjorie. *Ask Mr. Bear*. Illus. by author. New York: Macmillan Publishing Co., 1932.

Gag, Wanda. *Millions of Cats*. Illus. by author. New York: Coward, McCann and Geoghegan, Inc., 1928.

Galdone, Paul. *Henny Penny*. Illus. by author. New York: Seabury Press, Inc., 1968.

Grimm, Jakob, and Grimm, Wilhelm. Translated by Randall Jarrell. *The Fisherman and His Wife*. Illus. Margot Zemach. New York: Farrar, Straus and Giroux, 1980.

Hoban, Russell. *Bedtime for Frances*. Illus. by Garth Williams. New York: Harper & Row, Publishers, 1960.

Hoberman, Mary Ann. *Nuts to You & Nuts to Me: Alphabet of Poems*. Illus. by Ronni Solbert. New York: Alfred A. Knopf Inc., 1974.

Hogrogian, Nonny. *One Fine Day*. Illus. by author. New York: Macmillan Publishing Co., 1971.

Lear, Edward. *The Complete Nonsense Book*. New York: Dodd, Mead & Co., 1946.

Milne, A. A. *When We Were Very Young*. Illus. by E. H. Shepard. New York: E. P. Dutton & Co., Inc., 1924.

Mosel, Arlene. *Tikki Tikki Tembo*. Illus. by Blair Lent. New York: Holt, Rinehart and Winston, Inc., 1968.

Ness, Evaline, comp. *Amelia Mixed the Mustard and Other Poems*. Illus. by comp. New York: Charles Scribner's Sons, 1975.

Piper, Watty. *The Little Engine That Could*. Illus. by George Hauman and Doris Hauman. New York: Platt & Munk, 1954.

Prelutsky, Jack. *The Pack Rat's Day and Other Poems*. Illus. by Margaret Bloy Graham. New York: Macmillan Publishing Co., 1974.

——. *Toucans Two*. Illus. by Jose Aruego. New York: Macmillan Publishing Co., 1970.

Preston, Edna Mitchell. *Popcorn and Ma Goodness*. Illus. by Robert Andrew Parker. New York: Viking Press, 1969.

Quackenbush, Robert. *Go Tell Aunt Rhody*. Illus. by author. Philadelphia: J. B. Lippincott, 1973.

———. *Old MacDonald Had a Farm*. Illus. by author. Philadelphia: J. B. Lippincott, 1972.

Rockwell, Anne. *The Old Woman and Her Pig*. Illus. by author. New York: Thomas Y. Crowell, 1979.

Segal, Lore. *Tell Me a Mitzi*. Illus. by Harriet Pincus. New York: Farrar, Straus & Giroux, 1970.

Sendak, Maurice. *Chicken Soup with Rice* (in the Nutshell Library). Illus. by author. New York: Harper & Row Publishers, 1962.

———. *Pierre: a Cautionary Tale* (in the Nutshell Library). Illus. by author. New York: Harper & Row Publishers, 1962.

Watson, Clyde. *Father Fox's Pennyrhymes*. Illus. by Wendy Watson. New York: Thomas Y. Crowell Co., 1971.

Williams, Jay. *A Practical Princess and Other Liberating Fairy Tales*. Illus. by Rick Schreiter. New York: Four Winds, 1978.

STORIES TO BE READ AND SHOWN

Allard, Harry, and Marshall, James. *The Stupids Have a Ball*. Illus. by James Marshall. Boston: Houghton Mifflin, 1978.

Bemelmans, Ludwig. *Madeline*. Illus. by author. New York: Viking Press, 1939.

Carle, Eric. *The Very Hungry Caterpillar*. Illus. by author. Cleveland: William Collins and World Publishing Co., Inc., 1969.

Clifton, Lucille. *Amifika*. Illus. by Thomas DiGrazia. New York: E. P. Dutton and Co., Inc., 1977.

———. *Some of the Days of Everett Anderson*. Illus. by Evaline Ness. New York: Holt, Rinehart and Winston, Inc., 1970.

Cohen, Miriam. *When Will I Read?* Illus. by Lillian Hoban. New York: Greenwillow Books, 1977.

de Paola, Tomie. *Oliver Button Is a Sissy*. Illus. by author. New York: Harcourt Brace Jovanovich, Inc., 1979.

Duvoisin, Roger. *Petunia*. Illus. by author. New York: Alfred A. Knopf, Inc., 1950.

Emberley, Barbara. *Drummer Hoff*. Illus. by Ed Emberley. Englewood Cliffs, N.J.: Prentice-Hall, 1967.

Farber, Norma. *How Does It Feel to Be Old?* Illus. by Trina Schart Hyman. New York: E. P. Dutton & Co., Inc., 1979.

Freeman, Don. *Dandelion*. Illus. by author. New York: Viking Press, 1964.

Geisel, Theodor S. [Dr. Seuss]. *Horton Hatches the Egg*. Illus. by author. New York: Random House, 1940.

Gerrard, Roy. *Sir Cedric*. Illus. by author. New York: Farrar, Strauss & Giroux, 1984.

Hoban, Russell. *A Birthday for Frances*. Illus. by Lillian Hoban. New York: Harper & Row, Publishers, Inc., 1968.

Hoberman, Mary Ann. *A House Is A House for Me*. Illus. by Betty Fraser. New York: Viking Press, 1978.

Kraus, Robert. *Whose Mouse Are You?* Illus. by Jose Areugo. New York: Macmillan Publishing Co., 1980.

Lobel, Arnold. *Fables.* New York: Harper & Row, Publishers, Inc., 1980.

———. *A Rose in My Garden.* Illus. by Anita Lobel. New York: Greenwillow Books, 1984.

———. *A Treeful of Pigs.* Illus. by Anita Lobel. New York: Greenwillow Books, 1979.

Marshall, James. *George and Martha.* Illus. by author. Boston: Houghton Mifflin Co., 1972.

Moore, Clement. *The Night Before Christmas.* Illus. by Tomie de Paola. New York: Holiday House, 1980.

Noble, Trinka Hakes. *The Day Jimmy's Boa Ate the Wash.* Illus. by Steven Kellogg. New York: Dial Press, 1980.

Potter, Beatrix. *The Tale of Peter Rabbit.* Illus. by author. New York: Frederick Warne & Co., Inc., 1902.

Raskin, Ellen. *Nothing Ever Happens on My Block.* Illus. by author. New York: Atheneum, 1966.

Wildsmith, Brian. *Brian Wildsmith's Mother Goose.* Illus. by author. New York: Franklin Watts, Inc., 1964.

Zolotow, Charlotte. *William's Doll.* Illus. by William Pene du Bois. New York: Harper & Row, 1972.

STORIES TO BE LIVED BY SHARER (IN PRESENTATION AND POSSIBLY EXTENSION)

Aardema, Verna, ret. *Who's in Rabbit's House?* A Masai Tale. Illus. by Leo Dillon and Diane Dillon. New York: Dial Press, 1977.

Areugo, José. *Look What I Can Do.* Illus. by author. New York: Charles Scribner's Sons, 1971.

Balian, Lorna. *Humbug Witch.* Illus. by author. Nashville: Abingdon Press, 1965.

Brown, Marcia. *The Three Billy Goats Gruff.* Illus. by author. New York: Harcourt Brace World, 1957.

Burningham, John. *Mr. Grumpy's Outing.* Illus. by author. New York: Holt, Rinehart and Winston, 1971.

Burton, Virginia. *The Little House.* Illus. by author. Boston: Houghton Mifflin Co., 1942.

Chaucer, Geoffrey. *Chanticleer and the Fox.* Illus. by Barbara Cooney. New York: Harper & Row, Publishers, 1958.

de Paola, Tomie. *Strega Nona.* Illus. by author. Englewood Cliffs, N.J.: Prentice-Hall, Inc., 1975.

Ets, Marie Hall. *In the Forest.* Illus. by author. New York: Viking Press, 1944.

———. *Play With Me.* Illus. by author. New York: Viking Press, 1955.

Flack, Marjorie. *Ask Mr. Bear.* Illus. by author. New York: Macmillan Publishing Co., 1932 and 1958.

Freeman, Don. *The Chalk Box Story.* Illus. by author. Philadelphia: J. B. Lippincott Co., 1976.

Galdone, Paul, ret. and illus. *The Gingerbread Boy.* Boston: Houghton Mifflin Co., 1975.

————. *Monkey and the Crocodile.* Illus. by author. New York: Seabury Press, Inc., 1969.

Grimm Brothers. *King Grisly Beard.* Illus. by Maurice Sendak. New York: Farrar, Straus & Giroux, Inc., 1973.

Heide, Florence. *The Shrinking of Treehorn.* Illus. by Edward Gorey. New York: Holiday House, 1971.

Hobzek, Mildred. *We Came A-Marching One, Two, Three.* Illus. by William Pene DuBois. New York: Parents Magazine Press, 1978.

Hutchins, Pat. *Rosie's Walk.* New York: Macmillan Publishing Co., 1968.

Johnson, Crockett. *Harold and the Purple Crayon.* Illus. by author. New York: Harper & Row, Publishers, Inc., 1958.

Langstaff, John, comp. *Oh A-Hunting We Will Go.* Illus. by Nancy Winslow Parker. New York: Atheneum, 1974.

Mayer, Mercer. *What Do You Do with a Kangaroo?* Illus. by author. New York: Four Winds Press, 1973.

Sendak, Maurice. *Pierre: A Cautionary Tale.* (Nutshell Library.) Illus. by author. New York: Harper & Row, Publishers, Inc., 1962.

————. *Sign on Rosie's Door.* Illus. by author. New York: Harper & Row, Publishers, Inc., 1960.

Shulevitz, Uri. *One Monday Morning.* Illus. by author. New York: Charles Scribner's Sons, 1967.

Slobodkina, Esphyr. *Caps for Sale.* Illus. by author. Reading, Mass.: Addison-Wesley Publishing Co., Inc., 1947.

Udry, Janice May. *Let's Be Enemies.* Illus. by Maurice Sendak. New York: Harper & Row, Publishers, Inc., 1961.

Ungerer, Tomi. *The Beast of Monsieur Racine.* Illus. by author. New York: Farrar, Straus & Giroux, Inc., 1971.

Viorst, Judith. *Alexander and the Terrible, Horrible, No Good, Very Bad Day.* Illus. by Ray Cruz. New York: Atheneum, 1972.

————. *I'll Fix Anthony.* Illus. by Arnold Lobel. New York: Harper & Row, Publishers, Inc., 1969.

Willard, Nancy. *Simple Pictures Are Best.* Illus. by Tomie de Paola. New York: Harcourt Brace Jovanovich, Inc., 1977.

Wolkstein, Diane. *A Cool Ride in the Sky.* Illus. by Paul Galdone. New York: Alfred A. Knopf Inc., 1973.

Zemach, Margot. *Little Tiny Woman.* Illus. by author. Indianapolis: Bobbs-Merrill Co., Inc., 1965.

Chapter 4

The Feel of Literature: Design and Graphic Variations

RICH ENCOUNTERS

Donna scrambled through the toy box and pulled out Babar, hugged him tight, straightened him out, and crooned a lullaby.

"Would you like to know what happened to Babar today?" asked the teacher.

A nod of "yes" was followed with a correction. "King Babar. Tell me a story about King Babar."

●◆●

The four-year-old kindergarteners were in their story corner placing Raggedy Ann and Raggedy Andy on their separate rocking chairs. The children were a bit disturbed because Andy would not "sit up straight."

●◆●

Sally and Bobby were seated at a table sharing Robert Crowther's The Most Amazing Hide-and-Seek Counting Book.

"It's nine."

"No, it's ten!"

"Yessir!! Nine trees."

"Oh sure. But ten apples."

"And two something else," said Bobby, grinning.

"Two 'something else?'" Sally asked with a puzzled look. "What do you mean? Oh...," giggled Sally, "I see—two worms—in the apples and one worm can move."

Books of Diverse Design

Child Development

"Cutout books, pop-up books, peep shows, panoramas, printed toy theater play-books, and cutout sheets of theatrical scenes and characters belong to a world betwixt and between the world of children's books and that of toys."[1]

Very young children prefer toys they can cuddle and manipulate to any book they can hold. In nursery schools, playrooms, and libraries, visitors may find a large stuffed Paddington Bear, a Curious George, or a Babar being embraced and dressed before their adventures are attended to.

Developmentally, children move from the concrete stage where grasping, touching, and holding are the avenues of learning and loving. This is the stage where holdable, huggable toys are vital. In the next stage learning is accomplished largely through pictures. It is in the final or symbolic stage that numerals are recognized as labels for quantities of things and letters and words as the labels for real things. The feel of literature is likely to be attractive to children at all of these stages but the younger the child the greater the appeal of diverse design features and novel packaging.

Until recently, books with such features were fast disappearing. Today, in a period of resurgence, books of varied designs are available to young children — innovative die-cut overall shapes; folded pages, see-through pages, and pages of varying lengths; tiny books and large books with graphic and typographic variations; features such as "venetian blind" illustrations; strokeable, laceable, and even smellable pages; tugs, tabs, and strings which when pulled will reveal a fresh scene; "mechanicals" where figures move; revolving discs that produce a series of different scenes; and various three-dimensional or pop-up features. Indeed, some of Paddington the Bear's adventures are now in mini-pop-up form and John Goodall's familiar Paddy and Shrewbettina are also "popping up." Michael Hague's rendition of Clement Moore's *The Night Before Christmas* is a pop-up and Peter Spier's *Village Books* offer young children stand up "buildings," as does Tomie de Paola's *Giorgio's Village*. Books such as these are vulnerable to much happy handling and do need to be replaced frequently. Demonstration of the care needed in using such books is vital.

Place in Literature

"The trick three-dimensional book (pop-up, for example), though hardly part of literature, is nonetheless ingenious, satisfying, and a specific response to the child's desire to manipulate, change, and construct."[2]

However, there *are* some books of diverse design which, in addition to meeting the need of the young child to explore by touch, may stand the scrutiny of literary criticism and whose design features, in complementing the story, do much to communicate it. This *is* the

critical question in assessing such books: *Do* such features complement and enhance the content of the story?

Types of Diverse Design: Multiple Variations

The works of Eric Carle and Bruno Munari incorporate many
appealing design features that blend delightfully with story content.
Such features integrate story with design and are light-years away
from the cloth books infants "play-read."

Eric Carle's *The Very Hungry Caterpillar* is an all-time favorite and it
deserves its special niche. In it the hungry caterpillar eats his way
through the pages leaving behind a trail of holes. Each day of the week
is represented by the fractional fold of a page which the caterpillar
relentlessly munches through. Here is a natural blend of plot and
design that children return to often — to finger the different page
lengths, to poke their fingers through the holes, and to see and savor
the overall design.

After enjoying the caterpillar's adventures many times, some
children may wish to think of an animal around whose behavior they
can design a book; for example, a curious giraffe who continuously
cranes his neck into the next page or a cavorting otter who slips
through the hole in a page for a plunge into the sea.

In Carle's *The Grouchy Ladybug* and *The Secret Birthday Message*, varying page sizes, shapes, and holes abound that complement the story
content. In his more recent *The Honeybee and the Robber*, rightly called
a moving picture book, Carle places pull-outs, pop-ups, flaps, and a
"dancing" butterfly into the hands of the young child. It is thickened ink on the pages of *The Very Busy Spider* that Carle uses so that
young children can trace the web as they follow the industrious
spider.

Bruno Munari's books also represent marvels of design features.
The Elephant's Wish is found in a small camouflaged rectangle on one
page. Similarly, the wish of each animal appears on successive pages.
The plot is somewhat circular; the elephant starts by wishing to be a
bird and the ox concludes by wishing to be an elephant. Such features
propel a special kind of creative invention from young children when
the teacher asks, "What do you think each of the animals will wish
to be?"

If Dr. Seuss's *Horton Hatches the Egg* is shared with *The Elephant's Wish*,
young children will need little prodding to draw their perceptions of an
elephant-bird and give it a very special name. Munari's *Who's There?
Open the Door!* is another blend of design features that children delightedly touch and view.

Holidays rich in tradition and colorful customs are especially suitable for three-dimensional interpretation. Tasha Tudor's *A Book of Christmas* combines the pageantry of Christmas customs in various cultures and the biblical story of Christmas. Both are presented in three-dimensional colored pictures. Circuses, birthdays, and parades are also ideal topics for three-dimensional illustrations. In *Barbara's Birthday*, James Stevenson creates a pop-up book in keeping with the celebration. Young children may enjoy designing their own birthday flap book. After identifying the birthday surprises they would most like to receive, they can draw these through pre-cut flaps. Friends can guess and check the answers by lifting the flaps.

Many alphabet books such as Robert Crowther's *The Most Amazing Hide-and-Seek Alphabet Book* and Lisl Weil's *Owl and Other Scrambles* incorporate numerous unusual features and "paper engineering." Pop-ups, pull-outs, and flaps are found in the former title, and in the latter, Weil uses the letters in the words to create the pictures.

What's That? was designed for blind children, but sighted children can also enjoy it (especially if they close their eyes and listen to the text). A young child can follow the textures in the book with his or her fingers while listening to the story of Little Shaggy's game of hide-and-seek. The plot is not unlike Leo Lionni's *Little Blue and Little Yellow*. Little Shaggy runs to hide behind Little Smooth but his shaggy ends give him away. Shapes as well as textures can be learned through touching the textured portions on each page. This kind of book can generate innumerable creative tactile activities, including children designing their own *What's That?* book for different shapes with different textures. A similar format is Jensen's *Catching: A Book for Blind and Sighted Children with Pictures to Feel as Well as to See.*

Size

Sometimes size is the outstanding feature of a book. A considerable collection of books for young children are tiny. The mini format of Margot Zemach's *The Little Tiny Woman* is enjoyed by many two- and three-year-olds. The small size, the repetition of "Give me my bone," the surprising pull-out at the end of the book with enormous letters spelling TAKE IT, and the appropriate match between the tiny woman and the tiny book make this book especially endearing to young children who shout the final words with great glee.

A Folding Alphabet Book by Monika Beisner accordion folds into a compact 3" x 4" x 1/2" box. On one side of the strip are the capital letters and various objects or animals that begin with the same letter. On the other side, a capital and small letter sit at the bottom of each fold and the top three-fourths of each page houses the capital letter again. The unfolded horizontal strip confirms the sequential nature of the alphabet, just as the leporello style format complements the cumulative verse in Erika Schneider's *The 12 Days of Christmas.* Young children especially enjoy creating this particular design feature. They can make their own alphabet and counting books and even design their own train. In fact, they might enjoy comparing their own accordion-folded train with *The Train: The Amazing Train Chase That Unfolds into the Longest Book in the World.*

A classic and landmark in the field of variant design is Maurice Sendak's tiny (about 2½" x 4") Nutshell Library. The four mini volumes in their attractive sturdy case are deservedly lauded and loved. The attractive pen-and-ink and watercolor drawings illustrate *One Was Johnny,* a counting book; the contagiously melodic calendar book, *Chicken Soup with Rice;* the story of *Pierre* who didn't care; and the appealing alphabet book *Alligators All Around.*

Other *slightly* larger classics young children should see and hear are Beatrix Potter's books, which are easy to hold, appealing to view, and delightful to hear (particularly the nursery rhymes). In *Cecily Parsley's Nursery Rhymes,* the alternating verse and mini illustrations in color enable young children to match text with illustrations easily and to observe and discuss the many details the verse does not mention, such as a spinning wheel, shawl, shovel, rake, watering can, and even potato peelings.

Some of the books by Martha Alexander, Janice May Udry, Charlotte Zolotow, Lois Lenski, Mercer Meyer, Rosemary Wells, and others are tiny. Like the chapbooks[3] of yesteryear, they appeal to young children and are often found on the bottom shelves of children's rooms in homes, libraries, and classrooms, ready to be reached by small hands.

In contrast, some books are supersized, such as Fritz Eichenberg's *Dancing in the Moon,* a brightly illustrated, rhymed, counting book, and Clare Newberry's *The Kittens' ABC,* a rhymed picture book about kittens. There is also the giant *Ashanti to Zulu,* the glorious Caldecott winner full of African traditions and, only incidentally, an alphabet book fully appreciated by older children.

The books of the d'Aulaires, such as their Caldecott winner, *Abraham Lincoln* and the newly rewritten *The Terrible Troll Bird* (formerly *Ola and Blakken*), are large volumes awkward to hold (except in the lap) and beautiful to view. In these instances, the large pages permit Abe to look his natural tall self and the trolls and their bird to seem hugely horrendous and menacing.

Children can be challenged to think about what stories lend themselves to being tall books or small books. Young children quickly think of matching character size to book size; for example, a giant must have a tall book, a mouse needs only a tiny one.

Page Variations

Pages can also vary in design. In *Daisy,* Brian Wildsmith alternates half pages and full pages to tell the tale of an unhappy cow who sought and found adventure, and later happily returned to her own field.

The use of alternating pages to distinguish fact from fantasy is often employed. John Burningham does it in *Come Away from the Water, Shirley,* and Crosby Bonsall does it in *Who's Afraid of the Dark?* This juxtaposition of pages lends itself beautifully to the contrast of "real" and "imagination."

John Goodall's books feature the alternating or intermittent folded page. He combines this with a small rectangular shape and full-page "bleeds."[4] From his wordless picture books, young children enjoy telling *their* own stories of *Paddy Pork, Jacko, Creepy Castle* and *Naughty Nancy.* In *The Story of An English Village* Goodall uses a large book size and more pages yet preserves his alternating half pages. He presents a 600-year history of a rural village's change to urban clutter. An older child might better appreciate this picture book of what the centuries have wrought but young children will also note many of the details and enjoy labeling what they can recognize in the pictures while questioning what is new.

In *I Unpacked My Grandmother's Trunk: A Picture Book Game,* Susan Ramsay Hoguet uses split pages to differentiate the newest object unpacked from all of the previous items taken from Grandmother's trunk. The split page design complements the story content of gradual additions to the pile of unpacked items and subtraction to the items in the trunk.

Upper- and lower-page halves that have to be matched are used in Stephen Lewis's *Zoo City* and in *Graham Oakley's Magical Changes.* Helen Oxenbury takes page cutting one step further in her three books entitled *Curious Creatures, Merry Mixups,* and *Puzzle People.* Here pages are cut into three sections and by flipping the pages a great variety of stories, people, and animals can be created. Flip books such as these and Alan Benjamin's *1000 Inventions* lead children to imaginative excursions of their own—labeling and creating new adventures for the people and animals they flip and match. Such books do not offer the young child stories but rather the opportunity to create tales of their own.

In Maureen Roffey's *Door to Door* with humorous verses by Bernard Lodge, split pages show the reader what is going on inside and outside houses number one and number three, enabling the young viewer to perceive and appreciate the contrast which is basic to the story.

Seymour Chwast in *The House That Jack Built* imaginatively uses page size to help tell the tale. The page grows as the tale grows.

In Joyce Segal's *It's Time to Go to Bed*, young children, who never tire of inventing all sorts of excuses for postponing bedtime, will chuckle at the arrangement on opposite pages of the familiar bedtime reminders on one side and the equally familiar excuses on the other. Something of the same format is used in Bernard Most's *Turn Over* and in de Regnier's *It Does Not Say Meow!* wherein young children find the question on one page and the answer by turning the page.

Variations in Graphics and Typography

Due to great technical improvements in design and printing, variations in graphics and typography are quite frequent. In Ashok Davar's *Talking Words: A Unique Alphabet Book*, the author identifies an object's most outstanding quality and features it visually in illustrating the keywords for the letters of the alphabet. For example, the keyword for A is arrow. The letters that form ARROW are made up of small arrows. The word for Q is quilt and QUILT is made up of patchwork quilt squares. Third graders enjoy identifying and illustrating keywords of their own.

Fittingly, "SNARL" is much larger than "hsssssssssssss" in Kuskin's *Roar and More*. The former word shouts at you; the latter whispers. Unusual typography, which sometimes spans double pages, and the humorous verses make this book attractive to young children. In Peter Spier's *Crash! Bang! Boom!*, "BANG" is larger than "tweet-tweet." Every page is brimful of the sounds people and objects make and the lively detail of Peter Spier enables the reader to *feel* and *hear* the sound.

Ideally, all books encourage the young child's participation in that they stir ideas and feelings. Books of diverse designs may stimulate an especially active and overt participation. For instance, discussions on how to print and picture sounds leads to all kinds of experimentation in matching sounds with print size, shape, color, and texture.

Participation Books

Children: Solving Problems

Children can be invited to respond to books through the use of a variety of graphic or design features—color, texture, detail, and many of the features previously discussed. Participation is often the result of casting the child in the role of problem solver.

A die-cut hole in one page which challenges the child to look through it and guess the "whole" on the next page is a feature found in some of the older mass media books and is used by Tana Hoban in her *Look Again*, a classic concept book that tests a child's perceptions.

In Barry Miller's *Alphabet World* a transparent oversheet is used to confirm letter shapes that young children try to find in the pictures.

Size and perspective change in Roger Bester's *Guess What?* Children are challenged to solve the who-is-the-animal puzzles from photographic and design clues. Answers are provided through photographs of the whole animal.

In Allan and Janet Ahlberg's *Each Peach Pear Plum*, a Kate Greenaway Medal book,[5] young children are given textual clues to help find nursery rhyme friends in the illustrations. Young readers are to hunt for pigs in *Pigs in Hiding* by Arlene Dubanevich. The secret is divulged to the children and they know more than the hunter in the story.

In *Anno's Animals* (Mitsumasa Anno), *We Hide, You Seek* (José Aruego and Dewey Ariane), and *The Three Jovial Huntsmen* (Susan Jeffers), children also hunt for camouflaged animals. Of the three, *Anno's Animals* is the most demanding. Discovery is attended by chuckles and, in the case of *Three Jovial Huntsmen*, by a feeling of one-upsmanship; the reader is smarter than the characters in the story.

Something of the same feeling surfaces as the young child reads, listens, and sees Ellen Raskin's *Nothing Ever Happens on My Block*. All kinds of dramatic things *are* happening which the young reader quickly sees but the protagonist simply does not.

In Eric Carle's wordless *Do You Want to Be My Friend?* the mouse seeks a friend among many animals. The young child sees the tail of the animal being "questioned" (the mouse looks inquiringly) but does not know who is being questioned until the page is turned. The curly brown tail belongs to a monkey and the thick red one belongs to a fox. Lots of excited happy guesses pop from young children. This is another "open" book, that is, extension ideas flow naturally from it. Any zoo is full of many more animals to be questioned by the mouse. Some research on the characteristics of animals' tails will be needed but with a little thought a class might find several friends for Carle's lonely mouse.

In Beau Gardner's *The Turnabout Think About and Look About Book* children engage in turning the page and viewing it from four different directions, creating new content each time. Some young children will find Paul Zelinsky's *The Maid and the Mouse and the Odd-Shaped House* confusing, but slightly older children may delight in turning and twisting and thinking about the drawings that finally disclose that the house is indeed cat-shaped. *Round Trip* is most appropriately designed: A child is invited to proceed to the end of the book and then invert the book to make the return trip. This type of topsy-turvy design stirs much excited identification.

Anno in *Anno's Alphabet* continuously invites the book's readers or viewers to join in, requiring the young readers to match the huge letter on each page with objects in the border whose names start with the appropriate letter. A checklist is provided in the glossary which itemizes all the things there are to be found.

A participation book that stands alone in its field in that its sheer visual impact spurs creative responses from children is the far-from-recent but unique *It Looked Like Spilt Milk.* Children create all kinds of answers for the odd-looking cloud shapes on the startling blue background and quickly substitute their own solutions in the patterned refrain, "Sometimes it looked like...but it wasn't...."

A similar startling effect is achieved in Tana Hoban's *A, B, See!* Using photograms (white images against a black background), the artist-photographer features a letter of the alphabet with objects beginning with that letter. The young child is not asked the open-ended question generated by *It Looked Like Spilt Milk* but rather questions of identification.

Summary

In growing toward a love of books from a love of toys, young children encounter numerous rich and toy-like features in many books — variant page size, and graphic, typographic, and three-dimensional or paper "engineering" variations. When these design features are integral to the tale, they can entrance the young child and enhance the content.

Special challenges confront the young child to participate in such books; he or she must identify objects or animals, solve problems, or create new stories. The child can also extend or experiment with simpler design features.

Although the place in literature for some of these books is debatable, a case is made here for books whose content and variant design feature(s) *complement* each other, thereby succeeding in communicating the tale more effectively.

DISCUSSION ACTIVITIES

• Observe a group of preschoolers adventuring into *The Very Hungry Caterpillar.* What are their comments? How do they go about examining the book? What evidence exhibits that they have linked the text to the design (i.e., "The caterpillar made the holes.")? How many of their comments relate to the "feel" of the book?

• Share a Babar, Curious George tale, or *The Story of Peter Rabbit* while the stuffed "hero" is sitting next to you. Try another such story without the stuffed animal. Do children's reactions differ? In the former instance, what are the comments, if any, about the animal? Do children want to feel or hold it as you share the story? Are there noticeable differences in their post-sharing comments?

• Visit a bookstore or a children's book collection in a library. Study several Carle, Munari, Anno, Goodall, Oxenbury, Crowther books. Do all the design features enhance or reinforce the story? Do they, in fact, communicate the tale more effectively? If so, how?

NOTES

1. Dorothea Scott, "Pollock's Toy Theatres," *The Horn Book Magazine* (October 1979): 564.

2. Clifton Fadiman, "The Case for Children's Literature," *Children's Literature*, Vol. 5 (1976): 18.

3. Chapbooks of the seventeenth and eighteenth centuries were small, inexpensive (many were just a penny) books of greatly abbreviated, much distorted folk-fairy tales. Popular because of size, price, and action-filled plot, chapmen or peddlers had no trouble selling them. Their place in children's literature—whether famous or infamous—is often debated but their popularity is not.

4. *Bleeds* are illustrations which when printed "bleed" (go over) the very edges of the page.

5. The Kate Greenaway Medal is awarded annually by the British Library Association for the most distinguished work in illustration of a children's book first published in the United Kingdom during the preceding year.

PROFESSIONAL BIBLIOGRAPHY

Babcock, Janet E. "The Changing Look of Children's Books," *Book Production Industry* (November 1965): 42–45.

Bader, Barbara. *American Picturebooks from Noah's Ark to the Beast Within*. New York: Macmillan Publishing Co., Inc., 1976.

Fadiman, Clifton. "The Case for a Children's Literature," *Children's Literature*, Vol. 5 (1976) 9–21.

Freeman, Ruth S. *Children's Picture Books Yesterday and Today*. Watkins Glen, N.Y.: Century House, 1967.

Hektown, Faith H., and Rinehart, Jeanne R., eds. *Toys to Go: A Guide to the Use of Realia in Public Libraries*. Chicago: American Library Association, 1977.

Larrick, Nancy. "Design in Children's Books," *Library Journal* (October 15, 1950): 1776–1781.
Scott, Dorothea. "Pollock's Toy Theatres," *The Horn Book Magazine* (October 1979): 563–570.

CHILDREN'S BOOKS

Ahlberg, Allan, and Ahlberg, Janet. *Each Peach Pear Plum*. New York: Viking Press, 1979.
Anno, Mitsumasa. *Anno's Alphabet: An Adventure in Imagination*. New York: Thomas Y. Crowell Co., 1974.
——. *Anno's Animals*. New York: Philomel Books, 1979.
Aruego, José. *Look What I Can Do*. Illus. by author. New York: Charles Scribner's Sons, 1971.
Aruego, José, and Dewey, Ariane. *We Hide, You Seek*. New York: Greenwillow Books, 1979.
Beisner, Monika. *A Folding Alphabet Book*. New York: Farrar, Strauss and Giroux, 1981.
Benjamin, Alan. *1000 Inventions*. Illus. by Sal Murdocca. New York: Four Winds Press, 1980.
Bester, Roger. *Guess What?* New York: Crown Publishers Inc., 1980.
Bonsall, Crosby. *Who's Afraid of the Dark?* Illus. by author. New York: Harper & Row, Publishers, 1980.
Brown, Margaret Wise. *The City Noise Book*. Illus. by Leonard Wesigard. New York: Harper & Row, Publishers, 1939.
——. *The Country Noisy Book*. Illus. by Leonard Weisgard. New York: Harper and Row, Publishers, 1940.
——. *The Indoor Noisy Book*. Illus. by Leonard Weisgard. New York: Harper and Row, Publishers, 1942.
——. *The Quiet Noisy Book*. Illus. by Leonard Weisgard. New York: Harper and Row, Publishers, 1950.
——. *The Seashore Noisy Book*. Illus. by Leonard Weisgard. New York: Harper & Row, Publishers, 1941.
——. *The Summer Noisy Book*. Illus. by Leonard Weisgard. New York: Harper & Row, Publishers, 1951.
——. *The Winter Noisy Book*. Illus. by Charles Shaw. New York: Harper & Row, Publishers, 1976.
Burningham, John. *Come Away from the Water, Shirley*. New York: Thomas Y. Crowell Co., 1977.
Carle Eric. *Do You Want to Be My Friend?* New York: Thomas Y. Crowell Co., 1971.
——. *The Grouchy Ladybug*. New York: Thomas Y. Crowell Co., 1977.
——. *The Honeybee and the Robber*. New York: Philomel Books, 1981.
——. *The Secret Birthday Message*. New York: Harper & Row, Publishers, 1972.

———. *The Very Busy Spider.* Illus. by author. New York: Putnam Publishing, 1985.

———. *The Very Hungry Caterpillar.* Cleveland: Collins-World, 1969.

Chwast, Seymour. *The House That Jack Built.* New York: Random House, Inc., 1973.

Crowther, Robert. *The Amazing Hide-and-Seek Alphabet Book.* New York: Viking Press, 1978.

———. *The Most Amazing Hide-and-Seek Counting Book.* New York: Viking Press/ Kestrel Books, 1981.

d'Aulaire, Ingri, and d'Aulaire, Edgar Parin. *Abraham Lincoln.* New York: Doubleday & Co., Inc., 1939.

———. *The Terrible Troll Bird.* New York: Doubleday & Co., Inc., 1976.

Davar, Ashok. *Talking Words: A Unique Alphabet Book.* Indianapolis: The Bobbs-Merrill Company, Inc., 1969.

de Brunhoff, Jean. *Babar the King.* Illus. by author. New York: Random House, 1935.

de Paola, Tomie. *Giorgio's Village.* Illus. by author. New York: G. P. Putnam's Sons, 1982.

de Regniers, Beatrice Schenk. *It Does Not Say Meow!* Illus. by Paul Galdone. New York: Seabury Press, 1972.

Dubanevich, Arlene. *Pigs in Hiding.* Illus. by author. New York: Four Winds Press, 1983.

Eichenberg, Fritz. *Dancing in the Moon.* New York: Harcourt Brace, 1950.

Gardner, Beau. *The Turnabout Think About and Look About Book.* Graphics by author. New York: Lothrop, Lee and Shepard Co., Inc., 1980.

Garten, Jan. *The Alphabet Tale.* Illus. by Muriel Batherman. New York: Random House, 1964.

Geisel, Theodor [Dr. Seuss]. *Horton Hatches the Egg.* Illus. by author. New York: Random House, 1940.

Generowicz, Witold. *The Train: The Amazing Train Chase That Unfolds into the Longest Book in the World.* New York: Dial Press, 1983.

Goodall, John. *The Adventures of Paddy Pork.* New York: Harcourt Brace Jovanovich, Inc., 1968.

———. *Creepy Castle.* New York: Atheneum Publishers, 1975.

———. *Jacko.* New York: Harcourt Brace Jovanovich, Inc., 1971.

———. *Naughty Nancy.* New York: Atheneum Publishers, 1975.

———. *The Story of an English Village.* New York: Atheneum Publishers, 1979.

Hoban, Tana. *A, B, See!* New York: Greenwillow Books, 1982.

———. *Look Again.* Illus. by author. New York: Macmillan Publishing Co., 1971.

Hoguet, Susan Ramsay. *I Unpacked My Grandmother's Trunk: A Picture Book Game.* New York: E. P. Dutton, 1983.

Jeffers, Susan. *Three Jovial Huntsmen.* Illus. by author. New York: Bradbury Press, 1973.

Jensen, Virginia Allen, *Catching: A Book for Blind and Sighted Children with Pictures to Feel as Well as to See.* Illus. by author. New York: Philomel Books, 1984.

Jensen, Virginia Allen, and Haller, Dorcas Woodbury. *What's That?* New York: Collins and World Publishing Company, 1977.

Jonas, Ann. *Round Trip*. Illus. by author. New York: Greenwillow Books, 1983.

Kuskin, Karla. *Roar and More*. New York: Harper & Row, Publishers, 1956.

Lewis, Stephen. *Zoo City*. New York: Greenwillow Books, 1976.

Lionni, Leo. *Little Blue and Little Yellow*. New York: Astor-Honor Inc., 1959.

Meggendorfer, Lothar. *Surprise! Surprise!* New York: Viking Press Inc., 1982 (original 1899).

Miller, Barry. *Alphabet World*. New York: The Macmillan Company, 1971.

Moore, Clement. *The Night Before Christmas*. Illus. by Michael Hague. New York: Holt, Rinehart and Winston, Inc., 1981.

Most, Bernard. *Turn Over*. Englewood Cliffs, N.J.: Prentice-Hall, Inc., 1980.

Munari, Bruno. *The Elephant's Wish*. New York: The World Publishing Company, 1959.

———. *Who's There? Open the Door!* New York: World Publishing Co., 1957.

Musgrove, Margaret. *Ashanti to Zulu: African Traditions*. Illus. by Leo Dillon and Diane Dillon. New York: Dial Press, 1976.

Newberry Clare. *The Kittens' ABC*. New York: Harper & Row, Publishers, 1964.

Oakley, Graham. *Graham Oakley's Magical Changes*. New York: Atheneum Publishers, 1979.

Oxenbury, Helen. *Curious Creatures*. New York: Harper & Row, Publishers, 1980.

———. *Merry Mixups*. New York: Harper & Row, Publishers, 1980.

———. *Puzzle People*. New York: Harper & Row, Publishers, 1980.

Potter, Beatrix. *Cecily Parsley's Nursery Rhymes*. London: Frederick Warne & Co., Ltd., 1922.

Raskin, Ellen. *Nothing Ever Happens on My Block*. New York: Atheneum Publishers, 1966.

Roffey, Maureen, and Lodge, Bernard. *Door to Door*. Illus. by Maureen Roffey. New York: Lothrop, Lee and Shepard Co., Inc., 1980.

Schneider, Erika, illus. *The 12 Days of Christmas*. Calligraphy by Richard Lipton. Picture Book Studio, 1984.

Segal, Joyce. *It's Time to Go to Bed*. Ed. by Cindy Szekeres. Illus. by Robin Eaton. New York: Doubleday & Co., Inc., 1979.

Sendak, Maurice. *The Nutshell Library*. Including *Alligators All Around, Chicken Soup with Rice, One Was Johnny* and *Pierre*. New York: Harper & Row, Publishers, 1962.

Shaw, Charles Green. *It Looked Like Spilt Milk*. New York: Harper & Row, Publishers, 1947.

Spier, Peter. *Crash! Bang! Boom!* New York: Doubleday & Co., Inc., 1972.

———. *The Fox Went Out on a Chilly Night*. New York: Doubleday & Co., Inc., 1961.

———. *London Bridge Is Falling Down*. New York: Doubleday & Co., Inc., 1967.

———. *Peter Spier's Village Books*. New York: Doubleday & Co., Inc., 1981.

Stevenson, James. *Barbara's Birthday*. Illus. by author. New York: Greenwillow Books, 1983.

Tudor, Tasha. *A Book of Christmas*. New York: Philomel Books, 1979.

Weil, Lisl. *Owl and Other Scrambles*. New York: Elseview-Dutton Co., 1980.

Wildsmith, Brian. *Daisy*. Illus. by author. New York: Pantheon Books, Inc., 1984.

Zelinsky, Paul. *The Maid and the Mouse and the Odd-Shaped House*. New York: Dodd, Mead & Co., 1981.

Zemach, Margot. *The Little Tiny Woman*. Illus. by author. Indianapolis: Bobbs-Merrill Company, Inc., 1965.

Chapter 5

The Sound of Literature: Song and Poetry

RICH ENCOUNTERS

*"ABCDEFG
HIJKLMNOP
LMNOPQRST
UVWXYZ"*

As mother stood at the door of the child-care center, she heard the alphabet as lyrics.

●◆●

The kindergarteners were reciting from memory Vachel Lindsay's "The Little Turtle." On and on they went through the snapping and the catching to the final line. Then every one of the twenty-three, each in his or her own way, empha-sized the final words—with vigor of voice and gesture. Some children took both hands and pushed the turtle away; some gave an emphatic negative nod; some gave their shoulders a bit of a shrug; some frowned and shook an index finger; and some proudly turned their thumbs at themselves on the word me, *and at the same time nodded "no." Then they looked around and grinned at each other with pleasure and satisfaction.*

●◆●

Second graders have been introduced to David McCord's "Jamboree" and were sharing it for the umpteenth time. One side of the sitting group was posing the questions; the other side responded: in antiphonal chorus fashion.

"Who can rhyme ham?"

"How about spam?" *piped up Bobby. "Or* lamb?"

"Or ram?" *said Alice. "Is there really a ram? Can you eat a ram?"*

Somebody went for the dictionary. So the poem dialogue and rhyme extensions proceeded.

Jamboree

A rhyme for ham? Jam.
A rhyme for mustard? Custard.
A rhyme for steak? Cake.
A rhyme for rice? Another slice.
A rhyme for stew? You.
A rhyme for mush? Hush!
A rhyme for prunes? Goons.
A rhyme for pie? I.
A rhyme for iced tea? Me.
For the pantry shelf? Myself.

A Natural Affinity

The second graders just mentioned were becoming more sensitive to words and word patterns as they internalized the poem and were exercising a "...natural affinity [for] verse, song, puns, riddles, jokes, word-sounds, rhymes, chants and so on. Playing with words, inventing rules, enjoying patterns, and repetitions; imagining monsters, fairies, witches, talking animals, magical lands; the child's 'inward eye' and the poet's are more alike than we commonly realize."[1]

Poetry can touch young children in many ways—their imaginations are triggered and startled by the simple images; their sense of humor is tickled by word play; their curiosity is peaked by the content or story and the rhythmic, rhyming way it is told; their intelligence is promoted by the organization and compression of the words; and their emotions are stimulated by the poem's cadence and drama.

Young children meet the stimulations of poetry with an eagerness to capture lyric and lore, sound and story. Their response to the music of poetry is evident in their imitation of what they hear and their coinages of new words, heard by their own "inward ear." Witness their chuckles at word play, alliteration, onomatopoeia, and rhyme, and watch their bodies move to the rhythm of the poem.

The Music of Literature: Poetry

Poetry is the music of literature. It is the rhythm, form, figurative language, repetition, and, many times, rhyme that makes a poem music. Poetry is meant to delight the ear; like music, it must be heard.

For very young children the content of poetry is unimportant; it is the music — the rhythm and rhyme, the pattern of beat and sound — that delights them. As they grow, however, young children soon appreciate the content of poems and respond to it enthusiastically. They begin to link their experiences with the poem's substance, as did the young child who suffered from sibling woes and, in the pattern of Mary Ann Hoberman's "Brother," was heard to sigh, "I've got a bother of brothers." For young children this link between poetry content and their lives is riveted when poetry in print is infused with the intonation of speech. It is then that the music arrives and meaning is made. Music and poetry, song and poem, songwriter and poet are closely allied. Myra Cohn Livingston, a major poet, entitled her tribute to another major poet, David McCord, "The Singer, the Song, and the Sung."[2]

Poetry Selection

The teacher of young children is confronted with problems not of scarcity but of profusion in poetry. The wealth of poetry available is rich and divergent in form, content, rhythm, rhyme, and mood. How does one select amid such wealth? Answering the following questions helps in making a decision.

- *Does the poem sound good?* Does the linking and chunking of well-chosen, mood-generating words sound good enough to make young children hungry for more?
- *Is the rhythm of the poem pronounced?* Are young children likely to honor the poem with verbal participation stressing the beat or with a motoric response such as a foot tap, a hand clap, a sway, a hop, a jump, or a skip?
- *Are there brief and simple images in the poem?* Are there clear, sensory images that create pictures well within the experiences of young children?
- *Does the poem have substance?* Beyond the early musical nonsense, does the poem offer the young child an idea or feeling to chew on or delight in?
- *Is the poetry rhymed?* Does the poem offer to the young child the predictableness of rhyming words? Is he or she being invited to join in by a rhyming refrain, for example?
- *Does the poetry have some humor?* Much poetry presented to and loved by young children *is* humorous. Do the images, figurative language, or word play tickle the fancies of young children?

In addition, poems for very young children should be *brief*. Still, if the answer to the preceding six questions is "yes," young children will *attend* to a lengthy poem. They will want the story told and the mood sustained.

Children have little difficulty with poems that are frankly nonsense, but they also respond enthusiastically to poetry within their own actual experiences. The field for selection is broad.

Song ♪

Since the sound of poetry and the music it makes are likely to attract young children, they are especially quick to welcome poetry with melody, more commonly called song. Indeed, young children spontaneously sing poetry they like and easily learn an organized sequence of tones to match new poetry shared with them.

The young child's introduction to poetry and song is very often a Mother Goose rhyme simply chanted or set to music and presented in picture book form. A five-year-old sister may be found chanting "Pat-a-Cake" to her infant brother or a group of children spurred by the jolly story of King Cole may be found merrily pretending to be Old King Cole and his fiddlers three. Or several young children may accept the invitation to "Sing a Song of Sixpence," entranced by the silly text, the melody, and Tracey Campbell Pearson's bright, merry pictures, which give visual vivacity to Pearson's *Sing a Song of Sixpence*.

Collections of Songs

Collections of songs serve teachers well and Marie Winn's *The Fireside Book of Children's Songs* is still a most comprehensive, useful collection, as is the more recent *The Fireside Book of Fun and Game Songs*, but the one compiled especially for young children is *What Shall We Do and Allee Galloo: Playsongs and Singing Games for Young Children*. This has a great deal of word play, finger play, and follow-the-leader play. Karla Kuskin did the illustrations; children should *see* and *sing* this "book" as well as Timothy John's *The Great Song Book*. Full of over sixty-eight familiar English songs plus popular "Frere Jacques" and "Alouette" (in French lyrics), this book is illustrated with Tomi Ungerer's lively happy folk and offers teachers dance and play songs, nursery rhymes, farmers' songs, morning songs, evening songs, Christmas songs, and many others. Piano accompaniment and guitar chords are included.

Lullabies and Night Songs, edited by William Engvick and illustrated by Maurice Sendak, includes dozens of special night songs, some of which are set to music for the first time. Sendak's illustrations and sensitivity to the music reflect appropriately the theme of the collection.

Two holiday collection well worth sharing with young and older children are Robert Quackenbush's *The Holiday Song Book* and John Langstaff's *The Season for Singing.* The first includes a brief history of twenty-five holidays, and the second is a collection of Christmas songs and carols indigenous to many cultures and traditions. Black spiritual and gospel songs, Shaker, Moravian, Puerto Rican, Huron Indian, and the carols of many other cultures form this collection.

Langstaff's compilation of rounds—easy rounds about animals and birds—called *Sweetly Sings the Donkey: Animal Rounds for Children to Sing or Play on Recorders* invites participation as do Nancy Parker's illustrations. Young children love rounds and are delighted to hear themselves performing. Langstaff offers an initial suggestion on how to start "rounding."

Two worthy collections of folksongs include Nancy and John Langstaff's *Jim Along Josie: A Collection of Folk Songs and Singing Games for Young Children* and Ruth Seeger's *American Folk Songs for Children.*

Many of the songs young children will enjoy singing and acting are included in Jane Hart's *Singing Bee! A Collection of Favorite Children's Songs.* Children will also enjoy *seeing* this volume. The illustrations by Anita Lobel mirror the artist's love of the dramatic and theatrical. This volume offers a great deal to teachers of three- to eight-year-olds.

Individual Songs

Individual songs for young children abound. Fortunately teachers can now identify specific melodies do or should know via the *Index to Children's Songs.* This guide lists more than 5000 songs by title, first line, and subject.

Quackenbush, Spier, Aliki, Langstaff, and Pearson have presented in picture book form with full musical notation many of the more famous and popular *individual* folksongs and old nursery rhymes.

In *Hush Little Baby* by Aliki, colors, lullaby, and "pioneering" background blend well visually and verbally in presenting the old English folksong. Original music is included. Margot Zemach illustrated the same folk-lullaby. In her version, the "if" clauses are on the following page. Young children often enjoy supplying their own "if" clauses and can generate an endless stream of them.

Quackenbush's *Old MacDonald Had a Farm* always wins top honors with young children, and *Clementine, Skip to My Lou,* and *There'll Be a Hot Time in the Old Town Tonight* are not far behind. Quackenbush adds all sorts of pertinent details to his renditions. He tells us how to vacate a burning building in *There'll Be a Hot Time in the Old Town Tonight* and how to dance to "Skip to My Lou."

Tracey Campbell Pearson renders *Old MacDonald Had a Farm* and *We Wish You a Merry Christmas* with great verve, gusto, and humor. His hilarious illustrations "sing" joyously.

Frog Went A-Courtin', a Caldecott Award book, and *Oh, A'Hunting We Will Go* are two of the most popular of Langstaff's offerings. Children must see as well as sing both of these, and will wish to create new verses.

Peter Spier's *The Fox Went Out on a Chilly Night*, a Caldecott honor book, and *London Bridge Is Falling Down* are well-known picture books based on song. It is fitting to end the story and picture-sharing with the singing of the song; in fact, young children usually can't wait to start. In *London Bridge Is Falling Down*, in addition to the music, Spier includes a history of the bridge through the centuries. This is probably more than the three-year-old wants to know but the eight-year-old may be fascinated by the ice carnivals on the river and the houses and shops on the bridge in years past.

Both Quackenbush and Aliki have presented *Go Tell Aunt Rhody*. Young children will enjoy singing and seeing both versions of this plantive folksong or hearing it rendered by the New York City Opera Children's Chorus.[3] When the music is omitted from these picture-songbooks, it is sorely missed, as in *Fiddle-I-Fee: A Traditional American Chant*.

Hobzek's *We Came a-Marching One, Two, Three* has all the elements young children love in song — strong rhythm, rhyme, an invitation to participate, and a melody easy to learn. They will enjoy William Pene du Bois' marching illustrations too.

Edward Bangs's *Yankee Doodle* is fittingly full of Steven Kellogg's sprightful, light, and exuberant comic detail; it begins with history and concludes with song.

Jean Marzollo and Susan Jeffers (illustrator) present a happy "visible" blend of the lullaby *Close Your Eyes*. Here, what a child might dream about is interspersed with a father's humorously patient attempts to put his child to bed.

Literature and song meet in two song books: *The Pooh Song Book* and *The Songs of Peter Rabbit*. A Pooh or Peter story followed by their song(s) delights young children who may then go on to create special songs for their favorite animal characters.

Nursery and Mother Goose Rhymes

Nursery and Mother Goose rhymes join with song in introducing young children to poetry. The sheer endurance of nursery songs is remarkable. They have persevered for centuries. Given their tenacity, the purported claim of Mother Goose that "All imitators of my refreshing songs might well write a new Billy Shakespeare as another Mother Goose: we two great poets were born together and so shall go out of the world together,"[4] is not quite the unpardonable boast it appears to be. Unlike Humpty Dumpty it is not likely that the rhymes will have a great fall—or even a small one.

What are the origins of these much-loved rhymes and to what do they owe their hold on the fancies of children? The *origins* seem varied; their very diversity may explain in part their richness. It appears that origins of some of these rhymes are actually political squibs or fragments of folksongs or stage productions; some seem to be old street cries or maxims and proverbs. Some were born on the battlefield and some in meeting houses; some are rude jokes and some romantic sentiments.[5]

Nursery Rhymes and the Young Child ♪

Origins notwithstanding, young children love and chant nursery rhymes. Indeed, their very endurance is the result of young children wanting to hear them again and again told in the very same way. Such requests are surely due, in part or in whole, to the pleasure nursery rhymes give the ear. All the songs (for that is the term often used to describe them) have the strong rhythm and rhyme that make them singable.

Many nursery songs are alliterative, metaphorical, highly hyperbolic with that kind of exaggeration that the young child loves. The rhymes tell brief, very satisfying stories with children and animals as the heroes. Many are funny. Much of the humor is due to the comic actions of comic characters.

These nursery songs have appealed strongly to children's artists and have spurred a collective portfolio of children's literature illustrations unlike all others for richness of craftmanship and imagination. Young children take joy in *seeing* these songs.

The close developmental connection between motoric and linguistic activity is reinforced by these mini stories. From the very beginning of life, the infant can be exposed to nursery rhymes—cradled to "Rock-a-bye-Baby," trained in clapping to "Pat-A-Cake," or bounced to "Ride a Cock Horse to Banbury Cross."

Nursery rhymes trigger much verbal activity. Children can sing "Three Blind Mice" as a round and trip their tongues on "Peter, Peter Pumpkin Eater," "Peas Porridge Hot...," "Sing a Song of Sixpence," "Baa Baa Black Sheep," or "Goosey, Goosey Gander."

Nursery rhymes lodge deep in memory. Teachers of children's literature who have asked students to respond to a roll call with a nursery rhyme find students surprising themselves and remarking, "Why, I haven't thought of that in fifteen or twenty years."

Collections

Some of the best known collections of Mother Goose rhymes and nursery rhymes are distinguished by the size of the compilation, artistic excellence, and humorous or anachronistic characterization.

Artistic excellence is apparent in Marguerite de Angeli's *Book of Nursery and Mother Goose Rhymes*, illustrated in black and white and interspersed with a few full-color pages. This collection is laden with well-known and not-so-well-known verses; it includes many riddles, finger games, and word games.

Caldecott's several books of nursery rhymes, Arthur Rackham's *Mother Goose Nursery Rhymes*, Leonard Leslie Brooks's *Ring O'Roses*, and Kate Greenaway's *Mother Goose: or The Old Nursery Rhymes* are among many that should be shared with children. The life-like characteristics of Caldecott's figures, the quaintness and charm of Greenaway's humor, and the delicate look of Rackham's art should be seen by and discussed with children as the rhymes are shared.

In *Mother Goose*, Tasha Tudor's well-known gentle pastels and flowered frames illuminate familiar nursery characters.

Raymond Briggs's *The Mother Goose Treasury* — 408 rhymes and more than twice that number of illustrations — is a gigantic harvest of rhymes and has tremendous "explorability." This collection was a Greenaway Medal Winner.

Rojankovsky's *The Tall Book of Mother Goose* will keep young children occupied from the time they see Mother Goose strut forth in her button shoes, paisley shawl, umbrella, and elegant flower-and-lace bonnet opposite the title page, to the time they lay down the large but easy to hold, colored and black-and-white book. Illustrations vary; some characters look quaint and preserve folk charm of old, and some, like Simple Simon, look like a modern-day adolescent.

Kathleen Lines compiled *Lavender's Blue: A Book of Nursery Rhymes* which was illustrated by Harold Jones. The soft muted pictures of English village and country life contrast with Brian Wildsmith's *Mother Goose: A Collection of Nursery Rhymes* which is a glorious example of Wildsmith's riotous use of color. It is a harlequin, patchwork quilt of hues and shapes which overpowers the verses. Children need time to savor it.

Wallace Tripp's *Granfa' Grig Has a Pig and Other Rhymes Without Reason from Mother Goose* is a marvelous discussion motivator. Tripp's giant of "Fee, Fie, Fo, Fum" fame is fierce. His animals, as always, trigger reader emotion if not empathy. Children need time to probe his illustrations for their rich detail.

James Marshall's Mother Goose represents the illustrator's own favorite characters whom he selected and illustrated in simple, comic style. Children will enjoy his mix of people and animals as they will the contemporary family who go about their daily chores to the acco-contemporary family who go about their daily chores to the accompaniment of the verses in Pat Thompson's *Rhymes Around the Day.*

Quentin Blake selected a group of relatively unknown nursery rhymes and illustrated them in his own unique, droll fashion. Young children seem to sense that Blake laughs as he draws, and they give themselves up to enjoying hugely his characters in *Quentin Blake's Nursery Rhyme Book.*

Anne Rockwell's *Gray Goose and Gander and Other Mother Goose Rhymes* presents known and unknown rhymes—one per page—in a format children will like. The characters in this collection are exuberant and colorful.

All in all, Mother Goose's family is so large, spunky, droll, clever, fat, thin, naughty, timid, disobedient, and accident-prone that children can invent for them a wide variety of further adventures, different roles, and other settings. "What might happen..." or "if...then" games both verbal and pictorial can be played: What might Humpty Dumpty do *first* if indeed the kings' horses and men *did* put him back again? Or what might Little Miss Muffet and the spider discuss *if* they had become friends? What clothes would Mother Goose's family wear to King Cole's birthday party; what gifts would they offer the King? Why?

Single Nursery Rhyme Books

In addition to the many collections and anthologies, there are a host of single nursery rhyme books. These differ in artists' styles, in choice of protagonist, in the amount of detail, and in the focus of the grouping.

Margot Zemach's *Hush, Little Baby* differs in characterization from Aliki's. Zemach's parents are distressed, tired, and older, and the baby is screaming loudly. Aliki's parents are younger and more patient.

Sharing several versions of the same rhyme can stimulate areas of awareness in young children:

- They can identify differences and samenesses in each.
- They can appreciate that there is more than one way to illustrate the same rhyme (they themselves might think of a few).
- They can more easily remember the rhyme for sharing and dramatizing later.

In *London Bridge Is Falling Down* by Peter Spier, children will have much to discuss. The pictures include all the usual careful detail of Spier's work. There are people to locate, and ducks, pigs, and rowboats. Indeed, all sorts of things and creatures populate these pages (as they do in Spier's *To Market, To Market*). Included too are all eighteen verses of the song and the history of the bridge.

Maurice Sendak has illustrated two of the lesser known rhymes in *Hector Protector* and *As I Went Over the Water*. Here he displays his remarkable penchant for finding texts that are open to wide interpretation: "It's your story to do with as you please as a picture book illustrator."[6] What he pleases is a personal, highly entertaining improvisation.

Some nursery rhyme books have a basic focus. In the Blegvads' *Hark! Hark! The Dogs Do Bark!*, like *Mittens for Kittens and Other Rhymes About Cats* and *The Little Pig-a-Wig and Other Rhymes About Pigs*, verses about a specific animal are brought together. Susan Jeffers's focal animals are horses in *If Wishes Were Horses and Other Rhymes*.

Arnold Lobel's *Gregory Griggs and Other Nursery Rhyme People* focuses on the people in the rhymes. There is a marvelous folk quality about all his people but Griggs and his twenty-seven wigs and Theophilus Thistle atop his mountain are especially choice and encourage young children to identify their favorites and mime their actions.

In *From King Boggen's Hall to Nothing at All* Blair Lent illustrates some of the houses within the nursery rhymes in bright, colorful pictures. There is a pumpkin shell, the pastry crust, the bell, and Poll Parrot's Garret.

Rhyme books, whether anthologies, single rhyme, or special collections, are a rich source for sharing in classrooms. This spring never runs dry of possibilities for

chanting	creative movement	discussing
choral speaking	singing	questioning
skit planning	drawing	simple puppet making
miming	painting	verse additions

ABC Books ♪

According to Iona and Peter Opie, the "...only true nursery rhymes (i.e., rhymes composed especially for the nursery) are the rhyming alphabets, the infant amusements (verses which accompany a game) and the lullabies."[7]

Indeed, most of today's alphabet books are rhyming; some are puzzle or informational books. Not *primarily* designed to teach the alphabet, these books serve as vehicles for linguistic and artistic creations which certainly do attract the young child's attention and in so doing help to "teach" the child the alphabet if he or she does not already know it.

Illustrators and authors need to make several decisions when planning an alphabet book:

- Will the format be letter-object or letter-object-word?
- Where on the page will the letter appear and what size will the letter be?
- Will small *and* capital letters be included?
- Will visual or verbal humor be emphasized?
- What letters will represent certain sounds (i.e., for /g/ gate *or* giraffe)?
- How many objects or words will be associated with the letter?
- Will the rhyme or the story be focal?
- What artistic style or medium will be used?

Alphabet books range in complexity from the very simple *b is for bear* by Dick Bruna to the striking and highly informative Caldecott winner, *Ashanti to Zulu*. In Bruna's book the small letter in the usual manuscript form is given on the left-hand page, opposite a simple drawing of an appropriate person, animal, or thing on a bright background. Very young children have little difficulty with the identification of most of the drawings and the art work is simple and appealing, as it is in Matthiesen's *ABC: An Alphabet Book*.

Many alphabet books present the letters and keywords in some verse form so that the appeal to the eye and ear are assured. Two good examples are Greenaway's *A Apple Pie*, which illustrates the old nursery rhyme with unique old-fashioned but spirited children, and Mary Ann Hoberman's *Nuts to You & Nuts to Me: An Alphabet of Poems* in which the poems are cored around keywords like *balloons, ice cream slices, money, nuts,* and *pockets*.

In *If There Were Dreams to Sell,* Barbara Lalicki assembled quotations from diverse and rich sources (mostly poetic) so that each key letter of the alphabet begins a quotation. Sources of the quotations range from Mother Goose to Alfred Lord Tennyson. This compilation opens the young child's ears to new worlds of words. The illustrations will occasion much book talk. The pictures by Margot Tomes are colorful, quietly lively, whimsical, and apt.

Peter Piper's Alphabet by Marcia Brown will surface a look of recognition and giggles from many children who have met the Peter Piper who picked a peck of pickled peppers. Since the quatrains all follow the same pattern, third graders can begin to create a whole new set of updated alliterative silliness for themselves by dictating inserts to the teacher.

In *From A to Z: The Collected Letters of Irene and Hallie Coletta*, the authors use rhymes and rebuses to present the letters, and in *A Peaceable Kingdom: The Shaker ABECEDARIUS* by the Provensens, a verse pattern is followed that uses successive letters of the alphabet at the beginning of each line, such as:

"*Alligator,...*
Bobolink,...."

While the Provensens focused on the Shakers, Barbara Cooney designed her alphabet book around colonial Williamsburg and its games. *A Garland of Games and Other Diversions: An Alphabet Book* is a potpourri of rhymes and illustrations of cat's cradle, leap-frog, embroidery, etc.

Lear Alphabet—Penned and Illustrated by Edward Lear Himself is an exact reproduction of pages from Lear's original manuscript and rhymes. His "alphabetic," easily chantable verses appear in his actual handwriting.

Many alphabet books use animals as key figures. Clare Newberry features *large* kittens in *The Kittens' ABC*. Both Eric Carle and Fritz Eichenberg start off their books with an ape. Carle's ape is named Arthur (*All About Arthur*), an "absolutely absurd ape"; while Eichenberg's ape of *Ape in a Cape* is just one of many large, bold, brightly colored animals who dance and prance across the pages to a background of zany abbreviated verses. Bert Kitchen uses some lesser-known creatures, such as the quetzal and the dodo, among others, to form his pleasantly comic *Animal Alphabet*.

Sendak chose alligators. In *Alligators All Around: An Alphabet Book* (Nutshell Library), the capital letters are black block form. They sit on the page while the alligators engage in alliterative nonsense. Children will appreciate the illustrations which are in gray, blue, green, and splashes of yellow.

Peggy Parish's *A Beastly Circus* and Bernice Chardiet's *C Is for Circus* choose a circus focus for their animals, while Celestino Piatti's *Animal ABC* and Robert Barry's *Animals Around the World* present a variety of animals—all sizes, shapes, and personalities—to represent the letters.

Phyllis McGinley's *All Around the Town* and Rachel Isadora's *City Seen from A to Z* identify keywords relating to the city. The strength of the former book is its quick and witty rhymes; the strength of the latter is the startling and arresting illustrations.

Barry Miller (*Alphabet World*) uses city scenes to capitalize on letter shapes in the environment, which the young child will delight in discovering and then confirming by checking for the outline of the shape on a transparent paper cover on each page Another delightful "city" alphabet book is James Stevenson's *Grandpa's Great City Tour: An Alphabet Book*. Full of his usual surprises and adventures, Grandpa's tour is funny, exciting, and imaginative and his narrative is full of alliteration.

Graphic wonders are *Ed Emberley's ABC* and Baskin's *Hosie's Alphabet*. In Baskin's book, bright, full, large-page drawings contain letters that differ in size and style; graphics and content are integrated. The key-word for *T* is *toad*, a scholastic toad; lettering therefore looks medieval; *D* for *demon* is very large, but *F* for *fly* is tiny. In Emberley's book, a double page is devoted to each letter. Figure-ground problems are invited on some pages because the detail in the background makes the identification of the key letter difficult. This book may better suit the older child who can appreciate its scope and craft.

A good puzzle ABC book for older children is Rockwell's *Albert B. Cub and Zebra: An Alphabet Storybook*. The plot revolves around a zebra who is missing. Large and small letters are presented and full-color illustrations mark the mystery story. On each page a busy, active scene is featured in which numerous objects, people, and animals can be labeled with words beginning with the appropriate letter. Identifying *all* the words requires careful picture reading and a vocabulary many primary graders would not have acquired. Another kind of puzzle is posed in *Q Is For Duck: An Alphabet Guessing Game* by Mary Elting and Michael Folsom. This might confuse the very young child but four- and five-year-olds will see the connections (Q is for duck because a duck quacks). In Clyde Watson's *Applebet: An ABC*, a hidden apple must be discovered and children may be surprised to find that the farmer who journeys to the fair is *mother*. Not an apple but woodland creatures are hidden in Yolen's *All in the Woodland Early: An ABC Book*.

Another alphabet puzzle book is *Humbug Potion: A • B • Cipher* by Lorna Balian. This presents to seven- and eight-year-olds a recipe in code which must be cracked if the ingredients of the Magic Beauty Potion are to be discovered.

Beni Montresor's *ABC Picture Stories* are filled with glorious, riotous colors and a type of puzzle format. For example, everywhere a "B" word appears an arrow points to it. Young children will enjoy finding the arrows and identifying the objects, although the dark background can hamper quick identification.

Bruno Munari's ABC uses color freely, and variation in size and type characterize a good deal of his work. The large letter *B* may be followed by a fairly large blue butterfly, but bananas and boot are much smaller. Young children will find this confusing.

In Roger Duvoisin's *A for the Ark*, Noah calls the animals to the ark in alphabetical order; the alphabet is repeated up to the appropriate letter on each page. Letters are large and each has several associations.

There are many alphabet books built around a central theme such as Harry Milgrom's *ABC of Ecology*, Velma Ilsley's *M Is for Moving*, Deborah Boxe's *26 Ways to Be Somebody Else*, Donald Crews's *We Read: A to Z* (about concepts such as quarter, part, over, middle, left), Bruce McMillan's *The Alphabet Symphony: An ABC Book*, Anne Alexander's *ABC of Cars and Trucks*, and Deborah Niland's *ABC of Monsters*. Given young children's fascination with the world around them as well as with monsters, dragons, and dinosaurs, there is likely to be an alphabet book especially suited to every young child.

Two alphabet books unequaled for beauty and information about African life are *Jambo Means Hello: Swahili Alphabet Book* by Muriel and Tom Feelings, and *Ashanti to Zulu*, the Caldecott winner by Margaret Musgrove and Leo and Diane Dillon. The first presents twenty-four words to match each letter of the Swahili alphabet. It is also a treasure of traditional East African life. The second offers a mine of information, verbal and pictorial, about twenty-six African tribes. The illustrations of each tribe are masterpieces wrought from pastels, watercolors and acrylics and are framed on each page. Young children will find a great deal in these books to note and query but a full appreciation of content and design integration rests with older children.

In contrast to some of these large books is Trina Schart Hyman's delighful, diminutive *A Little Alphabet*, full of black and white line drawings of miniature children and objects.

There is also the zany *Applebet Story* by Byron Barton. Capital letters and simple drawings depict the apple's ludicrous journey. Tasha Tudor's *A Is For Annabelle* would be a delight to those children who have explored grandmother's attic (or wish they could).

An ABC in English and Spanish offers two words for each alphabet letter, one in English and one in Spanish; both words mean the same thing. A bilingual pronunciation guide for use by parents and teachers is provided.

Young children will enjoy the alphabetic antics of Gretz's *Teddybears ABC* and all children — young and old — can feast their eyes on Marcia Brown's *All Butterflies* and *On Market Street* by Arnold and Anita Lobel. *All Butterflies* is a marvel of doublespread colored woodcuts which young children want to touch as well as see. *On Market Street* is a glorious parade of tradespeople, such as a wigmaker, an appleman, etc., who exemplify the letters of the alphabet. Done in full color, children are intrigued to discuss the tradespeople of today who could be in such a book (i.e., jeansmakers, pizzamakers, etc.). Children need time to pore over this well-researched and beautiful book.

Alphabet books afford young children all kinds of visual and verbal pleasure. In addition to the extension activities mentioned throughout the chapter, the following suggestions for children are included:

- Design alphabet books of their own.
- Create many new keywords and key illustrations for the letters.
- Organize the alphabet around a theme — animal, place, sport, etc.
- Play simple word games (i.e., scramble the names of all the objects on a page and test each other).

• Solve alphabetic puzzles (i.e., complete the words that represent objects illustrated in given alphabet books).

The Young Child's World of Poetry ♪

Beyond the songs, nursery rhymes, and ABC books, the young child's world of poetry is as variegated in form as snowflakes and as diverse in content as an almanac — full of nonsense, bad and beguiling children, childhood, animals and nature, and snippets and smidgins of everything else.

Nonsense

As the rhythm of poetry sends young bodies moving and the rhyme of poetry sends young lips chanting, the nonsense of poetry sends giggles rippling. Nonsense is achieved through twists of language and logic, through portmanteau words and all kinds of repetitions of phrase and line that sustain music and lilt, as well as through exaggeration, personification, and onomatopoeia. All of these can create panoramas of impossible events and parades of preposterous people and animals.

Among the poets especially adept at mixing the ingredients of nonsense to young children's tastes are Jack Prelutsky, N. M. Bodecker, Dennis Lee, Eve Merriam, Mary Ann Hoberman, Shel Silverstein, John Ciardi, Mary O'Neill, Laura Richards, and Ogden Nash, all of whom join the company of those past masters of the art — Lewis Carroll and Edward Lear. Although a good deal of the work of Carroll and Lear is beyond the vocabulary and full appreciation of very young children, all of them will continue to giggle at the Jumblies and "The Owl and the Pussy-Cat" in their pea-green boat.

Older youngsters will chuckle at *The Scroobius Pip*, an unfinished manuscript of Edward Lear's that Ogden Nash was invited to complete.

Jack Prelutsky revels in rich, onomatopoetic, alliterative, strongly cadenced verse that young children love to hear and taste. His poetry rolls and somersaults along in such books as *Circus, The Mean Old Mean Hyena*, and *The Pack Rat's Day and Other Poems*. Children will enjoy the unexpected tidbits of advice in the *Pack Rat*, such as what you should do when you meet a skunk. Numbers of Prelutsky's poems have been collected in *Zoo Doings*. Even though very young children may not understand all the words, they appreciate the rhythm, rhyme, and "music."

In these books and the earlier *Toucans Two and Other Poems*, animals run rampant, while in *The Queen of Eene* and *The Sheriff of Rottenshot* it is zany characters who adorn the pages. Animals or people — the verse never slackens as chuckle-bait. *What I Did Last Summer* is less rollicking than some of Prelutsky's other collections, but it delightfully represents a young child's summer.

Delighting in the naughtiness of others, young children will chuckle at Lindgren's *The Wild Baby,* an adaptation by Prelutsky from a Swedish tale. Feelings of superiority (even a little age makes us wiser) will erupt as young children read about this perfectly rambunctious infant whose further adventures are recorded in *The Wild Baby Goes to Sea.*

In *It's Raining, Said John Twaining: Danish Nursery Rhymes,* N. M. Bodecker, translator, poet, and artist, offers young children the droll, gentle nonsense that were rhymes from his own Danish childhood.

The sounds of rhyming words are funny and fascinating in Nancy Patz's *Moses Supposes His Toeses are Roses and Seven Other Silly Old Rhymes,* as well as in Bruce Degan's *Jamberry.* The nonsensical singable rhymes in the first book and the word play and humor in the second stir great enthusiasm.

Like Laura Richards (*Tirra Lirra*) in such poems as "Eletelephony" and "Antonio," Dennis Lee (*Alligator Pie* and *Garbage Delight*) changes endings to suit the sound and look of the poem, creating strongly rhythmic, lilting lyrics.

Eve Merriam's intense love of words and concern about their sound, beat, and meaning show clearly in her three early books — *There Is No Rhyme for Silver, It Doesn't Always Have to Rhyme,* and *Catch a Little Rhyme.* She provides the rhythms that generate much movement, mime, and sound from young children. Her *Blackberry Ink* stirs chorusing and chuckles.

It is Mary Ann Hoberman's bouncy, swinging rhythms, easily singable and memorizable verse, and topics and titles close to the hearts of young children that draw young ears to her. Poems like "Brother," "Hello and Good-by," and "The Folk Who Live in Backward Town" and titles like *Bugs, Yellow Butter Purple Jelly Red Jam Black Bread, Nuts to You and Nuts to Me, I Like Old Clothes,* and *A House Is a House for Me* are likely to generate smiles before the books are even opened.

Shel Silverstein's zany creations in *Where the Sidewalk Ends* and *A Light in the Attic* stimulate endless requests for more from people of all ages. Although all of Silverstein's poems are not suited to young children, they giggle delightedly at Ann McKay in "Sick" and chuckle about poems of sibling frustrations such as "What a Day" and "For Sale." The zaniness of "Peanut Butter Sandwich," "Magical Eraser," "Spaghetti," and the "Recipe for a Hippopotamus Sandwich" bring on helpless laughter. Some of these poems can lead children to invent all sorts of culinary monstrosities.

In books like *I Met a Man* and *Fast and Slow: Poems for Advanced Children and Beginning Parents,* John Ciardi's wit and humor show through.

Particularly in poems by David McCord, John Ciardi, Myra Cohn Livingston, and Eve Merriam, children see form and content well blended and what is best in the art and craft thoroughly integrated. They need not accept second best. As seen at the beginning of this chapter, McCord's "Jamboree" with its antiphonal structure mandates choral rendition and invention.

In "Jump or Jiggle," creation becomes *motoric.*

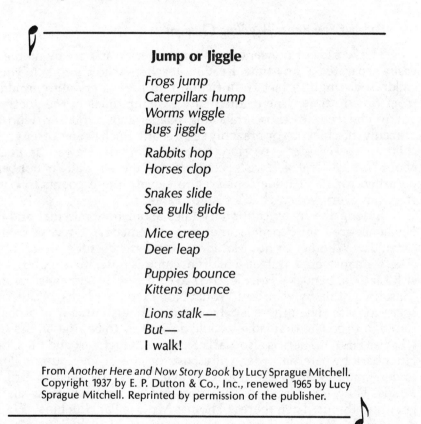

Jump or Jiggle

Frogs jump
Caterpillars hump
Worms wiggle
Bugs jiggle

Rabbits hop
Horses clop

Snakes slide
Sea gulls glide

Mice creep
Deer leap

Puppies bounce
Kittens pounce

Lions stalk —
But —
I walk!

From *Another Here and Now Story Book* by Lucy Sprague Mitchell. Copyright 1937 by E. P. Dutton & Co., Inc., renewed 1965 by Lucy Sprague Mitchell. Reprinted by permission of the publisher.

Mary O'Neill's *Hailstones and Halibut Bones: Adventures in Color* spurs young children to language and picture invention although the youngest may well miss some of the prolific and rich images the poetry evokes.

Ogden Nash's short poems about animals (the eel, the octopus, and many others) delight children, as do *The Adventures of Isabel,* a most fearless young lady, and *Custard the Dragon,* a most fearful creature. The sudden twists of many of the final lines produce smiles of appreciation. Older children are motivated to create short poems about animals, real or fanciful, after they have heard or read Nash's poems.

A master of longer strands of nonsense — book-length prose and poetry, in fact — is Theodor Geisel (Dr. Seuss). *And to Think That I Saw It on Mulberry Street, Horton Hatches the Egg, Five Hundred Hats of Bartholomew Cubbins,* and *Green Eggs and Ham,* to name a very few, keep young children glued for the climax. Zany illustrations, much repetition, fast-moving, weird adventures — all conspire to keep young children absorbed.

Bad but Sometimes Beguiling Children

The worlds of nonsense and sense overlap and are by no means easily separated at any time. Reading teachers who try to help young children distinguish fact from fiction find the waters quite muddied from time to time. One of the many twilight zones in the poetry of young children are those rollicking poems about children who are brazenly mischievous or brazenly self-reliant. Such poems offer young children special glee — possibly because they are viewed as poems about "me." A kind of "I wish I could do that but I'm glad I'm not being punished for it" attitude conspires to elevate these poems to honor status in every young child's Hall of Fame.

Among the many cautionary tales about how mischief and disobedience are punished and sometimes redeemed is F. Gwynne Evans's "Matilda." Whether or not Matilda will take the doctor's prescriptions is left unanswered but all children commiserate, to a point, with sick Matilda. Sendak's *Pierre* learned to care, but Silverstein's Sarah in "Sarah Cynthia Sylvia Stout Would Not Take the Garbage Out" was sorry too late. Then there is Silverstein's Pamela Purse who probably found out too late that ladies would do well *not* to be first all the time ("Ladies First"). There is also Karla Kuskin's "Hughbert and the Glue." Hughbert, by paternal order, will *not* use the glue again. Young children understand "Godfrey Gordon Gustavus Gore" by William Brighty Rands. They, too, forget to shut doors and like Jonathan Bing can forget other things. Then there is Thomas Mead in Pat Hutchins's *The Tale of Thomas Mead* whose response to every proposal, including an invitation to read, is, "Why should I?"

Many of these bad-to-beguiling children (or adults) are found in William Cole's *Beastly Boys and Ghastly Girls* and Eveline Ness's *Amelia Mixed the Mustard and Other Poems.* In general, both books are suited to an older audience but many seven- and eight-year-olds will laugh heartily at specific poems in these collections. Perhaps some of the ancestors of those rude and disobedient children are Heinrich Hoffman's *Struwwelpeter* where Solvenly Peter, Johnny Head-in-Air, and Augustus were introduced and severely punished — so severely punished that young children can wait indefinitely to be introduced to them.

Childhood

All poets of young children deal with childhood, nature, and animals in some form or other. There are, however, a number of poets — past and present — who bring *special* sensitivity to all stages of childhood. Dorothy Aldis, Walter de la Mare, A. A. Milne, Marchette Chute, and Eleanor Farjeon highlight fleeting moments of young years by capturing childhood's actions, fears, hopes, and play.

Walter de la Mare lauds the child's right to be himself in "Me," and to find his own "Somewhere." Dorothy Aldis speaks of siblings and everyday chores and play in "Little," "Our Silly Little Sister," "Setting the Table," and "Hiding." In poems such as the latter two, young children lived in a more leisured time and environment. This may require some discussion with young children of today.

Poems from de la Mare's *Now We Are Six* celebrate young years. "Us Two," a Winnie-the-Pooh poem, speaks to the special oneness of a child and his toy, as "Halfway Down" speaks of the special place a child can stop to think and wonder.

Marchette Chute captures many delights and wonders of childhood in poems like "My Dog" from *Rhymes About Ourselves* and "A Monkey" and "Spring Rain" from *Rhymes About the City.*

A Monkey

He likes to sit
With head in hand
Upon his little shelf.

A feeling I
Can understand.
I think a lot myself.

From *Rhymes About the City* by Marchette Chute. Copyright 1946 (Macmillan), renewal 1974 by Marchette Chute. By permission of the author.

In poems like Eleanor Farjeon's "Bedtime," the young child's determination to postpone bedtime is poetically monologued. In "Choosing," all the difficulties that beset the young child who has to make choices are chronicled and the ultimate happy solution recorded. Eleanor Farjeon's great sensitivity to rhythm is evident in her poems "Mrs. Peck Pigeon" and "Three Little Puffins." She speaks to many interests of children — real and fanciful — and their desire to explore them all in "There Isn't Time!"

The poems of Rose Fyleman, Harry Behn, and Robert Louis Stevenson bespeak childhood warmly, gently, and knowingly.

Two poets, both given the National Council of Teachers of English Award for Excellence in Poetry, have over the years offered to young children insights into self and nature with gentle, perceptive, spirit-reflective language. These are Karla Kuskin and Aileen Fisher.

From *Roar and More*, a benchmark in graphic design and "sound in print," through almost a score of books for children which she both wrote and illustrated, Karla Kuskin has presented childhood in its earliest joys, wonderments, and concerns. The simple, fitting images, love of words and the feelings they may tap, modest forms, and unpretentious illustrations comprise the quiet drawing card that is her poetry.

Poems like "Spring," "The Meal," her many "bug" poems, and the cumulative verse story about *A Boy Had a Mother Who Bought Him a Hat* especially touch young children. In *Dogs, Dragons, Trees, and Dreams* many verses from her earlier volumes have been brought together. Kuskin's *Any Me I Want to Be* and Lee Bennett Hopkins's *Girls Can Too! A Book of Poems* build for all young children the realization that the choices before them are many.

Animals and Nature

Aileen Fisher's keen love of nature permeates every poem she writes. She manages to offer children all sorts of information wrapped up in rhyme and rhythm about the way bugs and small and large woodland creatures live in *Cricket in a Thicket, Anybody Home?* and *Do Bears Have Mothers Too?* With a great deal of astute perception and understanding of children, she also identifies the questions that children think about and ask (*I Stood Upon a Mountain*) then she responds to them with simple lines, images, and rhymes true to the essence of childhood and nature.

Lids

It's good we have eyelids
that close at a touch
to keep out an insect
or sun that's too much.
Why don't we have earlids
for thunder and such?

From *Runny Days, Sunny Days* by Aileen Fisher. By permission of the author.

Feet

Feet of snails
are only one.
Birds grow two
to hop and run.
Dogs and cats
and cows grow four.
Ants and beetles
add two more.
Spiders run around
on eight,
which may seem
a lot, but wait—
Centipedes
have more than thirty
feet to wash
when they get dirty.

From *Cricket in a Thicket* by Aileen Fisher. By permission of the author.

Information, gentle humor, reflection, and some word play permeate her poetry.

Snippets and Smidgins of Everything Else

David McCord writes much of nature but also of snippets and smidgins of everything else. Word play abounds; humor is replete and the natural curiosity of the young child is both honored and spurred. Like Eve Merriam and Myra Cohn Livingston, McCord is well aware of the process of creating poetry and the discipline it requires. Of children's poetry he says, "Let's say that writing children's poetry is actually *being* with children inside a poem."[7]

Poems like "Jamboree," "And I Want You to Meet...," "Pickety Fence," and "The Song of the Train" exemplify word play and strong rhythm. In "The Grasshopper," he helps children see the *shape* of a poem—the wedding of an idea and its form on a page. But most of all, this poet gives children ideas to mull over—the need to be free, to climb a tree ("Every Time I Climb a Tree" from *Far and Few*), or find a rock ("This Is My Rock"); the need to be curious, raise questions ("The Shell"); and the need to play "Far Away." The very titles of his books lead children to wonder about the "was" and "is"—*Away and Ago, Far and Few, Take Sky, Every Time I Climb a Tree*, and *The Star in the Pail*.

Among the many other poets whose works young children should know are Lucille Clifton and Eloise Greenfield. The verse stories of Everett Anderson by Lucille Clifton beg for more of the same. Young children want to hear about Everett and how he copes with a number of things that beset a small boy. Eloise Greenfield's *Honey, I Love and Other Love Poems* is a collection of poems with a rhythmic, pulsating swing about love, friendship, family, and first adventures (like trying on mama's clothes, riding on a train, and watching a fast-running friend). The happiness of a secure childhood breathes through the poems and through the illustration by Diane and Leo Dillon.

Some of the excellent poems of Myra Cohn Livingston can be better understood by older children; however, her *Listen, Children, Listen: An Anthology of Poems for the Very Young* includes almost fifty poems to be read to young children.

Rose Fyleman writes of fairies, elves, and mice. "Mice" is one of the most popular of young children's poems and is always recited with a bit of bravado, possibly because children know that mice are not popular in many quarters.

Arnold Adoff's *Where Wild Willie* is about a joyful, effervescent child. It needs to be read aloud—the unusual poetic patterns and the syntax require that children hear the intonations the voice can give. Arnold Adoff is a skilled anthologist, especially of the poetry of Black America. Most of his compilations are better appreciated by older children.

Norma Farber's poetry—often book-length—deals with a wide range of topics: a response to *How Does It Feel to Be Old?* which represents a conversation-monologue between grandmother and granddaughter; *Where's Gomer?* a story of Noah's grandson who did not make it to the ark on time; and another Old Testament-based story that salvages the animals for whom there was no room on the ark, *How the Left-Behind Beasts Built Ararat*. Her *Small Wonders* and *Never Say Ugh to a Bug!* speak to children's small wonders (a bee, a snail) and larger ones (the sun, the moon). Her topics are broad, her imagery deft, and her rhythm and rhyme varied.

Collections and Anthologies

Two anthologists have done much to collect and compile poems for young children: Lee Bennett Hopkins and William Cole. The works of a third anthologist, Nancy Larrick, are more likely to be appreciated by the older child although within all of her compilations, especially *Piper Pipe That Song Again* and *When the Dark Comes Dancing*, are some poems clearly meant for young ears.

The topics for Lee Bennett Hopkins's anthologies range wide: *Elves, Fairies, and Gnomes, By Myself, Me: A Book of Poems, Zoo: A Book of Poems,* and holiday anthologies for Valentine's Day, Easter, Fourth of July, Halloween, Thanksgiving, and Christmas; and poems for bedtime, *Go to Bed!* and *Morning, Noon and Nighttime, Too.* Hopkins manages to collect and balance the better known and popular with the lesser known poems and poets. In *Surprises* the young beginning reader meets poems he or she can read and savor without adult aid.

William Cole's many anthologies speak to people of all ages; ones especially enjoyed by young children are *Dinosaurs and Beasts of Yore, Oh! What Nonsense, An Arkful of Animals* (many of these for older children), *The Book of Giggles,* and *I'm Mad at You.* His anthologies number many more but most of them are suited to the older child.

Two collections a young child will particularly enjoy are *A Rocket in My Pocket* by Withers and *Poems Children Will Sit Still For* by de Regniers. The first is full of brief nonsense verses and the second includes the poems of many famous poets, sense and nonsense side by side.

Once Upon a Rhyme: 101 Poems for Young Children, compiled by Sara and Stephen Corrin, serves many a humorous verse for five- to eight-year-olds by poets already mentioned, and Jill Bennett's *Tiny Tim: Verses for Children* serves the humor not only in words but also through the jolly, bright illustrations by Helen Oxenbury.

A large collection useful to primary and nursery teachers is Jack Prelutsky's *The Random House Book of Poetry for Children.* Illustrated by Arnold Lobel, the compilation is divided into topics dear to the hearts of children. It is a useful reference in any classroom.

Anthologies such as Helen Ferris's, *Favorite Poems Old and New,* May Hill Arbuthnot's *Time for Poetry,* and Elizabeth Sechrist's *One Thousand Poems for Children* are very valuable and comprehensive sources but need continuous updating and balancing with single poetry books.

Richard Lewis gathered children's own poems from several countries of the world in *Miracles.* The expressions of young children when they are told, "Michael, four years old, wrote this poem," is worth the sharing many times over.

For teachers needing to locate poems the *Index to Poetry for Children and Young People* is a vital resource. It is indexed by first line, author, and subject.

Summary ♪

Children have a natural affinity for the music of literature—poetry. Rhythm, rhyme, repetition, figurative language, and word play all excite enthusiastic movement, highly active listening, and verbal responses, even verbal creations, from young children.

Nursery children and primary graders should be immersed in song and poetry and all the spontaneous extensions these generate.

Single song-picture books and well-illustrated song compilations on which to feast tongue, ear, and eye are available.

Of all the songs of early childhood, none equal in popularity those highly repeatable mini verse stories — the nursery and Mother Goose rhymes. In presenting these to children all media and all artistic styles are available. The greatest of children's artists present Mother Goose in all her whimsy and variety. Collections and single nursery rhyme books abound. Versions of the same ones are available for sharing and comparing.

According to highly respected researchers Iona and Peter Opie, the only true nursery rhymes are the rhyming alphabets. Today such rhyming alphabets (and even unrhyming ones), innumerable and appealing, range from simple matches of object and letter to complex sophisticated cultural information books that only incidentally serve as alphabet books.

The young child's world of poetry is full of nonsense, nature, and the thoughts, feelings, and spirit of childhood. Poetry *must* be heard by young children. It stimulates their language, motion, and imagination; it is vital to the holistic development of each child.

DISCUSSION ACTIVITIES

• Share any of the poems by Mary Ann Hoberman or Eve Merriam. Observe the natural movement, mime, and echoic responses of young children to the words. Discuss the poems and observe and record the children's comments. Analyze these comments in terms of (1) words/figures of speech that elicit verbal/motoric responses, and (2) the number and kinds of word coinages children themselves produce.

• Identify three nursery rhymes with strong central characters, at least one of which is not well known. Share these with young children. Engage the children in creating fresh verses relating to other possible adventures the hero or heroine might have and help them to illustrate the verses in a leporello. Consider whether the further adventures of the characters exemplify children's own notable behaviors (Chapter 2).

• Select five alphabet books. Refer to page 92 and consider the decisions made by the authors and illustrators in the construction of each book.

NOTES

1. Michael Benton, "Poetry for Children: A Neglected Art," *Children's Literature in Education*, Vol. 19 (Autumn 1978): 113.

2. Myra Cohn Livingston, "The Singer, the Song, and the Sung," *Horn Book* (February 1979): 25.

3. "Sing Children Sing: Songs of the United States of America," Caedmon Records.

4. *The True Mother Goose* replica of the original *Mother Goose's Melodies: The Only Pure Edition,* published 1833 (New York: Merrimack Publishing Corp.). Original edition published by C. S. Frances and Company, New York and Boston, 1833, p. 2.

5. Iona and Peter Opie, eds., *The Oxford Dictionary of Nursery Rhymes* (London: Oxford University Press, 1951), pp. 22ff.

6. Selma G. Lanes, *The Art of Maurice Sendak.* (New York: Harry N. Abrams, Inc., 1980), p. 111.

7. Iona and Peter Opie, eds., *The Oxford Dictionary of Nursery Rhymes* (London: Oxford University Press, 1951), p. 47.

8. David A. Dillon quoting David McCord in "Perspectives," *Language Arts* (March 1978): 384.

♪ PROFESSIONAL BIBLIOGRAPHY

Apseloff, Marilyn. "Old Wine in New Bottles: Adult Poetry for Children," *Children's Literature in Education* (Winter 1979): 194–202.

Benton, Michael. "Poetry for Children: a Neglected Art," *Children's Literature in Education,* Vol. 19 (Autumn 1978): 113.

Burrows, Alvina Treut. "Profile: Karla Kuskin," *Language Arts* (November/December 1979): 934–940.

Clark, Leonard. "Poetry and Children," *Children's Literature in Education* (April 1978): 127–135.

———. "Poetry for the Youngest," *Horn Book Reflections,* edited by Elinor Whitney Field. Boston: Horn Book, 1969.

———. "Poetry Unfettered," *Children's Literature Association Quarterly* (Summer 1980): 12.

Dillon, David A., with McCord, David. "Perspectives," *Language Arts* (March 1978): 379–387.

Fisher, Carol J., and Natarella, Margaret A. "Of Cabbages and Kings: Or What Kinds of Poetry Young Children Like," *Language Arts,* Vol. 56, No. 4 (April 1979): 380–385.

Haviland, Virginia, and Smith, William Jay, comps. *Children and Poetry: A Selective Annotated Bibliography.* 2d rev. ed. Washington, D.C.: Library of Congress, 1979.

Kiah, Rosalie Black. "Profile: Eloise Greenfield," *Language Arts* (September 1980): 653–659.

Lanes, Selma G. *The Art of Maurice Sendak.* New York: Harry N. Abrams, Inc., 1980.

Livingston, Myra Cohn. "David McCord: The Singer, the Song, and the Sung," *The Horn Book* (February 1979): 25–39.

———. "Nonsense Verse: The Complete Escape," in *Celebrating Children's Books*, edited by Betsy Hearne and Marilyn Kaye. New York: Lothrop, Lee & Shepard, 1981.

McCord, David. "A Second Look: Tirra Lirra," *Horn Book* (December 1979): 690–694.

Opie, Iona, and Opie, Peter, eds. *The Oxford Dictionary of Nursery Rhymes*. London: Oxford University Press, 1951.

Painter, Helen W. *Poetry and Children*. Newark, Del.: International Reading Association, 1970.

Peterson, Carolyn Sue, and Fenton, Ann D., comps. *Index to Children's Songs*. New York: Wilson Company, 1979.

Sendak, Maurice. "Mother Goose's Garnishings," *Book Week* (Fall Children Issue) (October 31, 1965): 38–40.

Terry, Ann. *Children's Poetry Preferences: a National Survey of Upper Elementary Grades*. Urbana, Ill.: National Council of Teachers of English, 1974.

Tucker, Nicholas. "Why Nursery Rhymes?" *Where* (September 1969): 152–155.

♪ CHILDREN'S BOOKS

SONG

Aliki. *Go Tell Aunt Rhody*. Illus by author. New York: Macmillan Publishing Co., Inc., 1974.

———. *Hush Little Baby*. Illus. by author. Englewood Cliffs, N.J.: Prentice-Hall, Inc., 1968.

Bangs, Edward. *Yankee Doodle*. Illus. by Steven Kellogg. New York: Parents Magazine Press, 1976.

Engvick, William. *Lullabies and Night Songs*. Illus. by Maurice Sendak. New York: Harper & Row, Publishers, 1965.

Glass, Dudley (music). *The Songs of Peter Rabbit*. London: Frederick Warne & Co., Ltd., 1951.

Hart, Jane, comp. *Singing Bee! A Collection of Favorite Children's Songs*. Illus. by Anita Lobel. New York, Lothrop, Lee, & Shepard Books, 1982.

Hobzek, Mildred. *We Came a-Marching One, Two, Three*. Illus. by William Pene du Bois. New York: Four Winds Press, 1978.

John, Timothy, ed. *The Great Song Book*. Illus. by Tomi Ungerer. New York: Doubleday & Co., Inc., 1978.

Langstaff, John. *Frog Went A-Courtin'*. Illus. by Feodor Rojankovsky. New York: Harcourt Brace Jovanovich Inc., 1972.

———. *Oh, A' Hunting We Will Go*. Illus. by Nancy Winslow Parker. New York: Atheneum Publishers, 1974.

———, comp. *The Season for Singing: American Christmas Songs and Carols*. New York: Doubleday & Co., Inc., 1974.

————. *Sweetly Sings the Donkey: Animal Rounds for Children to Sing or Play on Recorders.* Illus. by Nancy Winslow Parker. New York: Atheneum Publishers, 1976.

Langstaff, Nancy, and Langstaff, John. *Jim Along Josie: A Collection of Folk Songs and Singing Games for Young Children.* Illus. by Jan Pienkowski. New York: Harcourt Brace Jovanovich Inc., 1970.

Marzollo, Jean. *Close Your Eyes.* Illus. by Susan Jeffers. New York: Dial Press, 1978.

Milne, A. A. *The Hums of Pooh.* New York: E. P. Dutton & Co., 1930.

————. *The Pooh Song Book.* New York: E. P. Dutton & Co., 1966.

Pearson, Tracey Campbell, illus. *Old MacDonald Had a Farm.* New York: Dial Press, 1984.

————, illus. *Sing a Song of Sixpence.* New York: Dial Press, 1984.

————, illus. *We Wish You a Merry Christmas.* New York: Dial Press, 1983.

Quackenbush, Robert. *Clementine.* Illus. by author. Philadelphia: J. B. Lippincott Co., 1974.

————. *Go Tell Aunt Rhody.* Illus. by author. Philadelphia: J. B. Lippincott Co., 1973.

————, ed. and illus. *The Holiday Song Book.* New York: Lothrop, Lee and Shepard, Inc., 1977.

————. *Old MacDonald Had a Farm.* New York: Harper & Row, Publishers, 1972.

————. *Skip to My Lou.* Illus. by author. Philadelphia: J. B. Lippincott Co., 1975.

————. *There'll Be a Hot Time in the Old Town Tonight.* Illus. by author. Philadelphia: J. B. Lippincott Co., 1974.

Seeger, Ruth. *American Folk Songs for Children.* Illus. by Barbara Cooney. New York: Doubleday & Co., Inc., 1980.

Spier, Peter. *The Fox Went Out on a Chilly Night.* New York: Doubleday & Co., Inc., 1961.

————. *London Bridge Is Falling Down.* Illus. by author. New York: Doubleday & Co., Inc., 1967.

Stanley, Diane. Illus. *Fiddle-I-Fee: A Traditional American Chant.* Boston: Little, Brown & Co., 1979.

Winn, Marie. *The Fireside Book of Children's Songs.* Illus. by John Alcorn. New York: Simon & Schuster, 1966.

————. *The Fireside Book of Fun and Game Songs.* Illus. by Whitney Darrow, Jr. New York: Simon & Schuster, 1974.

————, ed. *What Shall We Do and Allee Galloo: Playsongs and Singing Games for Young Children.* Illus. by Karla Kuskin. New York: Harper & Row, Publishers, 1971.

NURSERY RHYMES

Blake, Quentin, illus. *Quentin Blake's Nursery Rhyme Book.* New York: Harper & Row, Publishers, Inc., 1984.

Blegvad, Lenore. *Hark! Hark! The Dogs Do Bark!* Illus. by Eric Blegvad. New York: Atheneum Publishers, 1976.

————. *The Little Pig-a-Wig and Other Rhymes About Pigs.* Illus. by Eric Blegvad. New York: Atheneum Publishers, 1978.

————. *Mittens for Kittens and Other Rhymes About Cats.* Illus. by Eric Blegvad. New York: Atheneum Publishers, 1974.

Bodecker, N. M., trans. and illus. *It's Raining Said John Twaining: Danish Nursery Rhymes.* New York: Atheneum Publishers, 1973.

Briggs, Raymond. *The Mother Goose Treasury.* Illus. by author. New York: Coward, McCann & Geoghegan, Inc., 1966.

Brooks, Leonard Leslie. *Ring O' Roses.* New ed. New York: Frederick Warne & Co., Inc., 1977.

Caldecott, Randolph. *Randolph Caldecott's John Gilpin and Other Stories.* Illus. by author. New York: Frederick Warne & Co., Inc., 1977.

————. *Sing a Song of Sixpence.* Illus. by author. New York: Frederick Warne & Co., Inc., 1880.

de Angeli, Marguerite, comp. *Book of Nursery and Mother Goose Rhymes.* Illus. by author. New York: Doubleday & Co., Inc., 1954.

Greenaway, Kate. *Mother Goose: Or The Old Nursery Rhymes.* Illus. by author. New York: Frederick Warne & Co., Inc., 1882.

Jeffers, Susan, ed. and illus. *If Wishes Were Horses and Other Rhymes.* New York: E. P. Dutton & Co., 1979.

Lent, Blair. *From King Boggen's Hall to Nothing at All.* Illus. by author. Boston: Little, Brown & Co., 1967.

Lines, Kathleen. *Lavender's Blue: A Book of Nursery Rhymes.* Illus. by Harold Jones. New York: Franklin Watts Inc., 1954.

Lobel, Arnold. *Gregory Griggs and Other Nursery Rhymes People.* Illus. by author. New York: Greenwillow Books, 1978.

Marshall, James. *James Marshall's Mother Goose.* Illus. by author. New York: Farrar, Straus & Giroux, Inc., 1979.

Rackham, Arthur. *Mother Goose Nursery Rhymes.* Illus. by author. New York: F. Watts, 1969 (reprint of 1913 edition).

Rockwell, Anne. *Gray Goose and Gander and Other Mother Goose Rhymes.* New York: Harper & Row, Publishers, Inc., 1980.

Rojankovsky, Feodor. *The Tall Book of Mother Goose.* Illus. by author. New York: Harper & Row, Publishers, Inc., 1942.

Sendak, Maurice. *Hector Protector and As I Went Over the Water.* Illus. by author. New York: Harper & Row, Publishers, Inc., 1965.

Spier, Peter. *London Bridge Is Falling Down.* Illus. by author. New York: Doubleday & Co., Inc., 1967.

————. *To Market, To Market.* Illus. by author. New York: Doubleday & Co., Inc., 1967.

Thompson, Pat, Sel. *Rhymes Around the Day.* Illus. by Jan Ormerod. New York: Lothrop, Lee, & Shepard Books, 1983.

Tripp, Wallace. *Granfa' Grig Had a Pig and Other Rhymes Without Reason from Mother Goose.* Illus. by author. Boston: Little, Brown & Co., 1976.

Tudor, Tasha. *Mother Goose.* Illus. by author. New York: Henry Z. Walck, 1944.

Wildsmith, Brian. *Mother Goose: A Collection of Nursery Rhymes.* New York: Franklin Watts Inc., 1964.

Zemach, Margot. *Hush, Little Baby.* Illus. by author. New York: E. P. Dutton & Co., 1976.

ALPHABET

Alexander, Anne. *ABC of Cars and Trucks.* Pictures by Ninon. New York: Doubleday Company, Inc., 1971.

Balian, Lorna. *Humbug Potion: An A•B•Cipher.* Illus. by author. Nashville, Tenn.: Abingdon Press, 1984.

Barry, Robert. *Animals Around the World.* Illus. by author. New York: McGraw-Hill Book Co., 1967.

Barton, Byron. *Applebet Story.* New York: Viking Press, 1973.

Baskin, Hosea, et al. *Hosie's Alphabet.* Pictures by Leonard Baskin. New York: Viking Press, 1972.

Boxe, Deborah. *26 Ways to Be Somebody Else.* New York: Pantheon Books, Inc., 1960.

Brown, Marcia. *All Butterflies.* Illus. by author. New York: Charles Scribner's Sons, 1974.

―――. *Peter Piper's Alphabet.* Illus. by author. New York: Charles Scribner's Sons, 1959.

Bruna, Dick. *b is for bear: an ABC.* Illus. by author. New York: Methuen, 1972.

Carle, Eric. *All About Arthur.* Illus. by author. New York: Franklin Watts, 1974.

Chardiet, Bernice. *C Is for Circus.* Illus. by Brinton C. Turkle. New York: Walker & Co., 1971.

Coletta, Irene, and Coletta, Hallie. *From A to Z: The Collected Letters of Irene and Hallie Colletta.* Illus. by Hallie Colletta. Englewood Cliffs, N.J.: Prentice-Hall, Inc., 1979.

Cooney, Barbara. *A Garland of Games and Other Diversions: An Alphabet Book.* Illus. by author. Initial letters by Suzanne R. Morse. New York: Holt, Rinehart and Winston, Inc., 1969.

Crews, Donald. *We Read: A to Z.* Illus. by author. New York: Harper & Row, Publishers, Inc., 1967.

Duvoisin, Roger. *A For the Ark.* Illus. by author. New York: Lothrop, Lee & Shepard Co., 1952.

Eichenberg, Fritz. *Ape in a Cape.* Illus. by author. New York: Harcourt Brace Jovanovich Inc., 1952.

Elting, Mary, and Folsom, Michael. *Q Is For Duck: An Alphabet Guessing Game.* Illus. by Jack Kent. New York: Clarion Books, 1980.

Emberley, Ed. *Ed Emberley's ABC.* Illus. by author. Boston: Little, Brown & Co., 1978.

Feelings, Muriel, and Feelings, Tom. *Jambo Means Hello: Swahili Alphabet Book.* Illus. by Tom Feelings. New York: Dial Press, 1974.

Greenaway, Kate. *A Apple Pie.* Illus. by author. New York: Frederick Warne & Co., Inc., 1886.

Gretz, Susanna. *Teddybears ABC.* Chicago: Follett, 1975.

Hoberman, Mary Ann. *Nuts to You and Nuts to Me: An Alphabet of Poems.* Illus. by Ronni Solbert. New York: Alfred A. Knopf, Inc., 1974.

Hyman, Trina Schart. *A Little Alphabet*. Illus. by author. Boston: Little, Brown & Co., 1980.

Ilsley, Velma. *M Is for Moving*. New York: Henry Z. Walck, Inc., 1966.

Isadora, Rachel. *City Seen from A to Z*. Illus. by author. New York: Greenwillow Books, 1983.

Kitchen, Bert, illus. *Animal Alphabet*. New York: Dial Press, 1984.

Lalicki, Barbara, comp. *If There Were Dreams to Sell*. Illus. by Margot Tomes. New York: Lothrop, Lee and Shepard Books, 1984.

Lear, Edward. *Lear Alphabet — Penned and Illustrated by Edward Lear Himself*. New York: McGraw-Hill Book Company, 1965.

Lobel, Arnold. *On Market Street*. Illus. by Anita Lobel. New York: Greenwillow Books, 1981.

McGinley, Phyllis. *All Around the Town*. Drawings by Helen Stone. Philadelphia: J. B. Lippincott Company, 1948.

McMillan, Bruce. *The Alphabet Symphony: An ABC Book*. New York: Greenwillow Press, 1977.

Matthiesen, Thomas. *ABC: An Alphabet Book*. New York: Grosset & Dunlop Inc., 1981.

Milgrom, Harry. *ABC of Ecology*. Photos by Donald Crews. New York: The Macmillan Company, 1972.

Miller, Barry. *Alphabet World*. New York: The Macmillan Company, 1971.

Montresor, Beni. *A for Angel: Beni Montresor's ABC Picture Stories*. New York: Alfred A. Knopf Inc., 1969.

Munari, Bruno. *Bruno Munari's ABC*. Cleveland: The World Publishing Co., 1960.

Musgrove, Margaret. *Ashanti to Zulu: African Traditions*. Illus. by Leo Dillon and Diane Dillon. New York: Dial Press, 1976.

Newberry, Clare. *The Kittens' ABC*. Illus. by author. New York: Harper & Row, Publishers, Inc., 1965.

Niland, Deborah. *ABC of Monsters*. New York: McGraw-Hill Book Co., 1976.

Parish, Peggy. *A Beastly Circus*. Illus. by Arnold Lobel. New York: Macmillan Publishing Co., Inc., 1969.

Piatti, Celestino. *Celestino Piatti's Animal ABC*. New York: Atheneum Publishers, 1966.

Provensen, Alice, and Provensen, Martha. *A Peaceable Kingdom: The Shaker ABECEDARIUS*. New York: Viking Press, 1978.

Rockwell, Anne. *Albert B. Cub and Zebra: An Alphabet Storybook*. New York: Harper & Row, Publishers, Inc., 1977.

Sendak, Maurice. *Alligators All Around: An Alphabet Book*. (Nutshell Library.) Illus. by author. New York: Harper & Row, Publishers, Inc., 1962.

Stevenson, James. *Grandpa's Great City Tour: An Alphabet Book*. Illus. by author. New York: Greenwillow Books, 1983.

Tallon, Robert. *An ABC in English and Spanish*. New York: The Lion Press Inc., 1969.

Tudor, Tasha. *A Is For Annabelle*. Illus. by author. New York: Rand McNally Co., 1954.

Watson, Clyde. *Applebet: An ABC*. Illus. by Wendy Watson. New York: Farrar, Straus & Giroux, Inc., 1982.

Yolen, Jane. *All the the Woodland Early: An ABC Book*. Illus. by Jane B. Zalben. New York: Collins Publishers, 1979.

POETRY

Adoff, Arnold. *Where Wild Willie.* Illus. by Emily Arnold McCully. New York: Harper & Row, Publishers, Inc., 1978.

Aldis, Dorothy. "Hiding," "Little," "Our Silly Little Sister," and "Setting the Table," *Everything and Anything.* New York: Minton, Balch and Company, 1927.

Arbuthnot, May Hill, and Root, Shelton L., Jr., eds. *Time for Poetry.* 3rd ed. Illus. by Arthur Paul. Chicago: Scott, Foresman, 1968.

Behn, Harry. *The Little Hill.* Illus. by author. New York: Harcourt Brace Jovanovich, Inc., 1949.

Bennett, Jill. *Tiny Tim: Verses for Children.* Illus. by Helen Oxenbury. New York: Delacorte Press, 1982.

Beyer, Evelyn. "Jump or Jiggle," *Another Here and Now Storybook.* Edited by Lucy Sprague Mitchell. New York: E. P. Dutton and Company, 1937.

Bodecker, N. M., illus. *It's Raining Said John Twaining.* Illus. by author. New York: Atheneum Publishers, 1973.

Brewton, John E.; Blackburn, F. Meredith, III; and Blackburn, Lorraine A., comps. *Index to Poetry for Children and Young People 1976–1981.* Bronx, N.Y.: The H. W. Wilson Company.

Brown, Beatrice Curtis. *Jonathan Bing and Other Verses.* New York: Oxford University Press, 1936.

Chute, Marchette. "My Dog," *Rhymes About Ourselves.* New York: Macmillan Co., 1932.

———. "A Monkey," and "Spring Rain," *Rhymes About the City.* New York: Macmillan Co., 1946.

Ciardi, John. *Fast and Slow: Poems for Advanced Children and Beginning Parents.* Illus. by Becky Gaver. Boston: Houghton Mifflin Co., 1975.

———. *I Met a Man.* Illus. by Robert Osborne. Boston: Houghton Mifflin Co., 1961.

Clifton, Lucille. *Everett Anderson's Year.* Illus. by Ann Grifalconi. New York: Holt, Rinehart and Winston Co., 1974.

Cole, William. *An Arkful of Animals: Poems for the Very Young.* Illus. by Lynn Munsinger. Boston: Houghton Mifflin Co., 1978.

———, coll. *Beastly Boys and Ghastly Girls.* Drawings by Tomi Ungerer. New York: World Publishing Co., 1964.

———. *The Book of Giggles.* New York: Dell Publishing Co., 1980.

———, ed. *Dinosaurs and Beasts of Yore.* Illus. by Susanna Natti. New York: William Collins Publishers Inc., 1979.

———. *I'm Mad at You.* Illus. by George Macclain. New York: Philomel Books, 1978.

———, ed. *Oh! What Nonsense.* Illus. by Tomi Ungerer. New York: Viking Press, 1966.

Corrin, Sara, and Corrin, Stephen. *Once Upon a Rhyme: 101 Poems for Young Children.* Illus. by Jill Bennett. New York: Faber, 1982.

de la Mare, Walter. "Me," "Somewhere," and "Us Two," *Bells and Grass.* New York: Viking Penguin Inc., 1942.

de Regniers, Beatrice S. et. al., comps. *Poems Children Will Sit Still For.* New York: Scholastic Book Services, 1969.

Degan, Bruce. *Jamberry.* Illus. by author. New York: Harper & Row, Publishers, Inc., 1983.

Evans, F. Gwynne. "Matilda," *Puffin, Puma & Co.* New York: Macmillan & Co., undated.

Farber, Norma. *How Does It Feel to Be Old?* Illus. by Trina Schart Hyman. New York: E. P. Dutton & Co., 1979.

———. *How the Left-Behind Beasts Built Ararat.* Illus. by Antonia Frasconi. New York: Walker & Co., 1978.

———. *Never Say Ugh to a Bug!* Illus. by Jose Aruego. New York: Greenwillow Books, 1979.

———. *Small Wonders.* Illus. by Kazue Mitzumura. New York: Thomas Y. Crowell Co., 1979.

———. *Where's Gomer?* Illus. by William Pene du Bois. New York: E. P. Dutton & Co., 1974.

Farjeon, Eleanor. "Mrs. Peck Pigeon," "Bedtime," and "Choosing," *Over the Garden Wall.* Philadelphia: J. B. Lippincott Co., 1933.

———. "There Isn't Time," *Time to Shout Poems for You.* Compiled by Lee Bennett Hopkins and Misha Arenstein. Illus. by Lisl Weil. New York: Scholastic Book Services, 1973.

———. "Three Little Puffins," *The Silver Curlew.* New York: Viking Press, 1953.

Ferris, Helen. Comp. *Favorite Poems Old and New.* Illus. by Leonard Weisgard. New York: Doubleday & Co., Inc., 1957.

Fisher, Aileen. *Anybody Home?* Illus. by Susan Bonners. New York: Thomas Y. Crowell Co., 1980.

———. *Do Bears Have Mothers Too?* Illus. by Eric Carle. New York: Thomas Y. Crowell Co., 1973.

———. "The Handiest Nose," *Cricket in a Thicket.* Illus. by Feodor Rojankovsky. New York: Charles Scribner's Sons, 1963.

———. *I Stood Upon a Mountain.* Illus. by Blair Lent. New York: Thomas Y. Crowell Co., 1979.

Fyleman, Rose. "Mice," *Fifty One New Nursery Rhymes.* New York: Doubleday & Co., 1932.

Geisel, Theodor [Dr. Suess]. *And to Think That I Saw It On Mulberry Street.* New York: Vanguard Press, Inc., 1937.

———. *Five Hundred Hats of Bartholomew Cubbins.* New York: Vanguard Press, Inc., 1938.

———. *Green Eggs and Ham.* New York: Random House Inc., 1960.

———. *Horton Hatches the Egg.* New York: Random House Inc., 1940.

Greenfield, Eloise. *Honey, I Love and Other Love Poems.* Illus. by Diane and Leo Dillon. New York: Thomas Y. Crowell Co., 1978.

Hoberman, Mary Ann. "Brother," *Poems Children Will Sit Still For.* Compiled by Beatrice de Regniers et. al. New York: Scholastic Book Services, 1969.

———. *Bugs: Poems.* Illus. by Victoria Chess. New York: Viking Press, 1976.

———. "Hello and Good-by," and "The Folk Who Live in Backward Town," *Hello and Goodby.* Illus. by Norman Hoberman. Boston: Little, Brown & Co., 1959.

———. *A House is a House for Me.* Illus. by Betty Fraser. New York: Viking Press, 1978.

———. *I Like Old Clothes.* Illus. by Jacqueline Chwast. New York: Alfred A. Knopf, Inc., 1976.

———. *Nuts to You and Nuts to Me: An Alphabet of Poems.* Illus. by Ronni Solbert. New York: Alfred A. Knopf, Inc., 1974.

———. *Yellow Butter Purple Jelly Red Jam Black Bread.* Illus. by Chaya Burstein. New York: Viking Press, 1981.

Hoffmann, Heinrich. *Struwwelpeter: Merry Stories and Funny Pictures.* New York: Frederick Warne & Co., Inc., 1844. Translated (1848).

Hopkins, Lee Bennett, comp. *By Myself.* Illus. by Glo Coalson. New York: Thomas Y. Crowell Co., 1980.

———. comp. *Elves, Fairies, and Gnomes.* Illus. by Rosekrans Hoffman. New York: Alfred A. Knopf Inc., 1980.

———. *Girls Can Too! A Book of Poems.* Illus. by Emily McCully. New York: Franklin Watts, Inc., 1972.

———, comp. *Go To Bed! A Book of Bedtime Poems.* Illus. by Rosekrans Hoffman. New York: Alfred A. Knopf Inc., 1979.

———, ed. *Me: A Book of Poems.* Illus. by Talivaldis Stubis. Boston: Houghton Mifflin Co., 1970.

———, ed. *Merrily Comes Our Harvest in Poems for Thanksgiving.* Illus. by Ben Schecter. New York: Harcourt Brace Jovanovich Inc., 1978.

———. *Morning, Noon and Nighttime, Too.* Illus. by Nancy Hannans. New York: Harper & Row, Publishers, Inc., 1980.

———, ed. *Sing Hey for Christmas Day.* Illus. by Laura Jean Allen. New York: Harcourt Brace Jovanovich Inc., 1975.

———, comp. *Surprises.* Illus. by Megan Lloyd. New York: Harper & Row, Publishers, Inc., 1984.

———, ed. *Zoo: A Book of Poems.* New York: Crown Publishers, 1971.

Hutchins, Pat. *The Tale of Thomas Mead.* Illus. by author. New York: Greenwillow Books, 1980.

Kuskin, Karla. *A Boy Had a Mother Who Bought Him a Hat.* Boston: Houghton Mifflin Co., 1976.

———. *Any Me I Want to Be.* Illus. by author. New York: Harper & Row, Publishers, Inc., 1972.

———. *Dogs, Dragons, Trees, and Dreams.* New York: Harper & Row, Publishers, Inc., 1980.

———. "Hughbert and the Glue," *The Rose on My Cake.* New York: Harper & Row, Publishers, Inc., 1964.

———. "The Meal," *Alexander Soames: His Poems.* New York: Harper & Row, Publishers, Inc., 1962.

———. *Roar and More.* Illus. by author. New York: Harper & Row, Publishers, Inc., 1956.

———. "Spring," *In the Middle of the Trees.* New York: Harper & Row, Publishers, Inc., 1958.

Larrick, Nancy, ed. *Piper Pipe That Song Again.* Illus. by Kelly Oecholi. New York: Random House, Inc., 1965.

———, comp. *When the Dark Comes Dancing.* Illus. by John Wallner. New York: Philomel, 1983.

Lear Edward, and Nash, Ogden. *The Scroobius Pip.* Illus. by Nancy E. Burkert. New York: Harper & Row, Publishers, Inc., 1968.

Lee, Dennis. *Alligator Pie.* Illus. by Frank Newfeld. Boston: Houghton Mifflin Co., 1975.

———. *Garbage Delight.* Illus. by Frank Newfeld. Boston: Houghton Mifflin Co., 1978.

Lewis, Richard, ed. *Miracles: Poems by Children of the English Speaking World.* New York: Simon & Schuster, 1966.

Lindgren, Barbara. *The Wild Baby.* Adapted from the Swedish by Jack Prelutsky. Illus. by Eva Eriksson. New York: Greenwillow Books, 1981.

———. *The Wild Baby Goes to Sea.* Translated by Jack Prelutsky. Illus. by Eva Eriksson. New York: Greenwillow Books, 1983.

Lindsay, Vachel. "The Little Turtle," *Golden Whales.* New York: Macmillan Company, 1920.

Livingston, Myra Cohn, ed. *Listen, Children, Listen: An Anthology of Poems for the Very Young.* Illus. by Trina Schart Hyman. New York: Harcourt Brace Jovanovich Inc., 1972.

McCord, David. "And I Want You to Meet...," *Every Time I Climb a Tree.* Illus. by Marc Simont. Boston: Little, Brown & Co., 1967.

———. *Away and Ago: Rhymes of the Never Was and Always Is.* Illus. by Leslie Morrill. Boston: Little, Brown & Co., 1975.

———. "Every Time I Climb a Tree," "Far Away," "The Grasshopper," "Pickety Fence," "The Shell," "The Song of the Train," and "This Is My Rock," *Far and Few: Rhymes of the Never Was and Always Is.* Illus. by Henry B. Kane. Boston: Little, Brown & Co., 1952.

———. "Jamboree," *All Day Long.* Illus. by Henry B. Kane. Boston: Little, Brown & Co., 1965.

———. *The Star in the Pail.* Illus. by Marc Simont. Boston: Little, Brown & Co., 1975.

———. *Take Sky.* Illus. by Henry B. Kane. Boston: Little, Brown & Co., 1962.

Merriam, Eve. *Blackberry Ink.* Illus. by Hans Wilhelm. New York: William Morrow & Co., Inc., 1985.

———. *Catch a Little Rhyme.* Illus. by Imero Gobbato. New York: Atheneum Publishers, 1966.

———. *It Doesn't Always Have To Rhyme.* Illus. by Malcolm Spooner. New York: Antheneum Publishers, 1964.

———. *There Is No Rhyme for Silver.* Illus. by Joseph Schindelman. New York: Atheneum Publishers, 1962.

Milne, A. A. "Halfway Down," *When We Were Very Young.* Illus. by E. H. Shepard, New York: E. P. Dutton, 1924.

———. *Now We Are Six.* New York: E. P. Dutton & Co., 1927.

Nash, Ogden. "The Adventures of Isabel," and "The Eel," *Family Reunion.* Boston: Little, Brown & Co., 1936.

———. *Custard the Dragon.* Illus. by Linell Nash. Boston: Little, Brown & Co., 1961.

———. "The Octopus," *Good Intentions.* Boston: Little, Brown & Co., 1942.

Ness, Evaline. *Amelia Mixed the Mustard and Other Poems.* Illus. by author. New York: Charles Scribner's Sons, 1975.

O'Neill, Mary. *Hailstones and Halibut Bones: Adventures in Color.* Illus. by Leonard Weisgard. New York: Doubleday & Co., 1961.

Patz, Nancy. *Moses Supposes His Toeses Are Roses and Seven Other Silly Old Rhymes.* Illus. by author. New York: Harcourt Brace Jovanovich, Inc., 1983.

Peter Piper's Practical Principles of Plain and Perfect Pronunciation. New York: Dover Publications Inc., 1970. Unabridged and unaltered republication of the work published by LeRoy Phillips in Boston in 1911.

Prelutsky, Jack. *Circus.* Illus. by Arnold Lobel. New York: Macmillan Publishing Co., 1974.

———. *It's Christmas.* Illus. by MaryLin Hafner. New York: Greenwillow Books, 1981.

———. *It's Halloween.* Illus. by MaryLin Hafner. New York: Greenwillow Books, 1977.

———. *It's Thanksgiving.* Illus. by MaryLin Hafner. New York: Greenwillow Books, 1982.

———. *The Mean Old Mean Hyena.* Illus. by Arnold Lobel. New York: Greenwillow Books, 1978.

———. *The Pack Rat's Day and Other Poems.* Illus. by Margaret Bloy Graham. New York: Macmillan Publishing Co., 1974.

———. *The Queen of Eene.* Illus. by Victoria Chess. New York: Greenwillow Books, 1978.

———. *Rainy, Rainy Saturday.* Illus. by MaryLin Hafner. New York: Greenwillow Books, 1980.

———. *The Random House Book of Poetry for Children.* Illus. by Arnold Lobel. New York: Random House, 1983.

———. *The Sheriff of Rottenshot.* Illus. by Victoria Chess. New York: Greenwillow Books, 1982.

———. *Toucans Two and Other Poems.* Illus. by Jose Aruego. New York: Macmillan Publishing Co., 1967.

———. *What I Did Last Summer.* Illus. by Yossi Abolafia. New York: Greenwillow Books, 1984.

———. *Zoo Doings.* Pictures by Paul O. Zelinsky. New York: Greenwillow Books, 1983.

Rands, William Brighty. "Godfrey Gordon Gustavus Gore," *Liliput Lyrics,* edited by R. Bremley Johnson. London: Bodley Head, 1899.

Richards, Laura. "Antonio," and "Eletelephony," *Tirra Lirra.* Illus. by Marguerite Davis. Boston: Little, Brown & Co., 1955 (original 1902).

Sechrist, Elizabeth. *One Thousand Poems for Children.* Rev. ed. Illus. by Henry Pitz. Philadelphia: Macrae Smith Co., 1946.

Sendak, Maurice. *Pierre.* (Nutshell Library.) Illus. by author. New York: Harper & Row, Publishers, Inc., 1962.

Silverstein, Shel. "Ladies First," *A Light in the Attic.* New York: Harper & Row, Publishers, Inc., 1981.

———. "For Sale," "Magical Eraser," "Peanut Butter Sandwich," "Recipe for a Hippopotamus Sandwich," "Sarah Cynthia Sylvia Stout Would Not Take the Garbage Out," "Sick," "Spaghetti," and "What a Day," *Where the Sidewalk Ends.* New York: Harper & Row, Publishers, Inc., 1974.

Smith, William Jay. "The Toaster," *Laughing Time.* Illus. by Juliet Kepes. Boston: Little, Brown & Co., 1955.

Stevenson, Robert Louis. *A Child's Garden of Verses.* Illus. by Tasha Tudor. Chicago: Rand McNally & Co., Inc., 1981.

Tippett, James. "The Park," *I Live in a City*. New York: Harper & Bros., 1927.
Withers, Carl. *A Rocket in My Pocket*. Illus. by Susanne Suba. New York: Holt,
Rinehart and Winston, Inc., 1948.

Chapter 6

The Sound of Literature: Laughter

RICH ENCOUNTERS

There was a fence — not the wire kind but a good, old-fashioned picket fence — and Benjy had a stick. He couldn't resist. Prancing and giggling to the words of David McCord's "Pickety Fence," Benjy slid the stick against the pickets time and time again grinning with joy and resembling, for all the world, a pianist executing a successful glissando. His quick steps moved to the strong beat of the poem. As his mother looked out of the kitchen window to the yards beyond, she wondered what he was saying and laughing about. Benjy's teacher would know.

●◆●

"Where is George?" asked the teacher above the clamor of chuckles.

"He jumped up cause he was scared," Bobby said, pointing to a picture in George and Martha Rise and Shine.

"Of what?"

"Sam — the snake," replied Lisa.

"And he was only a stuffed snake, wasn't he?"

"Yes, it's so funny. You can just see George's feet," Lisa added as her class-mates giggled.

"Do you suppose Martha brought Sam out on purpose?" asked the teacher.

"Yes," answered Ryan, amidst more giggles, "She knew George was fibbing."

Humor

Humor is a powerful and proven bridge to literary appreciation for young children. It may be that we are all like Sid Fleischman, renowned lover of American folklore and writer of tall tales, in that our earliest literary memories are funny ones.[1] The poem, prose, or picture that aroused the first chuckles nestles deeply in one's memory.

No one doubts the need for humor. Indeed, "a world—or a literature—without mirth would be terrifying."[2] Humor *is* essential. To grow without laughter is to grow deprived, to exist merely and not to live fully.

Roald Dahl, the creator of many books for children, among them *The Enormous Crocodile* and *Charlie and the Chocolate Factory,* says about his writing for children, "And for children, humor is an absolute must. You can put lots of drama and tension in, but somewhere humor has to keep popping up. It's one of the first reactions of a child."[3]

It is because of the cruciality of laughter in life and because a child's love of literature may spring from early encounters with what is comic that this chapter is devoted to the humorousness in literature.

What is humor? Alvin Schwartz, master collector of verbal humor in all its guises, calls humor " . . . a slippery subject." Put simply, he says, "Humor is the comic quality in a person, experience, or idea that makes one laugh."[4]

Humor is indeed a slippery subject. Can one analyze a laugh? What is it that makes an adult or a child laugh? Are there comic elements that contribute to this "comic quality"? Answers to the first two questions are "slippery." Some light has been shed on the third question: There is little doubt that surprise, nonsense, contradiction, hyperbole, and illogic are elements in a definition of comic quality.

In terms of children and literature, however, *more important questions* are: To what other comic elements do young children respond? and How can adults help young children, over a period of time, to appreciate *many* kinds of humor?

Humor and Children

In the Rich Encounters at the beginning of this chapter, young children were responding to the tap-able, clap-able alliteration and onomatopoeia in "Pickety Fence." These sent Benjy into a laughing chant and bodily movement.

In *George and Martha Rise and Shine* the exaggerated reaction to the stuffed snake elicited giggles. Fear lifted George's feet well off the ground when he saw Sam the Snake. Children also responded happily to their own inference that Martha knew George was fibbing when he claimed snake-charming ability. Clearly children are not without appreciation for the ridiculous, the unreasonable, the exaggerated, and the variety of linguistic features that turn up lips and move hands and feet.

In response to the second question — How can adults help children to appreciate many kinds of humor? — there are innumerable works of prose, poetry, and picture that generate children's laughter. For the teacher concerned about selecting the best laughter-bait, exposing the young child to visual exaggeration, nonsense, surprise, incongruity, sheer slapstick, comic situations and problems as well as ludicrous events and diverse verbal humor is critical.

The younger child within the three- to eight-year range will respond more readily to slapstick and obvious alliteration and onomatopoeia than to subtle incongruity and comic but complex figurative language. Given exposure and, at times, discussion of what is read, however, these youngsters will soon develop an appreciation for more and more sophisticated word fun and visual and verbal contradictions. With further exposure, they may even begin to anticipate an author's or illustrator's punch line or "punch picture."

It has been suggested by Katharine Kappas in her analysis of children's responses to humor that a sense of humor is developmental and both parallels and depends upon intellectual and emotional development.[5] P. E. McGhee would agree.[6]

Developmental it may be, but it is also highly individual. Factors that shape a sense of humor have to do not only with intellectual and emotional development but sex, age, personality, cultural and social background and setting, education, and experience. A development of humor is both group and individually based; therefore, children within the same age group will probably laugh at the same things but children within any group will also laugh at different things.

Providing children with the variety of fare that will raise smiles and chuckles for a variety of reasons presents no problem today. Poets, writers, and illustrators have done and are doing their utmost to keep children laughing. The goal is to get children and books together. Of course, laughter purchased at the expense of harming people or animals should have no place in the literature for young children or indeed for adults.

Humor: Ways to Achieve It

How do authors and illustrators stir smiles, chuckles, and guffaws? They achieve humor in a variety of ways, some of which are:

- The cumulative buildup of a routine event to great exaggeration, as in *Right as Right Can Be* and *Simple Pictures Are Best*
- A totally surprising twist of plot at the end of the tale, as in *The Beast of Monsieur Racine*, *Love from Aunt Betty*, and *Love from Uncle Clyde*

- The use of the first person, as in *There's a Nightmare in My Closet*
- The combination of verbal and visual fun, as in *Squeeze a Sneeze*
- A contradiction of the verbal and visual, as in *The Christmas Camel* wherein the narrative is quite sober but the illustrations are lively and vibrant
- Incongruities and improbabilities as contrasted with the natural states of animate and inanimate things, as in *Animals Should Definitely Not Wear Clothes*, *Animals Should Definitely Not Act Like People*, or innumerable improbable facts, as in *The Improbable Book of Records* and *Perfect Pigs: An Introduction to Manners*
- Exaggeration in the reactions of characters, as in *The Stupids Have a Ball*
- Sheer nonsense and silliness, as in the Dr. Seuss books
- Ludicrous situations, as in *What Do You Do with a Kangaroo?*
- Word play, as in *Squash Pie*
- Slapstick, as in *Hush Up!*

See Table 6.1 for additional examples of such humor.

TABLE 6.1 *Books for Young Children: Their Major Comic Elements*

Comic Elements	Examples
Visual exaggeration	Tomi Ungerer. *One, Two, Where's My Shoe?* 3–5
Plot or character exaggeration	Harry Allard and James Marshall. *The Stupids Have a Ball.* 5–8 Bill Peet. *Cowardly Clyde.* 5–8 Marjorie Weinman Sharmat. *Mooch the Messy.* 5–8
Verbal exaggeration	Many of the poems in Chapter 5
Nonsense	Dr. Seuss's many books. 3–8 The limericks of Edward Lear. 5–8 N. M. Bodecker's books. 5–8
Surprise	Lorna Balian. *The Humbug Witch.* 3–8 Mercer Mayer. *There's a Nightmare in My Closet.* 3–8 Tomi Ungerer. *The Beast of Monsieur Racine.* 3–8 Rachel Isadora. *Max.* 5–8
Incongruity and illogic	Phyllis Krasilovsky. *The Cow Who Fell in the Canal.* 5–8 Ivor Cutler. *Elephant Girl.* 3–5 Grimm Brothers. "The Three Sillies." 5–8 Grimm Brothers. "The Bremen Town Musicians." 5–8

Comic Elements	Examples
	Anne Rose. *As Right as Right Can Be.* 5–8
	Noodlehead stories. 5–8
Ludicrous situations	Steve Kellogg. *There Was an Old Woman.* 3–8
	Mercer Mayer. *What Do You Do with a Kangaroo?* 5–8
	Gerta Mantinband. *Bing, Bong, Bang and Fiddle Dee Dee.* 5–8
	Phyllis Krasilovsky. *The Man Who Didn't Wash His Dishes.* 5–8
	Anne Laurin. *Little Things.* 3–8
	Peter Spier. *Oh, Were They Ever Happy!* 5–8
	James Flora. *The Great Green Turkey Creek Monster.* 5–8
	James Stevenson. *Yuck!* 3–8
Slapstick	Harry Allard and James Marshall. *The Stupids Have a Ball.* 5–8
	Jim Aylesworth. *Hush Up!* 5–8
Word play	Bill Morrison. *Squeeze a Sneeze.* 5–8
	Bill Peet. *Cowardly Clyde.* 5–8
	Paul Galdone. *Henny Penny.* 3–5
	Fred Gwynne. *The King Who Rained.* 5–8
	Fred Gwynne. *A Chocolate Moose for Dinner.* 5–8
	Fred Gwynne. *The Sixteen Hand Horse.* 5–8
	Edna Mitchell Preston. *PopCorn and Ma Goodness.* 5–8
	Wilson Gage. *Squash Pie.* 5–8
	Nonsense poems in Chapter 5

*

Poetry and Prose-Picture

Literature for the young child is amazingly rich in books full of humor—a humor often based on word play, ridiculous plots, zany characters, and/or pictures riotous and ingenious in color and line.

Examples of humorous books are not limited to this chapter. (Indeed, many of the tales of sibling frustrations in Chapter 9, for example, reflect humorous elements in their resolutions.) Titles cited here may well be found again in other chapters because many picture books that arouse laughter are the picture books of highest quality; the poetry that generates glee is often the poetry richest in the very elements that constitute poetry; and the prose that spurs chuckles is oftentimes the best writing. To share these titles is to offer a rich smorgasbord of humor to the young child.

Poetry

In addition to the numerous nonsense titles and collections noted in Chapter 5, there are various book-length poem narratives that generate laughter. In the following three texts the elements of surprise and strong characterization are evident.

Phoebe's Revolt, a poem story by Natalie Babbitt, recounts the WILL NOT'S of Phoebe Euphemia Brandon Brown, who will not wear frilly, lacey, "ruffley" clothes. Clothes like her father's are what she wants and she gets them in a surprise resolution of her demands by her father. Children today may not appreciate Phoebe's problem, which is no longer timely, but her sturdy independence and her father's comfortable solution will amuse young children.

In Norma Farber's *Where's Gomer?* the grandson of Noah, Gomer, blithely refuses to be troubled by time constraints. The ark may sail at 2:00 but there are umpteen things to investigate on land before that time. The ark does sail at 2:00 — without Gomer — but a surprise ending, which borrows from many Grecian tales, brings smiles and satisfaction to young listeners and viewers.

In Dr. Seuss's *Horton Hatches the Egg* and many of his other books, children are confronted with absurd situations, absurd characters, and a delightful surprise at the end. Here verbal and visual humor predominate, as they do in *Please Try to Remember the First of Octemder, Squeeze a Sneeze* and *What Do You Do with a Kangaroo?* The first of these will appeal to all children who cannot get their months straight; the second nudges laughter via ludicrous illustrations and equally ludicrous brief verse by Bill Morrison; and the third leaves children gasping at the silly illustrations as they savor the verse and echo the refrain. Stimulated by books like these, young children will attempt some verbal hilarity of their own. Teachers who show the illustrations first and ask young children to compose a suitable story or rhyme to match the picture find such tales produce much child-authored nonsense and giggles.

A droll situation is the basis of Quentin Blake's rhyming story, *Mister Magnolia*, whose search for his second boot is ridiculously funny. This tale and Beatrice de Regniers's *May I Bring a Friend?* have great visual beauty and surprise as well as strong verbal appeal. The Kate Greenaway Medal[7] was given to Quentin Blake for *Mister Magnolia* in 1981 and illustrator Beni Montresor received the Randolph Caldecott Medal for *May I Bring a Friend?* Introducing children to these books is to have them meet excellence in illustration as well as verbal humor in poetic form.

Judith Viorst's *If I Were In Charge of the World and Other Worries* includes much in its over forty poems that is beyond the primary-age child, yet there is also a good deal of humor here that young children will appreciate hearing and that might be expected from the author of *Alexander and the Terrible, Horrible, No Good, Very Bad Day* and *Alexander Who*

Used to Be Rich Last Sunday. Alexander's misery is remarkable in the former book and his philosophical though frustrated acceptance even more noteworthy. Young children need no nudging to relate their own terrible, horrible, no good, very bad days. This is one of many *open books* in the literature of the young child; it extends a strong invitation to the young child to share personal experiences like the protagonist's.

The Judge: An Untrue Tale by Harve Zemach is the rhyming tale of a silly judge who does not believe warnings about a monster and nearly gets his just desserts for his disbelief.

Two texts with an I-got-my-wish-but-I'm-not-happy theme are *Pig Tale* by Helen Oxenbury and *You Look Ridiculous Said the Rhinoceros to the Hippopotamus* by Bernard Waber. In the first, Briggs and Bertha, two pigs who dream of wealth, find it only to become disgruntled and most eager to return to their former lazy carefree lives after experiencing the luxuries and anxieties of the rich. *You Look Ridiculous Said the Rhinoceros to the Hippopotamus* records the sadness of a hippopotamus who, dissatisfied with her appearance, wishes she had parts of other animals only to find those completely unsuitable. Roger Duvoisin's *Donkey-Donkey* is a book with the same theme.

Waber's *Lovable Lyle*, the amiable crocodile, and his *An Anteater Named Arthur* also afford young children many laughing moments.

Clyde Watson's *Hickory Stick Rag* has a rhythm children will absorb quickly and a plot they will well understand. Energetic animals test their teacher almost to distraction and then do an about-face. Another story in rhyme that appeals to young children is Pat Hutchins's *Don't Forget the Bacon.* Any child who ever forgot a shopping item will understand the consternation caused by forgetting. This is another *open* plot that can lead to a number of "When I forgot..." stories.

Prose-Picture

In many of the following books, exaggeration, basic incongruities, or a felicitous integration of visual and verbal elements create the humor. There is hilarity in Judith Barrett's *Animals Should Definitely Not Wear Clothes* and *Animals Should Definitely Not Act Like People* or in *Bing, Bong, Bang, Fiddle Dee Dee* by Gerta Mantinband. In Viorst's *Alexander and the Terrible, Horrible, No Good, Very Bad Day,* and Steven Kellogg's *Much Bigger Than Martin,* the characters' response to events—their coping or not coping—is what furnishes the humor.

In Jim Aylesworth's *Hush Up!,* illustrated by Glen Rounds, the very largest and nastiest horsefly plagues Jasper, "the laziest man in Talula County." By biting a mule and starting a *very noisy* chain reaction that involves many other animals, the horsefly causes untold aggravation and clamor. Finally, in response to the din, Jasper yells "Hush Up!" and silences all the animals. In this exaggerated environment of "largest," "nastiest" "laziest," Glen Rounds, in the spirit of the tall tale, gives an almost diabolical expression to the horsefly: he looks his part. Jasper's exasperated "Hush Up!" could probably, for different reasons, equal the volume of the tiny woman's "Take it!" in Margot Zemach's *Little Tiny Woman*.

The cow heroine of Victoria Forrester's *The Magnificent Moo* would have been frightened by the shouts of Jasper and the tiny woman. Even her own moo disturbs her; it is too loud and too big. Gentle giggles greet this tale of the cow and her moo.

Lorna Balian's "Humbug" stories are also full of gentle surprises. To sit as *The Humbug Witch* is shared and watch the gradual revealing of the witch's identity is to watch suspense peak in a gasp and a grin.

Not only is Mooch messy, but he's irredeemable. In deference to his father in the first book by Marjorie W. Sharmat called *Mooch the Messy*, Mooch cleans up but his tidiness lasts only as long as his father's visit. In the second book, *Mooch the Messy Meets Prudence the Neat*, Mooch resists Prudence's compulsion to clean his home. Friendship is severely tried but Mooch and Prudence finally compromise and do remain friends. Mooch's untidiness is something to behold.

The surprise ending in *Much Bigger Than Martin* is one that every sibling understands. Steven Kellogg's pen and ink drawings with pale watercolors illustrate Henry's attempts to "best" his big brother and he succeeds in a perfectly delightful way.

Many other books by Steven Kellogg cause children to grin and giggle. His *The Mysterious Tadpole* and *The Mystery Beast of Ostergeest* are but two of these. Young children watch Louis's tadpole grow and wonder with Louis how the tadpole will ever find a home. The tadpole, it turns out, has come from Scotland and is clearly related to the Loch Ness monster. In *The Mystery Beast of Ostergeest*, the hysteria and confusion of the adults in Kellogg's detailed illustrations contrasted with the calm, wise child affords the comic contradiction and the ever-popular confirmation that sometimes children *are* smarter than adults.

In *Gustav the Gourmet Giant* by Lou Ann Gaeddert, young children chortle over Steven Kellogg's illustrations and the exaggeration of the eighty-seven servants marching up hill and down valley to serve Gustav his picnic.

For very young children the adventures of *Benjamin and Tulip* by Rosemary Wells afford much talk-bait. The patient forebearing boy raccoon, Benjamin, after incredibly nasty attacks from Tulip, a very aggressive, argumentative girl raccoon, finally wins out. Tulip gets her comeuppance and certain sex stereotypes are shaken.

Like Benjamin, Bill Peet's Pamela in *Pamela Camel* also wins in the end, but in the meantime it is difficult to overcome the labels unthinking people give her. However, her solution to the problem gives her instant stardom and her self-concept blossoms.

In Harry Allard's *Bumps in the Night* and Mercer Mayer's *There's a Nightmare in My Closet*, plots revolve around making friends of one's fears. In the former, James Marshall's illustrations complement the story so that the scariness of the first half of the book is as poignant as the relief of the last half — a relief accompanied by smiles and pleased sighs. This author-artist team fascinates young children with their adventures of *The Stupids* and the *Miss Nelson* stories.

Marshall's own George and Martha tales are another boon to comic literature for the young child who is much amused by the amiable hippopotamuses.

In Mayer's *There's a Nightmare in My Closet*, closet fears are vanquished; as a matter of fact, the nightmare is "tucked into bed." The final page effects another surprise which will bring on more giggles, as does the "almost wordless" picture book *Hiccup* by Mayer. Young children very excitedly tell *you* this story and shout "Hiccup" with glee at the ending. Numerous titles over the years by this author-illustrator have been selected by children as their favorites; such titles continue to appear in the International Reading Association's Children's Choices' lists each year.

The five adventures of Owl in Lobel's *Owl at Home* are rib-tickling. In one of these adventures, Owl, while in bed, sees two bumps at the end of his bed; he simply cannot figure them out. They frighten and frustrate him until he must resort to chair-sleeping instead of bed-sleeping. Many children of course know what the bumps are, most of them immediately, and enjoy being in on the secret. Being smarter than Owl is not the least of the joys for the young reader.

Tana Hoban's *Where Is It?* arouses laughter from the very young child via surprise. A very short rhyming sequence follows the rabbit in search of something. The clarity of the photographs and engaging antics of the rabbit as he pursues the search related in simple rhyme keep children's attention to the surprising end at which point broad smiles break out.

Some humor to which children respond is due to plot variations that in themselves are absurd. In Judi Barrett's *Animals Should Definitely Not Wear Clothes* and the later *Animals Should Definitely Not Act Like People*, the ludicrousness of happenings resulting from animals wearing clothes and acting like people is readily apparent.

For rollicking laughter, *The Stupids* earn a special niche. In Allard and Marshall's *The Stupids Have a Ball*, no child can resist helpless glee at the ridiculous illogic of any set of parents who would plan a ball to celebrate their children's *failing* all school subjects, but that is what Mr. and Mrs. Stupid do when Buster and Petunia Stupid bring home all-failing report cards.

Bing, Bong, Bang and Fiddle Dee Dee, by Gerda Mantinband, is the zany tale of an old farmer whose squeaky fiddle drives his wife to retaliate by banging a pan to drown out the squeak. The clamor reaches such a pitch that all the farm animals run away and the old couple must chase after them. Another lively story with a noisy plot is Wilson Gage's *Down in the Boondocks*. In this case the noise is beneficial; it frightens away a robber. A not-so-noisy tale, full of one-upmanship and trickery, is another Wilson Gage text, *The Crow and Mrs. Goddy*. Young children will "crow" over the antics of the bird and the woman as they bait each other.

Bernard Wiseman's adventures of Morris the Moose and Boris the Bear always produce laughs, and when Boris wants a bedtime story, *Morris Tells Boris Mother Moose Stories and Rhymes*, children will chortle.

The blatant selfishness of Jack Gantos's *Rotten Ralph* elicits all kinds of glee from young children. Ralph clearly does the kinds of things young children dream of doing but do not dare. Somehow Sarah loves Rotten Ralph just the same for all his wicked tricks. After some traumatic experiences, Ralph reforms, but young readers looking at Ralph on the final page wonder how permanent the reformation is. In *Worse Than Rotten Ralph*, Ralph *is* worse — nor does he behave much better in *Rotten Ralph's Rotten Christmas*.

Harry the Dirty Dog, by Eugene Zion, is a gentler adventure but one close to young hearts. Harry, a white dog with black spots, hates baths and for want of a bath becomes a black dog with white spots. Harry creates ambivalence in young children; they delight in his defiance of constraints and spirit of adventure but they very much want him to be recognized and welcomed by his family.

Don Freeman's mild, tender humor is evident in the silly *Mop Top*, the clever *Bearymore*, and the vain *Dandelion*, all of whom young children should meet. Gentle humor also prevails in Arnold Lobel's Frog and Toad stories and in Leatie Weiss's *My Teacher Sleeps in School*. The adventures of Frog and Toad as well as the young elephants who are certain that their teacher sleeps in school are firmly rooted in young children's own experiences.

Jokes and Riddles

Inasmuch as response to humor is dependent on intellectual and emotional development, which are themselves somewhat dependent on a number of cultural and social factors, the young child will have to grow into some of the famous compilations of folklore wit and humor, such as those by Alvin Schwartz although he or she will probably enjoy his *Ten Copycats in a Boat and Other Riddles*.

Joke and riddle books for primary children are available and Aidan Chambers, among others, urges that they be used. Writing specifically about the use of jokes, he says:

> *Jokes are the briefest form of narrative and are comments about life and the*
> *ways people live it....A teacher whose armor of humor is strong and unembarrassed*
> *will have little trouble getting the act going. But we are not all natural comics. So,*
> *again, an old saw comes to our aid: Trust the book to do its own work. Joke books*
> *are numerous....*[8]

Young children love riddles as well as jokes. Many of the collections of jokes include riddles and many of the riddles themselves have a good deal of humor in them. A number of the collections of riddle-joke-puzzle books have the older child as the target audience but they do include entries that the young child will ponder and enjoy.

Five Men Under One Umbrella and Other Ready-to-Read Riddles is written for the young child who will be fascinated by the riddles *and* the illustrations. Other collections by the same author-illustrator (Joseph Low) will please youngsters too—*A Mad Wet Hen and Other Riddles* and *Beastly Riddles; Fishy, Flighty and Buggy Too.*

Jane Sarnoff, a famous name in the riddle field, author of *I Know! A Riddle Book* and *What? A Riddle Book,* offers *Giants! A Riddle Book* and *Mr. Bigperson's Side: A Story Book.* There is the story of Mr. Bigperson on the right-hand side of the book and jokes and riddles printed atop cartoons of giants on the left-hand side. The combination of story, cartoons, and riddles make this a fun book.

Knock-knocks are always popular. William Cole's collections may be a bit beyond most young children, as are many of his jolly compilations of humor in prose and poetry, but a teacher of young children might use *Knockout Knock Knocks* by Caroline Anne Levine.

Riddle books run the gamut of topics, There are those about animals and animal life like William Gerler's *Pack of Riddles,* Charles Keller's *Llama Beans,* Bennett Cerf's *Book of Animal Riddles,* and David Adler's *The Carsick Zebra and Other Animals.* In this last, de Paola's page format of riddle drawing and answer assures fun and much feedback. There is even a riddle book about dinosaurs—those animals dear to the hearts of young children—*Tyrannosaurus Wrecks: A Book of Dinosaur Riddles* by Noelle Sterne. Fish also have their own riddle book—*Fishy Riddles* by Katy Hall and Lisa Eisenberg.

Lillian Morrison's riddles in *Black Within and Red Without* are challenging, easy to read, and fascinating because they are set in rhyme.

Duncan Emrich's popular *The Hodge Podge Book* is a little of everything, as is another volume full of jokes and word fun, *Scream Cheese and Jelly: Jokes, Riddles and Puns* by Victoria Gomez.

A Pocketful of Riddles and *The Riddle Pot* by William Wiesner are popular treasures and demanding of the young child, while Carl Withers and Sula Benet's *American Riddle Book,* an amazing compilation, is probably beyond them.

An unusual collection, some of which primary teachers may wish to share with young children, is *Laughing Together: Giggles and Grins from*

Around the Globe by Barbara Walker. The publishers, working with the United States Committee for UNICEF, compiled jokes, cartoons, riddles, rhymes, and short tales from six continents. This collection offers firm and jolly documentation that, overall, children laugh at many of the same things. Translating from diverse languages into English could not have been simple and jokes are easily lost in translation. Selective sharing of these should help young children to understand (though they will not appreciate all of the entries) that children the world over are very much alike.

The Upside Down Riddle Book, by Louis Phillips, attracts young children not only because of the puzzling riddles but because of the arresting graphics by Beau Gardner and the fact that the child can find out whether he or she is right by turning the page upside down.

Although many of the riddles in Alvin Schwartz's *Unriddling: All Sorts of Riddles to Puzzle Your Guessery* are meant for older children, this collection has much to offer young children aged seven or eight who will pore over the rebuses, pictures, jokes, and riddles.

All in all, there are many puzzle and riddle books that give young children mysteries to mull and many books full of humor to keep the sound of laughter rippling.

Summary

Humor is a quality difficult to define. It is not only dependent on developmental stage but on such factors as sex, age, personality, and cultural and social background. Surprise, nonsense, contradiction, hyperbole, illogic as well as word play are components of a definition of humor which young children can appreciate. For them, especially, surprise, exaggeration (verbal and visual), simple incongruities, slapstick, and word play bring smiles and chuckles.

Poetry, prose, and illustrations can be vehicles for humor. The rhythm, rhyme, and analogical and compressed nature of poetry can enhance the comic as visual humor intensify can the verbal. Indeed, humor is sometimes created by the contradiction between the visual and the verbal. In addition to the poems in Chapter 5, there are numbers of book-length poems—narratives that the young child will enjoy—and a greater number of wordless prose-picture books in which children recognize the comical.

Joke, riddle, and puzzle books exist in great supply. When used in classrooms, they afford the young child the comfort of a shared laugh, mental challenge, the fun of playing detective by identifying and integrating the clues, and they can generate the urge to collect or create more riddles, puzzles, and jokes.

The value of humor in the classroom is grossly underestimated and underutilized.

DISCUSSION ACTIVITIES

• Select five books from Table 6.1 and share them with three- to four-year-old children. Do all children respond enthusiastically to all five books? Were there any differences in reactions? To what do you attribute such differences? Consider comic elements identified in this chapter. What type of evaluative statements did children offer when they discussed the books? What conclusions can you make about the humor preferences of these children?

• Select eight to ten humor books — two or three by the same author-artist. Analyze them as to the basic comic elements involved. Note how authors and illustrators achieve their humor. (See the section on Humor: Ways to Achieve It.) Did authors and illustrators (singly or collectively) tend to use the same comic element each time?

• Share riddles with young children. If necessary, help them identify the clues. Note the riddles they guess quickly and the ones that give them difficulty. Compile a file of those useful with preschoolers or primary grade children. Do the same with jokes and puzzles.

NOTES

1. Sid Fleishman, "Laughter and Children's Literature," *The Horn Book Magazine* (October 1976): 466.

2. Ethel L. Heins, "A Cry for Laughter," *The Horn Book Magazine* (December 1979): 630.

3. Roald Dahl being quoted in Tom Bernagozzi's article, "Roald Dahl," *Early Years* (December 1981): 19.

4. Alvin Schwartz, "Children, Humor and Folklore," *The Horn Book Magazine* (October 1976): 281.

5. Katharine H. Kappas, "A Developmental Analysis of Children's Responses to Humor," *A Critical Approach to Children's Literature*, ed. Sara Innis Fenwick (Chicago: The University of Chicago Press, 1967), p. 69.

6. P. E. McGhee, "Cognitive Mastery and Children's Humor," *Psychological Bulletin* 81 (1974): 721–730. "Children's Appreciation of Humor: A Test of the Cognitive Congruency Principle," *Child Development* 47 (1976): 420–426.

7. The Kate Greenaway Medal is given by the British Library Association to the most distinguished work in the illustration of children's books first published in the United Kingdom during the preceding year.

8. Aidan Chambers, "Letter from England: Talking About Reading: Back to Basics?" Part II. *The Horn Book Magazine* (December 1977): 702.

✳ PROFESSIONAL BIBLIOGRAPHY

Barnagozzi, Tom. "Roald Dahl," *Early Years* (December 1981): 19–20.

Chambers, Aidan. "Letter from England: Talking About Reading: Back to Basics?" Part II. *The Horn Book* (December 1977): 700–708.

Cianciolo, Patricia, ed. *Picture Books for Children*. Chicago: American Library Association, 1973.

Fleischman, Sid. "Laughter and Children's Literature," *The Horn Book* (October 1976): 465–470.

Heins, Ethel L. "A Cry for Laughter," *The Horn Book* (December 1979): 630–631.

Kappas, Katherine H. "A Developmental Analysis of Children's Responses to Humor," *A Critical Approach to Children's Literature*. Edited by Sara Innis Fenwick. Chicago: The University of Chicago Press, 1967, pp. 67–77.

Livingston, Myra Cohn. "Nonsense Verse: The Complete Escape," in *Celebrating Children's Books*, edited by Betsy Hearne and Marilyn Kaye. New York: William Morrow & Co., Inc., 1981.

McGhee, P. E. "Children's Appreciation of Humor: A Test of the Cognitive Congruency Principle," *Child Development* 47 (1976): 420–426.

———. "Cognitive Mastery and Children's Humor," *Psychological Bulletin* 81 (1974): 721–730.

Schwartz, Alvin. "Children, Humor, and Folklore," *The Horn Book* (June 1977): 281–287. Part I and Part II (August 1977): 471–477.

✳ CHILDREN'S BOOKS

Adler, David. *The Carsick Zebra and Other Animal Riddles*. Illus. by Tomie de Paola. New York: Holiday House, 1983.

Allard, Harry. *Bumps in the Night*. Illus. by James Marshall. New York: Doubleday & Co., Inc., 1979.

———. *Miss Nelson Is Back*. Illus. by James Marshall. Boston: Houghton Mifflin Co., 1982.

———. *Miss Nelson Is Missing*. Illus. by James Marshall. New York: Scholastic Book Service, 1978.

Allard, Harry and Marshall, James. *The Stupids Have A Ball*. Illus. by James Marshall. Boston: Houghton Mifflin Co., 1978.

Aylesworth, Jim. *Hush Up!* Illus. by Glen Rounds. New York: Holt, Rinehart and Winston Inc., 1980.

Babbitt, Natalie. *Phoebe's Revolt*. Illus. by author. New York: Farrar, Straus & Giroux Inc., 1977.

Balian, Lorna. *The Humbug Witch.* Illus. by author. New York: Abingdon Press, 1965.

Barrett, Judith. *Animals Should Definitely Not Act Like People.* Illus. by Ron Barrett. New York: Atheneum Publishers, 1980.

———. *Animals Should Definitely Not Wear Clothes.* Illus. by Ron Barrett. New York: Atheneum Publishers, 1970.

Blake, Quentin. *Mister Magnolia.* Illus. by author. Bridgeport, Ct.: Merrimack Publishing Corp. (Jonathan Cape, England), 1980.

Blake, Quentin, and Yeoman, John. *The Improbable Book of Records.* Illus. by Quentin Blake. New York: Atheneum Publishers, 1976.

Brown, Marc, and Krensky, Stephen. *Perfect Pigs: An Introduction to Manners.* Illus. by Marc Brown. Boston: Little, Brown, 1983.

Cerf, Bennett. *Bennett Cerf's Book of Animal Riddles.* Illus. by Ray McKie. New York: Random House Inc., 1964.

Cole, William. *Knock Knocks: The Most Ever.* Illus. by Mike C. Thaler. New York: Franklin Watts Inc., 1976.

Cutler, Ivor. *Elephant Girl.* Illus. by Helen Oxenbury. New York: William Morrow & Co., Inc., 1976.

Dahl, Roald. *Charlie and the Chocolate Factory.* Illus. by Joseph Schindelman. New York: Alfred A. Knopf, Inc., 1964.

———. *The Enormous Crocodile.* Illus. by Quentin Blake. New York: Alfred A. Knopf, Inc., 1978.

de Regniers, Beatrice S. *May I Bring a Friend?* Illus. by Beni Montresor. New York: Atheneum Publishers, Inc., 1964.

Dovoisin, Roger. *Donkey-Donkey.* Illus. by author. New York: Parents Magazine Press, 1940.

Emrich, Duncan. *The Hodge Podge Book.* Illus. by Ib Ohlsson. New York: Four Winds Press, 1972.

Farber, Norma. *Where's Gomer?* Illus. by William Pene du Bois. New York: E. P. Dutton, 1974.

Flora, James. *The Great Green Turkey Creek Monster.* Illus. by author. New York: Atheneum Publishers, 1976.

Forrester, Victoria. *The Magnificent Moo.* Illus. by author. New York: Atheneuem Publishers, 1983.

Freeman, Don. *Bearymore.* Illus. by author. New York: Viking Press, 1976.

———. *Dandelion.* Illus. by author. New York: Viking Press, 1964.

———. *Mop Top.* Illus. by author. New York: Viking Press, 1955.

Gaeddert, Lou Ann. *Gustav the Gourmet Giant.* Illus. by Steven Kellogg. New York: Dial Press, 1976.

Gage, Wilson. *Down in the Boondocks.* Illus. by Glen Rounds. New York: Greenwillow Books, 1977.

———. *Squash Pie.* Illus. by Glen Rounds. New York: Greenwillow Books, 1976.

Galdone, Paul. *Henny Penny.* Illus. by author. Boston: Houghton Mifflin Co., 1968.

Gantos, Jack. *Rotten Ralph.* Illus. by Nicole Rubel. Boston: Houghton Mifflin Co., 1976.

———. *Rotten Ralph's Rotten Christmas.* Illus. by Nicole Rubel. Boston: Houghton Mifflin Co., 1984.

————. *Worse Than Rotten Ralph.* Illus. by Nicole Rubel. Boston: Houghton Mifflin Co., 1978.

Geisel, Theodor [Dr. Seuss]. *Horton Hatches the Egg.* Illus. by author. New York: Random House Inc., 1940.

Gerler, William. *Pack of Riddles.* Illus. by Guilio Maestro. New York: E. P. Dutton Co., 1975.

Gomez, Victoria. *Scream Cheese and Jelly: Jokes, Riddles and Puns.* Illus. by Joel Scheck. New York: Lothrop, Lee and Shepard, 1979.

Grimm Brothers. *The Bremen Town Musicians.* Illus. by Paul Galdone. New York: McGraw-Hill, 1968.

————. *The Three Sillies.* Illus. by Paul Galdone. Boston: Houghton Mifflin Co., 1981.

Gwynne, Fred. *A Chocolate Moose for Dinner.* Illus. by author. New York: Windmill Books, 1976.

————. *The King Who Rained.* Illus. by author. New York: Windmill Books, Inc., 1970.

————. *The Sixteen Hand Horse.* Illus. by author. New York: Windmill Books, 1980.

Hall, Katy, and Eisenberg, Lisa. *Fishy Riddles.* Illus. by Simms Taback. New York: Dial Press, 1983.

Hoban, Tana. *Where Is It?* Photographs by author. New York: The Macmillan Co., 1974.

Hutchins, Pat. *Don't Forget the Bacon.* Illus. by author. New York: Greenwillow Books, 1976.

Isadora, Rachel. *Max.* Illus. by author. New York: Macmillan Publishing Co., 1976.

Keller, Charles. *Llama Beans.* Illus. by Dennis Nolan. Englewood Cliffs, N.J.: Prentice-Hall, 1979.

Kellogg, Steven. *Much Bigger Than Martin.* Illus. by author. New York: Dial Press, 1976.

————. *The Mysterious Tadpole.* Illus. by author. New York: Dial Press, 1977.

————. *The Mystery Beast of Ostergeest.* Illus. by author. New York: Dial Press, 1971.

————. *There Was an Old Woman.* Retold and drawn by author. New York: Parents Magazine Press, 1974.

Krasilovsky, Phyllis. *The Cow Who Fell in the Canal.* Illus. by Peter Spier. New York: Doubleday & Co., Inc., 1950.

————. *The Man Who Didn't Wash His Dishes.* Illus. by Barbara Cooney. New York: Doubleday & Co., Inc., 1950.

Laurin, Anne. *Little Things.* Illus. by Marcia Sewell. New York: Atheneum Publishers, 1978.

Lear, Edward. *Lear's Nonsense Omnibus.* New York: Frederick Warne & Co., Inc., 1943.

Lessieg, Theodore. *Please Try to Remember the First of Octemter.* Illus. by Arthur Cumings. New York: Random House Inc., 1977.

Levine, Caroline Anne. *Knockout Knock Knocks.* Illus. by Guilio Maestro. New York: E. P. Dutton Co., 1978.

Lobel, Arnold. *Days with Frog and Toad.* Illus. by author. New York: Harper & Row, Publishers, Inc., 1979.

———. *Fables.* Illus. by author. New York: Harper & Row, Publishers, Inc., 1980.

———. *Frog and Toad All Year.* Illus. by author. New York: Harper & Row, Publishers, Inc., 1976.

———. *Frog and Toad Are Friends.* Illus. by author. New York: Harper & Row, Publishers, Inc., 1970.

———. *Frog and Toad Together.* Illus. by author. New York: Harper & Row, Publishers, Inc., 1972.

———. *Owl at Home.* Illus. by author. New York: Harper & Row, Publishers, Inc., 1975.

Low, Joseph. *Beastly Riddles: Fishy, Flighty and Buggy Too.* Illus. by author. New York: Macmillan Publishing Co., 1983.

———. *Five Men Under One Umbrella and Other Ready-to-Read Riddles.* Illus. by author. New York: Macmillan Publishing Co., 1975.

———. *A Mad Wet Hen and Oher Riddles.* Illus. by author. New York: Greenwillow Books, 1977.

McCord, David. "Pickety Fence," *Every Time I Climb a Tree.* Illus. by Marc Simont. New York: Little, Brown and Company, 1967.

Mantinband, Gerda. *Bing, Bong, Bang, and Fiddle Dee Dee.* Illus. by Anne Rockwell. New York: Doubleday & Co., Inc., 1979.

Marshall, James. *George and Martha Rise and Shine.* Boston: Houghton Mifflin Co., 1976.

Mayer, Mercer. *Hiccup.* Illus. by author. New York: Dial Press, 1978.

———. *There's a Nightmare in My Closet.* Illus. by author. New York: Dial Press, 1968.

———. *What Do You Do With a Kangaroo?* Illus. by author. New York: Four Winds Press, 1974.

Morrison, Bill. *Squeeze a Sneeze.* Illus. by author. Boston: Houghton Mifflin Co., 1977.

Morrison, Lillian. *Black Within and Red Without.* Illus. by Jo Spier. New York: Thomas Y. Crowell Co., 1953.

Oxenbury, Helen. *Pig Tale.* Illus. by author. New York: William Morrow & Co., Inc., 1973.

Parker, Nancy Winslow. *The Christmas Camel.* Illus. by author. New York: Dodd, Mead & Co., 1983.

———. *Love from Aunt Betty.* Illus. by author. New York: Dodd, Mead & Co., 1983.

———. *Love from Uncle Clyde.* Illus. by author. New York: Dodd, Mead & Co., 1977.

Peet, Bill. *Cowardly Clyde.* Illus. by author. Boston: Houghton Mifflin Co., 1979.

———. *Pamela Camel.* Illus. by author. Boston: Houghton Mifflin Co., 1984.

Phillips, Louis. *The Upside Down Riddle Book.* Graphics by Beau Gardner. New York: Lothrop, Lee & Shepard Books, 1982.

Pinkwater, Daniel. *The Big Orange Splot.* New York: Scholastic Book Services, 1977.

Preston, Edna Mitchell. *Pop Corn and Ma Goodness.* Illus. by Robert Andrew Parker. New York: Penguin Books Inc., 1969.

Rose, Anne. *As Right As Right Can Be.* Illus. by Arnold Lobel. New York: Dial Press, 1976.

Sarnoff, Jane. *Giants! A Riddle Book and Mr. Bigperson's Side: A Story Book.* Illus. by Reynold Ruffins. New York: Charles Scribner's Sons, 1977.

———. *I Know! A Riddle Book.* Illus. by Reynold Ruffins. New York: Charles Scribner's Sons, 1976.

———. *What? A Riddle Book.* Illus. by Reynold Ruffins. New York: Charles Scribner's Sons, 1974.

Schwartz, Alvin, comp. *Ten Copycats in a Boat and Other Riddles.* Illus. by Marc Simont. New York: Harper & Row, Publishers, Inc., 1980.

———, comp. *Unriddling: All Sorts of Riddles to Puzzle Your Guessery.* Illus. by Sue Truesdell. New York: J. B. Lippincott Co., 1983.

Sharmat, Marjorie Weinman. *Mooch the Messy.* Illus. by Ben Shecter. New York: Harper & Row, Publishers, Inc., 1976.

———. *Mooch the Messy Meets Prudence the Neat.* Illus. by Ben Shecter. New York: Coward, McCann & Gerghegan, Inc., 1979.

Spier, Peter. *Oh, Were They Ever Happy!* Illus. by author. New York: Doubleday & Co., Inc., 1978.

Sterne, Noelle. *Tyrannosaurus Wrecks: A Book of Dinosaur Riddles.* New York: Thomas Y. Crowell Co., 1979.

Stevenson, James. *Yuck!* Illus. by author. New York: Greenwillow Books, 1984.

Ungerer, Tomi. *The Beast of Monsieur Racine.* Illus. by author. New York: Farrar, Straus & Giroux, 1971.

———. *One, Two, Where's My Shoe.* New York: Harper & Row, Publishers, Inc., 1964.

Viorst, Judy. *Alexander and the Terrible, Horrible, No Good, Very Bad Day.* Illus. by Ray Cruz. New York: Atheneum Publishers, 1976.

———. *Alexander Who Used to Be Rich Last Sunday.* Illus. by Ray Cruz. New York: Atheneum Publishers, 1980.

———. *If I Were in Charge of the World and Other Worries.* Illus. by Lynne Cherry. New York: Atheneum Publishers, 1981.

Waber, Bernard. *An Anteater Named Arthur.* Illus. by author. Boston: Houghton Mifflin Co., 1967.

———. *Lovable Lyle.* Illus. by author. Boston: Houghton Mifflin Co., 1969.

———. *You Look Ridiculous Said the Rhinocerous to the Hippopotamus.* Illus. by author. Boston: Houghton Mifflin Co., 1966.

Walker, Barbara K., comp. *Laughing Together: Giggles and Grins from Around the Globe.* Illus. by Simms Taback. New York: Four Winds Press, 1977.

Watson, Clyde. *Hickory Stick Rag.* Illus. by Wendy Watson. New York: Thomas Y. Crowell Co., 1976.

Weiss, Leatie. *My Teacher Sleeps in School.* Illus. by Ellen Weiss. New York: Frederick Warne & Co., Inc., 1984.

Wells, Rosemary. *Benjamin and Tulip.* Illus. by author. New York: Dial Press, 1973.

Wiesner, William. *A Pocketful of Riddles.* Illus. by author. New York: E. P. Dutton, 1966.

———. *The Riddle Pot.* Illus. by author. New York: E. P. Dutton, 1973.

Willard, Nancy. *Simple Pictures Are Best.* Illus. by Tomie de Paola. New York: Harcourt Brace Jovanovich, Inc., 1977.

Wiseman, Bernard. *Morris Tells Boris Mother Moose Stories and Rhymes.* Illus. by author. New York: Dodd, Mead & Co., 1979.

Withers, Carl, and Benet, Sula, eds. *The American Riddle Book.* Illus. by Marc Simont. New York: Abelard-Schuman Ltd., 1954.

Zemach, Harve. *The Judge: An Untrue Tale.* Illus. by Margot Zemach. New York: Farrar, Straus & Giroux Inc., 1969.

Zemach, Margot. *Little Tiny Woman.* Illus. by author. Indianapolis: Bobbs-Merrill, 1965.

Zion, Eugene. *Harry the Dirty Dog.* Illus. by Margaret Bloy Graham. New York: Harper & Row, Publishers, 1956.

Chapter 7

The Sight of Literature:

RICH ENCOUNTERS

Two children are seated in a quiet corner giggling at the creatures Wallace Tripp invented for A Great Big Ugly Man Came Up and Tied His Horse to Me. Lewis is chuckling at the frog whose head rests on his school desk. The frog has obviously fallen asleep right in the middle of a lecture by the teacher.

"Can't she see him sleeping?" Lewis asks. "What'll she do when she finds out?"

"He'll probably have to sit on that high stool with that dunce hat on," replies Stan, pointing to a student frog eclipsed by a huge red hat labeled Dunce.

"Wait a minute," says Lewis, putting his hand down on the page, "Is that right?" pointing to the algorithm on the board that says: $1+3=5$.

"No," explodes Stan. "Good grief! That teacher is dumb. She doesn't see that mistake; she doesn't see the frog sleeping. She needs—nope—she's got 'em. But look where they are." Lewis closely inspects the page. The teacher's eyeglasses are too high and the alphabet too is all wrong. Stan and Lewis chuckle at the missequenced letters.

Some pages further on, a portly and angry bear pulls a mouse— a clothed in a bathing suit and life preserver—out of his stew.

"What's that he's holding?" asks John, looking at the picture the teacher is holding up for view.

"A mouse," says Amy. "He found it in his soup."

"Yuckee!" explodes Lewis.

After the teacher shares the verse about the epicure at Crewe and the children do some detective work on what epicure might mean, given the picture, Jim says disgustedly, "That ep-i-cure wouldn't want that mouse. Who would? Nobody, of course," asking and answering his own question.

"I can think of somebody who might," giggles Amy.

"Nobody," insists Jim. "Nobody!"

"You're not looking at the picture," says Amy, grinning.

Jim stares. "Oh, the cats. Well...."

In the meantime, Mary giggles at the next page as she observes the horse who thinks he is a fly, then sees the wall walk, the turrets, the knight on horseback, the sentinel and pennants, and says, "Oh, this is an old picture. Here's a knight in his armor. Not like the ep-i-cure; he looks like today."

Picture Books and the Young Child

Lewis and Stan are probing; so is Mary. They are examining and reexamining the illustrations, as Amy forces Jim to do. Such keen inspection yields better picture decoding and even some inferences ("He'll probably have to sit on that high stool...").

"When choosing a children's book, don't just look at it, stare at it."[1] This direction holds true for adults as well as children.

Young children are not used to looking deeply. Television's rapid pace mitigates against picture probes, as does the cultural love of haste and change. There is a need to balance such pressure with quiet reflection. Picture-savoring moments are reflective times. As picture books are shared, children are offered the time they need to develop a fuller appreciation of visual beauty and to build visual literacy (the understanding of visual stimuli in their surroundings)—a literacy sorely needed in light of the great amount of visual information we receive today.

Picture books offer rich materials for perceptual development and, representational as they are, form a bridge for young children between the concrete and abstract. There are also other areas in which picture books help young children.

• *Picture books meet children's needs for beauty, order, and information.* As an example, Tana Hoban's books feed the needs of young children
  1. *for beauty.* Her photographs and graphic art are sharp, uncluttered and honed to the theme.
  2. *for order.* All her works are focal. There is internal order in the central concentration; that is, one major concept such as color, shape, etc., is developed throughout the book.
  3. *for information.* Young children learn to *Take Another Look*, to label colors, to detect shapes, to recognize symbols, and so on.

• *Picture books help young children achieve greater visual discrimination.* Picture books help young children grow away from early misconceptions such as size constancy (an inability to take distance into account when judging size). They also aid children in becoming more adept at visual scanning and fixation, at subtler discriminations in more complex patterns, and at detecting "wholes" from smaller and smaller bits of visual information.

• *Picture books help children practice prereading/thinking skills.* Necessary reading skills—observing details, making inferences, drawing conclusions and making judgments, identifying cause and effect, sequence, and main idea—are prodded by picture books. In the Rich Encounters at the beginning of this chapter, Lewis, Stan, Amy, and Mary observed many details, inferred sequence, found the main idea (and others), drew conclusions, and made judgments.

Anno, Peter Spier and Wallace Tripp offer children rich opportunities to spot more and more of what one teacher calls "secrets in the story."[2] In the brief stories of George and Martha, James Marshall elicits chuckles based on recognition of sequence and cause-effect. Gerald McDermott's *Arrow to the Sun*, abstract art though it is, presents no problem to children in finding the main idea. There is no limit to the kinds and quality of inferences, conclusions, judgments, and creative and technical language that children can produce if time to savor and time to talk are provided.

• *Picture books help children to develop a sense of story through pictures.* No matter how simple in idea and design they are, picture books offer young children an opportunity to develop a sense of story structure. In Mercer Mayer's *Hiccup*, plot, characters, and setting are clear and the relationship among them creates the sequence that reflects the theme. Young children recognize and confirm their awareness by telling, retelling, and acting out this simple tale. Such consciousness of story structure builds expectancies about future stories.

• *Picture books (wordless picture and word-picture) help children to create stories and thereby refine children's language skills.* Young children are easily guided into book discussions. A teacher's questions and comments about a picture book are likely to generate from children *personal statements* and stories, *careful thinking* about the words they use to tell or describe the story and illustrations, more *creative expressions* as they fish in their own language pools for the word that says what they mean, and greater *awareness about how the pictures and story relate to each other.* It is doubtful that the expression "soft, swirly picture" (Chapter 1) or Mary's observation of medieval versus present settings (this chapter) would have been offered had these young children not been given reflective study time.

A book open to personal, imaginative associations is Eloise Greenfield's *Daydreams*, in which Tom Feelings's graceful pencil drawings invite the reflection that leads to creative expression.

• *Picture books help develop an understanding of how artists use art elements to achieve their purposes.* Normally young children will be aware of shape and color before any consciousness of line and space, texture, composition, or perspective is developed. It is with adult guidance that young children begin to develop the awareness that leads to appreciation for the craftsmanship of the artist. Such awareness lays the foundation for the shaping of personal discrimination and taste.

Young children also need guidance in going beyond the obvious details and in connecting visual and verbal information—plot and picture. In *One Monday Morning,* by Uri Shulevitz, for example, young children can be helped to see on the next to last page the connection between the playing cards shown lying about and the young boy's fantasy of royal visitors.

Development of Taste

Taste in selecting and understanding book illustration is teachable; it is shaped by:

- *artistic factors* ranging from the composite design features of books, various artists' styles, and the subject matter of illustrated books
- *developmental factors* such as the age and sex of the child, and breadth of experiential background
- *pedagogical factors* such as the methods used in sharing books and the frequency and variety of books shared.

Young children's growth in aesthetic development is accelerated by the quality, diversity, and quantity of pictures and art styles they see. Although on the whole, young children love color and quickly recognize representational art, they also respond to the black and white illustrations of Wanda Gag and some of Robert McCloskey's, to the abstract art of Gerald McDermott and some of Brian Wildsmith's, to the simplicity of James Marshall, and to the detail of Peter Spier. The dovetailing of art and narrative—how complete an integration the author-illustrator team makes—may be what matters. Such integration is beautifully accomplished in Arnold and Anita Lobel's *A Rose in My Garden,* Barbara and Ed Emberley's *Drummer Hoff,* Gerald McDermott's *Arrow to the Sun,* and Charles Martin's Island books.

If offered diverse, high-quality children's books and other visual media during preschool and school years, children's growing awareness becomes a knowledge base for judgments of excellence and for their own life preferences. It is continuous stimulation by the excellent and beautiful that develops discriminating taste in illustration and enriched personal meaning.

It may be that in presenting an artist's view of a tale to the child, a challenge to the child's imagination to invest the tale with his or her own "visuals" is forfeited and personal meaning is diminished. This is Bruno Bettleheim's view.[3] Yet, overall, it may be that the young child's exposure to excellence and variety in illustrations feeds his or her imagination and frees the child to create even richer personal meaning.

Picture Books Today

Picture books for children today are a glorious testament to the art and skill of illustrators and the technical improvement in publishing. In addition, they are a tribute to the illustrator's faithfulness to the "child within" himself or herself and to what Roger Duvoisin calls "...the abstract children who are watching over his [the artist's] shoulder."[4]

In being true to the "child within," some artists seem to be especially blessed with unusually clear memories of the events and impressions of their own childhood; these memories remain a fresh, vibrant treasury upon which they draw. Maurice Sendak often refers to such a treasury in *The Art of Maurice Sendak* by Selma G. Lanes. For others, the "watching children" are not abstract at all; they are their very own.

Whatever the resources, yesterday's illustrators have bequeathed an enormously rich legacy to the artists of today. A company among whom number Crane, Caldecott, and Cooney; Greenaway, Galdone, and Gag; the D'Aulaires, de Angeli, Duvoisin, and the Dillons; Seuss, Sendak, and Shulevitz; Lionni and Lobel; the Haders and Hague is as illustrious as it is divergent in style and philosophy. Young children need to meet all the members of this company.

Definition

The range of content, style, and design of picture books, as well as the number of genre with which they overlap, makes a comprehensive definition of picture books difficult. The distinguishing element usually offered is the number of pictures as compared to text.[5]

Closely allied to this quantitative measure — indeed, integral to it — is the part pictures bear in communicating the story. No matter what else it does, no matter how appealing it may be, the picture book should communicate. According to Walter Lorraine, an illustrator of many books of humor, a picture book "...must function rather than merely be pretty."[6]

In some cases the pictures communicate the whole story. Books for young children by John Goodall, Mercer Mayer, Fernando Krahn, and some of Pat Hutchins's work, among others, are of this type. In some other instances, such as the tales of owl, frog, and toad by Arnold Lobel, the pictures confirm and visualize details of the text but do not tell the entire story. This is also true of the illustrations of William Steig.

In still other instances, pictures clarify and extend the story to a significant degree. In the works of Randolph Caldecott, Maurice Sendak, Leo and Diane Dillon, for example, such use of pictures is made. An example of such clarification and extension is Trina Schart Hyman's illustrations of the Stepmother Queen in *Snow White*. The illustrations here tell far more than words about the slow deteriorative effect of jealousy. Such visual richness and subtlety bring depth and power to a tale. In Maurice Sendak's illustrations for *King Grisly-Beard:*

A Tale from the Brothers Grimm, the rendering of the tale as a play, which two children revel in performing, is an imaginative extension that enables children both to see and to move into the world of fantasy and to return to the real world at tale's end.

Art Style

The choice of medium and color, the use of line and shape, and the achievement of composition is the illustrator's; his or her restriction is the story. All decisions must be made with the tale in mind. This is a challenge most illustrators appreciate. Quentin Blake says, "Fortunately, it's the kind of restriction that squeezes new answers out of you."[7] There seems to be no end to the "new answers" being squeezed out or to the unique ways artists use their tools.

Some illustrators, among them Maurice Sendak, Ed Young, Barbara Cooney, and Marcia Brown, experiment a great deal with style and media in order to adjust both to the mood, plot, or characters of the story before them. They recognize that the fit of text and illustration is critical. "The first duty of a good illustrator is to know his manuscript cold," says Barbara Cooney.[8]

In addition to the specific tools and type of art they use, many illustrators of children's books do extensive research to achieve an integration of content, art style, and art media.

In *The Ox Cart Man* Barbara Cooney achieved a nineteenth-century setting, the era of the tale, in part by producing illustrations that look like paintings done on wood, a type of art characteristic of the period.

When illustrating folk tales Ed Young studies the culture that is the source of the tale and illuminates the story with an art form exempletive of that culture. His illustrations for *The Red Lion*, a Persian folk tale, are the result of the painstaking study of Persian tapestries.

Gerald McDermott studied thoroughly the Pueblo Indian culture to produce his dramatic geometrics for *Arrow to the Sun*. The Dillons's research to produce *Ashanti to Zulu* is richly apparent, as is Paul Goble's study of the Horseback Indians of the Plains, the background and setting for his Caldecott Award book, *The Girl Who Loved Wild Horses*.

Art is either representational and "real" or it is not. If it is real, it is very much like what we actually see. Precise and accurate illustrations (almost photographic), such as those found in many information books, are examples of representational or real art.

In other art styles — expressionism, impressionism, romanticism, and primitiveness, to identify a few — an artist's feelings, values, and perceptions are reflected. Here the "real" may become fleeting and changing; detail may be sacrificed to a general or blurred form. Some of Brian Wildsmith's work bears this quality. A portion of a picture may be accented or exaggerated to express the feelings or the humor of the artist or the protagonist, as in Tomi Ungerer's *One, Two, Where's My Shoe?*

Criteria

What is it about a picture book that *communicates*? Is a picture book an object of art, as some have suggested, or a literary work or both? How should picture books be evaluated? Are there standards that can be applied? First, it must be noted that the same concern for literary quality applies to the content of picture books (see Chapter 2). In addition, picture books demand that other questions be asked. Table 7.1 poses such questions.

TABLE 7.1 *Picture Book Criteria and Titles that Meet Them*

Questions	Examples
1. Are the illustrations and the text in harmony? Are they well-integrated and in balance?	Uri Shulevitz. *One Monday Morning.* 3–5 Alvin Tresselt. *White Snow, Bright Snow.* 3–5
2. Is there excellence in the art form and technique used?	Mary Azarian's woodcuts (all ages) and Ezra Jack Keats's collages (3–8)
3. Do the pictures move the plot and/or characters along?	Maurice Sendak. *Where the Wild Things Are.* 3–8 Peter Spier. *London Bridge is Falling Down.* 3–8
4. Do the pictures sustain the mood of the tale?	Harve Zemach. *Duffy and the Devil.* 5–8 Harry Allard. *The Stupids Have a Ball.* 3–8
5. Do the pictures clarify or exemplify the setting?	Arlene Mosel. *The Funny Little Woman.* 5–8 Gian Paolo Ceserani. *Marco Polo.* 5–8
6. Do they portray the characters with a faithfulness to the text and to their own interpretation?	Many "Mother Goose" artists.
7. If the illustrations go beyond the text, is the extension in keeping with the overall plot and the characterization?	Steven Kellogg. *The Mystery Beast of Ostergeest.* 5–8 Else Minarik. *Father Bear Comes Home.* 3–5
8. Is the style of the artist and the media selected sympathetic to the tale's mood and content? Is the placement of pictures consistent with the sequence of actions in the text?	James Riordan and Eileen Colwell. *Little Grey Neck.* 5–8 Eve Bunting. *Demetrius and the Golden Goblet.* 8 and up Arnold Lobel. *The Rose in My Garden.* 3–8 Vera Williams. *A Chair for My Mother.* 5–8

(continued)

TABLE 7.1 *Continued*

Questions	Examples
9. In the case of wordless picture books, are the design and pictorial features rich in nudging words and aesthetic responses? Can the child really tell the story from the illustrations?	Books by Mercer Mayer (3–8) and John Goodall (3–5).
10. Does the format of the book—shape, size, type, design, paper, binding—harmonize with the general content and theme of the book? Is the format suitable for young children? Is the binding reinforced and sturdy?	See Chapter 4.

Model Award Books

Just as young children find modeling a natural, potent way to learn, so modeling in another sense can be helpful in judging children's picture books. To become well acquainted with a variety of the best picture books is to create a comprehensive, rich, yet balanced frame of reference for the evaluation of all picture books. The award books and others that meet literary and artistic criteria serve as exemplars in aiding those who select books for young children.

Many exemplars exist. The most highly regarded Caldecott Award (for best illustrated book; see Appendix B) is an annual award of the American Library Association and is now, although not lessened in prestige, only one of the many annual, biennial, national, and international awards for excellence in the field of children's literature. Indeed, it requires a book to enumerate the number and variety of such prizes, some of which are based upon children's own choices.[9]

Special Groups of Picture Books

In addition to the nursery rhyme books and the alphabet books already mentioned, the breadth of subject and the variety of media and form in picture books are boundless. Discussion of them must therefore be focused.

The artists noted in this chapter are loved by young children. These individuals have contributed greatly to the literature of early childhood; they are known for their versatility of form and style and/or for a special talent with one medium. Many of the artists have been recognized for excellence by professional groups.

A Palette of Artists and Art

Line, space, color, shape, texture, composition, perspective — How do artists use these tools to create books loved by young children?

Dick Bruna uses simple, broad lines and bright colors for his small, sturdily bound books. In *b is for bear, I Can Count, I Can Read,* and the tales of Miffy and Snuffy, Bruna speaks directly to the young child. His illustrations relate clearly to the text and confirm it. Subjects are in the child's world — *The Apple, The Egg, The Fish,* and others. Places are also part of the world of children: Miffy goes to the zoo, the playground, the hospital and many other familiar places.

Donald Crews's books, *Freight Train, Truck, School Bus, Carousel,* and *Parade,* also show young children their own world. The text is slight. Illustrations in flat but lively colors are clear and simple of line, poster style, and sophisticated in composition. Highly focal, Crews's books help hone young children's concepts.

Virginia Burton's talent for telling a story through pictures is indicated in all her texts. Her machine subjects, a steam shovel in *Mike Mulligan and His Steam Shovel,* a snowplow in *Katy and the Big Snow,* and a cable car in *Maybelle the Cable Car,* have "personality," as does the special favorite of young children *The Little House.* Here text and illustration are closely allied, even to the winding of the road in the picture matching the winding of the prose on the opposite page.

Jose Aruego's line drawings and Ariane Dewey's very bright color additions for Robert Kraus's stories of *Herman the Helper, Milton the Early Riser,* and *Leo the Late Bloomer* offer young children bright, lovable characters who cope with problems they themselves understand.

Ludwig Bemelman's *Madeline,* the little girl in the Parisian convent school, is very much like a figure children would draw themselves, shapeless but recognizable. Lines are simple, colors few, and Madeline's adventures appealing.

Through use of color and facile lines, Roger Duvoisin (*Donkey-Donkey, Petunia, Veronica*) depicts silly, friendly, kindly animals and their friends and invests in each human qualities that are fetching and unforgettable.

In Wanda Gag's most famous picture book, *Millions of Cats,* many elements appealing to young children are found: a simple folk story format; melodious repetition; bold, direct drawings and hand lettering, and lots of animals — trillions of them in fact. This text is often used to document the fact that children are attracted to black and white drawings as well as color, but *Millions of Cats* is probably loved for its compilation of attractions.

Lois Lenski's Small Family stories, *The Little Auto*, and *The Little Farm*, are tales tucked into small, hand-lettered editions with cartoon-like figures that are familiar and comforting. Although the tales are no longer representative of today's family life, there is stability here for the young child.

Ingri and Edgar Parin d'Aulaire deserve their fame as stone lithographers. Primary children who listen to the d'Aulaires' narratives and study their appealing large lithographs learn of many American heroes and heroines in a most delightful way. The illustrated biographies of *Abraham Lincoln, Benjamin Franklin, Pocahantas*, and others contain full pages of color, arduous to produce, interspersed with black and white pictures. The d'Aulaires' works are milestones in picture-book illustration.

Stone lithography was also used by Robert McCloskey in his very popular *Make Way for Ducklings*, a story of how a family of ducks gently disrupted Boston. In his Caldecott Award book, *Time for Wonder*, McCloskey chose soft, pale watercolors on large pages to tell the quiet story of a part of the Maine seacoast.

Uri Shulevitz creates quiet serenity and great visual beauty with subtle shading in *Dawn*, but he uses sharp, clear, gem-shades in *The Treasure*. The use of the former inspires young children to look carefully and search for words to describe the subtle color changes.

Using pen and ink and watercolor, Maurice Sendak has created characters whose fantasies young children understand and whose return to reality they find comforting. His *Where the Wild Things Are*, *In The Night Kitchen*, and *Outside Over There* evidence diversity of style, endless experimentation, and increasing complexity of thought and technique. Young children will find enjoyment, adventure, and solace especially in *Where the Wild Things Are* and in Else Holmelund Minarik's stories of Little Bear in the historic *I Can Read* books. Here, Maurice Sendak created a viable, lovable family full of tenderness. As he says, "There couldn't be a safer place in all the world than Mother Bear's lap."[10] These are comforting, reassuring books, as are Arnold Lobel's Frog and Toad stories.

Fables, Arnold Lobel's Caldecott Award book, is a humorous set of Lobel-authored fables accompanied by full-page, full-color illustrations of animals usually wearing strange clothes or attempting unique ventures. Young children will smile at the strange appearances of the animals but they may have some problems with the tales. Until children have a background of traditional fables, this compilation is better introduced as a picture book rather than a fable book.

Beni Montresor's Caldecott Award book, *May I Bring a Friend?* written by Beatrice de Regniers, illustrated in bright, bold colors with an opera-backdrop setting, introduces a young boy and the animals he brings along to visit the King and the Queen. The turnabout at the end and the verse and refrain coupled with the impressive full-color illustrations earn it a special niche for read and read-again times. Here is another *open* book. Young children can draw their own zoo additions to the list of friends and carry on the verse through the next week.

Perhaps it was Kate Greenaway's early work for illustrated magazines and her creation of Christmas and Valentine cards that are responsible for her happy children in pastoral settings and the "framed" look of her art. Tasha Tudor also uses the frame in much of her work. *A Is for Annabelle, I Is One,* and *Mother Goose,* the last two Caldecott Honor books, are illustrated in her delicate watercolors and pastels with a yesteryear or country setting in a frame of floral chains. Here media, style, and content are harmonious.

Although no rabbit will ever supplant Peter, Beatrix Potter's *Tale of Peter Rabbit* is only one of an innumerable menagerie in children's picture books that have insinuated themselves into children's hearts. Potter's own zoological garden of ducks, mice, cats, badgers, foxes, rabbits, squirrels, pigs, and owls are lovingly presented in all their realistic liveliness in watercolor.

The Story of Babar, the lovable and wise French elephant with an international reputation, has had many an adventure since Jean de Brunhoff introduced him to children in 1933 and Laurent de Brunhoff continued to invent adventures for him. A simple, almost cartoon style predominates in presenting *Babar,* as it does in Don Freeman's most popular *Dandelion,* which charmingly but emphatically tells the young child to be himself or herself.

In pen and ink, line and wash, Don Freeman presents to young children all kinds of lovable bears — *Beady Bear, Bearymore,* and the most popular of Freeman's bears, *Corduroy,* the department store teddy bear waiting for someone to buy and love him. Young children rejoice when Lisa brings her piggy bank to the store and empties it to purchase Corduroy.

Bernard Waber's *Anteater Named Arthur; Lyle, Lyle Crocodile;* and *"You Look Ridiculous," Said the Rhinoceros to the Hippopotamus* are all suitably done in cartoon style and induce giggles, as do Fernando Krahn's picture books *The Great Ape, A Flying Saucer Full of Spaghetti,* and others with their simple line or line-and-wash drawings.

By using crayon, brush, and ink, Feodor Rojankovsky created a lively, bright and sportive frog for his Caldecott Award book, *Frog Went a Courtin'.* Here color and style make this lively ballad even merrier.

Edward Ardizzone, using pen and ink and watercolor, was able to create sea scenes alive with motion in his sea adventures of *Little Tim and the Brave Sea Captain.*

Ed Emberley is a master at using line effectively to depict lively action (*Klippity Klop*) and at creating sharp and stunning woodcut prints (*Drummer Hoff,* his Caldecott Award book). Both books beg to be chanted and dramatized. In addition, young children can construct their own *Drummer Hoff* books or leporellos. In this tale, each new officer and his rank are named as he takes part in loading the cannon, and a repetition of all the characters follows each new entry for a final explosive climax. Using this plot and format, children can have their favorite circus animals enter the big top one by one, repeating the menagerie after each addition for a rousing parade at the end.

In the humorous book, *The Enormous Crocodile* by Roald Dahl, Quentin Blake draws his cartoons in line and color wash to complement the tale about the crocodile who got what he deserved.

Ben Shecter uses the same media to illustrate Charlotte Zolotow's *A Father Like That*, but Shecter takes to his pencil for Marjorie Weinman Sharmat's *The Trolls of Twelfth Street*. Kay Chorao also deftly uses her pencil to illustrate *Albert's Toothache*, written by Barbara Williams.

The varied techniques in Leo Lionni's work demonstrate his own versatility as well as his desire to match story style and media. Whether he uses collage, crayon, felt pen, watercolor, or linoleum block, Lionni meshes media with tale in such books as *Inch by Inch*, *Alexander and the Wind-up Mouse*, *Swimmy*, and *Little Blue and Little Yellow*. These are unlikely to slip from the "bestseller list" of young children's picture books.

Theodor Geisel (Dr. Seuss) accomplishes remarkable things with a few lines; young children love the creatures that slide from his pen. *Horton Hatches the Egg*, *The Cat in the Hat*, *How the Grinch Stole Christmas*, and many more convulse them.

A totally different style for entirely different tales and moods is M. B. Goffstein's simple line drawings for *Two Piano Tuners* and *Sleepy People*, a most suitable pre-nap, pre-rest-period story.

Peter Spier and Steven Kellogg create great detail. Spier's Caldecott Award book *Noah's Ark* teems with detail for children to pore over and exclaim about. Young children can generate numerous tales about the twosomes that board and leave the ark.

Steven Kellogg uses very simple lines and little color in *The Mystery of the Missing Red Mitten* and *The Mystery of the Magic Green Ball*, but he becomes very detailed in such books as *Paul Bunyan*, *The Mystery Beast of Ostergeest* and Lou Ann Gaeddert's *Gustav the Gourmet Giant*.

Many of Mercer Mayer's wordless picture books are drawn with simple sketches in black and white (*Hiccup*, *The Great Cat Chase*, and *AH-CHOO!*), but he varies his style and media to suit stories such as Marianna Mayer's *Beauty and the Beast*, illustrated with full-color paintings in the style of some eighteenth-century artists, and Jay Williams's *Everyone Knows What a Dragon Looks Like*, illustrated in full-color, oriental style and with great detail.

For great precision of line, the works of David Macaulay are preeminent. Young children may not yet appreciate such careful craftsmanship; however, the anecdote in Chapter 1 indicates the vivid impression left upon a young child by the book *Cathedral*.

Ezra Jack Keats, well known for his books about young children in urban settings, uses collage to tell his tales. In *The Snowy Day*, a Caldecott

Award book and one of the first picture books with a black child as a protagonist, and *Goggles,* a Caldecott Honor book, Keats's talent with collage is evident, but it is in *Jennie's Hat,* the tale of a little girl who bemoans her too-plain bonnet, that Keats experiments with materials like dried leaves, strips of fabrics and even old valentines to enhance the content of the tale.

Janina Domanska, an illustrator of many folk tales, varies her style and media according to tale: collage for *The Best of the Bargain,* muted shades and folk art for *The Turnip,* stylized illustrations and very bright colors for *The Tortoise and the Tree,* and large, full-color paintings with some folk art for *King Krakus and the Dragon.*

The deft use of watercolor by Marguerite de Angeli is appreciated by young children who enjoy her *Book of Nursery and Mother Goose Rhymes* and the tales of a Pennsylvania Amish boy, *Yonie Wondernose,* and Amish girl, *Henner's Lydia.*

A prolific artist of fairy tales and folktales is Paul Galdone. He has illustrated that most famous trio of threesomes — *The Three Bears, The Three Little Pigs,* and *The Three Billy Goats Gruff* (to say nothing of his *Three Wishes* and Ron Roy's *Three Ducks Went Wandering*). Young children like his bright colors in *Henny Penny,* the vitality of *The Gingerbread Boy,* the large, funny illustrations of *The Three Bears,* the four-color illustrations of *The Princess and the Pea* (Hans C. Andersen), the cartoon-like illustrations of *What's in Fox's Sack? An Old English Tale,* and the full-color drawings of the Russian folktale, *A Strange Servant* (Blanche Ross).

Raymond Briggs is the winner of two Kate Greenaway medals for his *Mother Goose Treasury* and *Father Christmas.* His wordless picture book, *The Snowman,* subtly colored and, like *Father Christmas,* made up of various sized frames from double spreads to twelve frames per page, is a fantasy of a friendship between a boy and a snowman.

Tomie de Paola is one of the most prolific illustrators of children's books. In worded and wordless, fact-fiction and all fiction, folktales and other texts, he defines his characters with strong, usually thickened lines and captures the various settings of his tales by applying the findings of serious study to the buildings, customs, dress, and scenery of the relevant period — Renaissance for *The Clown of God;* mid-nineteenth-century New England for *The Night Before Christmas* (Moore), and sixteenth-century Mexico for *The Lady of Guadalupe.* His warm, squarish, generally happy folk people in *Pancakes for Breakfast, Strega Nona, Fin M'Coul,* and other stories bring smiles and delight to children.

Marcia Brown was awarded the Caldecott medal three times for her *Once a Mouse, Cinderella* (Charles Perrault), and *Shadow* (Blaise Cendrars). Noted for the imaginative matching of style and media to the particular story being told, Marcia Brown should be presented to children in all her variety. Her famous woodcuts are seen in *Once a Mouse,* a fable of fear and pride that young children understand, and in *All Butterflies: An ABC.* She uses crayon and gouache in *The Three Billy*

Goats Gruff, linoleum block prints in *Dick Whittington and His Cat*, restrained coloring of black, white, and peach in Hans C. Andersen's *The Wild Swans*, delicate colors and lines in *Cinderella*, and powerful collages in *Shadow* about which young children will have much to say although they will not understand the flow and sweep of words.

Trina Schart Hyman demonstrates versatility in the variety of genre she has illustrated, among which are *The Bread Book* (Caroline Meyer), *Sleeping Beauty* (Grimm Brothers), *On to Widecombe Fair*, (Patricia Gauch), *Listen Children Listen* (Myra Cohn Livingston), *How Does It Feel to Be Old* (Norma Farber), and *Will You Sign Here, John Hancock?* (Jean Fritz).

Her considerable talent shows especially in the way she uses her tools to create animation. The seven merry gentlemen on their way to Widecombe Fair are bouncing, rollicking, and robust—very much alive. The horses in *South Star* (Betsy Hearne) rival the wind; her *Peter Pan* (J. M. Barrie), somehow even while he is sitting and meditating, is charged with life; the Queen Stepmother in her *Snow White* (Grimm Brothers) reveals increasingly, in face and figure, her cancerous pride; and in her Caldecott Medal book, *Saint George and the Dragon*, adapted from Edmund Spenser's *Faerie Queene* by Margaret Hodges, the throes and exhaustion of battle are clearly and dramatically depicted.

Margot Zemach's clever use of line gives texture and substance to her settings. This is especially obvious in *Duffy and the Devil*, her Caldecott Award book, a variant of Rumplestiltskin.

Nancy Ekholm Burkert illustrates traditional literature with care and respect. Hans Christian Andersen's *The Nightingale* is cast in double spreads of three colors with hints of oriental art; for *Snow White and the Seven Dwarfs* (Grimm Brothers) medieval detail abounds; and for Edward Lear and Ogden Nash's *The Scroobious Pip* delicate and airy lines suit an odd, yet cerebral creature.

Another skilled illustrator of traditional literature is Susan Jeffers whose *Hansel and Gretel* (Grimm Brothers), *Thumbelina* (Hans C. Andersen), *The Wild Swans* (Hans C. Andersen), and *Hiawatha* (Henry W. Longfellow) will intrigue children. In the last text, the soft colors and the large, detailed paintings sustain the romantic mood. Young children will not understand the poem, but they will dwell on the paintings.

Thacher Hurd creates a lullaby of watercolors in *The Quiet Evening*, and Marie Hall Ets casts a woodland of stillness and peace in *Play with Me*.

Young Children and Picture Books: Broadening Their World

Young children can be stimulated to an awareness of other cultures through picture books of beauty like those of Gerald McDermott, Leo and Diane Dillon, and Muriel and Tom Feelings. McDermott's

Ashanti, Congo, Japanese, and Pueblo illustrated tales, Leo and Diane Dillon's many picture tales of African tribes, and Feelings's Swahili alphabet and counting book, and some of the works of Joe Lasker and Aliki, among others, speak forcefully to young children of the customs, dress, homes, economy, topography, climate, occupations, and entertainment of other people and other lands. It is the responsibility of teachers and parents to encourage discussion about these books so that the artists' choices of color, shape, line, and style are seen to be in keeping with the culture of the country and the folk of the tale.

Some books like Brinton Turkle's Obadiah stories about a Quaker boy and his family who live on the Island of Nantucket, Aliki's *Medieval Feast*, and the Provensens' *A Peaceable Kingdom*, the story of the Shakers, offer young children a visual banquet of other cultures and/or times. These generate much probing, sharing, and fresh vocabulary.

The Provensens' Caldecott Award book, *The Glorious Flight*, is the story of Louis Bleriot, the first person to fly across the English Channel. All of his trials are related here in words and stunning paintings that will raise many questions about flying and planes.

Illustrators can also present a way of life that may be unknown to many children. The Provensens' farm stories tell the urban child much about farm life, and their *Town and Country* presents to young children the differences between these settings with accuracy and imagination. Ezra Jack Keats's books give children of rural areas insights into urban living.

Illustrators also make facts visible. Tomie de Paola does this in *The Popcorn Book*, as do Arnold Lobel in Norma Farber's *As I Was Crossing Boston Common*, Aliki in *My Five Senses*, Peter Parnall in Byrd Baylor's books such as *Everybody Needs a Rock*, and Tana Hoban in her many concept books such as *Count and See*. Jill Krementz's sharp, clear photographs do the same in her *A Very Young* series based upon the day-to-day lives of children in a variety of careers. Anne and Harlow Rockwell's many books about things children experience every day illuminate these encounters—*Machines*, *My Kitchen*, and *I Like the Library* (see Chapter 10).

The various subjects treated in picture books have been indexed by subject, author, title, and illustrator by Carolyn W. Lima in *A to Zoo: Subject Access to Children's Picture Books*. Here is a valuable tool for teachers who wish to know of, and share, books appropriate to their curriculum and young children's interests.

Summary

Young children not only reap enjoyment from picture books but they learn visual discrimination, literacy, and appreciation. Picture books especially help to meet the young child's need for beauty, order, and information. They provide practice for pre-reading and thinking skills and for the development of a sense of story. In addition, they generate *original* story creations. The formation of taste is dependent upon artistic, developmental, pedagogical factors; it is spurred by the quality, diversity, quantity of pictures, and art styles the child sees.

Picture books must communicate; artists use all of their tools — media, color, line, shape, and composition — to accomplish this. Criteria for selecting high-quality picture books have to do with faithfulness to the tale and integration of picture and tale, excellence of form, and effect on characters, setting, and mood. Young children are likely to respond to picture books with personal statements, questions, and their own creative expressions. Today's young children have a rich array of picture books to probe.

DISCUSSION ACTIVITIES

• Select several of Peter Spier's or Steven Kellogg's books that contain pictures with great detail. Divide a group of children into pairs and give to each pair one of the Kellogg or Spier books to share. Listen to the various comments children make. What do they observe first? In terms of the artist's tools? In terms of literary components? Can you define any patterns from your data?

• Read a fairy tale (a well-illustrated version) to a small group of children without sharing the pictures. Then ask the children to describe the characters as they "see" them in their minds. List the words on the chalkboard then show the children the artist's view of the characters and discuss the artist's illustrations. Give children time to *stare* at the illustrations, and ask them if they can find other words to add to their list.

• After sharing many different artists with children discuss the samenesses and differences among them. From the children's observations, can you draw any conclusions as to the children's understanding and appreciation of the diverse ways artists use color, shape, and line?

NOTES

1. Betsy Hearne, "Picture Books: More Than a Story" (Part III), *Booklist*, Vol. 80, No. 7 (December 1, 1983): 577.

2. Barbara Kiefer, "Picture Books: More Than a Story" (Part II), *Booklist*, Vol. 80, No. 6 (November 15, 1983): 492.

3. Bruno Bettleheim, *The Uses of Enchantment* (New York: Alfred A. Knopf, 1977), pp. 59-60.

4. Roger Duvoisin, "Children's Book Illustration: The Pleasures and Problems," in *Children and Literature: Views and Reviews*, comp. Virginia

Haviland (Glenview, Illinois: Scott, Foresman and Company, 1973), p. 178 (Article 177-178). Original source: *Top of the News* 22 (November 1965): 31.

5. Zena Sutherland and Betsy Hearne, "In Search of the Perfect Picture Book Definition," *Wilson Library Bulletin* (October 1977): 158.

6. Walter Lorraine, "The Art of the Picture Book," *Wilson Library Bulletin* (October 1977): 145.

7. Quentin Blake, "Wild Washerwoman, Hired Sportsmen, and Enormous Crocodiles," *Horn Book* (October 1981): 508.

8. Barbara Cooney in Lee Kingman's *The Illustrator's Notebook* (Boston: The Horn Book, 1978), p. 13.

9. Children's Book Council, *Children's Books: Awards & Prizes* (New York: The Children's Book Council, Inc.), published every two years since 1969.

10. Maurice Sendak quoted in Selma G. Lanes, *The Art of Maurice Sendak* (New York: Harry N. Abrams, Inc., 1980).

✱ PROFESSIONAL BIBLIOGRAPHY

Alderson, Brian. *Looking at Picture Books,* 1973, catalog and commentary prepared for the National Book League in London.

Bader, Barbara. *American Picturebooks from Noah's Ark to the Beast Within.* New York: Macmillan Publishing Co., Inc., 1976.

Bettleheim, Bruno. *The Uses of Enchantment.* New York: Alfred A. Knopf, 1976.

Billington, Elizabeth T., sel. and ed. *The Randolph Caldecott Treasury.* New York: Frederick Warne, 1978.

Blake, Quentin. "Wild Washerwomen, Hired Sportsmen, and Enormous Crocodiles," *Horn Book* (October 1981): 505-513.

Children's Book Council. *Children's Books: Awards & Prizes.* New York: The Children's Book Council, Inc., 1981 edition.

Cianciolo, Patricia Jean. *Picture Books for Children.* 2d ed. Chicago: American Library Association, 1981.

Cooney, Barbara, in Lee Kingman's *The Illustrator's Notebook.* Boston: The Horn Book, 1978.

Degler, Lois Sauer. "Putting Words Into Wordless Books," *The Reading Teacher,* Volume 32, No. 4 (January 1979): 399-402.

Duvoisin, Roger. "Children's Book Illustration: The Pleasures and Problems," in *Children and Literature: Views and Reviews.* Comp. Virginia Haviland. Glenview, Ill.: Scott Foresman and Company, 1973, pp. 177-178.

Elleman, Barbara. "Picture Books: More Than a Story" (Part I), *Booklist* (October 1983): 292-294.

Freeman, Ruth S. *Children's Picture Book Yesterday and Today.* Watkins Glen, New York: Century House, 1967.

Gambrell, Linda B., and Sokolski, Carol. "Picture Potency: Use Caldecott Award Books to Develop Children's Language," *The Reading Teacher*, Volume 36, No. 9 (May 1983): 868–871.

Haviland, Virginia, comp. *Children and Literature: Views and Reviews*. Glenview, Ill.: Scott Foresman and Company, 1973.

Hearne, Betsy. "Picture Books: More Than a Story" (Part III), *Booklist* (December 1983): 577–578.

Hoffman, Miriam, and Samuels, Eva. *Authors and Illustrators of Children's Books*. New York: R. R. Bowker Company, 1972.

Hopkins, Lee Bennett. *Books Are by People*. New York: Citation Press, 1969.

Kiefer, Barbara. "Picture Books: More Than a Story" (Part II), *Booklist* (November 15, 1983): 492–494.

Kingman, Lee; Foster, Joanna; and Lantaft, Ruth Giles. *Illustrators of Children's Books, 1957–1960*. Boston: The Horn Book Inc., 1968.

—— and Hogarth, Grace Allen, and Quimby, Harriet. *Illustrators of Children's Books, 1967–1976*. Boston: The Horn Book Inc., 1978.

——, eds. *The Illustrator's Notebook*. Boston: The Horn Book Inc., 1978.

Lane, Margaret. *The Magic Years of Beatrix Potter*. New York: Frederick Warne, 1978. (This is an expansion of Lane's earlier biography (1908). *The Tale of Beatrix Potter*. First published in England.)

Lanes, Selma G. *The Art of Maurice Sendak*. New York: Harry N. Abrams, Inc., 1980.

Lima, Carolyn W., *A to Zoo: Subject Access to Children's Picture Books*. New York: R. R. Bowker Company, 1982.

Lorraine, Walter. "The Art of the Picture Book," *Wilson Library Bulletin* (October 1977): 144–147.

MacCann, Donnarae, and Richards, Olga. *The Child's First Books: A Critical Study of Pictures and Text*. New York: Wilson, 1973.

Sims, Rudine. *Shadow and Substance. Afro-American Experience in Contemporary Children's Fiction*. Urbana, Ill.: National Council of Teachers of English, 1982.

Sutherland, Zena, and Hearne, Betsy. "In Search of the Perfect Picture Book Definition," *Wilson Library Bulletin* (October 1977): 158–160.

Tudor, Bethany. *Drawn from New England: Tasha Tudor, A Portrait in Words and Pictures*. New York: Collins, 1979.

Viguers, Ruth Hill; Dolphin, Marcia; and Miller, Bertha Mahoney, comps. *Illustrators of Children's Books*. Boston: The Horn Book Inc., 1958.

Weiss, Ava. "The Artist at Work: The Art Director," *The Horn Book* (May/June 1985): 269–279.

✳ CHILDREN'S BOOKS

Aardema, Verna. *Why Mosquitoes Buzz in People's Ears*. Illus. by Leo Dillon and Diane Dillon. New York: Dial Press, 1975.

Aliki. *A Medieval Feast*. Illus. by author. New York: Thomas Y. Crowell Co., 1983.

————. *My Five Senses.* Illus. by author. New York: Thomas Y. Crowell Co., 1962.

Allard, Harry. *The Stupids Have a Ball.* Illus. by James Marshall. Boston: Houghton Mifflin, 1978.

Andersen, Hans C. *The Nightingale.* Trans. by Eva Le Gallienne. Illus. by Nancy Ekholm Burkert. New York: Holt, Rinehart and Winston, Inc., 1965.

————. *The Princess and the Pea.* Illus. by Paul Galdone. Boston: Houghton Mifflin Co., 1978.

————. *Thumbelina.* Amy Ehrlich, ret. Illus. by Susan Jeffers. New York: Dial Press, 1979.

————. *The Wild Swans.* Illus. by Marcia Brown. New York: Charles Scribner's Sons, 1963.

————. *The Wild Swans.* Amy Ehrlich, ret. Illus. by Susan Jeffers. New York: Dial Press, 1981.

Anno, Mitsumasa. *Anno's Counting Book.* Illus. by author. New York: Thomas Y. Crowell Co., 1977.

————. *Anno's Flea Market.* Illus. by author. New York: Philomel Books, 1984.

Ardizzone, Edward. *Little Tim and the Brave Sea Captain.* Illus. by author. New York: Oxford University Press, 1936. (1978 Oxford University reprint.)

Asbjornsen, P. C. *Three Billy Goats Gruff.* Illus. by Paul Galdone. Boston: Houghton Mifflin Co., 1957.

Azarian, Mary. *A Farmer's Alphabet.* Illus. by author. Boston: Godine Press, Inc., 1981.

Barrie, J. M. *Peter Pan.* Illus. by Trina Schart Hyman. New York: Charles Scribner's Sons, 1980.

Baylor, Byrd. *Everybody Needs a Rock.* Illus. by Peter Parnall. New York: Charles Scribner's Sons, 1974.

Bemelmans, Ludwig. *Madeline.* Illus. by author. New York: Viking Press, 1962 (original 1939).

Briggs, Raymond. *Father Christmas.* Illus. by author. New York: Coward, McCann & Geoghegan Inc., 1973.

————. *Mother Goose Treasury.* Illus. by author. New York: Coward, McCann & Geoghegan Inc., 1966.

————. *The Snowman.* Illus. by author. New York: Random House, Inc., 1978.

Brown, Marcia. *All Butterflies: An ABC.* Illus. by author. New York: Charles Scribner's Sons, 1974.

————. *Dick Whittington and His Cat.* Illus. by author. New York: Charles Scribner's Sons, 1950.

————. *Once a Mouse.* Illus. by author. New York: Charles Scribner's Sons, 1961.

————. *The Three Billy Goats Gruff.* Illus. by author. New York: Harcourt Brace Jovanovich, Inc., 1957.

Bruna, Dick. *The Apple.* Illus. by author. New York: Methuen Inc., 1965.

————. *b is for Bear.* Illus. by author. New York: Methuen Inc., 1971.

————. *The Egg.* Illus. by author. New York: Methuen Inc., 1964.

————. *The Fish.* Illus. by author. New York: Methuen Inc., 1975.

————. *I Can Count.* Illus. by author. New York: Methuen Inc., 1975.

————. *I Can Read.* Illus. by author. New York: Methuen Inc., 1975.

———. *Miffy.* Illus. by author. New York: Methuen Inc., 1975.

———. *Snuffy.* Illus. by author. New York: Methuen Inc., 1975.

Bunting, Eve. *Demetrius and the Golden Goblet.* Illus. by Michael Hague. New York: Harcourt Brace Jovanovich, Inc., 1980.

Burton, Virginia. *Katy and the Big Snow.* Illus. by author. Boston: Houghton Mifflin Co., 1943.

———. *The Little House.* Illus. by author. Boston: Houghton Mifflin Co., 1942.

———. *Maybelle the Cable Car.* Illus. by author. Boston: Houghton Mifflin Co., 1952.

———. *Mike Mulligan and His Steam Shovel.* Illus. by author. Boston: Houghton Mifflin Co., 1939.

Caldecott, Randolph. *The Caldecott Aesop, A Facsimile of the 1883 Edition.* New York: Doubleday & Co., Inc., 1978.

Cendrars, Blaise. *Shadow.* Illus. by Marcia Brown. New York: Charles Scribner's Sons, 1982.

Ceserani, Gian Paolo. *Marco Polo.* Illus. by Piero Ventura. New York: G. P. Putnam's Sons, 1977.

Crews, Donald. *Carousel.* Illus. by author. New York: Greenwillow Books, 1982.

———. *Freight Train.* Illus. by author. New York: Greenwillow Books, 1978.

———. *Parade.* Illus. by author. New York: Greenwillow Books, 1983.

———. *School Bus.* Illus. by author. New York: Greenwillow Books, 1984.

———. *Truck.* Illus. by author. New York: Greenwillow Books, 1980.

Dahl, Roald. *The Enormous Crocodile.* Illus. by Quentin Blake. New York: Alfred A. Knopf, Inc., 1978.

d'Aulaire, Ingri and d'Aulaire, Edgar Parin. *Abraham Lincoln.* Illus. by authors. New York: Doubleday & Co., Inc., 1957.

———. *Benjamin Franklin.* Illus. by authors. New York: Doubleday & Co., Inc., 1950.

———. *Pocahantas.* Illus. by authors. New York: Doubleday & Co., Inc., 1949.

de Angeli, Marguerite. *Book of Nursery and Mother Goose Rhymes.* Illus. by author. New York: Doubleday & Co., Inc., 1954.

———. *Henner's Lydia.* Illus. by author. New York: Doubleday & Co., Inc., 1936.

———. *Yonie Wondernose.* Illus. by author. New York: Doubleday & Co., Inc., 1944.

de Brunhoff, Jean. *The Story of Babar.* Illus. by author. New York: Random House, Inc., 1937.

de Paola, Tomie. *The Clown of God.* Illus. by author. New York: Harcourt Brace Jovanovich Inc., 1978.

———. *Fin M'Coul.* Illus. by author. New York: Holiday House, Inc., 1981.

———. *The Lady of Guadalupe.* Illus. by author. New York: Holiday House, Inc., 1980.

———. *Now One Foot, Now the Other.* Illus. by author. New York: Putnam Publishing Co., 1981.

———. *Pancakes for Breakfast.* Illus. by author. New York: Harcourt Brace Jovanovich, Inc., 1978.

———. *The Popcorn Book.* Illus. by author. New York: Holiday House Inc., 1978.

———. *Strega Nona.* Illus. by author. Englewood Cliffs, N.J.: Prentice-Hall, Inc., 1975.

de Regniers, Beatrice. *May I Bring a Friend?* Illus. by Beni Montresor. New York: Atheneum Publishers, 1965.

Domanska, Janina. *The Best of the Bargain.* Illus. by author. New York: Greenwillow Books, 1977.

———. *King Krakus and the Dragon.* Illus. by author. New York: Greenwillow Books, 1979.

———. *The Tortoise and the Tree.* Illus. by author. New York: Greenwillow Books, 1978.

———. *The Turnip.* Illus. by author. New York: Macmillan Publishing Co., Inc., 1969.

Duvoisin, Roger. *Donkey-Donkey.* Illus. by author. New York: Parents Magazine Press, 1940.

———. *Petunia.* Illus. by author. New York: Alfred A. Knopf, Inc., 1950.

———. *Veronica.* Illus. by author. New York: Alfred A. Knopf, Inc., 1961.

Emberley, Barbara. *Drummer Hoff.* Illus. by Ed Emberley. Englewood Cliffs, N.J.: Prentice-Hall, Inc., 1967.

Emberley, Ed. *Klippity Klop.* Illus. by author. Boston: Little, Brown & Co., Inc, 1974.

Ets, Marie Hall. *Play with Me.* Illus. by author. New York: Viking Press, 1955.

Farber, Norma. *As I Was Crossing Boston Common.* Illus. by Arnold Lobel. New York: E. P. Dutton & Co., 1975.

———. *How Does It Feel to Be Old?* Illus. by Trina Schart Hyman. New York: E. P. Dutton & Co., 1979.

Feelings, Muriel. *Jambo Means Hello: A Swahili Alphabet.* Illus. by Tom Feelings. New York: Dial Press, 1974.

Freeman, Don. *Beady Bear.* Illus. by author. New York: Viking Press, 1954.

———. *Bearymore.* Illus. by author. New York: Viking Press, 1976.

———. *The Chalk Box Story.* Illus. by author. New York: Harper and Row, 1976.

———. *Corduroy.* Illus. by author. New York: Viking Press, 1968.

———. *Dandelion.* Illus. by author. New York: Viking Press, 1964.

Fritz, Jean. *Will You Sign Here, John Hancock?* Illus. by Trina Schart Hyman. New York: Coward, McCann & Geoghegan, Inc., 1976.

Gaeddert, Lou Ann. *Gustav the Gourmet Giant.* Illus. by Steven Kellogg. New York: Dial Press, 1976.

Gag, Wanda. *Millions of Cats.* Illus. by author. New York: Coward, McCann & Geoghegan, Inc., 1928.

Galdone, Paul. *The Gingerbread Boy.* Illus. by author. Boston: Houghton Mifflin Co., 1975.

———. *Henny Penny.* Illus. by author. Boston: Houghton Mifflin Co., 1968.

———. *The Three Bears.* Illus. by author. Boston: Houghton Mifflin Co., 1972.

———. *The Three Billy Goats Gruff.* Illus. by author. Boston: Houghton Mifflin Co., 1973.

———. *The Three Little Pigs.* Illus. by author. Boston: Houghton Mifflin Co., 1970.

———. *Three Wishes.* Illus. by author. Boston: Houghton Mifflin Co., 1961.

———. *What's in Fox's Sack? An Old English Tale.* Illus. by author. Boston: Houghton Mifflin Co., 1982.

Gauch, Patricia L. *On to Widecombe Fair*. Illus. by Trina Schart Hyman. New York: Putnam Publishing Co., 1978.

Geisel, Theodor [Dr. Seuss]. *The Cat in the Hat*. Illus. by author. New York: Random House, Inc., 1957.

———. *Horton Hatches the Egg*. New York: Random House, Inc., 1940.

——— *How the Grinch Stole Christmas*. New York: Random House, Inc., 1957.

Goble, Paul. *The Girl Who Loved Wild Horses*. Illus. by author. New York: Bradbury Press, 1978.

Goffstein, M. B. *Sleepy People*. 2nd ed. Illus. by author. New York: Farrar, Straus & Giroux, Inc., 1979.

———. *Two Piano Tuners*. Illus. by author. New York: Farrar, Straus & Giroux, Inc., 1977.

Goodall, John S. *Shrewbettina Goes to Work*. Illus. by author. New York: Atheneum Publishers, 1981.

Greenaway, Kate. *A–Apple Pie*. Illus. by author. New York: Frederick Warne & Co., Inc., 1886.

Greenfield, Eloise. *Daydreamers*. Illus. by Tom Feelings. New York: Dial Press, 1981.

Grimm Brothers. *Hansel and Gretel*. Illus. by Susan Jeffers. New York: Dial Press, 1980.

———. *King Grisly-Beard: A Tale from the Brothers Grimm*. Trans. by Edgar Taylor. Illus. by Maurice Sendak. New York: Farrar, Straus & Giroux, Inc., 1973.

———. *Sleeping Beauty*. Illus. by Trina Schart Hyman. Boston: Little, Brown & Co., Inc., 1977.

———. *Snow White*. Trans. by Paul Heins. Illus. by Trina Schart Hyman. Boston: Little, Brown & Co., 1974.

———. *Snow White and the Seven Dwarfs*. Trans. by Randall Jarrell. Illus. by Nancy Ekholm Burkert. New York: Farrar, Straus & Giroux, Inc., 1972.

Hader, Berta, and Hader, Elmer. *The Big Snow*. New York: Macmillan Publishing Co., Inc., 1948.

Hall, Donald. *The Ox-Cart Man*. Illus. by Barbara Cooney. New York: Viking Press, 1979.

Hearne, Betsy. *South Star*. Illus. by Trina Schart Hyman. New York: Atheneum Publishers, 1977.

Hoban, Tana. *Count and See*. Illus. by author. New York: Macmillan Publishing Co., 1972.

———. *Take Another Look*. Illus. by author. New York: Greenwillow Books, 1981.

Hodges, Margaret, adap. *Saint George and the Dragon: A Golden Legend Adapted from Edmund Spenser's Faerie Queene*. Illus. by Trina Schart Hyman. Boston: Little, Brown & Co., 1984.

Hurd, Thacher. *The Quiet Evening*. Illus. by author. New York: Greenwillow Books, 1978.

Hutchins, Pat. *The Wind Blew*. Illus. by author. New York: Macmillan Publishing Co., Inc., 1974.

Jeffers, Susan. *Three Jovial Huntsmen*. New York: Bradbury Press, 1973.

Keats, Ezra Jack. *Goggles.* Illus. by author. New York: Macmillan Publishing Co., Inc., 1971.

———. *Jennie's Hat.* Illus. by author. New York: Harper & Row, Publishers, Inc., 1966.

———. *The Snowy Day.* Illus. by author. New York: Viking Press, 1962.

Kellogg, Steven. *The Mystery Beast of Ostergeest.* Illus. by author. New York: Dial Press, 1971.

———. *The Mystery of the Magic Green Ball.* Illus. by author. New York: Dial Press, 1981.

———. *The Mystery of the Missing Red Mitten.* Illus. by author. New York: Dial Press, 1974.

———. *Paul Bunyan.* Illus. by author. New York: William Morrow & Co., Inc., 1984.

Krahn, Fernando. *A Flying Saucer Full of Spaghetti.* Illus. by author. New York: E. P. Dutton & Co., 1970.

———. *The Great Ape.* Illus. by author. New York: Penguin Books, 1980.

Kraus, Robert. *Herman the Helper.* Illus. by Jose Aruego and Ariane Dewey. New York: Windmill Books, 1974.

———. *Leo the Late Bloomer.* Illus. by Jose Aruego and Ariane Dewey. New York: Windmill Books, 1971.

———. *Milton the Early Riser.* Illus. by Jose Aruego and Ariane Dewey. New York: Windmill Books, 1972.

Krementz, Jill. *A Very Young Gymnast.* Illus. by author. New York: Alfred A. Knopf Inc., 1978.

Langstaff, John. *Frog Went A'Courtin'.* Illus. by Feodor Rojankovsky. New York: Harcourt Brace Jovanovich Inc., 1955.

Lasker, Joe, and Lasker, David. *The Boy Who Loved Music.* Illus. by Joe Lasker. New York: Viking Press, 1979.

Lear, Edward and Nash, Ogden. *The Scroobious Pip.* Illus. by Nancy Ekholm Burkert. New York: Harper & Row, Publishers, Inc., 1968.

Lenski, Lois. *Cowboy Small.* Illus. by author. New York: Henry Z. Walck Inc., 1949.

———. *The Little Auto.* Illus. by author. New York: Henry Z. Walck, Inc., 1942.

———. *The Little Farm.* Illus. by author. New York: Henry Z. Walck, Inc., 1942.

Lionni, Leo. *Alexander and the Wind-up Mouse.* Illus. by author. New York: Pantheon Books, 1969.

———. *Inch by Inch.* Illus. by author. New York: Astor-Honor, 1962.

———. *Little Blue and Little Yellow.* Illus. by author. Astor-Honor, 1959.

———. *Swimmy.* Illus. by author. New York: Pantheon Books, 1963.

Livingston, Myra Cohen, ed. *Listen Children Listen.* Illus. by Trina Schart Hyman. New York: Harcourt Brace Jovanovich, Inc., 1972.

Lobel, Arnold. *Fables.* Illus. by author. New York: Harper & Row, Publishers, 1980.

———. *Frog and Toad Are Friends.* Illus. by author. New York: Harper & Row, Publishers Inc., 1979.

———. *The Rose in My Garden.* Illus. by Anita Lobel. New York: Greenwillow Books, 1984.

Longfellow, Henry W. *Hiawatha*. Illus. by Susan Jeffers. New York: Dial Press, 1983.

McCloskey, Robert. *Blueberries for Sal*. Illus. by author. New York: Viking Press, 1948.

———. *Make Way for Ducklings*. Illus. by author. New York: Viking Press, 1941.

———. *Time for Wonder*. Illus. by author. New York: Viking Press, 1957.

Macaulay, David. *Cathedral*. Illus. by author. Boston: Houghton Mifflin Co., 1973.

McDermott, Gerald, ret. *Arrow to the Sun: a Pueblo Indian Tale*. Illus. by author. New York: Viking Press, 1974.

Marshall, James. *George and Martha Back in Town*. Illus. by author. Boston: Houghton Mifflin Co., 1984.

Martin, Charles. *Island Winter*. Illus. by author. New York: Greenwillow Books, 1984.

———. *Island Rescue*. Illus. by author. New York: Greenwillow Books, 1985.

Mayer, Marianna, ret. *Beauty and the Beast*. Illus. by Mercer Mayer. New York: Four Winds Press, 1978.

Mayer, Mercer. *AH-CHOO!* Illus. by author. New York: Dial Press, 1976.

———. *The Great Cat Chase*. Illus. by author. New York: Scholastic Book Services, 1975.

———. *Hiccup*. Illus. by author. New York: Dial Press, 1978.

Meyer, Caroline. *The Bread Book*. Illus. by Trina Schart Hyman. New York: Harcourt Brace Jovanovich Inc., 1976.

Minarik, Else H. *Father Bear Comes Home*. Illus. by Maurice Sendak. New York: Harper & Row, Publishers, Inc., 1959 (an *I-Can-Read* book).

Moore, Clement. *The Night Before Christmas*. Illus. by Tomie de Paola. New York: Holiday House Inc., 1980.

Mosel, Arlene. *The Funny Little Woman*. Illus. by Blair Lent. New York: E. P. Dutton & Co., 1972.

Musgrove, Margaret. *Ashanti to Zulu*. Illus. by Leo and Diane Dillon. New York: Dial Press, 1980.

Perrault, Charles. *Cinderella*. Illus. by Marcia Brown. New York: Atheneum Publishers, 1954.

Potter, Beatrix. *Tale of Peter Rabbit*. Illus. by author. New York: Frederick Warne & Co., Inc., 1902.

Provensen, Alice, and Martin. *The Glorious Flight*. New York: Viking Press, 1983.

———. *A Peaceable Kingdom: The Shaker Abecedarius*. New York: Viking Press, 1978.

———. *Town and Country*. Illus. by authors. New York: Crown Publishers, Inc., 1985.

Riordan, James and Eileen Colwell. *Little Gray Neck*. Illus. by Caroline Sharpe. Reading, Mass.: Addison-Wesley Publishing Co., 1975.

Rockwell, Anne. *I Like the Library*. Illus. by author. New York: E. P. Dutton & Co., 1977.

———. *Machines*. Illus. by Harlow Rockwell. New York: Macmillan Publishing Co., 1972.

Rockwell, Harlow. *My Kitchen*. Illus. by author. New York: Greenwillow Books, 1980.

Ross, Blanche, ret. *A Strange Servant*. Illus. by Paul Galdone. New York: Alfred A. Knopf Inc., 1977.

Roy, Ron. *The Three Ducks Went Wandering*. Illus. by Paul Galdone. Boston: Houghton Mifflin Co., 1979.

Sendak, Maurice. *In the Night Kitchen*. Illus. by author. New York: Harper & Row, Publishers, Inc., 1970.

——. *The Nutshell Library*. Illus. by author. New York: Harper & Row, Publishers, Inc., 1962.

——. *Outside Over There*. Illus. by author. New York: Harper & Row, Publishers, Inc., 1981.

——. *Where the Wild Things Are*. Illus. by author. New York: Harper & Row, Publishers, Inc., 1963.

Sharmat, Marjorie Weinman. *The Trolls of Twelfth Street*. Illus. by Ben Schector. New York: Coward, McCann & Geoghegan Inc., 1979.

Shulevitz, Uri. *Dawn*. Illus. by author. New York: Farrar, Straus & Giroux, Inc., 1974.

——. *One Monday Morning*. Illus. by author. New York: Charles Scribner's Sons, 1967.

——. *The Treasure*. Illus. by author. New York: Farrar, Straus & Giroux, Inc., 1979.

Spier, Peter. *The Erie Canal*. New York: Doubleday & Co., Inc., 1970.

——. *London Bridge Is Falling Down*. Illus. by author. New York: Doubleday & Co., Inc., 1967.

——. *Noah's Ark*. Illus. by author. New York: Doubleday & Co., Inc., 1977.

Taylor, Edgar, trans. *King Grisly-Beard: A Tale from the Brothers Grimm*. Illus. by Maurice Sendak. New York: Farrar, Straus & Giroux, Inc., 1973.

Tresselt, Alvin. *White Snow, Bright Snow*. Illus. by Roger Duvoisin. New York: Lothrop, Lee & Shepard Books, 1947.

Tripp, Wallace. *A Great Big Ugly Man Came Up and Tied His Horse to Me: A Book of Nonsense Verse*. Illus. by author. Boston: Little, Brown & Co., Inc., 1973.

Tudor, Tasha. *A Is for Annabelle*. Illus. by author. Chicago: Rand McNally & Co., 1954.

——. *I Is One*. Illus. by author. Chicago: Rand McNally & Co., 1956.

——. *Mother Goose*. Illus. by author. New York: Henry Z. Walck, Inc., 1944.

Turkle, Brinton. *Obadiah the Bold*. Illus. by author. New York: Viking Press, 1965.

Ungerer, Tomi. *One, Two, Where's My Shoe?* Illus. by author. New York: Harper & Row, Publishers, Inc., 1964.

Waber, Bernard. *Anteater Named Arthur*. Illus. by author. Boston: Houghton Mifflin Co., 1967.

——. *Lyle, Lyle Crocodile*. Illus. by author. Boston: Houghton Mifflin Co., 1965.

——. *"You Look Ridiculous," Said the Rhinoceros to the Hippopotamus*. Illus. by author. Boston: Houghton Mifflin Co., 1966.

Wildsmith, Brian. *Brian Wildsmith's ABC*. Illus. by author. New York: Franklin Watts, Inc., 1963.

——. *Brian Wildsmith's Birds*. Illus. by author. New York: Franklin Watts, Inc., 1967.

——. *Brian Wildsmith's Mother Goose*. Illus. by author. New York: Franklin Watts, Inc., 1965.

————. *Brian Wildsmith's Wild Animals.* Illus. by author. New York: Oxford University Press, 1967.

————. *Circus.* Illus. by author. New York: Franklin Watts, Inc., 1980.

Williams, Barbara. *Albert's Toothache.* Illus. by Kay Chorao. New York: E. P. Dutton & Co., 1974.

Williams, Jay. *Everyone Knows What a Dragon Looks Like.* Illus. by Mercer Mayer. New York: Four Winds Press, 1976.

Williams, Vera. *A Chair for My Mother.* Illus. by author. New York: Greenwillow Books, 1982.

Wolkstein, Diane. *The Red Lion: A Persian Story.* Illus. by Ed Young. New York: Harper & Row, Publishers, Inc., 1977.

Zemach, Harve. *Duffy and the Devil.* Illus. by Margot Zemach. New York: Farrar, Straus & Giroux, Inc., 1973.

Zolotow, Charlotte. *A Father Like That.* Illus. by Ben Shecter. New York: Harper & Row, Publishers, Inc., 1971.

The Heart of Literature: Past

RICH ENCOUNTERS

"Billy! Why do you have to keep saying, 'Once upon a time'?"
"Cause that's the way stories start."

●◆●

In chorus, twenty voices repeat,
"I've run away from a little old woman,
A little old man,
A barn full...."
The class is indicating that they have learned the gingerbread boy's taunt and can deliver it in an equally mischievous manner.

●◆●

After listening to Jakob and Wilhelm Grimm's story, The Fisherman and His Wife, *the second graders were discussing it.*
"I think the flounder was right. She—the wife—was too fresh; she wanted everything. Just like my sister."
"Yes, she shouldn't have any nice house."
"What about the fisherman?" asked the teacher.
"Well," and here there was a pause for deliberation, "he kept bothering the fish," said Janie.
"But," insisted Danielle, "his wife kept asking and asking; it's mostly her fault."
"Yes, but he...." Then, emphatically from John, "The fish just got disgusted!"
On and on continues the discussion about who was at fault in this age-old tale whose ending, in some versions, sounds much like the biblical Adam and Eve.

Traditional Literature: Definition

Traditional literature consists of stories of, by, and from the people; such tales of the folk include the classic fairy tales. Generations of folk and centuries of events have shaped these stories, somehow preserving their core plots. Their beginnings may vary from the familiar "Once upon a time," to "Once there was and once there was not in the time before..." (Turkish) to "Long before the snow fell on the rock" (Majorcan), but their impact does not change. These stories mirror the dreams, the values, and the dilemmas confronting all of us. They stir the hearts and memories of those who hear or read them.

Although originally oral, fairy tales appear more and more in written collections, particularly since the time of the Grimm Brothers. In fact, according to Roger Sale, "In our reverence for fairy tales of the oral tradition, we must not think that written fairy tales are any less old." Sale then speaks of a written version of *Sleeping Beauty* in the Twentieth Dynasty in Egypt, a number of tales written in the *Pancha-tantra* of the fifth century (but in actual existence much earlier), and versions of some parts of *A Thousand and One Nights* written hundreds of years before importation into eighteenth-century Europe.[1]

Tracking down folklore figures demands curiosity, perseverance, and a great deal of detective skill. Gail Haley's "Everyman Jack and the Green Man" is a prime example of the intense work of a folklorist.[2] Jack of Beanstalk fame, Merlin (for a time), Robin Hood, Paul Bunyan, the Green Giant in the supermarkets—all are continuations or personifications of the spirit of Nature—the folkfigure of the Green Man.

Even in their written form, the tales at their best preserve their to-be-told character and thus come closest to meeting the major criterion of folklore. Idioms and customs are retained, and with the exception of myths and epics, conversation and narrative preserve a direct, terse informality.

The simplicity of folktales helps to intensify the optimism they radiate. For the most part, the tales give to young children the happy endings they expect. In speaking to the yearnings, hopes, and fears of all people, these stories communicate such values as:

- One must try.
- One is likely to succeed, at least ultimately, if one is good and kind.
- Impossible things can happen.
- Virtue is rewarded.
- Evil exists and is powerful but it can be overcome.

Bearing a variety of names and forms, folk literature includes folktales, fables, myths, legends, and epics. Such literature may also be characterized by its place or culture of origin; young children can therefore be introduced to American, British, German, African, Japanese, and a great assortment of tales from other countries. Involving children in such multi-cultural literature is to broaden greatly their base for making meaning about the world.

Folktales and Literary Components ♡

In folktales, *plots* are skeletal, brief (except for epics), and action-packed; they are easily told. Sometimes these actions are actually one repeated act, as in the Gingerbread Boy (see Galdone); sometimes they are a series of different acts, as in Patricia Lee Gauch's *Once Upon a Dinkelsbuhl.*

Characters, predictable in overall behavior if not in the specifics regarding it, are generally one-dimensional, never deviating from virtue or evil. Beauty remains kind; Cinderella, humble; Jack, brave; and the wolf remains true to his nature and devours two of the three little pigs.

Settings are vague and endlessly adaptable. Time is measured by the timeless clock of fantasy and, although palaces and woodlands abound, the actual locale may be here or anywhere. The goats in *The Three Billy Goats Gruff* may wander up *any* hill, and the fox in Hogrogian's *One Fine Day* could lose his tail in *any* wooded area.

Themes generally are few but pervasive. Protagonists consistently win over the great odds created by nature, events, other people, and sometimes themselves. One suffers if one disobeys rules or laws. Both Tikki Tikki Tembo (Mosel) and mythological Pandora (d'Aulaire) learn this.

The *mood* of folk-fairy tales is generally serious with *some* humor. Challenges, often overwhelming, must be faced. Yet, in the end, happiness eclipses the most trying, the most stressful dilemmas. Optimism holds and happiness is forever after. Rapunzel's tears restore her husband's sight; Elise restores her brothers and escapes burning in Hans Christian Andersen's *The Wild Swans;* and even in the noodlehead tale of the Grimm brothers' *Hans in Luck,* Hans believes he is the luckiest of fellows. Some cultural differences are apparent. For example, English folktales are generally more humorous than German ones.

Folktales and Young Children ♡

The behavioral characteristics of the young child and the nature of early childhood development substantiate the match of folk literature and young children. Indeed, early childhood is *the* time for folktales and fairy tales.

In his research, F. Andre Favat concluded "...that the characteristics of the fairy tales correspond precisely with the characteristics Piaget ascribed to children."[3] It is folk literature that responds to the characteristics of young children: curiosity, love of activity, impatience, imagination, and the need for stability. In fact, folktales meet many needs of the young child, as Table 8.1 indicates.

TABLE 8.1 *Value of Folktales to the Development of Young Children*

Child Development	Folktales' Value
Holistic	Teaches that people have always loved, hated, were born and died, were angry, happy, sad, glad
	Teaches that people need help but they also cope
Emotional	Provides a fantasy world in which young children can view their own fears and frustrations
Cognitive	Mirrors many cultures
	Reinforces the learning of story structure, thereby aiding comprehension and recall*†
Moral	Reflects values such as good will triumph, evil will be punished, and virtue is its own reward (but it is also recognized and compensated)
Language	Provides words for setting—"long, long ago," "once upon a time," "far, far away"—and an understanding of the fantasy land to which these words instantly introduce young children
	Offers children traditional refrains and cumulative tales to sing and remember
Social	Affords opportunities for choral and dramatic group work

*Young children's stories collected by Brian Sutton-Smith et al. in *The Folkstories of Children* show early chronicity (ability to sequence) and cultural and literary influences, as in the case of Danielle:
"A cow jumped over the...
Sleeping Beauty and the Prince
there was Kermit the frog
and he was making noise
that's all
and then there was water in the playground
and then what happened there was Sesame Street" (p. 70).

†See Muriel K. Rand, "Story Schema: Theory, Research and Practice," *The Reading Teacher*, Vol. 37, No. 4 (January 1984): 377–382.

♡

Young children come to recognize common elements in folktales. Familiar fairy tale staples such as the younger brother, the trickster or magician, the evil monster/giant, the heartless stepmother, and suffering children appear in their own stories.

As the patterns of the tales are learned, expectations are formed. For young children, the pleasures and the comfort of the tales rests to some extent on confirming these expectations.

Prime Years

Although fantasy is needed in all stages of life, there appears to be much agreement that a child's years for fairy tales and fantasy peak between ages six and eight.[4,5] During this prime period, some of the fairy tales of Grimm, Perrault, and Andersen, the simple folktales, the "beast" tales, the cumulative tales, tales full of humor, and a generous sharing of tales representing many countries and cultures can be presented to young children. After eight years of age, pretending and fanciful play and reading are gradually replaced by more realistic activities and stories.

Selection of Folk Literature

Care needs to be exercised in choosing traditional literature for young children. Compilations in which *all* the tales can be understood and appreciated by such children are not common. Certain collections stand out as source books in the field. Others have been translated with an older audience in mind. Neither of these types was written for *young* children, but they may contain some tales that can be shared as written and perhaps a few others that could be presented with some accommodation to the young child's limited knowledge and experience. They may also have *core* plots that are easily acted out. Such books will hereafter be designated with an * as comprehensive source books.

Fine single-tale editions abound. Here, too, selectivity needs to be exercised. Literary and developmental standards (Chapter 2) need to be applied. In addition, adherence of the story to its roots, content, language, and form must be considered.

Young children can listen to stories with understanding and appreciation long before they can read them. Literature for the pre-reader therefore must be selected, among other considerations, for its *ear appeal*. This is another reason why folk literature (the *oral* tradition) is so appropriate for young children. Some knowledge of the child's general experiential background and listening vocabulary is also helpful.

Issue: Violence and Stereotyping in Traditional Literature

In the selection of traditional literature for young children the stereotyping of characters and the violence in folktales, especially the classic fairy tales, are sometimes questioned. The nature of the stories themselves demand strong characters and strong action which is often followed by a justice meted out swiftly and violently. Like the morality plays of old, the characters represent some human characteristics such as goodness, evil, or innocence. In such characterization, good is very good, evil is very evil, and retribution can be very violent.

According to Bruno Bettelheim it is because the characters are all good, all innocent, all beautiful or all evil — actually stereotypes — that young children can profit from them. The very polarization helps children make choices about what and who they want to be. "This basic decision, on which all later personality development will build, is facilitated by the polarization of the fairy tale."[6]

There is also the thought that children are likely to meet cruelty and violence in their lives and that they need to see them "righted" with perseverance and courage, as in the fairy tales. Another argument for fairy tales advanced by some psychologists is that since we have within ourselves cruelty and violence, children need to see how these work to create much of the trouble in life.

Young children tend not to be troubled by violence in a tale when the story is shared in a sheltered, safe, calm environment. This very protection from personal harm — a distancing from the violence — actually heightens the enjoyment the young child feels about the tale and the justice levied in it. Certainly, young children are not surprised that when evil is gross, punishment is too. Still, the match of child and tale is critical.

Violence *in picture form* is another problem; here, too, the impact is keen. Illustrations like those of Dore in Perrault's fairy tales should give teachers cause to pause. Not everyone would agree with Christina Moustakis that once the monsters are pictured they become known and it is only the *unknown* terrors that are to be feared.[7] Young children can be frightened by both the known and unknown.

It is the role of modern realistic stories to present to children, as they grow older, diverse characters who are both good and bad, wise and silly, kind and ugly, beautiful and cruel, thoughtful and young, and to present this complexity in all races and both sexes. Therefore, all stepmothers are not unkind, all youngest sons are not brave, and so forth.

Sharing Folktales

The teacher of young children serves them and the lore best when folktales are told. Such sharing is not only true to the oral origins of the tale but the listening vocabulary of young children exceeds their reading word mastery so understanding is quickened by hearing the tales. Skilled story sharers *may* have to (1) repeat a phrase for emphasis when needed, (2) clarify or define a term when necessary, and (3) simplify narrative that is too compressed or complex. The eye-to-eye contact of the storyteller and story listener will quickly signal the need for clarification of traditional literature as well as the response of joy.

This is not to suggest that young children should not hear the sweep and lilt of the language of traditional literature at its best, but teachers of young children may find some syntactically difficult passages, some esoteric words, and some bewildering contexts. Traditional literature, after all, was not really children's literature but rather a type of adult literature. With this in mind, it is easy to understand why some adaptations might need to be made.

The beautiful illustrations of many tales can be shared when the tales are read but when the illustrations *wholly* eclipse the tale, as can easily happen, it is well to share the story without pictures and then exhibit them later during a retelling.

Major Types of Folk Literature

Within the broad field of folk literature some of the tales show special characteristics and are labeled accordingly.

Fables are brief tales with animals generally representing a single human trait. They are clearly didactic and their moral purpose is explicitly stated. There are differences among them, however. Many of the Aesop tales are much briefer than some of the Jataka fables from the East.

Legends are tales of historical figures to whose lives imaginative or fictional details have been added.

Myths are tales whose heroes and heroines are godlike or show supernatural traits and superhuman power. The language of myths tends to be formal; the content of them quite often offers an explanation of some natural phenomenon.

Epics are long narratives centering on one hero who battles against powerful human and superhuman odds. Language in epics mirrors the genre. Sentences are long; language is potent.

Young children are likely to find themselves most comfortable with the simple folktales and their variants and with some fables. The language, the length of plot, the somewhat involved symbols and images, and the "superfolk" heroes of myths, legends, and epics are more difficult for young children to understand and imaginatively role play or internalize.

Within the various types of folk literature, differences in such features as plot complexity, syntax, and length mandate careful selection for young children. Aesop's *A Lion and a Mouse* is a very brief, obvious tale of "We need each other no matter what appearances may be," whereas Paul Galdone's *The Monkey and the Crocodile* is a longer fable involving the schemes of both animals and the Crocodile's mother. The translation of La Fontaine's fables in rhyme can lead to complicated syntax; the wit can also be too subtle for young children.

Beast Tales and Fables

The first folktales presented to young children are likely to be brief and simple, many of them *beast tales* with the beasts assuming human traits in the fashion young children understand and enjoy. Young children who are very much at home with talking animals and toys adapt easily to such animism.

One of the most popular animated beast tales for young children is *The Three Bears*. Lorinda B. Cauley's *Goldilocks and The Three Bears* is handsome; Paul Galdone's *The Three Bears* is bright and bouncing with humor; and Lev Tolstoy's *The Three Bears*, published in Russia, has large full-color rustic folk-art pictures and a Goldilocks who looks like a peasant doll.

The Three Billy Goats Gruff, a most adored Norwegian tale, is available in many editions. Both Marcia Brown's gamboling, jaunting illustrations and Paul Galdone's large, colorful pictures are deservedly loved. This story has everything—simplicity, suspense, three lovable animals, and one hateful troll who gets his comeuppance.

Erik Blegvad's *The Three Little Pigs* is one of several versions of this bit of folklore. Using only pen, ink, and colored pencil, Blegvad balances his pictures and the tale well; the story is not lost in the artwork. This smallish book is easy to hold and enjoy. Paul Galdone's slightly larger version deserves the young child's affection. From the saddest mother sow ever seen waving goodbye to her three little pigs to the triumphant little pig who lives happily ever after, children hang on every word and picture. With varied illustration-text formats, Paul Galdone keeps interest at a peak. Another popular though obstinate pig is the one that would not jump over the stile. Patricia Lamont illustrates and retells this tale in *The Troublesome Pig*. This stubborn, lazy pig is totally unlike the very industrious *Little Red Hen* who justly enjoys the fruit of her labor to the chagrin of her friends. Margot Zemach's version is lively and gently comic.

Fables

Major fables—those from Greece and India—have found their way to children through translations and adaptations. The fables of Aesop which were added to by La Fontaine and the fables of the East as compiled, for example, in Marie Shedlock's *Eastern Stories and Legends* (Jataka tales), are available in collections and many single-tale editions, as indicated in Table 8.2.

Fairy-Folktales

The great folklorists, the Brothers Grimm (German), Charles Perrault (French), Peter Asbjornsen and Jorgen Moe (Norwegian),

* Source book

TABLE 8.2 *Collections and Single-Tale Editions of Fables*

Title	Type	Comment
Collections		
Eastern Stories and Legends (Shedlock)	(India)	Source book
Aesop's Fables (Untermeyer)	Aesop (Greece)	Well illustrated; giant-sized basic collection
The Turtle and the Two Ducks (Plante and Bergman)	La Fontaine tales	Bright, pastel illustrations by Rockwell; obvious humor
The Exploding Frog and Other Fables from Aesop (McFarland)	Aesop	Fable form blurred here by free retelling and droll illustrations
Once in a Wood (Rice)	Aesop	Especially suited to young children; can read independently
Borrowed Feathers and Other Fables (Stevens)	Aesop	Readily understood by young child
Twelve Tales from Aesop (Carle)	Aesop	Share traditional fables first; bright illustrations
Single Fables		
Once a Mouse (Caldecott book) (Marcia Brown)	(India)	Colored woodcuts striking; should be shared visually *and* verbally
Chanticleer and the Fox (Caldecott book) (Barbara Cooney)	Chaucer	Medieval setting; authentic to era; should be seen *and* heard
The Three Fox Fables and *The Monkey and the Crocodile* (Galdone)	Aesop	Gives young children taste of both great sources
The Lion and the Mouse (Young)	Aesop	Pencil drawings should be seen
The Cobbler's Song: A Fable (Sewall)	La Fontaine	Well illustrated and adapted; a fable without animals

— ♡ —

Joseph Jacobs (English), and Alexander Afanasyev (Russian), offer authors and illustrators of today vast treasuries of lore, and authors and illustrators have been eager to accept their research.

When using any of the great collections or the single tales that follow, the developmental characteristics of the young child must be kept in mind. The peak period of fantasy from six to eight years old notwithstanding, *all* tales are not equally suited to all young children.

Collections

If one had to identify the greatest contribution to the repository of folklore, the source book *Household Stories* would probably be cited. When the Grimm Brothers assembled the lore of their people, they served all people. Often called the classic fairy tales because they come from oral tradition as distinguished from those like Hans Christian Andersen's which were initially *written*, they are narrated and packaged and illustrated in diverse ways today. In Table 8.3, innumerable fairy tales from many regions of the world are identified, and appropriate extension activities for young children are suggested.

TABLE 8.3 *Tales from Many Cultures and Appropriate Extension Activities for Young Children*

Title	Comment/Extension Suggestion
English Fairy-Folktales Major Folklorist—Joseph Jacobs. The touch of humor in many of the following tales is obvious and much appreciated by children.	
Mr. Miacca (Ness)	Share illustrations.
Dick Whittington and His Cat (Brown)	Discuss linoleum cuts and share Marcia Brown's cuts.
Jack in the Beanstalk (Stobbs) (from Jacobs' collection)	Add other "Jack" tales.
The Three Sillies (Zemach)	Try "story theatre."
Duffy and the Devil (Zemach)	Share Grimm's "Rumpelstiltskin."
The Teeny Tiny Woman (Seuling) (from Joseph Jacobs' collection)	Practice refrain—each time a bit louder, then read story and invite participation.
The Hobyahs	Must be acted.
Parts of *Robin Hood*	Discuss different characteristics of Robin's Merry Men.
German Fairy-Folktales Major Folklorists—Jacob and Wilhelm Grimm. Comprehensive collections of the work of the Grimm Brothers total over 200 fairy-folktales.	
Cinderella (Hogrogian)	Share Hogrogian's pastel paintings. Read and contrast Brown's *Cinderella* (Perrault) from the French.
Bremen Town Musicians (Plume)	Compare Ilse Plume's *Bremen Town Musicians* with Helme Heine's *Friends* in which the mouse, not the donkey supports his friends.

Title	Comment/Extension Suggestion
German Fairy-Folktales (continued)	
The Table, The Donkey and the Stick	Discuss "magic objects" in other tales.
Hansel and Gretel (Adams)	Compare with Susan Jeffers's illustrations.
The Fisherman and His Wife (Grimm Brothers)	Compare with Godden's *The Old Woman Who Lived in a Vinegar Bottle* or McDermott's *The Stonecutter*.
Tom Thumb (Grimm Brothers)	Share Andersen's *Thumbelina*.
Hans in Luck (Grimm Brothers)	Share *The Triumph of Fuzzy Fogtop* (Rose) another noodlehead tale.
Snow White (Grimm Brothers)	Share Hyman and Burkert illustrations. Let children "stare."
The Sleeping Beauty (Grimm Brothers)	Compare Rackham and Hyman's illustrations.
Little Red Riding Hood (Grimm Brothers)	Share Hyman's illustrations in *Little Red Riding Hood* with Lisbeth Zwerger's illustrations in *Little Red Cap*. Discuss.
Once Upon a Dinkelsbuhl (Gauch)	Share with one of the tales from *Clever Gretchen and Other Forgotten Folktales* (Lurie).

French Fairy-Folktales
Major folklorist — Charles Perrault.
The fairy tales of Charles Perrault were meant for the French Court of the seventeenth century as the narrative shows. Cinderella's sisters had "parquet flooring" in their rooms (p. 58), "resplendent garments" (p. 60), and wore "Honiton lace" (p. 60).*

Cinderella (Perrault)	Share and discuss Galdone's, Brown's, and LeCain's *Cinderella*.
Puss in Boots (Perrault)	Encourage children to observe differences in illustrations and style.
Beauty and the Beast (de Beaumont)	Discuss Marianne Mayer's illustrations; compare with mood created by Dulac.
Balarin's Goat (Berson)	Enact.

*Charles Perrault, *Complete Fairy Tales*. Translated from the French by A. E. Johnson and others; illustrated by W. Heath Robinson. New York: Dodd, Mead and Co., 1961, pp. 58, 60, 63, 64.

(continued)

TABLE 8.3 *Continued*

Title	Comment/Extension Suggestion
French Fairy-Folktales (continued)	
Stone Soup (Brown)	Cook it.
Charles and Claudine (Berson, adap.)	Discuss (some children cannot accept the conclusion).
Scandinavian Fairy-Folktales	
Major Norwegian folklorists—Peter Asbjornsen and Joseph Moe. Eric Haugaard is a major translator of the Danish tales written by Hans Christian Andersen.	
The Cat on the Dovrefell (Asbjornsen and Moe)	Discuss trolls and other folklore figures.
The Terrible Troll Bird (d'Aulaires)	
The Princess and the Pea (Andersen)	Enjoy the scene of the maids toting mattresses to the Princess.
Thumbelina (Andersen)	Share Adams's, Jeffers's, Zwerger's illustrations.
The Emperor's New Clothes (Andersen)	Discuss the reasons the Emperor lied. Share Burton's version. Share also Weil's *The Foolish King*.
The Three Billy Goats Gruff (Galdone)	Enact.
"Why the Bear is Stumpy Tailed" "Why the Sea is Salt"	Discuss what other reasons might make bears stumpy-tailed and the sea salty.
The Cock and the Hen That Went to the Dovrefell (Asbjornsen)	Share with Galdone's *Henny Penny*.
The Ugly Duckling (Adams)	Discuss.
The Nightingale (Andersen)	The message may be lost on young children but the illustrations should be appreciated.
The Boy Who Ate More Than the Giant (Lofgren)	Compare with *The Three Billy Goats Gruff*.
"The Princess on the Glass Hill"	Compare with the Russian tale, *The Little Humpbacked Horse*.
Russian and Armenian Fairy-Folktales	
Major folklorist—Aleksander Afanasyev. Teachers of young children should share *Baba-Yaga* (Small) and *Vasilisa the Beautiful* (Afanasyev) from the major collections; *The Firebird*, a major Russian tale, is too complex for young children. Versions of the *Baba-Yaga* stories and the *Vasilisa* tales are continuously appearing. *Bony-Legs* (Cole) and *The Frog Princess* (Isele) are examples.	
The Woman of the Wood (Black)	Stop before the end and have children conclude the tale.

Title	Comment/Extension Suggestion
Russian and Armenian Fairy Folktales (continued)	
The Turnip (Domanska)	Discuss "teamwork."
The Bun (Brown)	Share with Gingerbread Boy.
Baboushka and the Three Kings (Robbins)	Share with *Old Befana* (de Paola).
Clay Pot Boy (Jameseon)	Discuss other objects that have come alive in stories.
The Fool of the World and the Flying Ship (Caldecott book) (Ransome)	Introduce other noodlehead stories.
Everyone Is Good for Something (de Regniers)	Read *Dick Whittington and His Cat* (Brown), too.
Good Morning Chick (Ginsburg)	Discuss mother hen's behavior.
One Fine Day (Caldecott book) (Hogrogian)	Help children understand the sequence and participate.
Translations of Russian tales by Mirra Ginsburg	Enact many of the briefer ones. Also enact *The Gossipy Wife* (Hall).
Bony-Legs (Cole)	Compare with *Hansel and Gretel* (Grimm).
Central, Eastern European Fairy-Folktales	
The Triumph of Fuzzy Fogtop (Rose)	Share with other noodlehead stories, like *The Three Sillies* (Zemach)
The Best of the Bargain (Domanska)	Read *The Tortoise and the Hare*, too.
The Three Poor Tailors (Ambrus)	Discuss the behavior of the tailors.
The Little Cockerel (Ambrus)	Discuss other stories in which the protagonist is little but smart.
The Little Girl and the Big Bear (Galdone)	Study pictures; much cultural influence here.
Chinese-Japanese Fairy-Folktales	
Tikki Tikki Tembo (Mosel)	Have children join in on the verse (they will naturally).
The Funny Little Woman (Mosel)	Compare the oni with the trolls.
The Legend of the Milky Way (Lee)	Study the illustrations. Discuss the Milky Way.
The Five Chinese Brothers (Bishop)	Enact.
The Fisherman Under the Sea (Miyoki)	*Not* a happy ending. Discuss.
Tye May and the Magic Brush (Bang)	Share *Liang and the Magic Paintbrush*. What are the differences between the tales?

(continued)

TABLE 8.3 *Continued*

Title	Comment/Extension Suggestion
Japanese-Chinese Fairy-Folktales (continued)	
The Stonecutter (McDermott)	Children will quickly learn the refrain and join in. (Marie Shedlock's version is "happier" than Gerald McDermott's.) Compare to *Fisherman and His Wife* (Grimm Brothers).
The Five Sparrows (Newton)	Discuss kindness and greed.
Italian Fairy-Folktales	
The Clown of God (de Paolo)	Share, too, *The Little Juggler* (Cooney). Discuss both.
The Prince of the Dolomites (de Paolo)	Share another pourquoi tale from *The Long Tailed Bear and Other Indian Legends* (Belting).
Strega Nona stories (de Paola)	Discuss characters Strega Nona and Big Anthony.
Indian Fairy-Folktales	
The Magic Cooking Pot (Towle)	Guide children in discussion of how art helps tell the story.
Kassim's Shoes (Berson)	Share P. L. Travers's *Two Pairs of Shoes*.
The Old Woman and the Rice Thief (Bang) *The Old Woman and the Red Pumpkin*	Try to find samenesses in both tales.
African Fairy-Folktales	
Verna Aardema has brought much African folklore to young children, all of it worth listening to and acting out.	
Who's in Rabbit's House (Aardema) *Bringing the Rain to Kapiti Plain* (Aardema) *What's So Funny Ketu? A Nuer Tale* (Aardema) *Why Mosquitoes Buzz in People's Ears* (Aardema)	Enact these with simple paper masks against a child-made mural backdrop.
Anansi Tales (Ghana) (McDermott)	Try Reader's Theatre for some of these.
American-Indian Fairy-Folktales	
Note Sternsland's *Literature by and about the American Indian*.	
Arrow to the Sun (Pueblo) (McDermott)	Contrast with Goble's *Star Boy*.
Annie and the Old One (Navajo) (Miles)	Share with older children; discuss "The Old One's" decision. (Though not a tale, this is full of the Navajo beliefs.)

Title	Comment/Extension Suggestion
American-Indian Fairy-Folktales (continued)	
The Angry Moon (Tlingit) (Sleator)	Have children study the illustrations.
Rat Is Dead and Ant Is Sad (Baker)	Enjoy the cumulative, rhythmic tale.
Other American Fairy-Folktales	
Amber Day (Galdone)	Guide children to think of other phrases in the pattern of "stubborn as a mule."
The Tailypo (Galdone)	Guide children to think of other animals who lost a tail.
The Cool Ride in the Sky (Wolkstein)	Enact.
Journey Cake, Ho! (Sawyer)	Share with other Gingerbread Boy variants.
John Henry: An American Legend (Keats)	Discuss "heroes" and "human legends."
A January Fog Will Freeze a Hog and Other Weather Folklore (Davis)	Discuss and add to weather folklore. Have children speak to grand-parents about additions.
Brer Rabbit by Margaret Wise Brown	Discuss the characteristics of the animals.
Tales from Other Cultures	
The Princess and the Pumpkin (Majorcan) (Duff)	Use with relevant social studies units.
Fin M'Coul (Irish) (de Paola)	
A Crocodile's Tale (Philippine) (Aruego and Dewey)	
A Fair at Kanta (Peru) (Llerena)	
The Thunder God's Son (Peru) (Dewey)	
It Could Always Be Worse (Yiddish) (Zemach)	Share with *Too Much Noise*.

The *Index to Fairy Tales* is a convenient tool for teachers who may wish to locate traditional literature on a special topic.

♡

In addition to the works of the other folklorists previously mentioned and the citations in the Professional Bibliography of Chapter 3, there are several major anthologies of children's literature of use to the classroom teacher as sources of folk-fairy tales.

* Griffith, John W., and Frey, Charles H. (eds.). *Classics of Children's Literature*. New York: Macmillan Company, Inc., 1981. A collection of classics in British children's literature from 1700-1920; available in paperback.

* Source book

* Johnson, Edna, et al. *Anthology of Children's Literature.* 5th ed. Boston: Houghton Mifflin Co., 1977. Comprehensive compilation; scholarly, extensive, with source-noted poems and tales from all over the world.

* Sutherland, Zena, and Livingston, Myra Cohn. *The Scott Foresman Anthology of Children's Literature.* Glenview, Illinois: Scott Foresman Co., 1984. Comprehensive and balanced compilation of selections from all genres; extensive bibliography and pronunciation guide.

In addition to these major anthologies is the extensive collection in *Favorite Fairy Tales Told in...* from various countries compiled by Virginia Haviland and illustrated by some of the most talented children's book illustrators. Virginia Haviland also selected a most worthy cross-section of children's literature for her *Fairy Tale Treasury* illustrated by Raymond Briggs.

Other rich compilations are Ruth Manning-Sanders's *A Choice of Magic,* *The Twelve Dancing Princesses and Other Fairy Tales* selected by Alfred David Meek and Mary Elizabeth Meek, and *One Hundred Favorite Folktales* chosen by Stith Thompson.

Of all these, Ann Rockwell's collections *The Three Bears and 15 Other Stories* and *The Old Woman and Her Pig and Ten Other Stories* are specially designed for young children. These two compilations, colorfully illustrated, offer story sharers twenty-seven better known fables from Aesop and La Fontaine as well as tales from the Brothers Grimm, and English and Norwegian folklore.

Single-Tale Versions

Young children have available to them not only diverse folktales but several versions of the same folktale from different parts of the world, many of them in well illustrated single-tale editions. Comparing Paul Galdone's *Gingerbread Boy* and Marcia Brown's *The Bun* enriches young children visually and linguistically, as does sharing Brown's *Cinderella* (Perrault) and Young's *Yeh Shen: A Cinderella Story from China* (Louie).

Myths

In the d'Aulaires' *Norse Gods and Giants* and *Book of Greek Myths* teachers of young children may be able to select a few tales and adapt others. Materials for the primary child in the great classical epics and myths are rare and, when present, tend to sound contrived or forced. Possible reasons for this are many: formal language, complex plots and subplots, and an aura of history beyond the child's ken. When any part of *Gilgamesh, Beowulf, Sundiata, Odyssey,* and *Iliad* or other myths or epics

* Source book

have been used with young children, the emphasis is likely to be the series of actions rather than the supernatural characters and their motives.

Some of the Indian and African myths are more easily understood than are the Greek and Roman ones; however, even from among the classical myths, selections can be made. The Persephone myth is readily presented to children as the way the Greeks answered the question of the differences in the seasons. Margaret Hodges's *Persephone and the Springtime* relates the tale for young children. The King Midas story is also one that young children can appreciate.

Margery Bernstein and Janet Kobrin's *The First Morning: An African Myth Retold* accounts for light coming to the world; this, presented with Anne Rose's *Spider in the Sky,* an American Indian myth that explains how fire and light came to the animals, gives young children an opportunity to contrast the way different cultures explained the same phenomenon. For older children, a telling of the Prometheus story broadens the base for contrast and discussion even further.

Bible Stories

The young child's curiosity is boundless; it embraces the world. In an age of space exploration the world grows larger. How did it come to be? Aileen Fisher's young child in *I Stood Upon a Mountain,* a verse tale, begins in curiosity about the natural wonders around her and ends in awe. It is nature also that breathes a sense of God in Florence Mary Fitch's book *A Book about God.*

Most biblical stories for young children are of specific figures like Noah and Jonah, specific religious holidays, or ways of worship.

Probably the most frequently shared Bible story in the literature of young children is *Noah's Ark,* one of the most recent (Peter Spier's) having earned the Caldecott Award. This is a highly detailed, colorful, humorous picture book of the voyage. A quite different version, *Noah and the Great Flood* (Warwick Hutton) matches the King James Bible text. A more imaginative, poetic account, *Where's Gomer?* (Norma Farber) focuses on Noah's grandson who missed the ark's sailing. There is also Max Bollinger's *Noah and the Rainbow: An Ancient Story,* rhythmically narrated and translated by Clyde Bulla.

The story of Jonah has also been retold a number of times. Beverly Brodsky's *Jonah: An Old Testament Story* is unusual because it is told in the first person. Norma Farber's *A Ship in a Storm on the Way to Tarshish* is an adaptation from part of the Book of Jonah, and Jan Wahl's *Runaway Jonah and Other Tales* includes several other Bible stories. Probably the most arresting of the Jonah books is Warwick Hutton's *Jonah and the Great Fish* with its dynamic full-color illustrations.

New Testament stories center upon the Nativity. Among such stories reverently told and well illustrated are Margaret Wise Brown's

Christmas in the Barn, illustrated by Barbara Cooney, and Edith Thatcher Hurd's *Christmas Eve*. Maud and Miska Petersham's *The Christ Child: As Told by Matthew and Luke* presents the young child with arresting illustrations and quotations directly from the Bible.

David Adler records the history of the Miracle of Light in *A Picture Book of Hanukkah*.

As children grow older they will appreciate two other books by Florence Mary Fitch: *One God: The Ways We Worship Him* and *Their Search for God*.

Rachel Field's *Prayer for a Child*, illustrated by Elizabeth Orton Jones, is the Caldecott Book that presents with gentle reverence and illustration a young child's prayer. Tasha Tudor's *First Prayers* help young children to think of different parts of the day as prayer times.

The picture book *Poems and Prayers for the Very Young* (Alexander) is a compilation of poems and prayers including, among others, Rossetti's inquiring poem "Clouds," Emerson's grateful "Father We Thank Thee," and a reverent version of "All things bright and beautiful..." by Cecil Alexander.

Another Caldecott "Bible" book is Dorothy P. Lathrop's *Animals of the Bible*. Portions of the King James version of the Bible are used and appropriately matched with the illustrations of the animals.

Pelagie Doane's *A Small Child's Bible* presents many Bible stories to the young child in a small, colorful edition.

Summary ♡

The many forms of traditional literature present humankind in all its richness and fullness, timeless history in the form of lore, and cultures in all their diversity. Such literature grips the attention of young children because it mirrors so well the hopes and fears, joys and sorrows, angers and comforts in each young heart, offering solace to the spirit and spurt to the imagination.

Adaptable, vague, timeless settings, skeletal plots, one-dimensional characters, and basic themes—serious but humorous too—characterize folktales. They support the young child's holistic development, especially his or her emotional, cognitive, moral, language, and social growth.

The one-dimensional figures are developmentally helpful to children and the violence is diluted by the child's distance from the tale and the supportive environment surrounding him or her when the tales are shared.

Of the major types of tales—fables, legends, myths, and epics—it is the simple folktales, beast tales, and some fables that young children *best* understand and relish.

Myriad extensions open up when fairy-folktales are shared and rich source books, collections, and single-tale editions are available; many of these are remarkably well illustrated. For young children, selection must be based on the child's background and developmental and conceptual stage. For the sake of future learning it is well to introduce young children to a genre in its traditional form (Aesop rather than the fable twists). Variations can be presented later.

There is no lack of folktales to support social studies objectives. Many examples are offered here.

Bible stories for young children center principally upon specific persons, specific religious holidays, and/or ways to worship.

DISCUSSION ACTIVITIES

• Select any of the extension activities in which children examine two or three versions of the same tale. Record discussion following sharing and analyze the bases for young children's comparison. Are such bases reflected in any of the types of stories they themselves tell?

• Share one of the fables with three or four children; suggest that they enact it. What parts of action and dialogue are represented in their own retelling? Consider the child's notable behaviors. Is this enactment what you would predict?

• Study several illustrated tales that are particularly rich in supplying cultural detail. Share with children and note what they observe in the pictures. Record comments and assess how observant or unobservant they were to such cultural details. Identify questions you might use in prodding a picture search.

NOTES

1. Roger Sale, *Fairy Tales and After from Snow White to E. B. White* (Cambridge, Mass.: Harvard University Press, 1978), p. 49.

2. Gail E. Haley, "Everyman Jack and the Green Man," *Proceedings of the Ninth Annual Conference of the Children's Literature Association,* University of Florida, March 1982, pp. 1–19.

3. F. Andre Favat, *Child and Tale* (Urbana, Ill.: National Council of Teachers of English, 1977), p. 25.

4. Ibid., p. 54.

5. Donald Baker, *Functions of Folk and Fairy Tales* (Washington, D.C.: Association for Childhood Education International, 1981), p. 21.

6. Bruno Bettleheim. *The Uses of Enchantment* (New York: Alfred A. Knopf, Inc., 1976), p. 9.

7. Christina Moustakis, "A Plea for Heads: Illustrating Violence in Fairy Tales," *Children's Literature Association Quarterly*, Vol. 7, No. 2 (Summer 1982): 26–30.

♡
PROFESSIONAL BIBLIOGRAPHY

Aquino, John. *Fantasy in Literature*. Washington, D.C.: National Education Association, 1977.

Baker, Donald. *Functions of Folk and Fairy Tales*. Washington, D.C.: Association for Childhood Education International, 1981.

Bettleheim, Bruno. *The Uses of Enchantment*. New York: Alfred A. Knopf, Inc., 1976.

Briggs, Katherine Mary. *The Vanishing People: Fairy Lore and Legends*. Illus. by Mary I. French. New York: Pantheon Books, 1978.

Clarkson, Atelia, and Cross, Gilbert B., comps. *World Folktales: A Scribner Resource Collection*. New York: Charles Scribner's Sons, 1980.

Favat, F. Andre. *Child and Tale*. Urbana, Ill.: National Council of Teachers of English, 1977.

Haley, Gail E. "Everyman Jack and the Green Man," *Proceedings of the Ninth Annual Conference of the Children's Literature Association*. University of Florida, March 1982.

Index to Fairy Tales. 1949–1972. Westwood, Mass.: Faxon, 1973.

Moustakis, Christina. "A Plea for Heads: Illustrating Violence in Fairy Tales," *Children's Literature Association Quarterly*, Vol. 7, No. 2 (Summer 1982).

Propp, V. *Morphology of the Folktale*. 2d ed. Austin: University of Texas Press, 1968.

Quinnam, Barbara. *Fables from Incunabula to Modern Picture Books*. Washington, D.C.: The Library of Congress, 1966.

Rand, Muriel K. "Story Schema: Theory, Research and Practice," *The Reading Teacher*, Vol. 37, No. 4 (January 1984): 377–382.

Sale, Roger. *Fairy Tales and After from Snow White to E. B. White*. Cambridge, Mass.: Harvard University Press, 1978.

Sutton-Smith, Brian, et al. *The Folkstories of Children*. Philadelphia: University of Pennsylvania Press, 1981.

Thompson, Stith, comp. *One Hundred Favorite Folktales*. Drawings by Franz Altshuler. Bloomington: Indiana University Press, 1968.

Travers, P. L. *About the Sleeping Beauty*. Illus. by Charles Keeping. New York: McGraw-Hill Company, 1975.

♡
CHILDREN'S BOOKS

Aardema, Verna. *Bringing the Rain to Kapiti Plain*. Illus. by Beatriz Vidal. New York: Dial Press, 1981.

————. *Half-a-Ball-of-Kenki*. Illus. by Diane Zuromskis. New York: Frederick Warne & Co., Inc., 1979.

————. *What's So Funny, Ketu? A Nuer Tale*. Illus. by Marc Brown. New York: Dial Press, 1982.

————. *Who's in Rabbit's House?* Illus. by Diane Dillon and Leo Dillon. New York: Dial Press, 1977.

————. *Why Mosquitoes Buzz in People's Ears*. Illus. by Leo Dillon and Diane Dillon. New York: Dial Press, 1975.

Adler, David. *A Picture Book of Hanukkah*. Illus. by Linda Heller. New York: Holiday House, 1982.

Aesop. *The Caldecott Aesop*. Illus. by Randolph Caldecott. Facsimile of 1883 edition. New York: Doubleday & Co., Inc., 1978.

————. *A Lion and a Mouse*. Illus. by Ed Young. New York: Doubleday and Co., Inc., 1980.

————. *Once in a Wood*. Adap. and ret. by Eva Rice. New York: Greenwillow Books, 1979.

Afanasyev, Alexander. *Vasilisa the Beautiful*. Trans. by Thomas P. Whitney. Illus. by Nonny Hogrogian. New York: Macmillan Publishing Co., Inc., 1970.

Alexander, Martha. *Poems and Prayers for the Very Young*. Illus. by author. New York: Random House, Inc., 1973.

Ambrus, Victor, ret. and illus. *The Little Cockerel*. New York: Harcourt, Brace and World, Inc., 1968.

————. *The Three Poor Tailors*. New York: Harcourt Brace Jovanovich Inc., 1965.

Andersen, Hans Christian. *The Emperor's New Clothes*. Illus. by Virginia Lee Burton. Boston: Houghton Mifflin Co., 1949.

————. *The Nightingale*. Trans. by Eva Le Gallienne. Illus. by Nancy E. Elkert. New York: Harper & Row, Publishers, 1965.

————. *The Princess and the Pea*. Illus. by Paul Galdone. New York: Seabury Press, 1978.

————. *Thumbelina*. Illus. by Adrienne Adams. New York: Charles Scribner's Sons, 1961.

————. *Thumbelina*. Retold by Amy Ehrlich. Illus. by Susan Jeffers. New York: Dial Press, 1979.

————. *Thumbelina*. Illus. by Lisbeth Zwerger. New York: William Morrow and Co., Inc., 1980.

————. *The Ugly Duckling*. Trans. by R. P. Keigwin. Illus. by Adrienne Adams. New York: Charles Scribner's Sons, 1965.

————. *The Wild Swans*. Illus. by Susan Jeffers. New York: Dial Press, 1981.

Aruego, Jose, and Dewey, Ariane. *A Crocodile's Tale*. New York: Charles Scribner's Sons, 1972.

Asbjornsen, Peter C., and Moe, Jorgen. *The Cat on the Dovrefell: A Christmas Tale*. Illus. by Tomie de Paola. New York: G. P. Putnam's Sons, 1979.

————. *East of the Sun and West of the Moon: Twenty-One Norwegian Folk Tales*. Ed. and Illus. by Ingri d'Aulaire and Edgar Parin. New York: Viking Press, 1969.

————. *Norwegian Folk Tales*. Trans. by Pat Shaw Iversen and Carl Norman. Illus. by Erik Werenskiold and Theodor Kittlesen. New York: Viking Press, 1960.

———. *The Three Billy Goats Gruff*. Illus. by Marcia Brown. New York: Harcourt Brace Jovanovich, 1957.

Baker, Betty. *Rat Is Dead and Ant Is Sad*. Illus. by Mamoru Funai. New York: Harper & Row, Publishers, Inc., 1981.

Bang, Betsy. *The Old Woman and the Red Pumpkin*. Illus. by Molly Bang. New York: Macmillan Publishing Co., 1975.

———. *The Old Woman and the Rice Thief*. Illus. by Molly Bang. New York: Greenwillow Books, 1978.

Bang, Molly. *Tye May and the Magic Brush*. Illus. by author. New York: Greenwillow Books, 1981.

Bernstein, Margery, and Kobrin, Janet. *The First Morning: An African Myth Retold*. Illus. by Enid Warner Romanek. New York: Charles Scribner's Sons, 1976.

Berson, Harold. *Balarin's Goat*. Illus. by author. New York: Crown Publishers, Inc., 1972.

———. *Charles and Claudine*. Illus. by author. New York: Macmillan Publishing Co., 1980.

———. *Kassim's Shoes*. Illus. by author. New York: Crown Publishers, Inc., 1977.

Belting, Natalie. *The Long-Tailed Bear and Other Indian Legends*. Illus. by Louis F. Cary. Indianapolis: Bobbs-Merrill Co., Inc., 1961.

Bishop, Claire Huchet. *The Five Chinese Brothers*. Illus. by Kurt Wiese. New York: Coward, McCann and Geoghegan, Inc., 1938.

Black, Algernon D. *The Woman of the Wood*. Illus. by Evaline Ness. New York: Holt, Rinehart and Winston, Inc., 1973.

Blegvad, Erik. *The Three Little Pigs*. Illus. by author. New York: Atheneum Publishers, 1980.

Bollinger, Max, ed. *Noah and the Rainbow: An Ancient Story*. Trans. by Clyde Robert Bulla. Illus. by Helga Aichinger. New York: Thomas Y. Crowell Co., 1972.

Briggs, Kathleen. *The Personnel of Fairyland*. Detroit: The Singing Tree Press, 1971.

Brodsky, Beverly. *Jonah: An Old Testament Story*. Illus. by author. Philadelphia: J. B. Lippincott Co., 1977.

Brown, Marcia. *The Bun*. Illus. by author. New York: Harcourt Brace Jovanovich, Inc., 1972.

———. *Dick Whittington and His Cat*. Illus. by author. New York: Charles Scribner's Sons, 1950.

———. *Once a Mouse*. Illus. by author. New York: Charles Scribner's Sons, 1961.

———. *Stone Soup*. Illus. by author. New York: Charles Scribner's Sons, 1947.

Brown, Margaret W. *Christmas in the Barn*. Illus. by Barbara Cooney. New York: Thomas Y. Crowell Co., 1952.

Bryan, Ashley, ret. *Beat the Story Drum, Pum-Pum*. Illus. by ret. New York: Atheneum Publishers, 1980.

Carle, Eric. *Twelve Tales from Aesop*. New York: Philomel Books, 1980.

Cauley, Lorinda B. *Goldilocks and the Three Bears*. Illus. by author. New York: G. P. Putnam's Sons, 1981.

Chandler, Robert, trans. *Russian Folk Tales*. Illus. by Ivan Bilibin. New York: Random House, 1980.

Cole, Joanna. *Bony-Legs*. Illus. by Dirk Zimmer. New York: Four Winds Press, 1983.

Cooney, Barbara. *Chanticleer and the Fox*. Illus. by author. New York: Thomas Y. Crowell Co., 1958.

———. *The Little Juggler*. Illus. by author. New York: Hastings House, 1961, 1982.

Dasent, George Webbe, trans. *East O' the Sun and West O' the Moon*. New York: Dover Publications Inc., 1970.

d'Aulaire, Ingri, and Parin, Edgar. *d'Aulaires' Book of Greek Myths*. Illus. by authors. Doubleday & Co., Inc., 1962.

———. *Norse Gods and Giants*. Illus. by authors. New York: Doubleday & Co., Inc., 1967.

———. *The Terrible Troll Bird*. Illus. by authors. New York: Doubleday & Co., Inc., 1976.

———. *d'Aulaires' Trolls*. Illus. by authors. New York: Doubleday & Co., Inc., 1972.

Davis, Hubert, ed. *A January Fog Will Freeze a Hog and Other Weather Folklore*. Illus. by John Wallner. New York: Crown Publishers, Inc., 1977.

de Beaumont, Madame. *Beauty and the Beast*. Trans. by Marianne Mayer. Illus. by Mercer Mayer. New York: Four Winds Press, 1978.

Demi. *Liang and the Magic Paintbrush*. Illus. by author. New York: Holt, Rinehart and Winston, Inc., 1980.

de Paola, Tomi. *Big Anthony and the Magic Ring*. Illus. by author. New York: Harcourt Brace Jovanovich, Inc., 1979.

———. *Clown of God*. Illus. by author. New York: Harcourt Brace Jovanovich, Inc., 1978.

———. *Fin M'Coul*. Illus. by author. New York: Holiday House, 1981.

———. *The Legend of Old Befana*. Illus. by author. New York: Harcourt Brace Jovanovich, Inc., 1980.

———. *The Prince of the Dolomites*. Illus. by author. New York: Harcourt Brace Jovanovich, Inc., 1980.

———. *Strega Nona*. Illus. by author. Englewood Cliffs, N.J.: Prentice-Hall, Inc., 1975.

———. *Strega Nona's Magic Lessons*. Illus. by author. New York: Harcourt Brace Jovanovich, Inc., 1982.

de Regniers, Beatrice. *Everyone Is Good for Something*. Illus. by Margot Tomes. Boston: Houghton Mifflin Co., 1980.

Dewey, Ariane. *The Thunder God's Son*. Illus. by author. New York: Greenwillow Books, 1981.

Doane, Pelagie, ed. *A Small Child's Bible*. Illus. by editor. New York: Henry Z. Walck Co., 1946.

Domanska, Janina. *The Best of the Bargain*. Illus. by author. New York: Greenwillow Books, 1977.

———. *The Turnip*. Illus. by author. New York: Macmillan Publishing Co., 1969.

Duff, Maggie. *The Princess and the Pumpkin*. Illus. by Catherine Stock. New York: Macmillan Publishing Co., Inc., 1980.

Farber, Norma. *A Ship in a Storm on the Way to Tarshish*. Illus. by Victoria Chess. New York: Greenwillow Books, 1977.

———. *Where's Gomer?* Illus. by William Pene du Bois. New York: E. P. Dutton Co., 1974.

Field, Rachel. *Prayer for a Child*. Illus. by Elizabeth Orton Jones. New York: Macmillan Publishing Co., 1944.

Fisher, Aileen. *I Stood Upon a Mountain*. Illus. by Blair Lent. New York: Harper & Row, Publishers, Inc., 1979.

Fitch, Florence Mary. *A Book About God*. Illus. by Leonard Weisgard. New York: Lothrop, Lee & Shepard Books, 1953.

———. *One God: The Ways We Worship Him*. New York: Lothrop, Lee & Shepard Books, 1944.

———. *Their Search for God*. New York: Lothrop, Lee & Shepard Books, 1947.

Gag, Wanda. *Gone is Gone*. Illus. by author. New York: Coward, McCann & Geoghegan, 1935.

Galdone, Joanna. *Amber Day*. Illus. by Paul Galdone. New York: McGraw-Hill Book Co., 1978.

———. *The Little Girl and the Big Bear*. Illus. by Paul Galdone. Boston: Houghton Mifflin Co., 1980.

———. *The Tailypo*. Illus. by Paul Galdone. New York: Clarion Books, 1977.

Galdone, Paul. *Cinderella*. New York: McGraw-Hill Book Co., 1978.

———. *The Gingerbread Boy*. New York: Seabury Press, 1975.

———. *Henny Penny*. Illus. by author. Boston: Houghton Mifflin Co., 1968.

———, ed. *The Monkey and the Crocodile: A Jataka Tale from India*. Illus. by editor. New York: Seabury Press, 1969.

———. *The Three Bears*. Illus. by author. New York: Seabury Press, 1972.

———. *The Three Billy Goats Gruff*. Illus. by author. Boston: Houghton Mifflin Co., 1973.

———. *The Three Aesop Fox Fables*. New York: Seabury Press, 1971.

———. *The Three Little Pigs*. Illus. by author. New York: Seabury Press, 1970.

Gauch, Patricia Lee. *Once Upon a Dinkelsbuhl*. Illus. by Tomie de Paola. New York: G. P. Putnam's Sons, 1977.

Ginsburg, Mirra. *Good Morning Chick*. Illus. by Byron Barton. New York: Greenwillow Books, 1980.

Goble, Paul, ret. *Star Boy*. Illus. by reteller. New York: Bradbury Press, 1983.

Godden, Rumer. *The Old Woman Who Lived in a Vinegar Bottle*. Illus. by Mairi Hedderwick. New York: Viking Press, 1972.

Grimm, Jakob, and Grimm, Wilhelm. *Bremen Town Musicians*. Illus. by Janina Domanska. New York: Greenwillow Books, 1980.

———. *Bremen Town Musicians*. Illus. and ret. by Ilse Plume. New York: Doubleday & Co., Inc., 1980.

———. *Cinderella*. Illus. by Nonny Hogrogian. New York: Greenwillow Books, 1981.

———. *Cinderella*. Illus. by Errol LeCain. New York: Puffin Books, 1976.

———. *The Fisherman and His Wife*. Trans. by Randall Jarrell. Illus. by Margot Zemach. New York: Farrar, Straus & Giroux, Inc., 1980.

———. *Hans in Luck*. Illus. by Felix Hoffman. New York: Atheneum Publishers, 1975.

———. *Hansel and Gretel*. Trans. by Charles Scribner. Illus. by Adrienne Adams. New York: Charles Scribner's Sons, 1975.

———. *Hansel and Gretel*. Illus. by Susan Jeffers. New York: Dial Press, 1980.

———. *Household Stories*. Trans. by Lucy Crane. Illus. by Walter Crane. New York: Macmillan Co., 1930.

———. *Little Red Cap*. Trans. by Elizabeth D. Crawford. Illus. by Lisbeth Zwerger. New York: William Morrow & Co., 1983.

———. *Little Red Riding Hood*. Ret. Illus. by Trina Schart Hyman. New York: Holiday House, 1983.

———. *The Sleeping Beauty*. Illus. by Trina Schart Hyman. Boston: Little, Brown and Co., 1977.

———. *The Sleeping Beauty*. Adap. by C. S. Evans. Illus. by Arthur Rackham. New York: Dover, 1920.

———. *Snow White*. Trans by Paul Heins. Illus. by Trina Schart Hyman. Boston: Little, Brown and Co., 1974.

———. *Snow White and the Seven Dwarfs*. Trans. by Randall Jarrell. Illus. by Nancy Ekholm Burkert. New York: Farrar, Straus & Giroux, 1972.

———. *The Table, the Donkey and the Stick*. Illus. by Paul Galdone. New York: McGraw-Hill Book Co., 1976.

———. *Tom Thumb*. Illus. by Felix Hoffman. New York: Atheneum Publishers, 1974.

Hall, Amanda, adap. *The Gossipy Wife*. Illus. by adapter. New York: Peter Bedrick Books, 1984 (first American edition).

Harris, Joel Chandler. *Brer Rabbit and Brer Fox*. New York: Philomel Books, 1969.

———. *Brer Rabbit: Stories from Uncle Remus*. Adap. by Margaret W. Brown. Illus. by A. B. Frost. New York: Harper & Row, Publishers, Inc., 1941.

Haugaard, Erik, trans. *The Complete Fairy Tales and Stories of Hans Christian Andersen*. New York: Doubleday & Co., Inc., 1974.

Haviland, Virginia. *Fairy Tale Treasury*. Illus. by Raymond Briggs. New York: Coward, McCann and Geoghegan, Inc., 1972.

———. *Favorite Fairy Tales Told in* ... (series). Illus. by many well-known illustrators. Boston: Little, Brown and Co., 1959.

Heine, Helme. *Friends*. Illus. by author. New York: Atheneum Publishers, 1982.

Hodges, Margaret. *Persephone and the Springtime*. Illus. by Arvis Stewart. Boston: Little, Brown & Co., 1973.

Hogrogian, Nonny. *One Fine Day*. Illus. by author. New York: Macmillan Publishing Co., Inc., 1971.

Hurd, Edith Thatcher. *Christmas Eve*. Illus. by Clement Hurd. New York: Harper & Row, Publishers, Inc., 1962.

Hutton, Warwick. *Jonah and the Great Fish*. Illus. by author. New York: Atheneum Publishers, 1984.

———. *Noah and the Great Flood*. Illus. by author. New York: Atheneum Publishers, 1977.

Isele, Elizabeth. *The Frog Princess*. Illus. by Michael Hague. New York: Thomas Y. Crowell Co., 1984.

Jacobs, Joseph, ed. *Mr. Miacca*. Illus. by Evaline Ness. New York: Holt, Rinehart and Winston, 1969.

Jameson, Cynthia, adap. *Clay Pot Boy*. Illus. by Arnold Lobel. New York: Coward, McCann and Geoghegan, 1973.

Keats, Ezra Jack. *John Henry: An American Legend*. New York: Pantheon Books, 1965.

Lamont, Priscilla, ret. *The Troublesome Pig: A Nursery Tale*. Illus. by author.

New York: Crown Publishers, Inc., 1985.

Lathrop, Dorothy, ed. *Animals of the Bible.* Illus. by editor. Philadelphia: J. B. Lippincott Co., 1969.

Lee, Jeanne, ret. *The Legend of the Milky Way.* Illus. by author. New York: Holt, Rinehart and Winston, 1982.

Llerena, Carlos. *A Fair at Kanta.* Illus. by author. New York: Holt, Rinehart and Winston, 1975.

Lofgren, Ulf, ret. Trans. from Swedish by Sheila La Farge. Illus. by author. *The Boy Who Ate More Than the Giant.* New York: Collier's & World, 1978.

Louie, Ai-Ling, ret. *Yeh-Shen: A Cinderella Story from China.* Illus. by Ed Young. New York: Philomel Books, 1982.

Lurie, Alison. *Clever Gretchen and Other Forgotten Folktales.* Illus. by Margot Tomes. New York: Harper & Row, Publishers, Inc., 1980.

McDermott, Gerald. *Anansi the Spider.* Illus. by author. New York: Holt, Rinehart and Winston, Inc., 1972.

———. *Arrow to the Sun.* Illus. by author. New York: Viking Press, 1974.

———. *The Stonecutter.* Illus. by author. New York: Viking Press, 1957.

McFarland, John. *The Exploding Frog and Other Fables from Aesop.* Illus. by James Marshall. Boston: Little, Brown and Co., 1981.

McGovern, Ann. *Robin Hood of Sherwood Forest.* Illus. by Tracy Sugarman. New York: Scholastic Book Services, 1970.

———. *Too Much Noise.* Illus. by author. Boston: Houghton Mifflin Co., 1967.

Manning-Sanders, Ruth. *A Choice of Magic.* Illus. by Robin Jacques. New York: E. P. Dutton & Co., Inc., 1971.

Meek, Alfred David, and Meek, Mary Elizabeth. *The Twelve Dancing Princesses and Other Fairy Tales.* Bloomington, Ind.: Indiana University Press, 1974.

Miles, Miska. *Annie and the Old One.* Illus. by Peter Parnall. Boston: Little, Brown & Co., 1971.

Miyoki, Matsutani. *The Fisherman Under the Sea.* English version by Alvin Tresselt. New York: Parents Magazine Press, 1969.

Mosel, Arlene, ret. *The Funny Little Woman.* Illus. by Blair Lent. New York: E. P. Dutton & Co., Inc., 1972.

———. *Tikki Tikki Tembo.* Illus. by Blair Lent. New York: Holt, Rinehart and Winston, Inc. 1968.

Newton, Patricia Montgomery, adapt. and illus. *The Five Sparrows: A Japanese Folktale.* New York: Atheneum Publishers, 1982.

Olenius, Elsa, sel. *Great Swedish Fairy Tales.* New York: Delacorte Press, 1973.

Petersham, Maud, and Petersham, Miska. *The Christ Child: As Told by Matthew and Luke.* Illus. by authors. New York: Doubleday & Co., Inc., 1931.

Perrault, Charles. *Cinderella.* Illus. by Marcia Brown. New York: Charles Scribner's Sons, 1954.

———. *Cinderella or The Glass Slipper.* Illus. by Errol LeCain. London: Faber and Faber, 1976.

———. *Perrault's Complete Fairy Tales.* Trans. by A. E. Johnson and others. Illus. by W. Heath Robinson. New York: Dodd, Mead and Company, 1961.

———. *Perrault's Fairy Tales.* Illus. by Gustave Dore. New York: Dover Publications, 1969.

———. *Puss in Boots.* Illus. by Marcia Brown. New York: Charles Scribner's Sons, 1952.

Plante, Patricia, and Bergman, David. *The Turtle and the Two Ducks*. Illus. by Anne Rockwell. New York: Thomas Y. Crowell, Co., 1981.

Provensen, Alice, and Provensen, Martin. *The Provensen Book of Fairy Tales*. Illus. by authors. New York: Random House, Inc. 1971.

Quiller-Couch, Sir Arthur, ret. *The Sleeping Beauty and Other Fairy Tales from the Old French*. Illus. by Edmund Dulac. New York: Aburis Books Inc., 1980.

Ransome, Arthur. *The Fool of the World and the Flying Ship*. Illus. by Uri Shulevitz. New York: Farrar, Straus & Giroux, Inc., 1968.

Robbins, Ruth. *Baboushka and the Three Kings*. Illus. by Nicolas Sidjakov. New York: Parnassus Press, 1960.

Rockwell, Anne. *The Old Woman and Her Pig and Ten Other Stories*. Illus. by author. New York: Harper & Row Publishers, 1979.

———, ed. *The Three Bears and 15 Other Stories*. Illus. by editor. New York: Thomas Y. Crowell Co., 1975.

Rose, Anne. *Spider in the Sky*. Illus. by Gail Ownes. New York: Harper & Row, Publishers, Inc., 1978.

———, ed. *The Triumph of Fuzzy Fogtop*. Illus. by Tomie de Paola. New York: Dial Press, 1979.

Ryder, Arthur, trans. *Panchatantra*. Chicago: University of Chicago Press, 1925.

Sawyer, Ruth. *Journey Cake, Ho!* Illus. by Robert McCloskey. New York: Viking Press, 1953.

Seuling, Barbara. *The Teeny Tiny Woman: An Old English Ghost Tale*. Illus. by author. New York: Viking Press, 1976.

Sewall, Marcia. *The Cobbler's Song: A Fable*. New York: E. P. Dutton & Co., 1982.

Shedlock, Marie. *Eastern Stories and Legends*. New York: E. P. Dutton & Co., Inc., 1920.

Sleator, William, ret. *The Angry Moon*. Boston: Little, Brown & Co., 1970.

Small, Ernest. *Baba Yaga*. Illus. by Blair Lent. Boston: Houghton Mifflin Co., 1966.

Smith, Doris, illus. *The Tortoise and the Hare*. New York: Alfred A. Knopf, Inc., 1979.

Spier, Peter. *Noah's Ark*. Illus. by author. New York: Doubleday & Co., Inc., 1977.

Stensland, Lee. *Literature by and about the American Indian*. Urbana, Ill.: National Council of Teachers of English, 1979.

Stern, Simon. *The Hobyahs*. Englewood Cliffs, N.J.: Prentice-Hall, Inc., 1977.

Stevens, Byrna. *Borrowed Feathers and Other Fables*. Illus. by Freire Wright and Michael Foreman. New York: Random House, Inc., 1977.

Still, James. *Jack and the Wonder Beans*. Illus. by Margot Tomes. New York: G. P. Putnam's Sons, 1977.

Stobbs, William. *Jack and the Beanstalk*. New York: Delacorte Press, 1969.

Sutherland, Zena, et al. *The Arbuthnot Anthology of Children's Literature*. 4th ed. Glenview, Ill.: Scott, Foresman and Company, 1976.

Sutton-Smith, Brian, et al. *The Folkstories of Children*. Philadelphia: University of Pennsylvania Press, 1981.

Taylor, Edgar, trans. *King Grisly Beard*. Illus. by Maurice Sendak. New York: Farrar, Straus & Giroux, Inc., 1973.

Tolstoy, Lev. *The Three Bears*. Drawings by Yuri Vasnetsov. Trans. by Ivy Litvinov. Moscow: Progress Publishers, 1979.

Towle, Faith M. *The Magic Cooking Pot*. Illus. by author. Boston: Houghton Mifflin Co., 1975.

Travers, P. L. *Two Pairs of Shoes*. Illus. by Leo Dillon and Diane Dillon. New York: Viking Press, 1980.

Tudor, Tasha. *First Prayers*. Illus. by author. New York: Henry Z. Walck, Inc., 1952.

Turner, Philip. *Brian Wildsmith's Bible Stories*. Illus. by Brian Wildsmith. New York: Franklin Watts, Inc., 1969.

Untermeyer, Louis, sel. *Aesop's Fables*. Illus. by Alice Provensen and Martin Provensen. New York: Golden Press, 1965.

Wahl, Jan. *Runaway Jonah and Other Tales*. Illus. by Uri Schulevitz. New York: Macmillan Publishing Co., Inc., 1968.

Weil, Lisl, ret. *The Foolish King*. Illus. by author. New York: Macmillan Publishing Co., 1982.

Wolkstein, Diane. *The Cool Ride in the Sky*. Illus. by Paul Galdone. New York: Alfred A. Knopf, Inc., 1973.

Yershov, P. *Little Humpbacked Horse*. Retold by Margaret Hodges. Illus. by Chris Conover. New York: Farrar, Straus & Giroux, 1980.

Young, Ed. *The Lion and the Mouse*. New York: Doubleday & Co., Inc., 1980.

Zemach, Harve. *Duffy and the Devil*. Illus. by Margot Zemach. New York: Farrar, Straus & Giroux, Inc., 1973.

Zemach, Margot. *It Could Always Be Worse*. Illus. by author. New York: Farrar, Straus & Giroux, 1976.

———. *Jake and Honeybunch Go to Heaven*. Illus. by author. New York: Farrar, Straus & Giroux, 1982.

———. *The Little Red Hen: An Old Story*. Illus. by author. New York: Farrar, Straus & Giroux, 1983.

———. *The Three Sillies*. New York: Holt, Rinehart and Winston, Inc., 1963.

♥

The Heart of Literature: Present

RICH ENCOUNTERS

"Just like my mom! I asked her if I could have a frog and she said 'No!'," George lamented as he sat shaking his head. In sympathy with experiences so like his in Steven Kellogg's Can I Keep Him?, *George just kept repeating,* "Just like my mom!"

◆◆◆

"Why do I have to wait until Saturday to see my daddy, Mr. Chalmers? Some other kids see their daddies every day."

"I'm not sure Joe, but of course when you see your daddy on Saturdays you have to make very special use of your time together, don't you? There's a story on our reading table about a boy who missed his father very much too." Mr. Chalmers handed Lexau's Me Day *to Mrs. Smith, his aide.* "Mrs. Smith, will you share this with Danny? I think he'll understand and appreciate it."

◆◆◆

"Me too!" declared Robin. "Why couldn't I be an only kid like you, Jack?" Robin questioned, imitating the title of Barbara Hazen's Why Couldn't I Be an Only Kid Like You, Wigger? *Tired of sharing and even more tired of being reminded to share, Robin understands the plight of children who suffer siblings.*

◆◆◆

"We just danced to 'Skip to My Lou' and you all looked as though you were having fun. Boys and girls like to dance, don't they?" asked Miss Shane. Second graders, still smiling from the music and exertion, clapped and nodded in vigorous affirmation. "Well, let me read you the story of Oliver who had some problems because he wanted to dance." The class was then invited into Tomie de Paola's delightful story of Oliver Button Is a Sissy. At the conclusion of the story, John piped up with, "It would be better if Oliver played baseball," and a very heated discussion began.

Realistic Literature, Modern Fantasy, and the Young Child

Realistic literature confronts squarely the problems of everyday existence—problems that are embedded firmly in direct and vicarious experiences. *Fantasy literature* provides other worlds one can inhabit for a time while personal problems are held in abeyance. Here the opportunity to "live away" affords young children time to kindle their imaginations, integrate their emotions, and allow their problems to take on a different perspective.

These problems are bipolar for young children. Many of them spiral around each child's own development. These have to do with the young child's growth toward independence: easing into more and larger social groups; understanding the role he or she plays in family and peer groups; learning self-control and self-discipline; sharpening motor, linguistic, and cognitive skills; and absorbing and seeking more and more information. In facing these problems, the young child's "copability quotient" is raised and lowered by the way he or she responds to stimulation, situations, and choices.

At the other end of the spectrum are problems related to the impact society and culture have on the child. In coping with these problems, the young child's choice may be limited by competition and conflict, which are soon apparent. These molders of personality—choice, competition, and conflict—inhabit nursery and primary classrooms as much as they do the world at large. The young child deals with these more emotionally than intellectually, and in such emotional reactions develops his or her personality.

"As far as we now understand, personality is grounded in the emotional history of an individual."[1] Realistic fiction and modern fantasy can play an important part in that history of each child because of the *sharp* reactions they generate and the way stations they provide for imagining and coping. The impact on the reader is strong: the emotional response is likely to be quick and keen.

For young children, realistic tales and modern fantasy span a vast array of plots about protagonists who experience simple constraints (Byars's *Go and Hush the Baby*) to protagonists who must cope with emotions like jealousy (Alexander's *Nobody Asked Me If I Wanted a Baby Sister*), events like death (Cohen's *Jim's Dog Muffins*), and needs like love and support (Moeri's *Star Mother's Youngest Child* and Potter's *The Tailor of Gloucester*).

Rare is the problem not treated in children's literature. Economic constraints and their effects, for example, are treated in Hazen's *Tight Times*, while child disappearance and inferred abuse are the themes of Goldner and Vogel's *The Dangers of Strangers*. Today, realistic books speak of a myriad of pollutions and the quickened deterioration of human relationships as seen in divorce, separation, war, and personal and social violence. No shield exists that can spare young children confrontation with such reality. Indeed, characteristic of the times is an ever-diminishing attempt to do so.

According to Russell Hoban, who created among other books the delightfully apt tales of Frances, the charming young badger, "...today's children do not live in an expurgated world. With their elders they must endure sudden deaths and slow ones, bombs and fire falling from the sky, the poisoning of peaceful air and the threatened extinction of this green jewel of Earth. They must endure the reality of mortal man."[2] Robert Cole adds, "To be sure, stories, heard or read, and told and told again, often help children to resolve in their minds worries or fears or anxieties—to come closer to a difficulty through a story of which that difficulty is the subject matter."[3]

The role of fantasy in the life of the young child has been investigated by Bruno Bettleheim, Jerome and Dorothy Singer, and Eric Klinger, among others. All agree that fantasy helps the child toward an emotional integration. It is not only a way to project and handle the child's more violent feelings but it legitimates wonder and spurs divergent thinking.

Bibliotherapy is likely to be more effective with these genres than with others. Because the young child whose world is very much self-centered can easily see himself or herself as the protagonist in realistic fiction and modern fantasy, the way is opened for whatever modification of attitudes or behaviors books can effect. These are the books that are much handled, read, discussed, and even quoted. "Realistic fiction and nonfiction are at the foundation of bibliotherapy."[4] The impact of these books is great; their selection should be especially choice. General and basic literary criteria (see Chapter 2) and accuracy must also be considered when selecting these tales. In addition, sensitive topics call for an awareness of not only the child's maturity but the values and attitudes of family and community.

Criteria ♥

In his "A Letter from a Critic," Robert Moore says, "Those who select children's books should consider more than literary merit. What will be the impact of the book on a child's self-image, personality, and image of others? Will it contribute to liberating or restricting a child's imagination and striving? Will it enhance or inhibit a child's ability to relate humanely with other human beings? Will it encourage the development of human or anti-human values in the next generation?"[5]

A fact that makes evaluative criteria *sorely* needed here and excellence in these genres particularly important is that some balance must be provided for today's young child, who looks at this unexpurgated world for hours through a television screen that flashes scenes in a highly vivid, explicit, rapidly paced form. Such rapid-fire stimulation cannot be processed fully by the young child. "...When subjected to very rapid presentations of novel material piled on top of novel material, the child lacks the time to replay this material mentally in the 'echo box' of the short-term memory system and thus transfers it to the longer-term memory system, where it can later be retrieved."[6]

Among other results of this lack of time, according to the Singers, is a kind of "mindless watching"—an uncritical look and a less imaginative play which may mean more aggressive behavior. Still another result is a kind of configuration residue; that is, for instance, the child remembers that an aggressive act was performed but recalls nothing of the intentions of the characters.[7]

Realistic fiction and modern fantasy can play a potent role in balancing if not counteracting some of the negative effects of television. The process is self-pacing: tales are rich in imagining potential, and effect a *mind-full* rather than *mindless* engagement.

In selecting literature in these genres, the *criteria* identified in Chapter 2 apply. In addition, the following questions need to be addressed in examining these titles:

- Is the story of reality presented without sensationalism?
- Is the "reality" or "fantasy" appropriate to the developmental stage of the listener/reader?
- Is the tale believable? (Even in fantasy, is the tale consistent with the viewpoint adopted, the characters depicted, and the fantasy world created?)
- Is the characterization free of stereotypes?

In many stories for young children, events, no matter how painful, are presented clearly, honestly, without euphemisms, and with sensitivity to the developmental age of the young child. Grandpa has died in Zolotow's *My Grandson Lew,* Barney dies in Viorst's *The Tenth Good Thing About Barney,* as does Nana in de Paola's *Nana Upstairs and Nana Downstairs.* Grandpa had a stroke in *Now One Foot Now the Other* (Tomie de Paola) and is quite ill for a very long time. George in *George the Babysitter* (Shirley Hughes) is not a mother substitute. Mother cannot give up smoking in Tobias's *The Quitting Deal,* nor can the daughter give up thumbsucking. Evan has no place to call his own at the beginning of Hill's *Evan's Corner;* Peter is being usurped in Keats's *Peter's Chair;* and *Amifika* (Lucille Clifton) and *Stevie* (John Steptoe) feel rejected. In these books there is no attempt to hide death, illness, fear, jealousy, or human frailties. There is also no attempt to exaggerate reality. Indeed, it is the reasonableness of the reality that tugs the heart and grips the emotions. The realities are clear, the problems are plausible, and the method of coping is understandable and organic to the tale.

Fantasy must have an internal consistency and be credible. "A successful story, no matter how soaring the fantasy or how offbeat the science, must be believable."[8] In *Charlotte's Web*, a classic fantasy for the older child in this age group, E. B. White violates nothing of what is known about human or animal behavior. This multilevel tale is honest throughout in its farm setting, characterization, and realistic plot.

In selecting these books for young children, it is especially important that the story sharer know something of the background experience and general maturity of young children. A child who is ready for the story of a dead bird may not be able to cope at all with the death of a fictional child. A young child who may understand something of the problems of aging because he or she has met that charming turtle *Edgemont* (Marjorie Sharmat) is not necessarily ready for the nuances of Farber's *How Does It Feel to Be Old?* A young child can understand and "live" *Where the Wild Things Are* (Maurice Sendak) but is unlikely to appreciate fully Sendak's much more complex fantasy *Outside Over There.*

Characters who are stereotypes create prejudice in young children at a time when children are most vulnerable to the formation of stereotypes, and can straitjacket children's understandings and appreciations of the rich variability and humanness in all persons. For example, until recently grandparents were highly stereotyped in literature. Today, in books like Farber's *How Does It Feel to be Old?* and Eisenberg's *A Mitzvah Is Something Special*, grandmothers are presented with the variability characteristic of any group of human beings.[9]

Numerous books exist today in which young children see both sexes working and playing at a wide variety of occupations and hobbies. In Ernst's *Sam Johnson and the Blue Ribbon Quilt*, for example, Sam proves that he and his friends can produce quilts as fine as any quilts their wives can make. In *Benjamin and Tulip* (Rosemary Wells), Benjamin proves that boys can be gentle and considerate; Tulip shows that girls can be very aggressive.

Work to balance the literature available to children so that sexual stereotypes lessen is continuously being pursued. Searches have been made for strong female heroines, and books like Lurie's *Clever Gretchen and Other Forgotten Folktales* and Phelps's *Tatterhood and Other Tales* resulted. Today, children can read about Clever Gretchens and Clever Jacks; a *Train for Jane* (Norma Klein) and *William's Doll* (Charlotte Zolotow).

Tools of Authors and Illustrators ♥

Creators of realistic and fantasy literature for young children are likely to:

- Use illustration as much as narrative.
- Employ animal protagonists more often than human ones.
- Balance their realities, even the most tragic ones, with some humor and gentle joy.

Use of Illustration

The great use of illustration is no doubt a response to the need of pre-readers. Still, the creators employ a variety of design and artistic strategies for distinguishing and for merging the real world and the fantasy world.

Sometimes the major difference between the real and the fanciful world is shown by color or its absence. The real world is dull and bleak in Keeping's *Willie's Fire Engine* and Shulevitz's *One Monday Morning*, and the fantasy world is cast in bright colors. It is size that is a factor in *Where The Wild Things Are* by Maurice Sendak. As Max gives vent to his imagination and as his fantasy grows, pictures become larger. In Seuss's *To Think That I Saw It On Mulberry Street*, pages become busier and more cluttered as the fantasy continues.

Employment of Animal Protagonists

The tendency of the young child to animate toys and animals is reflected in innumerable stories.

Collectively, these animals face the constraints of life: the pangs of growing up (Minarik's *Little Bear*); the pain of being different (Leaf's *Ferdinand* and Lionni's *Frederick*); the penalties of disobedience (Potter's *Peter Rabbit* and Gantos's *Rotten Ralph*); the trauma of leaving home (the three little pigs and Molly in Pearson's *Molly Moves Out*); the disorientation of a totally new situation (William Steig's Amos, Boris, and Sylvester); the joys and annoyances of friendship (Lobel's Frog and Toad, Vincent's Ernest and Celestine, and Marshall's George and Martha); even the facing of death (Charlotte in E. B. White's *Charlotte's Web*).

The inconsistencies, interdependencies, and frailties of all of us are represented. In the process, an egotistical level versus a social level of living is easily discernible: self-centeredness is contrasted with the selflessness friendship requires. Young children struggling to understand why they must share and consider the thoughts and feelings of others commiserate with the tribulations of these book friends.

Humor in Reality

In literature for young children, reality is balanced with humor or joy; tragedy is rarely left to dominate.

In *The Quarreling Book*, by Charlotte Zolotow, the pictures by Arnold Lobel give humor to the tale, and a day that begins unhappily ends well.

In Amy Schwartz's *Bea and Mr. Jones*, weary of their respective roles, father and daughter change places. Bea becomes an advertising executive and father becomes a kindergartener—a humorous solution to the tedium of the daily schedule.

The annoyance of being told to take care of a younger child is aptly coped with in *Go and Hush the Baby* by Betsy Byars. In this case, the clever older brother wants to play baseball, so he sings, feeds, performs magic, and engineers a race to "hush" the baby.

Humor permeates Ellen Raskin's *Spectacles* and Marc Brown's *Arthur's Eyes,* yet having to wear glasses is generally viewed as anything but funny by young children.

Grandpa's deafness is sad and unfortunate, but in *I Dance in My Red Pajamas* by Edith Hurd, granddaughter understands grandpa's plight, has fun, and is even praised by her grandfather for the *noisy,* happy day they had together.

The Needs of Young Children and Book Clusters

The quantity, diversity, and richness of the genres of modern fantasy and realistic fiction have been noted. There are many titles on almost every subject awaiting young children's eyes, hands, and hearts. Some of these book clusters follow, categorized according to the emotional or social needs of young children.

Need to be Safe, Protected, and Loved

The feeling that someone will take care of them—that they are safe and protected—is crucial to young children. This feeling is fed via many genres. In folktales like Paul Galdone's *The Three Billy Goats Gruff,* the biggest billy goat will surely contest and conquer the wicked troll, and in Gerald McDermott's *Arrow to the Sun,* the father will oversee the safety and success of his son. In countless realistic stories, young children are assured that harm will not come their way, the goblins won't get them, and even nightmares "in the closet" may be coped with—indeed may be friendly and lovable.

Family Stories   It is within the family that the safety and protection from which independence grows are first offered to young children. Stories of close family ties abound.

The strong interdependence that exists among family members if family happiness is to be preserved is clearly depicted in Charlotte Zolotow's *The Quarreling Book* and, despite economic problems, in Vera Williams's *A Chair for My Mother, Something Special for Me,* and *Music, Music for Everyone.* In stories such as these, young children easily see themselves between the covers of the book. They see in print and picture their daily routines and the love given and taken by each family member.

"Series" books, such as Beverly Cleary's Ramona stories (for older children) and books about Little Bear, Frances, and Obadiah (for younger children), bespeak the understanding needed by each member if families are to function for the happiness of all.

Literally hundreds of single books exist about affectionate human and animal families, such as *Black Is Brown Is Tan* (Arnold Adoff), *Evan's Corner* (Elizabeth Hill), *Amifika* (Lucille Clifton), *Peter's Chair* (Ezra Keats), *The Quitting Deal* (Tobi Tobias), *First Pink Light* (Eloise Greenfield), *Begin at the Beginning* (Amy Schwartz), *Owliver* (Robert Kraus), and *Sylvester and the Magic Pebble* (William Steig). No matter what problem is in these tales, its resolution is accomplished in a climate of strong, solid family love.

Some of these tales are marked by straightforward actions and dialogue, as in *The Quitting Deal.* Here, mother and daughter try to support each other in breaking a habit. Mother promises to stop smoking and daughter promises to stop sucking her thumb. They try all kinds of reward systems, and eventually they decide on a less rigorous detachment in an effort to "sneak up on quitting." Discussion on habits we would like to break and how we might do it naturally stem from the sharing of this book.

In keeping with the changed family structure in so many homes, there is an increasing number of stories of single-parent families, such as Charlotte Zolotow's *A Father Like That,* Gloria Skurzynski's *Martin by Himself,* and, for the slightly older child, Joan Lexau's *Striped Ice Cream.* In such books, the single parent is warm, loving, patient, understanding, and aware of the young child's problems of adjustment. In *Everett Anderson's 1, 2, 3* (Lucille Clifton), Everett deals with the problem of trying to love another father; in Judith Vigna's *She's Not My Real Mother,* Miles tries to love his new stepmother; and Ron boasts about a father he wants so much that he imagines him in *My Dad Is Really Something,* by Lois Osborn.

The loneliness a child feels when parents are separated and the child sees one parent infrequently is expressed well in Jeannette Caines's *Daddy* and in Joan Lexau's *Me Day*.

Sensitively expressed, too, are the fears that arise when the acts and words of love are even momentarily withdrawn or unstated, as in *My Mother Didn't Kiss Me Good-Night* (Charlotte Herman), *You Make the Angels Cry* (Denys Cazet), and *Say It!* (Charlotte Zolotow). In the first story, mother had a cold; in the second, the reason the cookie jar broke is explained and mother assures Albert that indeed he "makes the sun shine," and in the last, mother realizes her daughter needs to *hear* words of love. Books like these open the doors to discussion on how we let people know we love them and why we should do that often.

At times, it is natural that the hunger for love and approval will conflict with the drive toward independence. In books like Steptoe's *Daddy Is a Monster...Sometimes* and Alexander's *And My Mean Old Mother Will Be Sorry, Blackboard Bear*, children vent their annoyance at parental constraint by chatting out their problems with real and imaginary friends. From such books, young children learn that being annoyed with prohibitions is not unique and that talking to friends may help.

Stories about Grandparents　There are numerous stories today of grandparents who in a very special way provide young children with the stable love they need. In the process, young children grow to understand something of the aging process, and the problems and special joys it brings. Not the least of the joys is that sometimes grandparents have time to play (Borack's *Grandpa*), to talk and listen and read (Adler's *A Little at a Time*, Alexander's *The Story Grandmother Told Me*), to laugh (Hurd's *I Dance in My Red Pajamas*), or even to share a walk with you (Hest's *The Crack-of-Dawn Walkers*). Helen Buckley's *Grandfather and I* and *Grandmother and I* and Kathryn Lasky's *My Island Grandma* beautifully celebrate the happy experiences of young children and their grandparents savoring life together.

In Ron Brooks's *Timothy and Gramps*, Gramps appears at Timothy's school to share a story, and in Tomie de Paola's *Watch Out for the Chicken Feet in Your Soup*, much to Joey's surprise, his old-fashioned grandmother engages the affection of his own friend, Eugene.

Some of the problems that can accompany aging are realistically presented and coped with in stories such as Patricia MacLachlan's *Through Grandpa's Eyes*, Tomie de Paola's *Now One Foot, Now the Other*, and Edith Hurd's *I Dance in My Red Pajamas*.

The first tale shares how blind grandfather teaches his grandson a new "way of seeing": Grandpa lets his fingers and his ears see. In the de Paola book, the need for love and support by both grandfather, who has apparently suffered a severe stroke, and Bobby, his grandson, is recounted. In *I Dance in My Red Pajamas*, the most lighthearted of the three books, Grandpa, who is somewhat deaf, and Jenny have fun dancing and stomping together to Grandma's music. Joy and merriment radiate from Emily McCully's illustrations.

Sometimes grandparents are depicted as the only people who understand the young child's problem (or the problems the young child is creating). William wants a doll; only his grandmother understands and gives it to him in Zolotow's *William's Doll*. Jeremy doesn't want to take a bath; grandmother gently outwits him in Yolen's *No Bath Tonight*. In Howard Knotts's *Great Grandfather, the Baby and Me*, another generation is spanned; it is great grandfather who helps his great grandson cope with the arrival of a new sister, and in James Stevenson's Grandpa stories (*Worse than Willie* and others) it is grandpa, wise, jolly, and creative, who resolves problems with much humor.

Need to Conquer Fear; Need to Be Successful

Allied to the need for love is the fear of its diminution or disappearance. A well-known stimulus to such fear is the birth of a sibling. An abundance of books treat the ways young children cope with this event, and the special patience and understanding needed by adults to still such fear and ease the pain of sharing. Many of these tales are realistically presented, balanced, and humorous.

Stories about Siblings Books range from laments at the introduction of a sibling into the household as in Hutchins's *The Very Worst Monster*, Alexander's *Nobody Asked Me If I Wanted a Baby Sister*, and Zolotow's *If It Weren't For You* to joyous plans for doing things together as in Zolotow's *Do You Know What I'll Do?* For the very young child two of Martha Alexander's books, *When the New Baby Comes, I'm Moving Out* and *Nobody Asked Me If I Wanted a Baby Sister*, mirror especially well the fears attendant upon the coming of a sibling. In such books a young child's feelings before and after a new baby arrives are treated with realism and humor. One or two sentences to a page, these books and Alexander's *I'll Be the Horse If You'll Play with Me*, wherein young Bonnie struggles against being imposed upon by an older sibling, are simply illustrated and reflective of the feelings and actions of the young child. In many of these tales, humor is introduced when the younger child solves his problems by imposing, in turn, upon the newest/youngest member of the family, as in *You'll Soon Grow Into Them, Titch* (Pat Hutchins) wherein it is Titch's turn to "hand down" *his* clothes.

Sibling tensions are apparent in Frances's relationship with Gloria (*A Baby Sister for Frances* by Russell Hoban), in *Rachel and Obadiah* by Brinton Turkle, in *I'll Fix Anthony* by Judith Viorst, in *Much Bigger than Martin* by Steven Kellogg, in *Marty McGee's Space Lab, No Girls Allowed* by Martha Alexander, in *Keep Running Allen* by Clyde Bulla, in *It's Not My Fault* by Franz Brandenberg, in *Stanley and Rhoda* by Rosemary Wells, in *I Hate My Brother Harry* by Crescent Dragonwagon, and in *My Brother Never Feeds the Cat* by Reynold Ruffins.

In many of these tales it is not only fear of loss of parental love that creates anxiety but it is the impatience of the older child for instant independence. In Clyde Bulla's *Keep Running Allen,* the opposite is true. Allen keeps seeking companionship, and his older siblings, at least at first, wish to be independent of him.

Sometimes sibling problems lead to wishes like *Why Couldn't I Be an Only Kid Like You, Wigger?* (Barbara Hazen) wherein it's apparent that sibling frustrations have reached the saturation point. At times, such frustrations are imaginatively solved, as in Kellogg's *Much Bigger than Martin* and Wells's *A Lion for Lewis.*

Sometimes the tale is of sibling love rather than sibling tension. Stories of gentle but sincere affection are Pomerantz's *The Half-Birthday Party* and McPhail's *Sisters.*

In John Steptoe's *Stevie,* the love to be shared is not that of siblings; rather, Robert is jealous of the love and attention lavished on Stevie whom Robert's mother cares for while Stevie's mother works. The struggle against jealousy is especially poignant here.

Time heals but it doesn't lessen initial pain when special friends move away, as *Janey* relates in the work by Charlotte Zolotow and Robert finds out in Aliki's *We Are Best Friends.*

"Firsts" The lives of young children are full of "firsts," and anxieties inevitably accompany these experiences. The first days at school, the first hospital or doctor's visit, the new home, a new parent, a new friend—all raise concern. Many books deal with these initial experiences. Sharing them offers young children coping mechanisms and food for thought. Sometimes factual presentations such as the books of the Rockwells—*My Doctor, My Dentist, My Nursery School*— alleviate fear by their very straightforward simple narration and illustration. From them, children learn what to expect.

The *first* days in nursery school, kindergarten, or first grade have been chronicled in many books for young children. Miriam Cohen's series about Jim and his classmates (*When Will I Read?, First Grade Takes a Test, Will I Have a Friend?, Jim Meets the Thing, No Good in Art, Lost in the Museum,* and *So What?*), illustrated by Lillian Hoban, speaks squarely to first schooling experiences, questions, and concerns. In Cohen's *See You Tomorrow, Charles,* the first-grade class meets Charles, a blind boy, and learns as much from him—if not more—than he learns from them.

In *Jim Meets the Thing*, Jim, who is embarrassed because he is fearful of television monsters, observes classmate Danny who is fearless of monsters but who takes fright when he finds a praying mantis on his shoulder. Jim courageously removes the insect. Later, when the children can discuss their own personal fears, relief sweeps the group as they all realize that no one is exempt from some fear or anxiety. Jim and Danny's fears form a solid base for classroom talk about fears and how to cope with them. Not only does Miriam Cohen have unusual insight in identifying the hopes and fears of children and in accurately describing them, but she also weaves into her story reasonable resolutions and coping mechanisms.

In Jones's *The Biggest, Meanest, Ugliest Dog in the Whole Wide World*, fear of the dog next door is conquered by playing ball with him.

In her many books for younger children, Rosemary Wells treats their problems with insight. In *Timothy Goes to School*, Timothy's tensions grow because classmate Claude is perfect. Solution? Find a more fallible friend—Timothy does. He discovers Violet, who is having difficulty bearing with the perfection of Grace.

In Andersen's *What's the Matter, Sylvie, Can't You Ride?* not only is Sylvie suffering self-depreciation because she cannot ride a bicycle, but her friends keep asking, "What's the matter, Sylvie, can't you ride?"

Alfie, in *Alfie's Feet* (Shirley Hughes) learns to match foot with boot; the *Carrot Seed* (Ruth Kraus) finally does grow; Willie eventually whistles in *Whistle for Willie* (Ezra Keats); Sam finally and safely reaches David's house in *Try It Again, Sam* (Judith Viorst), and the bacon is finally brought home in *Don't Forget the Bacon!* (Pat Hutchins). Young children learn from these tales that patience and perseverance are rewarded.

The great mobility of society forces children to cope with new locations. In *Gila Monsters Meet You at the Airport*, Marjorie Weinman Sharmat addresses the preconceptions that a young boy holds about the West, where he will soon move. In any classroom this prompts all kinds of stories about "when we moved...."

Nighttime Stories Nighttime brings with it special fears and a delightful, if annoying, array of creative efforts to stave off bedtime. *Clyde Monster* (Robert Crowe), who is afraid of the dark *and* humans, has patient, comforting parents to help him, but in *There's a Nightmare In My Closet*, Mercer Mayer's hero determines to rid himself of the nightmare in his closet by confronting it himself.

In *Simon's Book*, authored by Hendrik Drescher, Simon *creates* his own monster on paper and carries it into his dream.

Probably the classic story encompassing the varied reasons

young children summon to delay going to bed is Hoban's *Bedtime for Frances.* Each of Frances's ploys is met with patient understanding until father is goaded into being very firm. Illustrations here are choice.

Bedtime books that help the young child appreciate that he or she is one with nature in resting at night are such books as Margaret Wise Brown's *A Child's Good Night Book,* the earlier *Good Night Moon,* and Eve Rice's *Goodnight, Goodnight.* In the first two books, animals and/or children quietly prepare to sleep; in the last, night sweeps over a town. The two-page spreads in gray and black and the text record the ways people in their homes and shopkeepers in their stores get ready for nightfall.

Stories about Death Death is frightening and mysterious to youngsters. It is a great tribute to a number of authors and illustrators of children's books that death has been made less frightening and mysterious because it is treated more honestly. This is so in such books as Clifton's *Everett Anderson's Goodbye,* Brown's *The Dead Bird,* Viorst's *The Tenth Good Thing About Barney,* Zolotow's *My Grandson Lew,* de Paola's *Nana Upstairs and Nana Downstairs* for younger children, and Smith's *A Taste of Blackberries* and Miles's *Annie and the Old One* for older children.

Oftentimes a child's initial contact with death is the death of a pet. In Margaret Wise Brown's *The Dead Bird* (a picture book), Judith Viorst's *The Tenth Good Thing About Barney,* and Carol Carrick's *The Accident* children deal with the deaths of animals—the first, a stray dead bird; the second, a pet cat, and the third, a pet dog.

In *My Grandson Lew, Nana Upstairs and Nana Downstairs,* and *Annie and the Old One,* young children cope with the deaths of grandparents.

Simply but honestly illustrated and narrated, these tales and others, such as *Now One Foot, Now the Other* (Tomie de Paola) in which the devastating effects of a stroke are clear, offer young children an opportunity to experience vicariously pain and separation. They provide a vital early *distancing* from the actuality and so plant the seeds of understanding and compassion. They also pave the way for fruitful discussions of events that affect young lives.

Stories about Everyday Frustrations Along with the graver human problems, young children, in their hungry reach for independence and success, have to cope with those everyday nuisances that beset all of us. They have no trouble relating to Alexander who suffered his Terrible, Horrible, No Good, Very Bad Day (Judith Viorst) with a kind of rebellious stoicism. Alexander contemplated moving to Australia but ended up remembering that his mom said you can find days "like this" even in Australia.

Need to Love Others as Well as Ourselves

Stories of Friendship and Giving   It is often through the tales of animal twosomes in literature—Frog and Toad, George and Martha, Ernest and Celestine, Amos and Boris—that young children learn something of the give and take of friendship.

In the surge of literature about older people and people with special needs, children learn that friendship has no age barriers (Thomas's *Hi, Mrs. Mallory!* Clifton's *My Friend Jacob*, and Rylant's *Miss Maggie*), and no handicap limits (Cohen's *See You Tomorrow, Charlie* and Rosenberg's *My Friend Leslie*), and no cultural or racial boundaries (Getz's *Tar Beach*).

The yearning young children feel in wanting to *give* help and love and gifts is exemplified in the simple, repetitive, gentle story by Marjorie Flack, *Ask Mr. Bear*, an all-time favorite, and in Charlotte Zolotow's *Mr. Rabbit and the Lovely Present.* In both books the quest is a present for mother and in each a perfect gift is found with the help of an understanding animal.

In *Happy Mother's Day* by Steve Kroll, no one needs advice about a gift for mother. What mother clearly needs is help around the house—and she gets it.

In Frank Asch's fantasy, *Happy Birthday, Moon*, it is a gentle understanding animal who himself finds the gift he very much wants to give to the moon—a top hat.

A happy, tender story of children's giving to each other is Charlotte Zolotow's *The White Marble.* Another warm, inspiring story is *Miss Rumphius* (Barbara Cooney) in which a child is challenged to give something to the world to make it more beautiful.

Young children want to help. This is partially because they want to be near those they love but also because they themselves must be doing and testing. In Lasker's *The Do-Something Day*, Bernie's help is *finally* accepted, and in Herold's *The Helping Day* David settles for helping the ants, worms, and butterflies until father suggests that David help him buy ice cream cones.

In Evaline Ness's *Yeck Eck*, Tana, a little girl who has love to give and wants a baby more than anything else in the world, thinks she has finally found a baby when her friend offers one of his brothers or sisters to her *free.* She decides on the one who comes to her and says, "Yeck eck," which Tana is sure means "Take me."

In books like Carle's *Do You Want to Be My Friend?* Cohen's *Will I Have a Friend?* Kellogg's *Won't Somebody Play with Me?* and Ets's *Play With Me*, the need to be loved seems uppermost but the need to give love is also focal.

Sometimes children balk at the demands of love, yet offer it nonetheless. In Skorpen's *Bird*, a young boy finds a baby bird that needs nurturing. He mumbles and grumbles while he cares for it, yet he obviously loves it. In Turkle's *Thy Friend, Obadiah*, Obadiah is clearly annoyed at first by the seagull that befriends him, but when it flies off, he misses it and keeps looking for its return.

A book of marvelously clear photographs, *The Shadow Book* (de Regniers) exemplifies the kind of imaginative play between friends that flexes both muscles and imagination.

Children's relationships run the usual cycle of friendships— whole, broken, and mended. Such relationships are depicted humorously and realistically in books such as *Let's Be Enemies* by Janice May Udry, *Meet M and M* by Pat Ross, and *Rosie and Michael* by Judith Viorst. In the first book, the friendship between James and John is broken, then mended as, in the final picture, they skate off on *one* pair of skates, each waving his half of a pretzel. In the latter two books, close friendships suffer setbacks but are strong enough to survive.

A friendship that should not and does not continue is the theme of Snyder's *Come On Patsy*. In the name of companionship, Patsy takes orders, abuse, and all kinds of dictation, but she finally realizes that this friendship is not worth keeping.

Stories of Loving Ourselves—Realistic Self-Concept Sometimes in comparing themselves with others, young children will believe themselves to be quite deficient in looks or skills, and so will settle for being anybody else. At these times, especially, they appreciate tales like *Donkey-Donkey* by Roger Duvoisin, *Humphrey, the Dancing Pig* by Arthur Getz, and *You Look Ridiculous Said the Rhinoceros to the Hippopotamus* by Bernard Waber.

Donkey-Donkey hates his ears until a little girl praises them. Humphrey wants to be unpig-like, slim, and trim, but the maintenance of a streamlined self is too exhausting. In the third book, a hippopotamus who wishes to look unlike herself finally admits her natural self is best.

Young children need the reassurance that it is acceptable—even admirable—to be themselves. They continuously battle anxieties about being different. Alexander's *Sabrina* is bothered by her different name; so is Alison in Waber's *But Names Will Never Hurt Me*. Benjie fights shyness (*Benjie* by Joan Lexau); so does Anne in Krasilovsky's *The Shy Little Girl*. *Crow Boy* (Yashima) seems to have no talents; *The Ugly Duckling* (Andersen), no beauty. Iris Fogel must wear glasses (Raskin's *Spectacles*), Tom must cope with his own mental retardation (Larsen's *Don't Forget Tom*), Janet deals with spina bifida (White's *Janet at School*), and Allen copes with not being able to run as fast as his siblings (Bulla's *Keep Running, Allen*). In a humorous tale, *Otto Is Different* by Franz Brandenberg, Otto Octopus discovers that although his eight arms make him different, they *do* have their uses.

There are also the tales of children or animals who staunchly hold on to their selfhood. Lionni's *Frederick* diligently stores words for winter as his friends store food, and Lionni's *Cornelius*, the crocodile, unlike his friends, walks *upright*, and Ferdinand *will* smell the flowers in *The Story of Ferdinand* by Munro Leaf.

Owliver (Kraus), while ostensibly preparing for the career his parents have selected for him, quietly and emphatically chooses his own. Bemelmans's *Madeline* is very much her own person, as is Babbitt's Phoebe *(Phoebe's Revolt)*, Ambrus's *Mishka*, and Avi's Emily in *Emily Upham's Revenge* (for older children). These characters—animals and children who are staunch, straight, square and persevering—have faith in themselves.

At times, to continue faith in oneself, one must be by oneself. "We need to respect the different social needs and styles of different children, including the real need that many children have for privacy and solitude."[10] To achieve such faith in oneself it is sometimes necessary to move. Molly does this in *Molly Moves Out* (Pearson), as Jenny does in *Higglety Pigglety Pop!* (Sendak). *In My Treehouse* (Schertle) also expresses joy in the quiet and privacy of a treehouse, and Katie in *Katie in the Morning* (Dragonwagon) savors every second of her solitary early morning walk.

Sometimes what one is, is less than desirable and children recognize in these stories the need for change. In Bottner's *Messy*, Harriet knows she needs to change and manages to do it. *Grumley the Grouch* (Sharmat) finds that he must become less crotchety, and *Cowardly Clyde* (Peet) is forced into bravery.

Stories like Clyde Bulla's *Daniel's Duck* celebrate the joy of having ridicule turned to praise. In his usual strong, clear, narrative, Bulla relates the tale of Daniel's woodcarving, a duck whose head looked backward. This was jeered at only to be later praised by a famed woodcarver who wanted to buy it. Young children need such tales to bolster their belief in their own ideas and efforts.

Need for Fantasy and Adventure

Fantasy literature for young children is prolific with (1) personified animals and toys, and (2) worlds of wish fulfillment.

Sometimes the animals or toys do little but listen. Indeed, as in the case of the Blackboard Bear stories, the bear is nothing more than an imaginary quiet friend who moves into the child's world at his command and listens sympathetically to his woes and ideas.

On the other hand, sometimes the tale is told from the viewpoint of the personified toy or animal. Here, adventures are controlled by the human hero or heroine, as in the cases of *Impunity Jane* (Godden) and *The Velveteen Rabbit* (Bianco), but the animal or toy thinks and feels and, depending upon the skill of the writer, is a highly plausible, believable creature. Often the animals are people, thinly disguised.

In Milne's *Winnie-the-Pooh*, the characterization of each toy animal is so unique and consistent that each lives in the young child's imagination as an individual friend, as do the animals in Grahame's *The Wind in the Willows* (for older children) and some of Kipling's characters in *Just So Stories* and *The Junglebook*.

Fantasies of worlds where wishes come true are a rich and varied lot, as in *Oh, What a Noise* (Schulevitz) where you can make all the noise you want. For young children full of yearnings and balking at restrictions, what is more natural than the creation of fanciful worlds where enemies are vanquished, adventures await, and the child reigns supreme?

Martin in Blos's *Martin's Hats* creates jolly and exciting worlds for himself as he dons various hats. *Where the Wild Things Are* (Sendak) is Max's heaven for establishing his own independence. In *Sam, Bangs and Moonshine* (Ness), Sam conjures up all kinds of adventures as she travels about in her dragon-drawn chariot (really, the transformed "ragged old rug on the doorstep.")

In *Willie's Fire Engine* (Keats), Willie's ideal world is peopled by yesterday's firemen and their horse-drawn engines; that is the world where his heroes are. Harold's purple crayon creates a garden rich in adventures (*Harold and the Purple Crayon* by Johnson) and in John Burningham's *Come Away from the Water, Shirley*, Shirley's fantasy world removes her from mother's many admonitions into a world of pirates, adventures, treasures, and conquests. The *Knight of the Golden Plain* (Hunter) records a young boy's fantasies of bravery and courage of dragon slaying and witch exiling.

In Sendak's *In the Night Kitchen*, hungry Mickey travels from the night kitchen or bakery up to the Milky Way in a plane of dough and then back to his bed.

In Briggs's *Snowman*, a boy takes off into the snowman's world for a glorious ride, and in *James and the Giant Peach* (Dahl), James enters another world as he crawls into the peach. In all of these fantasies, the heroes and heroines find their wishes fulfilled or transformed.

Some fantasy worlds in literature exist less as places where wishes come true than as new and different lands to inhabit for a while. In *Winnie-the-Pooh* (Milne), the nursery-turned-100-Aker-Wood and the farm and the barn in White's *Charlotte's Web* are places where animals talk and have adventures.

Other times the imaginative lands seem not so near and familiar. Few are the titles of science fiction for young children, but Louis Slobodkin's *The Space Ship Under the Apple Tree* and Eleanor Cameron's *The Wonderful Flight to the Mushroom Planet*, as well as some of the Matthew Looney tales by Jerome Beatty and the Danny Dunn stories by Jay Williams can intrigue the older children in this age group into investigating several strange but believable worlds. For slightly younger children, the adventures of that redoubtable, inquisitive, energetic Miss Pickerell (MacGregor's *Miss Pickerell Harvests the Sea*) are appealing.

Summary ♥

Realistic literature offers young children a storyland full of characters coping with problems they themselves must face and solve. Modern fantasy offers children a way station, at which to fuel their imaginations before returning to the tasks, frustrations, concerns, and problems that may trouble them. The role of fantasy and realistic fiction in the lives of young children has been documented as vital.

Realistic literature for young children must be devoid of sensationalism and stereotypes, appropriate to their holistic development, and believable. In presenting realistic books and fantasies to young children, authors and illustrators use illustration as much as narrative, employ animal protagonists more often than human ones, and balance their realities, even the most tragic ones, with some humor or gentle joy.

Numerous titles meet the needs of young children for safety, love, acceptance, success, and adventure.

DISCUSSION ACTIVITIES

• Share Joan Lexau's *I Should Have Stayed in Bed* and Judith Viorst's *Alexander and the Terrible, Horrible, No Good, Very Bad Day* and generate with several young children a discussion on how each child— Alexander and Sam—solves his problem *and* ask what else each might have done. Have children twist the theme and draw scenes of Alexander and His Perfectly Marvelous, Joyously Great, Very Good Day or Sam's I'm So Glad I Got Out of Bed Today.

• Identify a problem common to young children (having to share, needing to feel positive about themselves) and consult Selection Aids *A to Zoo: Subject Access to Children's Picture Books* and *The Bookfinder: A Guide to Children's Literature* (see Chapter 11) to assemble a bibliography of eight to twelve books dealing with the problem. Read and plan to use in your classroom.

• Share several fantasies with young children. Discuss these. Suggest that children build their own special "wish world." Discuss the people, animals, and places they might want in this special place, stressing that they think of places they cannot see on a map. Help the children express and describe this "wish world." Then, as Harold had, give them a purple crayon; ask them to show in crayon their very special world.

NOTES

1. David Bleich, *Readings and Feelings* (Urbana, Ill.: National Council of Teachers of English, 1975), p. 4.
2. Russell Hoban, "Thoughts on Being and Writing," in *The Thorny Paradise*, ed. Edward Blishen (New York: Penguin Books, 1975), p. 75.
3. Robert Coles, "Children's Stories: The Link to a Past," *Children's Literature*, Vol. 8 (New Haven: Yale University Press, 1980), p. 144.
4. Mary Renck Jalongo, "Bibliography: Literature to Promote Socioemotional Growth," *The Reading Teacher*, Vol. 36, No. 8 (April 1983): 800.
5. Robert B. Moore, "A Letter from a Critic," *Children's Literature*, Vol. 10 (New Haven: Yale University Press, 1982), p. 213.
6. Jerome L. Singer and Dorothy C. Singer, "Television and Reading in the Development of Imagination," *Children's Literature*, Vol. 9 (New Haven: Yale University Press, 1981), p. 128.
7. Ibid., pp. 127, 129, 131.
8. Madeleine L'Engle, "Childlike Wonder and the Truths of Science Fiction," *Children's Literature*, Vol. 10 (New Haven: Yale University Press, 1982), p. 106.
9. Nancy A. Mavrogenes, "Positive Images of Grandparents in Children's Picture Books," *The Reading Teacher*, Vol. 35, No. 8 (May 1982): 896–901.
10. Zick Rubin, *Children's Friendships* (Cambridge, Mass.: Harvard University Press, 1980), p. 11.

♥
PROFESSIONAL BIBLIOGRAPHY

Bleich, David. *Readings and Feelings.* Urbana, Ill.: National Council of Teachers of English, 1975.

Blount, Margaret. *Animal Land: The Creatures of Children's Fiction.* New York: William Morrow Co., Inc., 1975.

Bond, Nancy. "Conflict in Children's Fiction," *The Horn Book* (June 1984): 297–306. (From a speech given March 12, 1983, in Madison, Wisconsin.)

Coles, Robert. "Children's Stories: The Link to a Past," *Children's Literature*, Vol. 8. New Haven: Yale University Press, 1980.

Enright, Elizabeth. "Realism in Children's Literature," *The Horn Book* (April 1967): 165–170.

Higgins, James. *Beyond Words.* New York: Teachers College Press, 1970.

Hoban, Russell. "Thoughts on Being and Writing," in *The Thorny Paradise*, edited by Edward Blishen. New York: Penguin Books, 1975.

Jalongo, Mary Renck. "Bibliotherapy: Literature to Promote Socioemotional Growth," *The Reading Teacher* (April 1983): 796–803.

L'Engle, Madeleine. "Childlike Wonder and the Truths of Science Fiction,' *Children's Literature,* Vol. 10. New Haven: Yale University Press, 1982

Moore, Robert. "A Letter from a Critic," *Children's Literature,* Vol. 10. New Haven: Yale University Press, 1982.

Rubin, Zick. *Children's Friendships.* Cambridge, Mass.: Harvard University Press, 1980.

Segal, Elizabeth. "Picture Books and Princesses: the Feminist Contribution," *Proceedings of the Eighth Annual Conference of the Children's Literature Association.* University of Minnesota, March 1981, pp. 77–83.

Singer, Jerome, ed. *The Child's World of Make Believe.* New York: Academic Press, 1973.

Singer, Jerome, and Singer, Dorothy C. "Television and Reading in the Development of Imagination," *Children's Literature,* Vol. 9. New Haven: Yale University Press, 1981.

Waddey, Lucy. "Home in Children's Fiction: Three Patterns," *Children's Literature Association Quarterly* (Spring 1983): 13–15.

Wigutoff, Sharon. "The Feminist Press: Ten Years of Nonsexist Children's Books," *The Lion and the Unicorn,* Vol. 3, No. 2 (Winter 1979–80): 57–63.

Wood, James Playsted. "The Honest Audience," *The Horn Book* (October 1967): 612–616.

♥ CHILDREN'S BOOKS

Adler, David. *A Little at a Time.* Illus. by N. M. Bodecker. New York: Random House, Inc., 1976.

Adoff, Arnold. *Black Is Brown Is Tan.* Illus. by Emily A. McCully. New York: Harper & Row, Publishers, 1973.

Alexander, Martha. *And My Mean Old Mother Will Be Sorry, Blackboard Bear.* Illus. by author. New York: Dial Press, 1972.

———. *I'll Be the Horse If You'll Play With Me.* Illus. by author. New York: Dial Press, 1975.

———. *Marty McGee's Space Lab, No Girls Allowed.* Illus. by author. New York: Dial Press, 1981.

———. *Nobody Asked Me If I Wanted a Baby Sister.* Illus. by author. New York: Dial Press, 1971.

———. *Sabrina.* Illus by author. New York: Dial Press, 1971.

———. *The Story Grandmother Told.* Illus. by author. New York: Dial Press, 1969.

————. *When the New Baby Comes, I'm Moving Out.* illus. by author. New York: Dial Press, 1979.

Aliki. *We Are Best Friends.* Illus. by author. New York: Greenwillow Books, 1982.

Ambrus, Victor. *Mishka.* Illus. by author. New York: Frederick Warne & Co., Inc., 1978.

Andersen, Hans C. *The Ugly Duckling.* Illus. by Adrienne Adams. Trans. by R. P. Kergwin. New York: Charles Scribner's Sons, 1965.

Andersen, Karen Born. *What's the Matter, Sylvie, Can't You Ride?* Illus. by author. New York: Dial Press, 1981.

Asch, Frank. *Happy Birthday, Moon.* Englewood Cliffs, N.J.: Prentice-Hall, Inc., 1982.

Avi. *Emily Upham's Revenge.* Illus. by Paul D. Zelinsky. New York: Pantheon Books, 1978.

Babbitt, Natalie. *Phoebe's Revolt.* Illus. by author. New York: Farrar, Straus & Giroux, 1977.

Beatty, Jerome. *Matthew Looney and the Space Pirates.* Illus. by Gahan Wilson. Reading, Mass.: Addison-Wesley Publishing Co., Inc., 1972.

Bemelmans, Ludwig. *Madeline.* New York: Viking Press, 1939.

Bianco, Margery Williams. *The Velveteen Rabbit.* Garden City, N.Y.: Doubleday and Co., 1926.

Blos, Joan. *Martin's Hats.* Illus. by Marc Simont. New York: William Morrow and Co., Inc., 1984.

Borack, Barbara. *Grandpa.* Illus. by Ben Shecter. New York: Harper & Row, Publishers, 1967.

Bottner, Barbara. *Messy.* Illus. by author. New York: Delacorte Press, 1979.

Brandenberg, Franz. *It's Not My Fault.* Illus. by Aliki. New York: Greenwillow Books, 1980.

————. *Otto Is Different.* Illus. by James Stevenson. New York: Greenwillow Books, 1985.

Briggs, Raymond. *Snowman.* Illus. by author. New York: Random House Inc., 1978.

Brooks, Ron. *Timothy and Gramps.* Illus. by author. New York: Bradbury Press, 1979.

Brown, Marc. *Arthur's Eyes.* Illus. by author. Boston: Little, Brown and Co., 1979.

Brown, Margaret Wise. *A Child's Good Night Book.* Illus. by Jean Charlot. New York: Albert Whitman & Co., 1943.

————. *The Dead Bird.* Illus. by Remy Charlip. Reading, Mass.: Addison-Wesley Publishing Co., Inc., 1958.

————. *Good Night Moon.* Illus. by Clement Hurd. New York: Harper & Row Publishers, 1947.

Buckley, Helen E. *Grandfather and I.* Illus. by Paul Galdone. New York: Lothrop, Lee & Shepard Books, 1959.

————. *Grandmother and I.* Illus. by Paul Galdone. New York: Lothrop, Lee and Shepard Books, 1961.

Bulla, Clyde. *Daniel's Duck.* New York: Harper & Row, Publishers, Inc., 1979.

————. *Keep Running, Allen.* Illus. by Satomi Ichikawa. New York: Thomas Y. Crowell Co., 1978.

Burnett, Frances Hodgson. *A Little Princess.* Illus. by Tasha Tudor. Philadelphia: J. B. Lippincott Co., 1962 (original 1905).

Burningham, John. *Come Away from the Water, Shirley.* Illus. by author. New York: Harper & Row, Publishers, Inc., 1977.

Byars, Betsy. *Go and Hush the Baby.* Illus. by Emily McCully. New York: Viking Press, 1971.

Caines, Jeannette. *Daddy.* Illus. by Ronald Himler. New York: Harper & Row, Publishers, Inc., 1977.

Cameron, Eleanore. *The Wonderful Flight to the Mushroom Planet.* Illus. by Robert Henneberger. Boston: Little, Brown & Co., 1954.

Carle, Eric. *Do You Want to Be My Friend?* Illus. by author. New York: Thomas Y. Crowell Co., 1971.

————. *The Mixed Up Chameleon.* Illus. by author. New York: Thomas Y. Crowell Co., 1975.

Carrick, Carol. *The Accident.* Illus. by Donald Carrick. New York: Seabury Press Inc., 1976.

Cazet, Denys. *You Make the Angels Cry.* Illus. by author. New York: Bradbury, 1983.

Child Study Children's Book Committee at Bank Street. *Friends Are Like That: Stories to Read Yourself.* Illus. by Leigh Grant. New York: Thomas Y. Crowell, 1979.

Cleary, Beverly. *Ralph S. Mouse.* Illus. by Paul Zelinsky. New York: William Morrow & Co., Inc., 1982.

————. *Ramona the Pest.* Illus. by Louis Darling. New York: William Morrow & Co., 1968.

Clifton, Lucille. *Amifika.* Illus. by Thomas DeGrazia. New York: E. P. Dutton Co., 1977.

————. *Everett Anderson's Goodbye.* Illus. by Ann Grifalconi. New York: Holt, Rinehart and Winston, Inc., 1983.

————. *Everett Anderson's 1-2-3.* Illus. by Ann Grifalconi. New York: Holt, Rinehart & Winston, Inc., 1977.

————. *My Friend Jacob.* Illus. by Thomas DeGrazia. New York: E. P. Dutton Co., 1980.

Cohen, Miriam. *First Grade Takes a Test.* Illus. by Lillian Hoban. New York: Greenwillow Books, 1980.

————. *Jim Meets the Thing.* Illus. by Lillian Hoban. New York: Greenwillow Books, 1981.

————. *Jim's Dog Muffins.* Illus. by Lillian Hoban. New York: Greenwillow Books, 1979.

————. *Lost in the Museum.* Illlus. by Lillian Hoban. New York: Greenwillow Books, 1979.

————. *No Good in Art.* Illus. by Lillian Hoban. New York: Greenwillow Books, 1980.

————. *See You Tomorrow, Charles.* Illus. by Lillian Hoban. New York: Greenwillow Books, 1983.

————. *So What?* Illus. by Lillian Hoban. New York: Greenwillow Books, 1982.

———. *When Will I Read?* Illus. by Lillian Hoban. New York: Greenwillow Books, 1977.

———. *Will I Have a Friend?* Illus. by Lillian Hoban. New York: Macmillan Publishing Co., 1967.

Cooney, Barbara. *Miss Rumphius.* Illus. by author. New York: Viking Press, 1982.

Crowe, Robert. *Clyde Monster.* Illus. by Kay Chorao. New York: E. P. Dutton, Inc., 1976.

Dahl, Roald. *James and the Giant Peach.* Illus. by Nancy E. Burkert. New York: Alfred A. Knopf, Inc., 1961.

de Paola, Tomie. *Nana Upstairs and Nana Downstairs.* Illus. by author. New York: G. P. Putnam's Sons, 1973.

———. *Now One Foot, Now the Other.* Illus. by author. New York: G. P. Putnam's Sons, 1981.

———. *Oliver Button Is a Sissy.* Illus. by author. New York: Harcourt, Brace Jovanovich, Inc., 1979.

———. *Watch Out for the Chicken Feet in Your Soup.* Illus. by author. Englewood Cliffs, N.J.: Prentice-Hall, Inc., 1974.

de Regniers, Beatrice Scheck. *The Shadow Book.* Photographs by Isabel Gofdon. New York: Harcourt, Brace and World, 1960.

Dragonwagon, Crescent. *I Hate My Brother Harry.* Illus. by Dick Gackenbach. New York: Harper & Row, Publishers, Inc., 1983.

———. *Katie in the Morning.* Pictures by Betsy Day. New York: Harper & Row, Publishers, Inc., 1983.

Drescher, Hendrik. *Simon's Book.* New York: Lothrop, Lee and Shepard, 1983.

Duvoisin, Roger. *Donkey-Donkey.* Illus. by author. New York: Parents Magazine Press, 1968.

Eisenberg, Phyllis R. *A Mitzvah Is Something Special.* Illus. by Susan Jeschke. New York: Harper & Row, Publishers, 1978.

Ernst, Lisa Campbell. *Sam Johnson and the Blue Ribbon Quilt.* Illus. by author. New York: Lothrop, Lee and Shepard, 1983.

Ets, Marie Hall. *Play With Me.* New York: Viking Press, 1955.

Farber, Norma. *How Does It Feel to Be Old?* Illus. by Trina S. Hyman. New York: E. P. Dutton Co., 1979.

Flack, Marjorie. *Ask Mr. Bear.* Illus. by author. New York: Macmillan Publishing Co., 1932.

Galdone, Paul. *The Three Billy Goats Gruff.* New York: Seabury Press Inc., 1973.

Gantos, John B. *Rotten Ralph.* Illus. by Nicole Rubel. Boston: Houghton Mifflin Co., 1976.

Geisel, Theodor S. [Dr. Seuss]. *And To Think That I Saw It On Mulberry Street.* Illus. by author. New York: Vanguard Press Inc., 1937.

Getz, Arthur. *Humphrey, the Dancing Pig.* Illus. by author. New York: Dial Press, 1980.

———. *Tar Beach.* Illus. by author. New York: Dial Press, 1979.

Godden, Rumer. *Impunity Jane: The Story of a Pocket Doll.* Illus. by Adrienne Adams. New York: Viking Press, 1954.

Goffstein, M. B. *Fish for Supper.* Illus. by author. New York: Dial Press, 1976.

Goldner, Kathryn A., and Vogel, Carol G. *The Dangers of Strangers*. Minneapolis: Dillon Press, 1983.

Grahame, Kenneth. *The Wind in the Willows*. Pictures by John Burningham. New York: Viking Press, 1983 (orig. 1908).

Greenfield, Eloise. *First Pink Light*. Illus. by Moneta Barnett. New York: Thomas Y. Crowell Co., 1976.

Hazen, Barbara. *Tight Times*. Illus. by author. New York: Viking Press, 1979.

———. *Why Couldn't I Be an Only Kid Like You, Wigger?* Illus. by Leigh Grant. New York: Atheneum Publishers, 1975.

Herman, Charlotte. *My Mother Didn't Kiss Me Good-Night*. Illus. by Bruce Degen. New York: E. P. Dutton Co., 1980.

Herold, Ann Bixby. *The Helping Day*. Illus. by Victoria de Larrea. New York: Coward, McCann & Geoghegan Inc., 1980.

Hest, Amy. *The Crack-of-Dawn Walkers*. Illus. by Amy Schwartz. New York: Macmillan Publishing Co., Inc., 1984.

Hill, Elizabeth S. *Evan's Corner*. Illus. by Nancy Grossman. New York: Holt, Rinehart and Winston Inc., 1967.

Hoban, Russell. *A Baby Sister for Frances*. Illus. by Lillian Hoban. New York: Harper & Row, Publishers, Inc., 1964.

———. *Bedtime for Frances*. Illus. by Garth Williams. New York: Harper & Row, Publishers, Inc., 1960.

Hughes, Shirley. *Alfie's Feet*. Illus. by author. New York: Lothrop, Lee & Shepard Co., 1983.

———. *George the Babysitter*. Illus. by author. Englewood Cliffs, N.J.: Prentice-Hall, Inc., 1977.

Hunter, Mollie. *The Knight of the Golden Plain*. Illus. by Marc Simont. New York: Harper & Row, Publishers, Inc., 1983.

Hurd, Edith. *I Dance in My Red Pajamas*. Illus. by Emily McCully. New York: Harper & Row, Publishers, Inc., 1982.

Hutchins, Pat. *Don't Forget the Bacon!* Illus. by author. New York: Greenwillow Books, 1976.

———. *The Tale of Thomas Mead*. Illus. by author. New York: Greenwillow Books, 1980.

———. *The Very Worst Monster*. Illus. by author. New York: Greenwillow Books, 1985.

———. *You'll Soon Grow Into Them Titch*. Illus. by author. New York: Greenwillow Books, 1983.

Johnson, Crockett. *Harold and the Purple Crayon*. Illus. by author. New York: Harper & Row, Publishers, Inc., 1958.

Jones, Rebecca. *The Biggest, Meanest, Ugliest Dog in the Whole Wide World*. Illus. by Wendy Watson. New York: Macmillan Co., 1982.

Keats, Ezra Jack. *Peter's Chair*. Illus. by author. New York: Harper & Row, Publishers, Inc., 1967.

———. *Whistle for Willie*. Illus. by author. New York: Viking Press, 1964.

Keeping, Charles. *Willie's Fire Engine*. Illus. by author. New York: Oxford University Press, 1980.

Kellogg, Steven. *Can I Keep Him?* Illus. by author. New York: Dial Press, 1971.

———. *Much Bigger Than Martin*. Illus. by author. New York: Dial Press, 1976.

————. *Won't Somebody Play With Me?* Illus. by author. New York: Dial Press, 1972.

Kipling, Rudyard. *The Jungle Book.* Illus. by Kurt Wiese. New York: Doubleday & Co., 1952.

————. *Just So Stories.* Illus. by Victor Ambrus. Skokie, Ill.: Rand McNally and Co., 1982 (orig. 1902).

Klein, Norma. *A Train for Jane.* Illus. by Miriam Schottland. Old Westbury, N.Y.: Feminist Press, 1974.

Knotts, Howard. *Great Grandfather, the Baby and Me.* Illus. by author. New York: Atheneum Publishers, 1978.

Krasilovsky, Phyllis. *The Shy Little Girl.* Illus. by Trina Schart Hyman. Boston: Houghton Mifflin Co., 1970.

Kraus, Robert. *Owliver.* Illus. by Jose Aruego and Ariane Dewey. New York: Windmill Books, 1974.

Krauss, Ruth. *The Carrot Seed.* Illus. by Crockett Johnson. New York: Harper & Row, Publishers, 1945.

Kroll, Steven. *Happy Mother's Day.* Illus. by Marilyn Hofner. New York: Holiday House, Inc., 1985.

————. *That Makes Me Mad!* Illus. by Hilary Knight. New York: Pantheon Books, 1976.

Larsen, Hanne. *Don't Foget Tom.* New York: Thomas Y. Crowell Co., 1978.

Lasker, Joe. *The Do-Something Day.* Illus. by author. New York: Viking Press, 1982.

Lasky, Kathryn. *My Island Grandma.* Illus. by Emily McCully. New York: Frederick Warne & Co., Inc., 1979.

Leaf, Munro. *The Story of Ferdinand.* New York: Viking Press, 1936.

Lexau, Joan. *Benjie.* Illus. by Don Bolognese. New York: Dial Press, 1964.

————. *I Should Have Stayed in Bed.* Illus. by Syd Hoff. New York: Harper & Row, Publishers, 1965.

————. *Me Day.* Illus. by Robert Weaver. New York: Dial Press, 1971.

————. *Striped Ice Cream.* Illus. by John Wilson. Philadelphia: J. B. Lippincott, Co., 1968.

Lionni, Leo. *Cornelius.* Illus. by author. New York: Pantheon Books, 1983.

————. *Frederick.* Illus. by author. New York: Pantheon Books, 1966.

Lobel, Arnold. *Frog and Toad Are Friends.* Illus. by author. New York: Harper & Row, Publishers, Inc., 1979.

Lurie, Alison. *Clever Gretchen and Other Forgotten Folktales.* New York: Thomas Y. Crowell Co., 1980.

MacGregor, Ellen. *Miss Pickerell Harvests the Sea.* New York: McGraw-Hill Book Co., 1969.

MacLachlan, Patricia. *Through Grandpa's Eyes.* Illus. by Deborah Rey. New York: Harper & Row, Publishers, Inc., 1980.

Marshall, James. *George and Martha Rise and Shine.* Boston: Houghton Mifflin Co., 1976.

Mayer, Mercer. *There's a Nightmare in My Closet.* Illus. by author. New York: Dial Press, 1968.

McDermott, Gerald. *Arrow to the Sun.* Illus. by author. New York: Viking Press, 1974.

McPhail, David. *Sisters.* Illus. by author. New York: Harcourt, Brace Jovanovich, Inc., 1984.

Miles, Miska. *Annie and the Old One.* Boston: Little, Brown & Company, 1971.

Milne, A. A. *Winnie-the-Pooh.* Illus. by E. H. Shepard. London: Methuen Inc., 1926.

———. *Winnie the Pooh.* Illus. by Ernest Shepard. New York: E. P. Dutton Co., 1971.

Minarik, Else Holmelund. *Little Bear.* Illus. by Maurice Sendak. New York: Harper and Row, Publishers, 1957.

Moeri, Louise. *Star Mother's Youngest Child.* Illus. by Trina Schart Hyman. Boston: Houghton Mifflin Co., 1975.

Ness, Evaline. *Sam, Bangs and Moonshine.* Illus. by author. New York: Holt, Rinehart and Winston, Inc., 1966.

———. *Yeck Eck.* Illus. by author. New York: E. P. Dutton Co., 1974.

Osborn, Lois. *My Dad Is Really Something.* New York: Whitman Publishers, 1983.

Pearson, Susan. *Molly Moves Out.* Illus. by Steven Kellogg. New York: Dial Press, 1979.

Peet, Bill. *Cowardly Clyde.* Illus. by author. Boston: Houghton Mifflin Co., 1979.

Phelps, Ethel Johnston. *Tatterhood and Other Tales.* Old Westbury, N.Y.: Feminist Press, 1978.

Pomerantz, Charlotte. *The Half-Birthday Party.* Illus. by Dy Anne D. Ryann. Boston: Houghton Mifflin Co., 1984.

Potter, Beatrix. *The Tailor of Gloucester.* Illus. by author. London: Frederick Warne & Co., Inc., 1903.

———. *The Tale of Peter Rabbit.* Illus. by author. New York: Atheneum Publishers, 1968 (orig. 1901).

Raskin, Ellen. *Spectacles.* Illus. by author. New York: Atheneum Publishers, 1968.

Rice, Eve. *Goodnight, Goodnight.* Illus. by author. New York: Greenwillow Books, 1980.

Rockwell, Harlow. *My Dentist.* Illus. by author. New York: Greenwillow Books, 1975.

———. *My Doctor.* Illus. by author. New York: Macmillan Publishing Co., 1973.

———. *My Nursery School.* Illus. by author. New York: Greenwillow Books, 1976.

Rosenberg, Maxine B. *My Friend Leslie.* Photographs by George Ancona. New York: Lothrop, Lee & Shepard Co., 1983.

Ross, Pat. *Meet M and M.* Illus. by Marylin Hafner. New York: Pantheon Books, 1980.

Ruffins, Reynold. *My Brother Never Feeds the Cat.* Illus. by author. New York: Charles Scribner's Sons, 1979.

Rylant, Cynthia. *Miss Maggie.* Illus. by Thomas DeGrazia. New York: E. P. Dutton Co., 1983.

———. *Begin at the Beginning.* Illus. by author. New York: Harper & Row, Publishers, Inc., 1983.

Schwartz, Amy. *Bea and Mr. Jones.* Illus. by author. New York: Bradbury Press, 1983.

Schertle, Alice. *In My Treehouse.* Illus. by Meredith Dunham. New York: Lothrop, Lee & Shepard Co., 1983.

Sendak, Maurice. *Higglety Pigglety Pop!* Illus. by author. New York: Harper & Row, Publishers, Inc., 1967.

———. *In the Night Kitchen.* Illus. by author. New York: Harper & Row, Publishers, Inc., 1970.

———. *Outside Over There.* Illus. by author. New York: Harper & Row, Publishers, Inc., 1981.

———. *Where the Wild Things Are.* Illus. by author. New York: Harper & Row, Publishers, Inc., 1963.

Sharmat, Marjorie W. *Edgemont.* Illus. by Cyndy Szekeres. New York: Thomas Y. Crowell Co., 1976.

———. *Gila Monsters Meet You at the Airport.* Illus. by Byron Barton. New York: Macmillan Publishing Co., 1980.

———. *Grumley the Grouch.* Illus. by Kay Chorao. New York: Holiday House, 1980.

Sharmat, Mitchell. *Gregory the Terrible Eater.* Illus. by Jose Aruégo and Ariane Dewey. New York: Four Winds Press, 1980.

Shulevitz, Uri. *Oh, What a Noise.* Illus. by author. New York: Macmillan Co., 1971.

———. *One Monday Morning.* Illus. by author. New York: Charles Scribner's Sons, 1967.

Skorpen, Liesel. *Bird.* New York: Harper & Row, Publishers, Inc., 1976.

Skurzynski, Gloria. *Martin by Himself.* Illus. by Lynn Munsinger. Boston: Houghton Mifflin Co., 1979.

Slobodkin, Louis. *The Space Ship Under the Apple Tree.* Illus. by author. New York: Macmillan Publishing Co., 1952.

Smith, Doris Buchanan. *A Taste of Blackberries.* Illus. by Charles Robinson. New York: Thomas Y. Crowell Co., 1973.

Snyder, Zilpha Keatley. *Come On Patsy.* Illus. by Margot Zemach. New York: Atheneum Press, 1982.

Steig, William. *Amos and Boris.* Illus. by author. New York: Farrar, Straus & Giroux, 1971.

———. *Dr. De Soto.* Illus. by author. New York: Farrar, Straus & Giroux, 1982.

———. *Sylvester and the Magic Pebble.* Illus. by author. New York: Simon & Schuster, 1969.

Steptoe, John. *Daddy Is a Monster . . . Sometimes.* Illus. by author. Philadelphia: J. B. Lippincott Co., 1980.

———. *Stevie.* Illus. by author. New York: Harper & Row, Publishers, 1969.

Stevenson, James. *Worse Than Willy.* Illus. by author. New York: Greenwillow Books, 1984.

Thomas, Ianthe. *Hi, Mrs. Mallory!* Illus. by Ann Toulmin-Rothe. New York: Harper & Row, Publishers, Inc., 1979.

Tobias, Tobi. *The Quitting Deal.* Illus. by Trina S. Hyman. New York: Viking Press, 1975.

Turkle, Brinton. *Rachel and Obadiah.* Illus. by author. New York: E. P. Dutton Co., 1978.

————. *Thy Friend, Obadiah.* Illus. by author. New York: Viking Press, 1969.

Udry, Janice May. *Let's Be Enemies.* Illus. by Maurice Sendak. New York: Harper & Row, Publishers, Inc., 1961.

Vigna, Judith. *She's Not My Real Mother.* Illus. by author. Chicago: Albert Whitman & Co., 1980.

Vincent, Gabrielle. *Ernest and Celestine's Picnic.* New York: Greenwillow Books, 1982.

————. *Smile, Ernest and Celestine.* New York: Greenwillow Books, 1982.

Viorst, Judith. *Alexander and the Terrible, Horrible, No Good, Very Bad Day.* Illus. by Ray Cruz. New York: Atheneum Publishers, 1972.

————. *I'll Fix Anthony.* Illus. by Arnold Lobel. New York: Harper & Row, Publishers, Inc., 1969.

————. *Rosie and Michael.* Illus. by Lorna Tomei. New York: Atheneum Publishers, 1974.

————. *The Tenth Good Thing About Barney.* Illus. by Erik Blegvad. New York: Atheneum Publishers, 1971.

————. *Try It Again, Sam.* Illus. by Paul Galdone. New York: Lothrop, Lee & Shepard Books, 1970.

Waber, Bernard. *But Names Will Never Hurt Me.* Illus. by author. Boston: Houghton Mifflin Co., 1976.

————. *You Look Ridiculous Said the Rhinoceros to the Hippopotamus.* Illus. by author. Boston: Houghton Mifflin Co., 1966.

Wells, Rosemary. *Benjamin and Tulip.* Illus. by author. New York: Doubleday & Co., Inc., 1973.

————. *A Lion for Lewis.* Illus. by author. New York: Dial Press, 1982.

————. *Stanley and Rhoda.* Illus. by author. New York: Dial Press, 1978.

————. *Timothy Goes to School.* Illus. by author. New York: Dial Press, 1981.

White, E. B. *Charlotte's Web.* Illus. by Garth Williams. New York: Harper & Row, Publishers, 1952.

White, Paul. *Janet at School.* Illus. by Jeremy Finlay. New York: Thomas Y. Crowell Co., 1978.

Williams, Jay, and Abrashkin, Raymond. *Danny Dunn and the Smallifying Machine, No. 1.* Illus. by Paul Sagsoorian. New York: McGraw-Hill Co., 1969.

Williams, Vera. *A Chair for My Mother.* Illus. by author. New York: Greenwillow Books, 1982.

————. *Music, Music for Everyone.* Illus. by author. New York: Greenwillow Books, 1984.

————. *Something Special for Me.* Illus. by author. New York: Greenwillow Books, 1983.

Yashima, Taro. *Crow Boy.* Illus. by author. New York: Viking Press, 1955.

Yolen, Jane. *No Bath Tonight.* Illus. by Nancy W. Parker. New York: Harper & Row, Publishers, 1977.

Zolotow, Charlotte. *A Father Like That.* Illus. by Ben Schecter. New York: Harper & Row, Publishers Inc., 1971.

————. *Do You Know What I'll Do?* Illus. by Garth Williams. New York: Harper & Row, Publishers, Inc., 1958.

————. *If It Weren't For You.* Illus. by Ben Schecter. New York: Harper & Row, Publishers, Inc., 1966.

———. *Janey.* Illus. by Ronald Himler. New York: Harper & Row, Publishers, Inc., 1973.

———. *Mr. Rabbit and the Lovely Present.* Illus. by Maurice Sendak. New York: Harper & Row, Publishers, Inc., 1977.

———. *My Grandson Lew.* Illus. by William Pene du Bois. New York: Harper & Row, Publishers, Inc., 1974.

———. *The Quarreling Book.* Illus. by Arnold Lobel. New York: Harper & Row, Publishers, Inc., 1963.

———. *Say It!* Illus. by James Stevenson. New York: Greenwillow Books, 1980.

———. *The White Marble.* Illus. by Deborah K. Ray. New York: Thomas Y. Crowell Co., 1963.

———. *William's Doll.* Illus. by William Pene du Bois. New York: Harper & Row, Publishers, Inc., 1972.

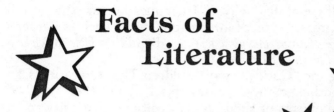

Chapter 10

Facts of Literature

RICH ENCOUNTERS

"I told you! I told you! The whale is bigger than any animal—even the elephant. It says so here!" shouted John, intrigued with John Quinn's *Nature's World Records,* a book beyond his reading level but one he reached for because he was fact hungry—and because he wanted to prove to Dan that he was right.

•◆•

"It must be great to be a famous ballet dancer," whispered Betty as she looked at Rachel Isador's *My Ballet Class.*

"Yes, but my mother says I'm clumsy so I'm going to be a cook—a good cook and make all the things in this book," asserted Donna, holding up Eva Moore's *The Seabury Cook Book for Boys and Girls.* *"I wonder—do you have to go to college to be a good cook?"*

•◆•

Ray, sitting back on his heels, Ed Emberley's *Drawing Book of Faces* at his side, was bursting with pride. *"I made them. I made them. I made them. Look at all my faces,"* and he scrolled out for Pam's benefit his panorama of square, round, rectangular, oval, triangular, smiling, frowning, bearded, and bald faces.

"Gosh, they're good," praised Pam, *"But wait—just wait till you see my dinosaur. It's even better than this one,"* and she pointed to the *Dryosaurus* by Anthony Rao in Helen Sattler's *Dinosaurs of North America.*

Miss Byrd, who heard the conversation, complimented both Ray and Pam, and silently apologized to Mr. Rao whose detailed illustrations set straight the history and types of dinosaurs.

Curiosity of Young Children: Impetus

Young children live in a land of "I wonder." They inhale questions and exhale even more of them. For them, inquisitiveness, the very touchstone of learning, runs at full tilt. Initially self-centered, this inquisitiveness is nondiscriminating. *Everything* the young child perceives and feels generates "whys?" Their questions are the natural propeller for the presentation of information books such as Berger's *Why I Cough, Sneeze, Shiver, Hiccup and Yawn*, Bendick's *How to Make a Cloud*, and Cole's *Cars and How They Go*.

In discussing the "Curiosities of Children That Literature Can Satisfy," Roy Toothaker encompasses this and all other "worlds" when he cites the objects of children's curiosity as: "curiosity about themselves, the natural world, people and places, machines and how they work, facts and proofs of facts, the ideals by which men live, creative experiences, the world of make-believe, the unknown world, and the social world."[1]

High-quality information books can not only supply many answers to these curiosities but should generate more questions. What constitutes *high quality* in information books?

Criteria

Books that offer young children information about natural phenomena, that clarify relationships, and that present historical, biographical, mathematical, and myriad other facts must have the following criteria:

- Accuracy
- Purposeful integration of narrative and illustration
- Clear focus
- Relevance to the young child's experience and development (for instance, pictorial maps first)
- Clear syntax (syntax that is not too embedded)
- Terms explained visually and verbally
- Sound and logical organization
- No anthropomorphism
- Print size that is sufficiently large and clear
- Uncluttered/balanced pages

The accuracy of information books for young children is especially critical not only because of their early development but because their experience of the world is too limited to protect them against misinformation and their experience with books may carry with it an aura of infallibility.

Illustrations in science and concept books for young children must be placed close to the text to which they apply and must be carefully labeled. The concepts young children form will be confused if pages are cluttered and if illustrations and text are not clearly allied.

According to Margery Fisher, "Formally or informally, an informational book sets out to teach."[2] Good teaching demands accuracy, focus, and care in presentation. To present facts in simple but honest form requires the best in writing and illustrating. It necessitates identifying core concepts and information, then focusing on these, so that text and graphic and design features combine to clarify the central ideas and to present them in accurate simplicity.

Good teaching and good information books also make demands of the child. "A good nonfiction book as it marshals facts, should create a challenge. It should encourage a child to think—to relate one fact to another and test a familiar idea against a new idea—until at last he or she is able to weave a pattern of increased understanding. What begins as idle curiosity should end as independent thinking."[3]

Value of Information Books

In the process of sharing information books, children will

- Increase their knowledge of things, people, and events.
- Improve the range and quality of the questions they continually raise about the world around them.
- Develop their critical thinking, problem solving, and "reference" skills.
- Clarify early misconceptions.
- Accelerate the development of certain skills via relevant books (for example, the how-to books).

In addition to the young child's fund of general background information, the appropriateness and subsequent success of helping a young child move from one informational title to others is dependent upon several factors, such as:

- The strength of the child's motivating "why?"
- The teacher's and librarian's knowledge of the child and informational books
- The accessibility of informational books.

Easy access to sources by both the teacher and the child is critical. Motivation may wither as distance between question and answer increases. Optimum service to young children is achieved when they have at hand well-stocked school libraries serviced by well-informed librarians who keep their library doors open and their shelves inviting and who alert and involve teachers in book selection. Children's interests and the school curriculum are well served in these environments.

Variation in Information Books   ☆

Information books for young children differ widely in several areas:

- Subject or topic
- Amount of narrative versus pictorial material
- Provision of a "story frame"
- Depth to which content is treated

Range of Content

The *Subject Guide to Children's Books in Print* and *A to Zoo: Subject Access to Children's Picture Books* (see Chapter 11) list a vast range and diversity of nonfiction books for young children, as do many other selection aids. Young children can explore everything from arts and crafts or activity books to those about endangered species, diverse ethnic groups, sports, secret codes, scarecrows, and the weather. Table 10.2, presented later in this chapter, gives a sense of the scope of information books available to the three- to eight-year-olds as they reach for more and more information; it includes only a very small portion of the great variety of subjects treated and titles available.

In the "natural progression" chart (Table 10.1), books that move children on to a deeper, broader, more divergent treatment of a topic are presented. Several representative and recommended titles are included for each broad topic.

Narrative Versus Pictorial Material

Because their reading ability is limited and many of their questions can be answered, if not wholly by pictorial content then certainly strongly supported by it, it is likely that information books for young children will contain even more pictorial and graphic material than the subject itself may warrant.

Children need and expect such material; pictures are a natural bridge in the development from things to words. In addition, the television "immersion" of today's young children may well have made them particularly picture-dependent.

Young children are deeply involved in naming their world. Accurate identification and labeling are as developmentally critical to young children as they are academically critical to the noted scientist. Elements vital to the identification and classification of any given topic must be provided in informational books even when production costs are high. Color in books, for example, raises costs yet many books require it, such as Allen's *Everyday Wildflowers* and Millicent Selsam and Joyce Hunt's *A First Look at Birds*. It is interesting to note that neither book is done completely in color; in the former the front and back covers contain the full-color illustrations of each wildflower discussed throughout the text, and in the latter the critical red and blue are introduced when the red-winged blackbird and the bluejay require it.

In books like Tana Hoban's *Dig, Drill, Dump, Fill*, photographs do the informing; they must be clear and sharp.

In Patricia Lauber's *What's Hatching Out of That Egg?* there is much young children can cull from the sharp, clear photographs that chronicle the ways eleven very different animals are born. Don Bolognese's illustrations for Jean George's *All Upon a Sidewalk* render the ant's view of the world and its own hazardous adventure. The illustrations by Su Zan Swain in Dorothy Shuttlesworth's *The Story of Ants* are large, clear, in natural color, and well labeled. This is a book young children refer to for picture identification, the "mining" of pictorial detail, and the matching of "specimens" with pictures Appreciation of the narrative would come during the middle grades, possibly after such a title as *A Look at Ants* by Ross E. Hutchins had been shared. In Hutchins's book the photographs are numerous and clear and the general syntax of the narrative is in keeping with young children's needs and understanding. For this and many other information books, the teacher's careful reading of the narrative and exhibiting of photographs or drawings can be the best kind of initial sharing procedure.

Information in a Story Frame

Unfortunately, when selecting books for class sharing, information books are often neglected: a good-for-reference-work-but-not-for-sharing attitude seems to prevail. Such an attitude may have influenced some writers to frame their information in a story.

In Francine Jacobs's *Supersaurus*, the story and facts are true. Children who dote on dinosaurs will appreciate the facts and bits of humor in this well-written true tale of "Dinosaur Jim" Jensen.

Sometimes a child narrator is provided, as in Anne and Harlow Rockwell's *How My Garden Grew*. In Margaret Bartlett's *Where Does All the Rain Go?* a child is illustrated who experiences the book content and the story is told in the second person.

Depth of Content

The depth of content to be treated in books for young children is a major and critical decision. The oft-quoted statement by Jerome Bruner seems as applicable to information books for young children as it does to curriculum in general: "We begin with the hypothesis that any subject can be taught effectively in some intellectually honest form to any child at any stage of development."[4]

The task of assuring a clear, simple, and honest presentation of complex ideas and concepts is demanding and engrossing, yet many authors, illustrators, and editors (like Roma Gans, Franklyn Branley, Millicent Selsam, Tana Hoban, Aliki, Anne and Harlow Rockwell, Brinton Turkle, F. N. Monjo, Mae Freeman, the D'Aulaires, Byrd Baylor, Clyde Bulla, Martha and Charles Shapp, Gail Gibbons, Illa Podendorf, Joanna Cole, and Jerome Wexler) have succeeded in accomplishing the task in a great number of informational areas. Depth is more easily achieved when the topic is highly focal, as in *The 100-Year-Old Cactus* by Anita Holmes or *I, Christopher Columbus* by Lisl Weil.

Natural Progressions ☆

Once piqued, the young child's curiosity grows and, over time, a natural progression of books can fuel an increasing hunger. The young child may seek greater detail, more and more comprehensiveness, a broader or a narrower perspective, or content that is more technical.

Taking advantage of the first dandelion a child sees or picks can lead to a sharing of *The Amazing Dandelion* by Millicent Selsam and Jerome Wexler. The arrival of a letter calls forth questions about mail, which Gail Gibbons's *The Post Office Book* may answer. Units of study on transportation bridge naturally into such books as *Truck* by Donald Crews or *Wheels* by Byron Barton. Eating popcorn or stringing it on a Christmas tree can lead to questions answered by Selsam's *Popcorn*. A newspaper clipping or telecast about a rocket commented on in class raises the whys that Branley and Vaughn's *Rockets and Satellites* (for older children) can answer.

Progressions can start with fiction and move to fact; they can begin with poetry and end in prose. Some examples of such progressions are shown in Table 10.1.

Sometimes progressions seem "unnatural" but they are nonetheless quite effective. In "On Fact with Fancy: An Approach to Science Books," Jane Granstrom details an interesting, imaginative program in which tradebooks were used to develop science concepts. *The Three Billy Goats Gruff*, performed as a shadow play, was then used

TABLE 10.1 *Natural Progressions in Information Books for the Young Child*

The Tiny Seed by Eric Carle	Can Lead To	*The Hidden Magic of Seeds* by Dorothy Shuttlesworth
The Cloud Book by Tomie de Paola		*How to Make a Cloud* by Jeanne Bendick
Whose Little Bird Am I by Leonard Weisgard		*Birds* by Arnold Adoff or *A First Look at Birds* by Millicent Selsam and Joyce Hunt
Greg's Microscope by Millicent Selsam		*Exploring with a Microscope* by Seymour Simon
Mickey's Magnet by Franklyn Branley and Eleanor K. Vaughn		*Junior Science Book of Magnets* by Rocco Feravolo
A Tree Is a Plant by Clyde Bulla		*Maple Tree* by Millicent Selsam
Exploring as You Walk in the City by Phyllis Busch		*All Upon a Sidewalk* by Jean George
Lambing Time by Jane Miller		*Born in a Barn* by Elizabeth Gemming
Maple Hill Farm books by the Provensons		*Ten Big Farms* by Dahlov Ipcar
		The Tool Book by Gail Gibbons
Thanksgiving Day by Gail Gibbons		*The Thanksgiving Story* by Alice Dalgliesh
Truck by Donald Crews		*Trucks of Every Sort* by Ken Robbins
The Lion and the Mouse, Aesop		*The Lion Family* by Gladys Conklin
I, Christopher Columbus by Lisl Weil		*Columbus* by Ingri and Edgar D'Aulaire
The Glorious Flight by the Provensons		*Flight: A Panorama of Aviation* by Melvin Zisfein
Baby Dinosaurs by Helen Roney Sattler		*Dinosaurs of North America* by Helen Roney Sattler
Mike Mulligan and His Steam Shovel by Virginia Lee Burton		*Heavy Equipment* by Jan Adkins

to develop an understanding of shadows. "The Blind Man and the Elephant" was told as a feltboard story and helped to build an understanding and an appreciation of shapes.[5]

Here is the rich merging of fiction and fact, literature and science, which expands awareness or confirms concepts.

Two Special Categories of Information Books

Among the great range of information books, two types seem particularly designed for young children: the concept book and the counting book. They will be treated here in some detail.

Concept Books

Early information books are likely to be concept books; that is, they deal with relationships. For example, books that compare shapes, sizes, colors, and seasons qualify as concept books. In this sense, alphabet and counting books, founded as they are on sequential relationships, are also concept books. Alphabet books have been treated with nursery rhymes because of their early association with the nursery and song; counting books are treated here, following concept books.

The chief criterion pertinent to a concept book is whether it adheres to one focus—one generalization—and whether this is presented clearly without visual or narrative distraction. In a number of concept and counting books an especially apt blend of narrative and graphic design exists.

In *Is It Red? Is It Yellow? Is It Blue?* Tana Hoban tells her tale through breathtakingly bright and beautiful color photographs. Balls of bright colors dot the bottom of each page and match objects in the pictures. Following the Hoban book, Leo Lionni's *Little Blue and Little Yellow* can be presented and discussed; the merging of two primary colors to effect a secondary one is made beautifully clear.

A simple, focal presentation of *Colors* is made by John Reiss. He presents each color and its possible shades and changes.

In *Shapes and Things*, Tana Hoban uses white on black, and creates the impression that the white shapes are "alive." Extensive examples are given; circles are found in links, necklaces, and a turtle. In her *Round & Round & Round*, young children look carefully to identify the many items that *go* round and *are* round.

In *Shapes, Circles, Triangles, and Squares*, Hoban employs black and white photographs of everyday functional objects, again to help children generalize about the shapes they see and the shapes within shapes.

Jeanne Bendick's *Shapes* goes well beyond the sheer recognition of basic forms. Children make shapes and answer questions about them. The illustrations are many—perhaps too many for clear page design and for the very young child.

Primary teachers spend a great deal of their time working to develop children's understanding of such words as *over, before, after, under, through,* etc. For teachers who have had children step *over* the rug swatch, go *under* the table, and *through* a tunnel of classmate's upraised arms, Hoban's *Over, Under &Through* can further instill these concepts via photographs in which children's activities exemplify the words singly or together. *On* and *in; around, across,* and *between; beside* and *below; against* and *behind* are also treated. Young children can mimic many of the activities pictured and *feel* these relationships. In Hoban's

One Little Kitten, through, behind, and *inside* are the focal concepts and in *Is It Larger? Is It Smaller?* size relationships are the core.

Concepts of size are humorously and accurately illustrated in *Bigger and Smaller.* In this book, Robert Froman uses many surprising but relevant comparisons to clarify *bigger* and *smaller,* and Gioia Fiammenghi's illustrations further document the difference.

The young child is probably helped most when the variables change one at a time in a concept book. For example, to demonstrate a difference in size, a bigger paint spot in the same color keeps the concept central. In Froman's book, both size and color initially change. On the whole, however, the book will help the young child understand size differences.

Thomas O'Brien's *Odds and Evens* is a clear presentation with relevant practical examples of what makes numbers odd and even, and when and why one may be preferable to the other. Children are nudged toward generalizations regarding the addition of such numbers.

In *Big Ones, Little Ones,* Tana Hoban's photographs of young and mature animals differentiate sizes effectively and also picture the care animals show for each other. Animals are generally shown side by side or close together to facilitate concept formation. Pictures are not labeled, but on the final page the entire collection is identified in mini-photographs, and the easily labeled elephant and not-so-readily-known zebu are shown.

In Eve Merriam's *Small Fry,* the same differentiation between mature and young animals is the focus, but the accent is on the names of the young animals which are presented in brief verse form.

Big Rigs by Hope Marston helps young children identify parts of tractor-trailers and to recognize different kinds of trucks.

In *All Aboard the Train,* Ethel and Leonard Kessler distinguish among train types and car types.

Dig, Drill, Dump, Fill (Tana Hoban) is also about heavy machines—what they do and how their names often reflect their jobs. Guiding children's "photo reading" here will help them describe the operation and begin to learn synonyms for the work of these machines.

In *Look Again!* and *Take Another Look,* Hoban encourages second, more careful viewing. In these treasures of photographs, every other sheet is white with a small peephole. Children guess what the object is by studying what is visible through the hole. Helping children to articulate their guesses before they turn the page to confirm or reject their hypotheses can lead to more precise looking.

Ielo and Enzo Mari's *The Apple and the Moth* is a wordless picture-book illustrating brightly and simply the cycle of a worm in an apple to butterfly, to egg, and back to a worm in an apple. The pictures tell all—simply and beautifully.

Janina Domanska's *What Do You See?* helps children understand that everyone may have different opinions and that no one need be all right or all wrong. A difficult understanding—that the view depends upon the point of view—is presented here for young children.

Patricia Lauber's *What's Hatching Out of That Egg?* involves young children in identifying an animal by its egg. The description of each egg or nest contains clues, and answers can be checked.

Change is a difficult concept for young children to master. Pat Hutchins's *Changes, Changes* is a classic in the field. She uses different formations of building blocks to illustrate change. Hoban's *Push, Pull, Empty, Full* and Spier's *Fast-Slow, High-Low* are both subtitled "a book of opposites" and are often used to help young children understand antonyms. For the very young child, Bruce McMillan's *Here a Chick, There a Chick* illustrates in color on facing pages contrasts such as straight and crooked, stand and sit, and so on.

Counting Books

Young children need to touch and manipulate actual objects—blocks, discs, sticks, rods—to learn fundamental mathematical concepts. Fingers and even toes can help in counting. Indeed, many of the early fingerplays, "This Little Men" and "The Counting Lesson," are games in which children use their fingers as counters. The progression from concrete objects to picture to numeral is pedagogical and developmentally sound. Given many such manipulative experiences, counting books can confirm the accuracy of these direct experiences by offering children pictorial proof in colorful, diverse, imaginative ways. Counting books are perforce participation books, and teachers have all sorts of ways to involve children in them.

Some counting books "tell" the addition story; some the subtraction story. Still others illustrate the inverse nature of the two.

Counting books can help introduce and deepen such mathematical concepts as number sequence, one-to-one correspondence, grouping, place value, and sets. Some are works of art and aesthetic treasures rather than simple concept books; some tell the number story via a merry, rhyming tale.

The simplest and clearest counting books are of the Dick Bruna type in *I Can Count*, one numeral and matching object on each double page.

Another simple counting book for very young children—one with a story—is Rosemary Wells's *Max's Toys: A Counting Book*. Max is a plump, little rabbit who has adventures with his first word, his new suit, and a jaunt in a baby carriage. The book is a laminated board book, tiny in size, and printed in clear, bold colors. Very young children will delight in it and will begin counting by ones the objects on each page. The simple story with its sibling "you-can't-have-it" feature will be appreciated too.

Young children will also like *Roll Over! A Counting Song* (Merle Peek), which begins with ten and works back to one. Nine animals share the bed with a toddler, and one by one they leave to tuck themselves away for the night. Music is attached so children can sing the counting song. Another subtraction bedtime story is the Caldecott Honor book *Ten, Nine, Eight* by Mollie Bang. Pictures are bright and bespeak tenderness and love. In John Becker's *Seven Little Rabbits*, young children have another "backward" counting book, this one illustrated in color by Barbara Cooney.

One of the most praised of all counting books is Mitsumasa's *Anno's Counting Book* which is a remarkable treasury of aesthetic and mathematical pleasure, although complicated for the very young child. The watercolor landscapes depict seasonal and regional changes that offer all kinds of counting and grouping possibilities.

Like his ABC book, Fritz Eichenberg's *Dancing in the Moon: Counting Rhymes* is large and full of bright colors and zany rhymes: 7 raccoons dancing in the moon, or 2 moose scaring a papoose. Numerals go to twenty, so place value is reinforced. Moltke Weissman's *Numbers: A First Counting Book* is simple, clear, colorful, and an easy matching book for the young child. Tasha Tudor's delicate *1 Is One* also facilitates matching.

Maurice Sendak's *Seven Little Monsters* is presented in a small rectangular text to allow for the parading seven who are more mischievous than monsterish and who end up proceeding in chains (to what might be a jail) in fitting punishment for their antics. Children can count the monsters here, but the book that Sendak actually calls "a counting book" is *One Was Johnny*, a delightful story of Johnny who lived alone and liked it but was invaded by eight visitors who disturbed his peace in all sorts of ways. This is a participation book; children are eager to model Johnny.

Lentil Soup by Joe Lasker teaches cardinal and ordinal concepts and the sequence of the days of the week in a funny story of a farmer and his wife.

Another "farmer" story is Sandra Russell's *A Farmer's Dozen*, which is told in verse and contains borders of *sets* of fruits or vegetables. The couplets will be easily repeatable by young children who will learn them quickly and happily.

In *We Came A-Marching...1 2 3* by Mildred Hobzek, with illustrations by William Pene Du Bois, the accent is on counting to three in twelve different languages to the tune of a Slavic folksong. The illustrations are merry, the accompaniment to the folksong is included, and flags depict the different nations.

Not a concept or counting book in the *strict* sense, Eric Carle's *The Very Hungry Caterpillar* can reinforce counting skills and the concept of sets.

Eric Carle's *1, 2, 3 to the Zoo* marches a series of animals, double-page size, across its pages in circus cars in ever-increasing numbers—one elephant, two hippopotomuses, and so on, up to ten birds. On the bottom left-hand corner of each page a tiny replica of the circus cars on the previous pages are represented so the child can count up to the present page. Both cardinal and ordinal relationships are thereby reinforced. Pictures are gloriously bright and large as befits a circus.

Young children used to a story hour will understand the setting and number concepts in *1, 2, 3 for the Library* by Mary E. Little. Children are counted as they arrive for storytime.

John J. Reiss's *Numbers* begins with a hopscotch diagram on a background of black. Numerals appear almost luminous and you have to hop around to achieve order. Sometimes the number of things that matches the appropriate numerals are part of one whole, as five starfish arms; other times, they are discrete, as seven ravens. Drawings are simple and bright, and the counting goes to one thousand.

In Helen Oxenbury's *Numbers of Things* the illustrations are clear, distinct, cheerful, and meander comfortably between home, circus, playground, zoo, or park. Children can count by tens from ten to fifty and join the young child on the last page who asks, "How many stars?"

One Snail and Me by Emilie Warren McLeod is the hilarious cumulative tale of an amazing bathtub which seems to expand to accommodate eight alligators, seven bears, six kangaroos, five whales, four seals, and so on.

Children also enjoy Margaret Friskey's *Chicken Little, Count to Ten* in which none of the ten animals she meets can tell Chicken Little how to take a drink. Young children giggle greatly at the suggestions given.

Brian Wildsmith's 1, 2, 3 is a medley of his harlequin patterns made from bright basic shapes which join to form the numerals appropriate to the objects. The left-hand page is occupied by an enormous numeral and the number name in capital and small letters. The right-hand page forms familiar large shapes from the small basic shapes. Careful looking is needed.

An Invitation to the Butterfly Ball: A Counting Rhyme by Jane Yolen is a fantastic, whimsical, cumulative verse tale of an elf who offers invitations to ten different families of animals to attend the Butterfly Ball. At the end, there is a marvelous opportunity to count all the families and their members. The verse is cumulative, children will quickly join in.

Catherine Barr's story of *Seven Chicks Missing* is accompanied by simple illustrations that depict the chick's penchant for succumbing to curiosity. As mother hen takes them about, the chicks vanish one by one to investigate their own puzzlements. A young boy brings them back. This is a subtraction then an addition story, an unusual sequence.

Sixes and Sevens (Yeoman and Blake) is a counting book of Barnaby's adventures as captain of the raft that picks up and deposits villagers going to Limber Lea. The child reader sees the raft becoming filled with an amazing number of people and animals, and marvels at its ability to support everyone. The way Barnaby solves the problems of accommodating everyone is masterly. Children can be helped to hypothesize about ways to keep the raft afloat.

In *One, Two, Buckle My Shoe: A Book of Counting Rhymes,* Gail Haley selected nursery rhymes dealing with numbers from one to ten.

In her recording, *Counting Games and Rhythms for the Little Ones,* Ella Jenkins compiles several counting nursery rhymes and directs contagious counting rhythmic exercises to go with them.

One White Crocodile Smile (Richard Hefter) is full of bright colors, huge numerals, childlike drawings, and cumulative verse. Numerals are arranged to match specific things in pairs, vertically, horizontally, or in simple graph form. Children can enjoy the verse, the easy-to-count objects, and the inventive format of numeral presentation.

Three other funny counting books in verse are *Hippos Go Beserk* by Sandra Boynton, *Up the Down Elevator* by Norma Farber, and *Kitten from One to Ten* by Mirra Ginsburg.

Erika Weihs's *Count the Cats* gives young children who like cats (very energetic ones) an opportunity to follow lovingly a simple text and crayon drawings of cats and their adventures. Ducks are the creatures being counted in Pomerantz's colorful *One Duck, Another Duck.*

Haris Petie focuses on bugs—*Billions of Bugs.* Large-number concepts are taught by illustration and the child travels by tens to 100 and onto 1000. Small and rectangular in size, the book is about the kinds of bugs children could meet in everyday settings.

Simple city scenes illustrate *Counting Carnival* by Feenie Ziner and Paul Galdone. Place value is introduced; count goes from 1 to 12. Numerals appear in bright red with a brief couplet, such as, "Just one no fun."

Tana Hoban's *Count and See* is full of her usual remarkably clear photographs, which help to establish correspondences with numbers 1 through 15 but she also continues to 100. Young children can very easily recognize and count the objects pictured and go on to counting the objects in their surroundings.

Guilio Maestro's *One More and One Less: A Number Concept Book* is a clear, simple, colorful representation of the addition and subtraction processes and the manner in which one undoes the other. Characters are clear, identifiable, and perhaps whimsical. Animals sit in a row, thereby making it easy to count them.

Moja Means One is a Swahili counting book by Muriel and Tom Feelings. Beautiful double-spread, detailed paintings give life to the Swahili culture. Pronunciation of the number names in Swahili are given.

Ballet, Bugs, and Benjamin Franklin ☆

A selective sampling of the diversity of topic and title available in information books for the three- to eight-year-old follows. Many of these books are perfect matches for the "whys" of children; others are initially triggered by the "whys" of teachers, librarians, parents, and friends.

TABLE 10.2 *A Selective Sampling of Information Books for the Young Child*

Topic	Title
Science	Vicki Cobb. *Fuzz Does It.* 5-8
	Gwynne Vevers. *Animal Homes* (series on animals). 5-8
	Patricia Lauber. *What's Hatching Out of That Egg?* 5-8
	Joanna Cole and Jerome Wexler. *A Frog's Body* (series) 5-8
	Atsushi Komori. *Animal Mothers.* 3-5
	Roma Gans. *Icebergs.* 5-8
	Millicent Selsam. *Is This a Baby Dinosaur and Other Science Puzzles?* 5-8
	Millicent Selsam. *A First Look at* Series. 3-8
	Anne and Harlow Rockwell. *How My Garden Grew.* 3-8
	Linda Girard. *You Were Born on Your Very First Birthday.* 5-8
	Gail Gibbons. *Paper, Paper Everywhere.* 5-8
	Jim Arnosky. *Watching Foxes.* 6-8
Holidays	Alice Dalgliesh. *The Thanksgiving Story.* 5-8
	Tomie de Paola. *The Family Christmas Tree Book.* 5-8
	David A. Adler. *A Picture Book of Hanukkah.* 3-8
Health, Food, and Nutrition	Paul Showers. *No Measles No Mumps for Me.* 5-8
	Tomie de Paola. *The Popcorn Book.* 5-8
	Aliki. *Corn Is Maize.* 5-8
Art and Music	Leonard Weisgard. *Treasures to See: A Museum Picture Book.* 5-8
	Sergei Prokofiev. *Peter and the Wolf.* 3-8
Careers	Byron Barton. *Building a House.* 3-5
	Roger Bester. *Fireman Jim.* 5-8

Topic	Title
	Rachel Isadora. *My Ballet Class.* 5-8 Jill Krementz. *The Very Young.* series 5-8 Herbert Zim. *What Can She Be* series. 5-8 Byrd Baylor. *Sometimes I Dance Mountains.* 5-8
History and Biography	Aliki. *A Weed Is a Flower: The Life of George Washington Carver.* 5-8 Aliki. *Fossils Tell of Long Ago.* 5-8 Brinton Turkle. *The Obadiah* books. 5-8 Olaf Baker. *Where the Buffaloes Begin.* 7-8 Ingri and Edgar d'Aulaire. *Benjamin Franklin.* 6-8 F. N. Monjo. *Me and Willie and Pa.* 7-8 Peter Spier. *Tin Lizzie.* 7-8 John Kaufmann. *Little Dinosaurs and Early Birds.* 5-8 Cynthia Basil. *How Ships Play Cards: a Beginning Book of Homonyms.* 5-8
Geography	Sally Cartwright. *What's in a Map.* 5-8
Sports	Marshall Burchard. *Sports Hero: Rod Carew.* 8 up George Sullivan. *Willie Mays.* 8 up
Ecology	Jeanne Bendick. *Ecology.* 7-8 Margaret Bartlett. *The Clean Brook.* 5-8
Health and the Senses	Paul Showers. *How You Talk.* 5-8 Paul Showers. *Hear Your Heart* (and many other titles by the same author). 5-8 Herbert S. Zim. *What's Inside Me?* 5-8 Aliki. *My Five Senses.* 5-8 Harlow Rockwell. *My Doctor.* 3-8 Harlow Rockwell. *My Dentist.* 5-8 Joanne Bernstein. *When People Die.* 5-8 Margaret Sheffield. *Where Do Babies Come From.* 5-8
Today's World/ Environment	Eve Merriam. *Mommies at Work.* 5-8 Donald Crews. *Truck.* 3-8 Donald Crews. *Harbor.* 3-8 Donald Crews. *Light.* 3-8 Roy Wulffson *The Invention of Ordinary Things.* 8 up Anne and Harlow Rockwell. *The Supermarket* (and many other Rockwell titles). 3-5 Ron and Nancy Goor. *In the Driver's Seat.* 5-8 Tana Hoban. *I Walk and Read.* 3-5
Hobbies and Crafts	Harlow Rockwell. *I Did It* and *Look at This.* 6-8 Hou-Tien Cheng. *Scissor Cutting for Beginners.* 6-8 Anne Rockwell. *The Toolbox.* 3-5 Ed Emberley's books. 5-8

(continued)

TABLE 10.2 *Continued*

Topic	Title
Language and Communication	John W. Stewig. *Sending Messages.* 5-8
	Antonio Franconi. *See and Say: a Picture Book in Four Languages.* 7-8
	Esther Hautzig. *In the Park: An Excursion in Four Languages.* 5-8
	Gail Gibbons. *The Post Office Book: Mail and How It Moves.* 5-8
	Byron Barton. *Airport.* 5-8
Reference Books	Melvin Zisfein. *Flight: A Panorama of Aviation.* 8 up
	Helen Sattler. *Dinosaurs of North America.* 7 up
	John Quinn. *Nature's World Records.* 7 up
	Franklyn Branley's books. For older children
Safety	Dorothy Chlad. *Matches, Lighters, Firecrackers Are Not Toys.* 5-8

Summary

Books can both respond to many of the curiosities of young children and nurture ever-new "whys." They can feed the need for information as well as fantasy, thereby keeping young children learning the known, envisioning the unknown, and shaping, on the way to their Somewhere, the merging of the two.

Accuracy is vital in all information books; it is especially critical for young children whose early development makes them vulnerable to misinformation because their experience of the world is so limited and their experience with books may carry with it an aura of "book infallibility."

Criteria in judging information books are accuracy, integration of narrative and illustration, focus, relevance to the young child's experience and development, clear syntax, well-defined terms, logical organization, sufficiently large print, and uncluttered pages. Information books help young children increase their knowledge of things, people, events; improve the range and quality of their questions; further their critical thinking, problem-solving, and study skills.; clarify their misconceptions; and teach various skills.

Information books for young children are richly diverse in subject and depth of treatment, full of pictorial material, and sometimes framed in a story.

If curiosity is ignited and maintained, young children will continue to seek more and more information and a natural progression of books, *over a period of time,* can be shared and/or given to them that will supply greater detail, more comprehensiveness, a broader perspective, and more technical content. Such progressions may start with fact and end in fiction or start with fiction and end in fact.

Two major information categories for young children are concept and counting books; the former are highly focal, the latter are often less concerned with teaching number sequence than with merry or rhyming stories and attractive illustrations.

DISCUSSION ACTIVITIES

• Share Eric Carle's *The Rooster Who Set Out to See the World* as a flannelboard story. (Or use any counting book that treats both addition and subtraction; Sendak's *One Was Johnny,* for example.) Have children retell it, then encourage them to paraphrase their understanding of the story. From the retelling and the paraphrase, assess whether children do understand the inverse relationship of addition and subtraction.

• Share Byron Barton's *Building a House* and Martha Alexander's *How My Library Grew* (or any two books that contrast information versus information-in-a-story book). Discuss at length. Note the children's reactions. What kinds of observations do children make about each?

• Share Jim Arnosky's *Crinkleroot's Book of Animal Tracks and Wildlife Signs.* If possible, identify real animal footprints from the chart in the book. Explore other books about differences in animals' beaks, feet, and so on, with the children. After considerable sharing, encourage them to play "detective" by using slides or pictures.

NOTES

1. Roy Eugene Toothacker, "Curiosities of Children That Literature Can Satisfy," *Childhood Education* (March 1976): 262–267.

2. Margery Fisher, "Matter of Fact," *Appraisal,* Vol. 8, No. 1 (Winter 1975): 1.

3. Jo Carr, Writting the Literature of Fact," in *Beyond Fact: Nonfiction for Children and Young People* (Chicago: American Library Association, 1982), p. 4.

4. Jerome Bruner, *The Process of Education* (Cambridge, Mass.: Harvard University Press, 1960), p. 33.

5. Jane Granstrom, "On Fact With Fancy: An Approach to Science Books," *Appraisal,* Vol. 7, No. 1 (Winter 1974): 1–4.

☆
PROFESSIONAL BIBLIOGRAPHY

Carr, Jo. "Clarity in Science Writing," *Appraisal,* Vol. 15, No. 1 (Winter 1982): 4–13.
————. *Beyond Fact: Nonfiction for Children and Young People.* Chicago: American Library Association, 1982.
Fisher, Margery. "Matter of Fact," *Appraisal,* Vol. 8, No. 1 (Winter 1975): 1–4.
————. *Matters of Fact: Aspects of Non-Fiction for Children.* New York: Thomas Y. Crowell Company, 1972.
Giller, Pamela. "Science Books for Young Children," *Appraisal* , Vol. 13, No. 1 (Winter 1980): 1–5.
Granstrom, Jane. "On Fact With Fancy: An Approach to Science Books," *Appraisal,* Vol. 7, No. 1 (Winter 1974): 1–4.
Russell, David. *Children's Thinking.* Boston: Ginn & Co., 1956.
Toothacker, Roy Eugene. "Curiosities of Children That Literature Can Satisfy," *Childhood Education* (March 1976): 262–267.
Wann, Kenneth D.; Dorn, Miriam Selchen; and Liddle, Elizabeth Ann. *Fostering Intellectual Development in Young Children.* New York: Teachers College, 1962.

☆
CHILDREN'S BOOKS

Adkins, Jan. *Heavy Equipment.* Illus. by author. New York: Charles Scribner's Sons, 1980.
Adler, David. *A Picture Book of Hanukkah.* Illus. by Linda Heller. New York: Holiday House, 1982.
Adoff, Arnold. *Birds.* Illus. by Troy Howell. New York: Harper & Row, Publishers, Inc., 1982.
Aesop. *The Lion and the Mouse.* Illus. by Ed Young. New York: Doubleday & Co., Inc., 1980.
Ahlberg, Janet, and Ahlberg, Allan. *The Baby's Catalog.* Illus. by authors. Boston: Little, Brown & Co., 1983.
Alexander, Martha. *How My Library Grew.* New York: Wilson, 1983.
Aliki. *Corn Is Maize.* Illus. by author. New York: Thomas Y. Crowell Co., 1976.
————. *Fossils Tell of Long Ago.* Illus. by author. New York: Harper & Row Publishers, 1972.
————. *My Five Senses.* Illus. by author. New York: Harper & Row Publishers, 1962.
————. *A Weed Is a Flower: The Life of George Washington Carver.* Illus. by author. Englewood Cliffs, N.J.: Prentice-Hall, Inc., 1965.
Allen, Gertrude E. *Everyday Wildflowers.* Illus. by author. Boston: Houghton Mifflin Co., 1965.

Arnosky, Jim. *Crinkleroot's Book of Animal Tracks and Wildlife Signs*. Illus. by author. New York: G. P. Putnam's Sons, 1979.

———. *Watching Foxes*. Illus. by author. New York: Lothrop, Lee and Shepard Books, 1985.

Baker, Olaf. *Where the Buffaloes Begin*. Illus. by Stephen Gammell. New York: Frederick Warne Co., Inc., 1981.

Barton, Byron. *Airport*. Illus. by author. New York: Harper & Row, Publishers, 1982.

———. *Building a House*. Illus. by author. New York: Greenwillow Books, 1981.

———. *Wheels*. Illus. by author. New York: Thomas Y. Crowell Co., 1979.

Bartlett, Margaret. *The Clean Brook*. Illus. by Aldren A. Watson. New York: Harper & Row, Publishers, Inc., 1960.

———. *Where Does All the Rain Go?* Illus. by Patricia Collins. New York: Coward, McCann & Geoghegan Inc., 1974.

Basil, Cynthia. *How Ships Play Cards: A Beginning Book of Homonyms*. Illus. by Janet McCaffrey. New York: William Morrow & Co., Inc., 1980.

Baylor, Byrd. *Sometimes I Dance Mountains*. Illus. by Kenneth Longtemps. New York: Charles Scribner's Sons, 1973.

Bendick, Jeanne. *Ecology*. Illus. by author. New York: Franklin Watts, Inc., 1975.

———. *How to Make a Cloud*. Illus. by author. New York: Parents Magazine Press, 1971.

———. *Shapes*. Illus. by author. New York: Franklin Watts, Inc., 1968.

Berger, Melvin. *Why I Cough, Sneeze, Shiver, Hiccup & Yawn*. Illus. by Holly Keller. New York: Thomas Y. Crowell Co., 1983.

Bernstein, Joanne. *When People Die*. New York: E. P. Dutton Co., 1977.

Bester, Roger. *Fireman Jim*. Illus. by author. New York: Crown Publishers, Inc., 1981.

Branley, Franklyn M., and Vaughn, Eleanor K. *Mickey's Magnet*. Illus. by Crockett Johnson. New York: Thomas Y. Crowell Co., 1956.

———. *Rockets and Satellites*. Illus. by Al Nagy. New York: Thomas Y. Crowell Co., 1970.

Bulla, Clyde. *A Tree Is a Plant*. Illus. by Lois Lignell. New York: Harper & Row, Publishers, Inc., 1960.

Burchard, Marshall. *Sports Hero: Rod Carew*. Illus. by author. New York: Putnam Publishing Co., 1978.

Busch, Phyllis. *Exploring as You Walk in the City*. Illus. by author. Philadelphia: J. B. Lippincott Co., 1972.

Carle, Eric. *The Tiny Seed*. Illus. by author. New York: Thomas Y. Crowell Co., 1970.

Cartwright, Sally. *What's in a Map*. Illus. by Dick Gackenbach. New York: Coward, McCann & Geoghegan, Inc., 1976.

Cheng, Hou-Tien. *Scissor Cutting for Beginners*. Illus. by author. New York: Holt, Rinehart & and Winston, Inc., 1978.

Chlad, Dorothy. *Matches, Lighters and Firecrackers Are Not Toys*. Illus. by Lydia Halverson. New York: Children's Press, 1982.

Cobb, Vicki. *Fuzz Does It*. Illus. by Brian Schatell. New York: Harper & Row, Publishers, Inc., 1982.

Cole, Joanna. *Cars and How They Go*. Illus. by Gail Gibbons. New York: Thomas Y. Crowell Co., 1983.

———. *A Frog's Body*. Photographs by Jerome Wexler. New York: William Morrow & Co., 1980. (One of a series.)

Conklin, Gladys. *The Lion Family*. Illus. by Joseph Cellini. New York: Holiday House, 1973.

Crews, Donald. *Harbor*. Illus. by author. New York: Greenwillow Books, 1982.

———. *Light*. Illus. by author. New York: Greenwillow Books, 1981.

———. *Truck*. Illus. by author. New York: Greenwillow Books, 1980.

Dalgliesh, Alice. *The Thanksgiving Story*. Illus. by Helen Sewell. New York: Charles Scribner's Sons, 1954.

d'Aulaire, Ingri, and d'Aulaire, Edgar. *Benjamin Franklin*. Illus. by authors. New York: Doubleday & Co., 1950.

———. *Columbus*. New York: Doubleday & Co., Inc., 1955.

de Paola, Tomie. *The Cloud Book*. Illus. by author. New York: Holiday House 1975.

———. *The Family Christmas Tree Book*. Illus. by author. New York: Holiday House, 1980.

———. *The Popcorn Book*. Illus. by author. New York: Holiday House, 1978.

———. *The Quicksand Book*. Illus. by author. New York: Holiday House, 1977.

Domanska, Janina. *What Do You See?* Illus. by author. New York: Macmillan Publishing Co., Inc., 1974.

Emberley, Ed. *Drawing Book of Faces*. Illus. by author. Boston: Little, Brown and Co., 1975.

Feravolo, Rocco. *Junior Science Book of Magnets*. Illus. by Evelyn Urbanowich Champaign, Ill.: Garrard Publishing Co., 1960.

Frasconi, Antonio. *See and Say: A Picture Book in Four Languages*. Illus. by author. New York: Harcourt Brace Jovanovich, Inc., 1955.

Froman, Robert. *Bigger and Smaller*. Illus. by Gioia Fiammenghi. New York: Thomas Y. Crowell Co., 1971.

Gans, Roma. *Icebergs*. Illus. by Vladimir Bobri. New York: Thomas Y. Crowell Co., 1964.

Gemming, Elizabeth. *Born in a Barn: Farm Animals & Their Young*. Illus. by Klaus Gemmings. New York: Coward, McCann & Geoghegan, Inc., 1974.

George, Jean. *All Upon a Sidewalk*. Illus. by Don Bolognese. New York: E. P. Dutton Co., Inc., 1974.

Gibbons, Gail. *Paper, Paper Everywhere*. New York: Harcourt Brace Jovanovich, 1983.

———. *The Post Office Book: Mail and How It Moves*. New York: Thomas Y. Crowell Co., 1982.

———. *Thanksgiving Day*. Illus. by author. New York: Holiday House, 1983.

———. *The Tool Book*. Illus. by author. New York: Holiday House, 1982.

Girard, Linda. *You Were Born on Your Very First Birthday*. Illus. by Kathy Tucker. New York: Albert Whitman & Co., 1983.

Goor, Ron, and Goor, Nancy. *In the Driver's Seat*. Photographs by author. New York: Thomas Y. Crowell Co., 1982.

Hautzig, Esther. *In the Park: An Excursion in Four Languages*. Illus. by Ezra Jack Keats. New York: Macmillan Publishing Co., Inc., 1968.

Hoban, Tana. *Big Ones Little Ones*. Illus. by author. New York: Greenwillow Books, 1976.

———. *Circles, Triangles, and Squares*. Illus. by author. New York: Macmillan Publishing Co., Inc., 1974.

———. *Dig, Drill, Dump, Fill*. Illus. by author. New York: Greenwillow Books, 1975.

———. *I Walk and Read*. Illus. by author. New York: Greenwillow Books, 1984.

———. *Is It Larger? Is It Smaller?* Illus. by author. New York: Greenwillow Books, 1985.

———. *Is It Red? Is It Yellow? Is It Blue?* Illus. by author. New York: Greenwillow Books, 1978.

———. *Look Again!* Illus. by author. New York: Macmillan Publishing Co., Inc., 1971.

———. *One Little Kitten*. Illus. by author. New York: Greenwillow Books, 1979.

———. *Over, Under & Through*. Illus. by author. New York: Macmillan Publishing Co., Inc., 1973.

———. *Push, Pull, Empty, Full*. Illus. by author. New York: Macmillan Publishing Co., Inc., 1972.

———. *Round & Round & Round*. Illus. by author. New York: Greenwillow Books, 1983.

———. *Shapes and Things*. Illus. by author. New York: Macmillan Publishing Co., Inc., 1970.

———. *Take Another Look*. Illus. by author. New York: Greenwillow Books, 1981.

Holmes, Anita. *The 100-Year-Old Cactus*. Illus. by Carol Lerner. New York: Four Winds Press, 1983.

Hutchins, Pat. *Changes, Changes*. Illus. by author. New York: Macmillan Publishing Co., Inc., 1971.

Hutchins, Ross E. *A Look at Ants*. New York: Dodd, Mead & Co., 1978.

Ipcar, Dahlov. *Ten Big Farms*. Illus. by author. New York: Alfred A. Knopf, Inc., 1958.

Isadora, Rachel. *My Ballet Class*. Illus. by author. New York: Greenwillow Books, 1980.

Jacobs, Francine. *Supersaurus*. Illus. by D. D. Tyler. New York: Putnam Publishing Co., 1982.

Kaufmann, John. *Little Dinosaurs and Early Birds*. Illus. by author. New York: Thomas Y. Crowell Co., 1977.

Kessler, Ethel, and Kessler, Leonard. *All Aboard the Train*. Illus. by author. New York: Doubleday & Co., Inc., 1964.

Komori, Atsushi. *Animal Mothers*. Illus. by Masayuki Yabuuchi. New York: Philomel Books, 1983.

Krementz, Jill. *The Very Young* ------ *Series*. New York: Alfred A. Knopf, Inc.

Lauber, Patricia. *What's Hatching Out of That Egg?* Illus. by author. New York: Crown Publishers, Inc., 1979.

Lionni, Leo. *Little Blue and Little Yellow*. Illus. by author. New York: Astor-Honor, 1959.

McMillan, Bruce. *Here a Chick, There a Chick*. New York: Lothrop, Lee & Shepard, 1983.

Mari, Iela, and Mari, Enzo. *The Apple and the Moth*. Illus. by Iela Mari. New York: Pantheon Books, 1970.

Marston, Hope. *Big Rigs*. Illus. by author. New York: Dodd, Mead & Co., 1980.

Merriam, Eve. *Mommies at Work*. Illus. by Beni Montresor. New York: Scholastic Book Services, 1973.

––––––. *Small Fry*. Illus. by Garry MacKenzie. New York: Alfred A. Knopf, Inc., 1965.

Miller, Jane. *Lambing Time*. Illus. by author. New York: Methuen Inc., 1978.

Monjo, F. N. *Me and Willie and Pa*. Illus. by Douglas Gorsline. New York: Simon & Schuster Inc., 1973.

Moore, Eva. *The Seabury Cook Book for Boys and Girls*. Illus. by Talivaldis Stubis. New York: Deabury Press, 1971.

O'Brian, Thomas. *Odds and Evens*. Illus. by Allan Eitzen. New York: Thomas Y. Crowell Co., 1971.

Prokofiev, Sergei. *Peter and the Wolf*. Illus. by Erna Voight. New York: David R. Godine Publishers Inc., 1980.

Provensen, Alice, and Provensen, Martin. *The Glorious Flight Across the Channel with Louis Bleriot*. Illus. by authors. New York: Viking Press, 1983.

––––––. *Maple Hill Farm* books. New York: Atheneum Publishers.

Quinn, John R. *Nature's World Records*. New York: Walker & Co., 1977.

Reiss, John. *Colors*. Illus. by author. New York: Bradbury Press, 1969.

Robbins, Ken. *Trucks of Every Sort*. Illus. by author. New York: Crown Publishers Inc., 1981.

Rockwell, Anne. *The Toolbox*. Illus. by Harlow Rockwell. New York: Macmillan Publishing Co., Inc., 1974.

Rockwell, Anne, and Rockwell, Harlow. *How My Garden Grew*. Illus. by authors. New York: Macmillan Publishing Co., Inc., 1982.

––––––. *The Supermarket*. Illus. by authors. New York: Macmillan Publishing Co., Inc., 1979.

Rockwell, Harlow. *I Did It*. Illus. by author. New York: Macmillan Publishing Co., Inc., 1974.

––––––. *Look at This*. Illus. by author. New York: Macmillan Publishing Co., Inc., 1978.

––––––. *My Dentist*. Illus. by author. New York: Macmillan Publishing Co., Inc., 1975.

––––––. *My Doctor*. Illus. by author. New York: Macmillan Publishing Co., Inc., 1973.

Sattler, Helen. *Baby Dinosaurs*. Illus. by Jean Day Zallinger. New York: Lothrop, Lee & Shepard Books, 1984.

––––––. *Dinosaurs of North America*. Illus. by Anthony Rao. New York: Lothrop, Lee & Shepard, 1981.

Selsam, Millicent E. *Greg's Microscope*. Illus. by Arnold Lobel. New York: Harper & Row, Publishers, Inc., 1963.

––––––. *Is This a Baby Dinosaur and Other Science Puzzles?* Illus. by author. New York: Harper & Row, Publishers, Inc., 1972.

––––––. *Maple Tree*. Illus. by Jerome Wexler. New York: William Morrow & Co., Inc., 1968.

––––––. *Popcorn*. Illus. by Jerome Wexler. New York: William Morrow & Co., Inc., 1976.

Selsam, Millicent E., and Hunt, Joyce. *A First Look at Birds*. New York: Walker & Co., 1973. (One of a series.)

Selsam, Millicent E., and Wexler, Jerome. *The Amazing Dandelion*. Illus. by Jerome Wexler. New York: William Morrow & Co., Inc., 1977.

Sheffield, Margaret. *Where Do Babies Come From*. Illus. by Sheila Bewley. New York: Alfred A. Knopf, Inc., 1973.

Showers, Paul. *Hear Your Heart*. Illus. by Joseph Low. New York: Harper & Row Publishers, 1975.

———. *How You Talk*. Illus. by Robert Galster. New York: Harper & Row, Publishers, Inc., 1967.

———. *No Measles No Mumps for Me*. Illus. by Harriet Barton. New York: Harper & Row, Publishers, Inc., 1980.

Shuttlesworth, Dorothy. *The Hidden Magic of Seeds*. Emmaus, Pa.: Rodale Press, Inc., 1976.

———. *The Story of Ants*. Illus. by Su Zan Swain. New York: Doubleday & Co., Inc., 1964.

Simon, Seymour. *Exploring with a Microscope*. New York: Random House Inc., 1969.

Stewig, John W. *Sending Messages*. Illus. by author. Boston: Houghton Mifflin Co., 1978.

Spier, Peter. *Fast-Slow, High-Low*. Illus. by author. New York: Doubleday & Co., Inc., 1972.

———. *Tin Lizzie*. Illus. by author. New York: Doubleday & Co., Inc., 1975.

Sullivan, George. *Willie Mays*. Illus. by David Brown. New York: Putnam Publishing Co., 1973.

Testa, Fulvio. *If You Take a Pencil*. Illus. by author. New York: Dial Press, 1982.

Turkle, Brinton. The *Obadiah* books. New York: Viking Press.

Vevers, Gwynne. *Animal Homes*. Illus. by Wendy Branell. London: Bodley Head, 1982.

Weil, Lisl. *I, Christopher Columbus*. New York: Atheneum Publishers, 1983.

Weisgard, Leonard. *Treasures to See: A Museum Picture Book*. Illus. by author. New York: Harcourt, Brace Jovanovich, 1956.

———. *Whose Little Bird Am I*. Illus. by author. New York: Frederick Warne & Co., Inc., 1965.

Wulffson, Don. *The Invention of Ordinary Things*. Illus. by Roy Doty. New York: Lothrop, Lee & Shepherd, 1981.

Zim, Herbert S. *What Can She Be* Series. New York: Lothrop, Lee & Shepherd.

———. *What's Inside Me?* Illus. by Herschel Wartik. New York: William Morrow & Co., Inc., 1952.

Zisfein, Melvin B. *Flight: A Panorama of Aviation*. Illus. by Robert A. Parker. New York: Pantheon Books, 1981.

COUNTING BOOKS

Anno, Mitsumasa. *Anno's Counting Book*. Illus. by author. New York: Thomas Y. Crowell Company, 1977.

Bang, Mollie. *Ten, Nine, Eight*. Illus. by author. New York: Greenwillow Books, 1983.

Barr, Catherine. *Seven Chicks Missing*. New York: Henry Z. Walck, Inc., 1962.

Becker, John. *Seven Little Rabbits*. Illus. by Barbara Cooney. New York: Walker & Co., 1973.

Bendick, Jeanne. *How Much and How Many: The Story of Weights and Measures*. Illus. by author. New York: McGraw-Hill Book Company, 1960.

Boynton, Sandra. *Hippos Go Beserk*. Illus. by author. Boston: Little, Brown & Co., 1979.

Bruna, Dick. *I Can Count*. Illus. by author. New York: Methuen Co., 1975.

Carle, Eric. *1, 2, 3 to the Zoo*. Cleveland: The World Publishing Co., 1968.

———. *The Rooster Who Set Out to See the World*. New York: Franklin Watts, Inc., 1972.

———. *The Very Hungry Caterpillar*. Illus. by author. New York: Philomel Books, 1969.

Eichenberg, Fritz. *Dancing in the Moon: Counting Rhymes*. New York: Harcourt, Brace Jovanovich Inc., 1955.

Farber, Norma. *Up the Down Elevator*. Illus. by Annie Gusman. Reading, Mass.: Addison-Wesley Publishing Co., 1979.

Feelings, Muriel. *Moja Means One: Swahili Counting Book*. Illus. by Tom Feelings. New York: The Dial Press, 1971.

Friskey, Margaret. *Chicken Little, Count to Ten*. Illus. by Katherine Evans. New York: Children's Press, 1946.

Ginsburg, Mirra. *Kittens from One to Ten*. Illus. by Guilio Maestro. New York: Crown Publishers, 1980.

Haley, Gail E., illustrator. *One, Two, Buckle My Shoe: A Book of Counting Rhymes*. New York: Doubleday & Company, Inc., 1964.

Hefter, Richard. *One White Crocodile Smile*. New York: Strawberry Books, 1974.

Hoban, Tana. *Count and See*. Illus. by author's photographs. New York: Macmillan Co., 1972.

Hobzek, Mildred. *We Came A-Marching . . . 1 2 3*. Illus. by William Pene Du Bois. New York: Parents Magazine Press, 1978.

Jenkins, Ella. *Counting Games and Rhymes for the Little Ones*. Scholastic Records.

Lasker, Joe. *Lentil Soup*. Illus. by author. Chicago: Albert Whitman & Co., 1977.

Little, Mary E. *1, 2, 3 for the Library*. Illus. by author. New York: Atheneum Publishers, 1974.

McLeod, Emilie Warren. *One Snail and Me*. Illus. by Walter Lorraine. Boston: Little, Brown & Co., 1961.

Maestro, Guilio. *One More and One Less: A Number Concept Book*. New York: Crown Publishers, 1974.

Oxenbury, Helen. *Numbers of Things*. New York: Franklin Watts, Inc., 1968.

Peek, Merle. *Roll Over! A Counting Song*. Illus. by author. Boston: Houghton Mifflin, 1981.

Petie, Haris. *Billions of Bugs*. Englewood Cliffs, N.J.: Prentice-Hall, Inc., 1975.

Pomerantz, Charlotte. *One Duck, Another Duck*. Illus. by Jose Aruego and Ariane Dewey. New York: Greenwillow Books, 1984.

Poulsson, Emilie. *Finger Plays for Nursery and Kindergarten*. Illus. by L. J. Bridgman. New York: Dover Publications Inc., 1971.

Reiss, John J. *Numbers*. Scarsdale, N.Y.: Bradbury Press, 1971.

Russell, Sandra. *A Farmer's Dozen*. Illus. by author. New York: Harper & Row, Publishers, Inc., 1982.

Sendak, Maurice. *One Was Johnny: A Counting Book*. New York: Harper & Row, Publishers, Inc., 1962.

———. *Seven Little Monsters*. New York: Harper & Row, Publishers, Inc., 1977.

Tudor, Tasha. *1 Is One*. New York: Henry Z. Walck, Inc., 1956.

Weihs, Erika. *Count the Cats*. New York: Doubleday & Co., Inc., 1976.

Weissman, Moltke, photographer. *Numbers: A First Counting Book*. Text by Robert Allen. New York: Platt & Munk, 1968.

Wells, Rosemary. *Max's Toys: A Counting Book*. New York: Dial Press, 1979.

Wildsmith, Brian. *Brian Wildsmith's 1, 2, 3's*. New York: Franklin Watts, Inc., 1965.

Yeoman, John, and Blake, Quentin. *Sixes and Sevens*. New York: Macmillan Publishing Co., Inc., 1971.

Yolen, Jane. *An Invitation to the Butterfly Ball: A Counting Rhyme*. Illus. by Jane Breskin Zalben. New York: Putnam Publishing Group, 1983.

Ziner, Feenie, and Galdone, Paul. *Counting Carnival*. New York: Coward, McCann & Geoghegan, 1962.

Chapter **11**

Literature in the Early Childhood Program: Staple and Syllabub

RICH ENCOUNTERS

"Look at me. I'm eating it, too."

"I'm dancing and prancing and pounding like the elephants in that Circus poem."

"He's going to get it, isn't he, Miss Smith? Isn't he? He's being so-o-o fresh!"

"That's so funny when he's running up and down the steps to keep up with himself."

"Do you think he learned his lesson now?"

"Nope, he was silly before and he'll probably be silly again."

"In the movie the dwarfs were funnier but these are more dwarfy...."

"Is that really paper he just cut? Mine doesn't look like that."

"Who ever heard of an elephant school?"

Evidence of Responses

The above comments and questions of young children follow close on literary sharing. They range from:

- Fantasizing about being the caterpillar in Carle's *The Very Hungry Caterpillar*
- Dramatizing some of Prelutsky's *Circus* poems
- Seeking assurance that Sendak's *Pierre* will be punished
- Convulsing at Lobel's owl in *Owl at Home*
- Deciding that Big Anthony in de Paola's books will *never* learn
- Comparing Trina Schart Hyman's drawings of the seven dwarfs (*Snow White*) with the Walt Disney motion picture
- Doubting Lionni's use of cut paper in *Frederick*

- Querying dubiously about an elephant school after hearing John Stewart's *Elephant School.*

These encounters are *rich* and *alive.* Literary mines are tapped and the gold that is found is greeted with gusto and questions.

Lively, varied responses to literature are evident in a variety of behaviors. Teachers know literature is being appreciated and internalized when the following occurs:

- Children return on their own to the books that have been shared.
- They seek other books that are similar to their favorites.
- They talk about their favorite titles and suggest that other children read them.
- They dramatize, sing, and construct in response to literature.
- They freely choose to use their time to read or listen to tales.
- They beg to have more stories shared.

To achieve such responses, young children's thoughts and feelings must be fully engaged; the linkage between child and book must be strong.

Truisms Basic to Rich Encounters

Awareness and commitment to the following truisms help to weld strong links between child and book:

- *Children need books.* Books for young children are not a luxury; they are staple *and* syllabub.
- *Young children need book sharers.* They owe to sharers the first sounds of literature—the feel, sight, heart, and facts of it, too.
- *Young children need time to listen, read, and respond to literature.* Their time is managed and supervised by others. If such management is wise, frequent literary hours are built in.
- *Young children need to share their reactions with each other.* Sometimes, especially with books filled with humor, half the joy is in the sharing.
- *Young children need to see and feel books.* Attention-getting exhibits and browsing time are vital.
- *Young children need a broad range of carefully culled books.* Books should represent *every* genre to meet fully each child's needs. Young children also need time to choose their own title.
- *An apt literary response or an array of responses from young children is depen-*

dent on the teacher's knowledge.   Such knowledge is evident in (a) the recognition of a class's teachable moment, and (b) the reaction to a young child's spontaneous question or comment.

- *Literary rubbish is most easily counteracted by filling young children's minds, hands, ears, eyes, and hearts with a broad spectrum of the highest-quality books and planned "shared" time.*

Working to Effect Rich Responses

Various factors combine to effect rich responses from young children. Consideration of the following questions will enable a teacher to determine whether such factors or conditions exist in the classroom:

- Does the classroom beckon the child into books? Are books handle-able and visible? Are stories audible as well as readable? Are there some book friends to cuddle?
- Does the air ring and sing with the music of literature?
- Are there quiet moments to think and browse, to experience the joy of selecting a book that promises to entertain?
- Are there other quiet moments when everyone savors his or her own book *together* as in the USSR-type programs (see Chapter 3)?
- Is the school day saturated with storytelling, story reading, and story living activities wherein the young child not only listens and reads but composes and tells his or her very own tales?
- Are books used to extend and enhance units of study, class projects, and programs so that young children see them continuously employed in school living?
- Is time provided to visit library media-centers so that the young child knows *all* the book collections available to him or her in the classroom, school, and community?
- Do young children ever have an opportunity to buy books at book fairs, through book clubs, in bookstores?
- How rich is the classroom in divergent extensions of literary experiences in attending? Acting? Brainstorming? Composing? Chorusing? Constructing? Dramatizing? Demonstrating? and so on through an alphabet of involvement?
- How often are local taletellers and yarn spinners invited into the school to share stories?

Long-term, continuous rich encounters are not happenstance; they are the result of loving and knowing and creating the kind of setting nurturant of a range of responses.

Range of Responses

In demonstrating an internalization of literature, young children react in four basic ways:

- *Children may respond with silence.* Sometimes the best way to savor a tale or poem is by quietly "feeling" it. Mood books like Shulevitz's *Dawn* and poems like Eleanor Farjeon's "The Night Will Never Stay," full of metaphors, require some silent minutes following sharing.

- *Children may respond with questions and comments.* A teacher's open-ended questions—How did the poem/story make *you* feel? What did it make you think about? What pictures are in your mind now?—invite a personal "feeling" and "thinking" response. Assuming that the sharing has been at a pace such that the child can savor the story, such questioning can bring forth highly individual and thoughtful responses, which will ripple through a group.

- *Children may respond via an art form.* There are many ways a child can extend his or her personal reaction to internalizing literature. Some include:

    Dramatizing Babbitt's "The Monkey and the Crocodile"

    Sculpting one's own "wild thing" (Sendak)

    Dictating a new adventure for Obadiah (Turkle)

    Writing an answer to Robert Louis Stevenson's questions to the wind in "The Wind"

    Trimming or drawing *Jennie's Hat* (Keats)

    Putting one of Frances's songs to music (Hoban)

    Constructing *Donkey-Donkey's* (Duvoisin) different ear styles, or *Jack in the Beanstalk's* (Stobbs) infinite beanstalk, or *Pinocchio's* (Collodi) amazingly flexible nose.

- *Children may respond with movement.* Physical movements, so natural and joyous for young children, can deepen and intensify book experiences in a number of ways. For example:

    Aping Aruego's *Look What I Can Do*

    Charading Mayer's *What Would You Do With a Kangaroo?*

    Playing the chipmunk in Jarrell's "The Chipmunk's Day"

    Offering a ferocious rendition of Lewis's lion in *A Lion for Lewis.*

Spurring such responses cannot be left to chance. To a knowledge of children and literature, the teacher must add knowledge of the vehicles through which a continuity of literary experiences for the young child may be assured. In addition to the daily schedule, which can be permeated with poetry, story sharing, "book looks," and book probes, there are two basic vehicles teachers may use to assure young children of a continuity of literature experiences: story "hours" and a literature-rich curriculum.

The establishment of literary links in the lives of young children is initially dependent on the sharing done by parents, siblings, grand-parents, and other caring adults; teachers continue and enrich such sharing. Such links are reinforced through aspects of the school program.

In effect, the young child's development of a love of literature and refinement of literary taste broadens with greater and greater immersion in the feel, sounds, sight, heart, and facts of literature. See Figure 11.1.

Story Hours

Time for literature is assured when a story time is scheduled each day. Stories then become an established part of the program. The very allocation of story time and story space by the teacher communicates to young children that their own pleasure in hearing stories is highly legitimate and soundly seconded by the teacher. The teacher is both time provider and tale sharer, offering young children a sampler of stories. This sampler assures highly active listening when the teacher

FIGURE 11.1 *Nurturance of Literary Taste in the Young Child*

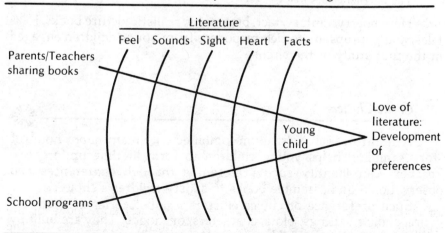

is well prepared and when the hour balances (1) traditional and modern literature, (2) poetry and prose, and (3) tales of varying length. It is from such rich and balanced story hours that young children hone their own preferences.

A Literature-Rich Curriculum

Sampler experiences are perforce, discrete, and divergent. The identification and use of stories and poems that are core to themes or units currently part of the curriculum of early years provides depth in one area and a developing awareness that all kinds of books may relate to one topic. For example, children studying the circus can experience the following activities:

- Listen, move, sway, and dance to Prelutsky's *Circus* poems while they giggle at Arnold Lobel's illustrations.
- Enjoy the adventures of Don Freeman's *Bearymore*, or Syd Hoff's *Henrietta Circus Star*, or Crockett Johnson's Harold in *Harold's Circus*.
- Study the photographs in Powledge's *Born on the Circus*, about a circus family.
- "Ooh" and "ah" over Brian Wildsmith's radiant illustrations in *The Circus*.
- Follow the schedule of Tato in Jill Krementz's *A Very Young Circus Flyer*, or of the clowns in Harriet Sobol's *Clowns*.
- Join Hoffman's Circus with *Mishka* (Victor Ambrus) and start the painstaking climb to success.
- Enjoy the feel of the famous pop-up book by Meggendorfer, *The International Circus*.

Here poetry, fantasy, fact, biography, realistic picture books, folktales, and pop-ups invite rich responses from young children engaged in the unit study of the circus.

Choice Clusters

A literature-rich curriculum combined with many happy hours of story sampling helps young children to form lifetime preferences. Teachers can identify such preferences through conferences and observations[1] and assemble books to satisfy children's choices.

Such preference or choice clusters *may* be stories of the same genre, similar settings, plots, characters, or moods. They are built by teachers who observe children's reactions to tales and poems, record such reactions, and then scout out similar titles for exhibit, comment, or sharing. These clusters respond to the young child's "I want another book like that!" (that is, a book of the same type [plot or genre], same character, or same setting).

For example, the teacher may cluster, for a range of children, a variety of mysteries—some very simple, and some more complex and demanding strong reading skills. The young child may travel from the simple picture books by Steven Kellogg, *The Mystery of the Missing Red Mitten* and *The Mystery of the Magic Green Ball*, to Kellogg's *The Mystery Beast of Ostergeest* to Crosby Bonsall's *The Case of the Double Cross* or William Hooks's *The Mystery on Bleeker Street* which pairs a young boy and his seventy-eight-year-old friend. Or the young child may start with Ezra Jack Keats's *Maggie and the Pirate* or some of the Nate the Great mysteries, and later go on to the Piet Potter mysteries (Quackenbush), and, as the child grows older into Rumer Godden's *The Rocking Horse Secret*.

A preference cluster may also be a character cluster. The young child having sampled one Frances book, one George and Martha, one Nate the Great, one Paddington the Bear (for older children in this group), and one Harold book often wants to read *all* the books about that particular character.

Preference clusters may also be "setting" clusters. A young child who is first intrigued by Lobel's *On the Day Peter Stuyvesant Sailed into Town* goes on to other colonial stories—perhaps Peter Spier's *The Legend of New Amsterdam*, or the question-answer book by Anne McGovern *If You Sailed on the Mayflower*, or later to Jean Fritz's *Who's That Stepping on Plymouth Rock?*

The range of literature shared during story hours, within curriculum units and through choice clusters, helps to provide the breadth and to initiate the depth children need in order to develop a life-long reading habit and a discriminating taste.

The young "whodunit" fan who starts with Kellogg, Lauber, and Sharmat can, as he or she grows older, go on to space mysteries like Franklyn Branley's *A Book of Flying Saucers for You*, or later to Isaac Asimov's *The Key Words and Other Mysteries* (five short stories), or the child can proceed from Natalie Babbitt's gothic *Goody Hall* to, much later, Nina Bawden's well-written mystery, *Devil by the Sea* and Katherine Paterson's mystery set in historical Japan, *The Master Puppeteer*.

Selected Sources for Planning a Literature-Rich Curriculum and Choice Clusters

There are many references available to teachers who are engaged in planning a rich curriculum in literature and in compiling clusters of titles relating to young children's preferences, such as:

• The comprehensive *Children's Catalog* (H. W. Wilson Co.) is updated four times annually and reissued every five years.

• *The Elementary School Library Collection* is most valuable to those establishing new library facilities or resource centers.

• *Children's Books in Print* (R. R. Bowker Company) is an author-title-illustrator listing of children's books in print; it is updated annually. *The Subject Guide to Children's Books in Print* (R. R. Bowker Co.) arranges the titles included in the annual *Children's Books in Print* (R. R. Bowker Co.) by subject.

• For more information about authors, teachers will find much valuable information in *Something About the Author* (Gale Research), and for biographical sketches of famous children's illustrators the *Illustrators of Children's Books* volumes published by Horn Book are a useful and handy reference.

• Sharon Dreyer's *The Bookfinder: A Guide to Children's Literature* (American Guidance Service) offers teachers extensive lists of children's books in a variety of areas in which children may need guidance and direction: death, serious illness, fears, etc. A special reference by Barbara Baskin, *More Notes from a Different Drummer: A Guide to Juvenile Fiction Portraying the Disabled* (Bowker), provides annotations on fiction about disabilities.

• Tway, Eileen, ed. *Reading Ladders for Human Relations.* 6th ed. American Council on Education and the National Council of Teachers of English. Washington, D.C.: American Council on Education, 1981. This provides annotated book suggestions about human relationships organized under topics such as "Developing a Positive Self-Image," and "Friendships."

• Cullinan, Bernice, and Carmichael, Carolyn W., eds. *Literature and Young Children.* Urbana, Ill.: National Council of Teachers of English, 1977. This compilation of articles presents numerous book titles for young children, as well as offers a strong rationale for the need of books in early years and how to present them to children.

• White, Mary Lou, ed. *Adventuring with Books.* New Edition. Urbana, Ill.: National Council of Teachers of English, 1981. This is an extensive annotated book list, pre-K through grade 6, arranged by genre. It also includes categories like social studies, sciences, art, and language, which can be of help to teachers in building choice clusters or curriculum units.

• Lima, Carolyn W. *A to Zoo: Subject Access to Children's Picture Books.* New York: R. R. Bowker Company, 1982. Picture books are indexed under titles like "Behavior" and "Behavior—sibling rivalry." The book is not annotated, but it contains complete bibliographic information and a most comprehensive list of all possible categories under which each title could be indexed.

• Gillespie, John T., and Gilbert, Christine B., eds. *Best Books for Children. Preschool Through the Middle Grades.* 2nd ed. New York: R. R. Bowker Company, 1981. This is a genre- and subject-indexed listing of selected books for the preschool through middle-grade child. Brief annotations are given.

• Butler, Francelia. *Sharing Literature with Children.* New York: David McKay Company, Inc., 1977. Although many of the selections excerpted or offered in full in this anthology are well beyond the young child, this is a thematic approach to a compilation. Teachers will find an array of genres categorized and collected under titles like "Toys and Games," "Shadows," and "Circles."

Summary

Rich literary responses from young children require their immersion in song and story. A checklist for the design of such an immersion program involves not only the classroom but the entire school.

Responses from young children range from silence, to questions and comments, to artistic, motoric, linguistic, and dramatic activities.

Story hours and a literature-rich curriculum can lead young children to a life-time love of literature and the development of personal preferences. Many selection aids are available to help teachers create settings for rich encounters.

DISCUSSION ACTIVITIES

• Select a unit of study usually taught to young children. Using appropriate selection aids, identify a variety of books suitable for young children and germane to the unit topic. Check to be sure that many genres are represented. Then consider the probable responses to these titles that children might make. Which titles would deserve some silent minutes? Which would deserve some discussion? Art activity? Movement? Try to select a range of books that will invite a variety of responses.

• Prepare a "balanced" story hour. Select two brief stories (at least one that invites participation), two poems (at least one that invites motor response), and a song. Evaluate the impact of your hour in terms of student attention, questions and comments, and dramatic or motor activity.

• For a period of several days observe children as they choose books. Note their preferences. With the librarian, prepare several choice clusters based upon children's selections. Then note how many children other than those initially observed come to use the cluster. Also note how frequently the original group of children return for more books.

NOTE

1. For recording young children's reactions during and after a literary experience, see Jessie A. Roderick, "Responses to Literature," in *Literature and Young Children* (Urbana, Ill.: National Council of Teachers of English, 1977), pp. 142–154.

CHILDREN'S BOOKS

Aruego, Jose. *Look What I Can Do.* Illus. by author. New York: Charles Scribner's Sons, 1971.

Asimov, Isaac. *The Key Words and Other Mysteries.* Illus. by Rod Burke. New York: Walker & Co., 1978.

Ambrus, Victor. *Mishka.* Illus. by author. New York: Frederick Warne & Co., Inc., 1978.

Babbitt, Ellen C., ret. "The Monkey and The Crocodile," *Jataka Tales.* Englewood Cliffs, N.J.: Prentice-Hall, Inc., 1940.

Babbitt, Natalie. *Goody Hall.* Illus. by author. New York: Farrar, Straus & Giroux, Inc., 1971.

Bawden, Nina. *Devil by the Sea.* Philadelphia: J. B. Lippincott Co., 1976.

Bonsall, Crosby. *The Case of the Double Cross.* Illus. by author. New York: Harper & Row, Publishers, Inc., 1980.

Branley, Franklyn. *A Book of Flying Saucers for You.* Illus. by Leonard Lessler. New York: Harper & Row, Publishers, Inc., 1973.

Carle, Eric. *The Very Hungry Caterpillar.* Illus. by author. Cleveland: William Collins Publishers, Inc., 1969.

Collodi, Carlo. *Pinocchio.* Trans. by Walter S. Cramp. Illus. by Charles Copeland. Boston: Ginn and Company, 1904.

de Paola, Tomie. *Big Anthony and the Magic Ring.* Illus. by author. New York: Harcourt Brace Jovanovich, Inc., 1979.

———. *Strega Nona.* Englewood Cliffs, N.J.: Prentice-Hall Inc., 1975.

Duvoisin, Roger. *Donkey-Donkey.* Illus. by author. New York: Grosset & Dunlap, Inc., 1940.

Farjeon, Eleanor. "The Night Will Never Stay," *Eleanor Farjeon's Poems for Children.* Philadelphia: J. B. Lippincott Company, 1951. Originally from *Gypsy and Ginger.*

Freeman, Don. *Bearymore.* Illus. by author. New York: Viking Press, 1976.

Fritz, Jean. *Who's That Stepping on Plymouth Rock?* Illus. by J. B. Handelsman. New York: Coward, McCann & Geoghegan, Inc., 1975.

Godden, Rumer. *The Rocking Horse Secret*. Illus. by Juliet Stanwell Smith. New York: Viking Press, 1978.

Grimm Brothers. *Snow White*. Trans. by Paul Heins. Illus. by Trina Schart Hyman. Boston: Little, Brown & Co., 1974.

Hoban, Russell. *A Baby Sister for Frances*. Illus. by Lillian Hoban. New York: Harper & Row, Publishers, Inc., 1964.

Hoff, Syd. *Henrietta Circus Star*. New York: Garrard Publishing Co., 1978.

Hooks, William H. *The Mystery of Bleeker Street*. Illus. by Susanna Natti. New York: Alfred A. Knopf, 1980.

Jarrell, Randall. "The Chipmunk's Day," *The Bat Poet*. Illus. by Maurice Sendak. New York: Macmillan Publishing Co., Inc., 1964.

Johnson, Crockett. *Harold's Circus*. Illus. by author. New York: Harper & Row Publishers, 1959.

Keats, Ezra Jack. *Jennie's Hat*. Illus. by author. New York: Harper & Row Publishers, 1966.

———. *Maggie and the Pirate*. Illus. by author. New York: Four Winds Press, 1979.

Kellogg, Steven. *The Mystery Beast of Ostergeest*. Illus. by author. New York: Dial Press, 1971.

———. *The Mystery of the Magic Green Ball*. Illus. by author. New York: Dial Press, 1978.

———. *The Mystery of the Missing Red Mitten*. Illus. by author. New York: Dial Press, 1974.

Krementz, Jill. *A Very Young Circus Flyer*. Photographs by author. New York: Alfred A. Knopf, Inc., 1979.

Lionni, Leo. *Frederick*. Illus. by author. New York: Pantheon Books, 1966.

Lobel, Arnold. *On the Day Peter Stuyvesant Sailed into Town*. Illus. by author. New York: Harper & Row, Publishers, Inc., 1971.

———. *Owl at Home*. New York. Harper & Row, Publishers, Inc., 1975.

Loeper, John. *Going to School in 1776*. New York: Atheneum Publishers, 1973.

McGovern, Ann. *If You Sailed on the Mayflower*. Illus. by J. B. Handelsman. New York: Scholastic, Inc., 1970.

Mayer, Mercer. *What Do You Do with a Kangaroo?* Illus. by author. New York: Four Winds Press, 1974.

Meggendorfer, Lothar. *The International Circus*. New York: Viking Press, 1980 (reproduction of original pop-up book).

Paterson, Katherine. *The Master Puppeteer*. Illus. by Haru Wells. New York: Thomas Y. Crowell Co., 1976.

Powledge, Fred. *Born on the Circus*. Photographs by author. New York: Harcourt Brace Jovanovich, Inc., 1976.

Prelutsky, Jack. *Circus*. Illus. by Arnold Lobel. New York: Macmillan Publishing Co., Inc., 1974.

Quackenbush, Robert. *Piet Potter's First Case*. Illus. by author. New York: McGraw-Hill, 1980.

Sendak, Maurice. *Pierre*. Illus. by author. New York: Harper & Row, Publishers, Inc., 1962. (Part of the Nutshell Library.)

———. *Where the Wild Things Are*. Illus. by author. New York: Harpel & Row, Publishers, Inc., 1963.

Sharmat, Marjorie Weinman. *Nate the Great and the Phony Clue*. Illus. by Marc Simont. New York: Coward, McCann & Geoghegan, Inc., 1977.

Shulevitz, Uri. *Dawn*. Illus. by author. New York: Farrar, Straus & Giroux, Inc., 1974.

Sobol, Harriet. *Clowns*. New York: Coward, McCann & Geoghegan, Inc., 1982.

Spier, Peter. *The Legend of New Amsterdam*. Illus. by author. New York: Doubleday & Co., 1979.

Stevenson, Robert Louis. "The Wind," *A Child's Garden of Verses*. Illus. by Brian Wildsmith. New York: Franklin Watts, Inc., 1966 (original 1905).

Stewart, John. *Elephant School*. Photographs by author. New York: Pantheon Books, 1982.

Stobbs, William. *Jack and the Beanstalk*. New York: Delacorte Press, 1969.

Turkle, Brinton. *Thy Friend, Obadiah*. Illus. by author. New York: Viking Press, 1969.

Wells, Rosemary. *A Lion for Lewis*. Illus. by author. New York: Dial Press, 1982.

Wildsmith, Brian. *The Circus*. Illus. by author. New York: Oxford University Press, Inc., 1970.

Selecting, Adapting, and Preparing Stories for Telling
by Gwendolyn Jones

Dewey Chambers[1] tells us, "Regardless of how we may try to standardize the teller's selection process, storytelling is still not only an art but a highly personal one. And as an art, it often contradicts standardization."

Each storyteller has his or her unique approach to "learning" a story. I have found the following method successful. Just as I have culled ideas from others, I hope that sharing my approach with you may prove helpful.

SELECTING (How I Select a Story for Telling)

After reading many stories I suddenly know that a particular story is one I want to make "my own." I want it to be mine free and unfettered—no aids, no props, no books. I want to be able to tell it in a train, on a bus, in a car, on the playground, around a campfire; anywhere at anytime. The only way this can be done is by *knowing it completely.*

ADAPTING (How I Adapt a Story for Telling)

My next decision is whether or not to adapt the story from the original source. In using the word *original*, please understand that the version I have selected may be far removed from the original source. For instance, I favor Marie Shedlock's retelling of Hans Christian Andersen's *The Swineherd*. And of course fairy tales collected and recorded by the Brothers Grimm have been retold so many times that adapted sources are infinite. After a few readings I decide whether or not I want to remain with the original text or whether I want to make the main points of the story and add my own connecting narrative. However, in the case of literary fairy tales or traditional folk and fairy tales, the stories really need to be internalized. I use the term *internalized* as opposed to *memorized* because in the telling, the story should flow or surge from the teller's lips, not limp lamely forth because a particular phrase or word cannot be recalled. How does the storyteller internalize the tale? I use both of the following methods.

PREPARING (How I Prepare a Story for Telling) ◇

A. HOLISTIC-TAPING METHOD (Auditory Emphasis)

Step I: I read and reread the chosen story until I can visualize the whole narrative. Scenes and people pass before my eyes. Visualization helps me to forget myself. I am merely the instrument through which the story unfolds. Any gestures I use are involuntary because they are gestures of the characters themselves. I am told that my face reflects the emotions of the tale. My small niece would always say, "Tell me a story with your face." She did not want the book to come between us.

Step II: I now tape the story and listen. I may find stresses that I wish to change. Usually I don't, as I have "felt" the story through repeated readings before taping. I then listen to the tape as I drive to and from work until I can anticipate each succeeding event.

Step III: Now comes the test! I tape the story from memory and listen to it intently. I listen for hesitations or passages that do not flow. If I detect such errors, I correct them by going back to my original recording.

Step IV: Next I tell myself the tale aloud—again, usually as I am driving to work. I aim for fluency—no hesitations. The pictured events and my own voice recalled from the recordings guide me throughout the narrative. (I might add that I get strange glances from passing motorists. A State Trooper once stopped me to ask if I were not well. I *think* I convinced him of my sanity—at least he didn't arrest me!)

Step V: I now feel confident enough to tell the tale to an audience. It no longer consists of words that first appeared in cold black print. It is now a tale to be told; an experience to be shared. One decision remains. I must decide if it needs a short introduction—an "associational setting"—so that my listeners can more fully share the experience. Often a brief direct statement is sufficient; for example, "This is a story of..." or "Our tale today is about..." or "Have you ever heard of the...?" Then the tale unfolds!

B. HOLISTIC-PRINT METHOD (Visual Emphasis)

In this method I write the whole story on 8 x 5 cards, separating the tale into its natural sequential episodes. Dewey Chambers[2] suggests the following categories (which dramatists call *melodrama*) that refer to the structure of the tale. They are:

- Exposition
- Problem
- Rising action
- Climax or denouement
- Falling action
- Conclusion.

As most folktales and fairy tales fall into these classifications, my "natural sequential episodes" automatically follow his suggestion. I might add that Chambers says it is a good rule *never* to memorize a story for telling. However, I subscribe to the notion that storytelling is a highly personal art, therefore I choose the method that is most successful for me.

C. MAINTAINING (How I Keep the Story Alive)

As my storytelling repertoire increases and a throng of step-mothers, giants, fairies, simpletons, princes, princesses, and countless others take residence in my mind, I need to put them in some kind of framework so that I can recall the major details of each tale wherein they all belong. The following outline, in sequential form, quickly reacquaints me with the characters and the plot of a particular tale.

Outline Example

Tale: "Mother Hollee" Brothers Grimm (1824 translation)
Widow and 2 daughters: pretty/thrifty   ugly/idle
Pretty daughter–spins by well–side of highroad
Pricks finger–blood on spindle–tries to wash it in well–falls in
Mother scolds her–tells her to get it back
Daughter sorrow-filled, throws self in well
Emerges in meadow–2 good deeds–bread from oven–apples from tree
Arrives at Mother Hollee's cottage–shakes feather bed–snow below
Daughter wishes to go home–receives gift–returns–rooster crows:
"Cock-a-doodle-do—Our golden lady's come again."
Mother and sister jealous– mother sends ugly sister on same journey
Ugly sister doesn't help bread or tree
Does poor work for Mother Hollee
Receives departing gift—kettleful of "dirty pitch" (tar)
Rooster greets her: "Cock-a-doodle-do! Our dirty slut's come home again."

With this "bare bones" outline and my accompanying tape or text (or both), I can quickly re-create the *entire* tale. In this way I keep my repertoire alive and well, and when someone says, "Tell me a story," I am ready and willing.

NOTES

1. Dewey W. Chambers, *The Oral Tradition: Storytelling and Creative Drama* (Dubuque, Iowa: Wm. C. Brown Company, 1977), pp. 17–18.
2. Ibid., p. 18.

Randolph Caldecott Medal Books

1938

Animals of the Bible. Helen Dean Fish. Illus. by Dorothy P. Lathrop. Lippincott.

1939

Mei Li Thomas Handforth. Doubleday.

1940

Abraham Lincoln. Ingri and Edgar Parin d'Aulaire. Doubleday.

1941

They Were Strong and Good. Robert Lawson. Viking.

1942

Make Way for Ducklings. Robert McCloskey. Viking.

1943

The Little House. Virginia Lee Burton. Houghton.

1944

Many Moons. James Thurber. Illus. by Louis Slobodkin. Harcourt.

1945

Prayer for a Child. Rachel Field. Illus. by Elizabeth Orton Jones. Macmillan.

1946

The Rooster Crows (tradition Mother Goose). Illus. by Maud and Miska Petersham. Macmillan.

1947

The Little Island. Golden MacDonald. Illus. by Leonard Weisgard. Doubleday.

1948

White Snow, Bright Snow. Alvin Tresselt. Illus. by Roger Duvoisin. Lothrop.

1949

The Big Snow. Berta and Elmer Hader. Macmillan.

1950

Song of the Swallows. Leo Politi. Scribner.

1951

The Egg Tree. Katherine Milhous. Scribner.

1952

Finders Keepers. William Lipkind. Illus. by Nicolas Mordvinoff. Harcourt.

1953

The Biggest Bear. Lynd Ward. Houghton.

1954

Madeline's Rescue. Ludwig Bemelmans. Viking.

1955

Cinderella, or the Little Glass Slipper. Charles Perrault. Trans. and illus. by Marcia Brown. Scribner.

1956

Frog Went a-Courtin'. Edited by John Langstaff. Illus. by Feodor Rojankovsky. Harcourt.

1957

A Tree is Nice. Janice May Udry. Illus. by Marc Simont. Harper.

1958

Time of Wonder. Robert McCloskey. Viking.

1959

Chanticleer and the Fox. Adapted from Chaucer. Illus. by Barbara Cooney. Crowell.

1960

Nine Days to Christmas. Marie Hall Ets and Aurora Labastida. Illus. by Marie Hall Ets. Viking.

1961

Baboushka and the Three Kings. Ruth Robbins. Illus. by Nicolas Sidjakov. Parnassus/Houghton.

1962

Once a Mouse.... Marcia Brown. Scribner.

1963

The Snowy Day. Ezra Jack Keats. Viking.

1964

Where the Wild Things Are. Maurice Sendak. Harper.

1965

May I Bring a Friend? Beatrice Schenk de Regniers. Illus. by Beni Montresor. Atheneum.

1966

Always Room for One More. Sorche Nic Leodhas. Illus. by Nonny Hogrogian. Holt.

1967

Sam, Bangs and Moonshine. Evaline Ness. Holt.

1968

Drummer Hoff. Barbara Emberley. Illus. by Ed Emberley. Prentice.

1969

    The Fool of the World and the Flying Ship. Arthur Ransome. Illus. by Uri Shulevitz. Farrar.

1970

    Sylvester and the Magic Pebble. William Steig. Windmill/Simon & Schuster.

1971

    A Story—A Story: An African Tale. Gail E. Haley. Atheneum.

1972

    One Fine Day. Nonny Hogrogian. Macmillan.

1973

    The Funny Little Woman. Retold by Arlene Mosel. Illus. by Blair Lent Dutton.

1974

    Duffy and the Devil. Harve Zemach. Illus. by Margot Zemach. Farrar.

1975

    Arrow to the Sun. Adap. and illus. by Gerald McDermott. Viking.

1976

    Why Mosquitoes Buzz in People's Ears. Retold by Verna Aardema. Illus. by Leo and Diane Dillon. Dial.

1977

    Ashanti to Zulu: African Traditions. Margaret Musgrove. Illus. by Leo and Diane Dillon. Dial.

1978

    Noah's Ark. Peter Spier. Doubleday.

1979

    The Girl Who Loved Wild Horses. Paul Goble. Bradbury.

1980

    Ox-Cart Man. Donald Hall. Illus. by Barbara Cooney. Viking.

1981

    Fables. Arnold Lobel. Harper.

1982

    Jumanji. Chris Van Allsburg. Houghton.

1983

    Shadows. Blaise Cendrars. Illus. by Marcia Brown. Scribner.

1984

    The Glorious Flight Across the Channel with Louis Bleriot. Alice and Martin Provensen. Viking.

1985

    Saint George and the Dragon. Retold by Margaret Hodges. Illus. by Trina Schart Hyman. Little, Brown.

From Teachers to Parents

The following sources are helpful when teachers and librarians confer with parents about the young child's need to be read to, to feel, hear, and see the literature that is theirs.

NEWSLETTERS FOR PARENTS

• *News for Parents from IRA.* Published three times a year for use by International Reading Association members; permission is not required to reprint newsletter items. A practical list of suggestions for parents on spurring children's interest in reading and books. Each issue includes a recommended booklist. May be subscribed to through the International Reading Association, 800 Barksdale Road, P.O. Box 8139, Newark, Delaware 19711.

• *Parents' Choice.* Published four times a year. A review of all media for children—includes television, movies, music, story records, toys, games and books. May be subscribed to through Parents' Choice Foundation, *Parents' Choice*, P.O. Box 185, Waban, Mass. 02168.

• *Why Children's Books?* Sources are given to parents regarding material relating to selecting and sharing books with children. Many suggested book titles are included in each issue. May be ordered from The Horn Book, Inc., Park Square Bldg., Boston, Mass. 02116.

LEAFLETS/ BROCHURES

• *Choosing a Child's Book.* Contains criteria for selecting books for children of various age levels. Also contains booklists and periodical listings that would be helpful in selection. May be obtained by writing to The Children's Book Council, 67 Irving Place, New York, N.Y. 10003. Enclose SASE.

• *The International Reading Association series of pamphlets.* Geared for parents; include such titles as: Why Read Aloud to Children? What Books and Records Should I Get for My Preschooler? What Is Reading Readiness? How Can I Help My Child Get Ready to Read? How Can I Encourage My Primary-Grade Child to Read? and others. These are avilable for a small charge. International Reading Association, 800 Barksdale Road, P.O. Box 8139, Newark, Delaware 19711.

BOOKS

• Arbuthnot, May Hill. *Children's Reading in the Home.* New York: Lothrop, Lee & Shepard, 1969. Practical, comprehensive, annotated guide to books recommended for sharing in the home.

• Butler, Dorothy. *Babies Need Books.* New York: Atheneum Publishers, 1980. Practical guide to book choices for very young children. Author obviously has had much experience in introducing young children to books.

• Glazer, Susan Mandel, and Brown, Carol Smullen. *Helping Children Read: Ideas for Parents, Teachers and Librarians.* New Jersey Reading Association, 1980. Compilation of practical articles on books, the library, and informal techniques for intriguing children with literature.

• Johnson, Ferne, ed. *Start Early for an Early Start: You and the Young Child.* Chicago: American Library Association, 1976. Several sections devoted specifically to parents desirous of helping children experience literature in the home, library, and classroom.

• Larrick, Nancy. *A Parent's Guide to Children's Reading.* 4th rev. ed. New York: Doubleday and Co., 1975. A comprehensive practical source book for parents. There are hundreds of recommended titles.

• Magini-Rossi, Mary Jane. *Read to Me! Teach Me!* Wauwatosa, Wis.: American Baby Books, 1982. A comprehensive guide to hundreds of picture books for children up to six years old; categorized as titles useful from infancy to one year, one to two years, two to three years, etc.

• Monson, Dianne L., and McClenathan, Day Ann K., eds. *Developing Active Readers: Ideas for Parents, Teachers and Librarians.* Newark, Del.: International Reading Association, 1979. This reference is not limited to the young child but does contain relevant articles on book selection, library use, and the involvement of children in literature. Mary Simpson's chapter on "Parents and Teachers Share Books with Young Children" is particularly helpful.

• Roser, Nancy, and Frith, Margaret, eds. *Children's Choices: Teaching with Books Children Like.* Newark, Del.: International Reading Association, 1983. Numerous suggestions of books children have themselves chosen.

• Trelease, James. *The Read-Aloud Handbook.* New York: Penguin Books, Inc., 1982. Highly readable and enthusiastic suggestions on how to read books to children; includes many titles to be shared.

• White, Dorothy. *Books Before Five.* Portsmouth, N.H.: Heinemann Educational Books, 1984 (first published in 1954). A classic account of a mother's "record" of sharing books with her daughter from her daughter's second year to her sixth year. Many titles and responses are carefully noted.

Index